The New Suburban History

HISTORICAL STUDIES OF URBAN AMERICA

Edited by Kathleen N. Conzen, Timothy J. Gilfoyle, and James R. Grossman

The New
Suburban History

EDITED BY

KEVIN M. KRUSE AND

THOMAS J. SUGRUE

The University of Chicago Press   Chicago and London

The University of Chicago Press, Chicago 60637
The University of Chicago Press, Ltd., London
© 2006 by The University of Chicago
All rights reserved. Published 2006
Printed in the United States of America

15 14 13 12 11 10 09 08 07   2 3 4 5

Chapter 6, by Matthew D. Lassiter, draws mainly from chapter 7 of *The Silent Majority: Suburban Politics in the Sunbelt South* (Princeton: Princeton University Press, forthcoming) and is used by permission of the publisher.

ISBN: 0-226-45662-5 (cloth)
ISBN: 0-226-45663-3 (paper)

Library of Congress Cataloging-in-Publication Data

The new suburban history / edited by Kevin M. Kruse and Thomas
J. Sugrue.
    p.   cm.—(Historical studies of urban America)
    Based on a conference held at Princeton University in Feb. 2004.
    Includes bibliographical references and index.
    ISBN 0-226-45662-5 (cloth : alk. paper)—ISBN 0-226-45663-3 (pbk. :
alk. paper)
    1. Suburbs—United States—History—Congresses.   2. Metropolitan
areas—United States—History—Congresses.   I. Kruse, Kevin Michael,
1972–   II. Sugrue, Thomas J., 1962–   III. Series.
HT352.U6N48   2006
307.76′0973—dc22   2005029658

Contents

Acknowledgments

This collection had its origins in the lively conversations at a conference convened at Princeton University titled City Limits: New Perspectives in the History of American Suburbs. Over the course of two days in February 2004, the participants exchanged their cutting-edge work in suburban history and, more important, their thoughts on the new paths and possibilities emerging in the field. We would like to thank them, first and foremost, for their many insights that weekend and the conversations we've continued with them since. We would also like to thank colleagues who, through their service as chairs, commentators, and panelists, enriched both our conversations and the collection that has resulted: Elizabeth Blackmar, Sheryll Cashin, Gary Gerstle, James Goodman, Elizabeth Lunbeck, Stephen Macedo, Adam Rome, Christine Stansell, and Thorin Tritter. For their generous funding of the conference, we would like to thank the university's Council of the Humanities, the Princeton Environmental Institute, the Program in African-American Studies, the Program in American Studies, the Program in Law and Public Affairs, the University Center for Human Values and, most of all, the Shelby Cullom Davis Center for Historical Studies. Special thanks to Jennifer Houle for her diligent work in coordinating the conference and to Gyan Prakash for his support.

For their encouragement and assistance, we would like to thank our editor at the University of Chicago Press, Robert Devens, and his excellent staff. Three anonymous readers for the press offered enthusiastic and thoughtfully critical reviews of the papers that certainly helped strengthen the collection as a whole. Of course, tremendous thanks are due to our contributors, who survived multiple rounds of our editorial intrusions promptly and cheerfully.

—Jersey City and Philadelphia, June 2005

Introduction

The New Suburban History

KEVIN M. KRUSE AND THOMAS J. SUGRUE

In the still-developing history of the postwar United States, suburbs belong at center stage. The rise and dominance of suburbia in America after the Second World War is inescapable. In 1950, a quarter of all Americans lived in suburbs; in 1960, a full third; and by 1990, a solid majority.[1] The transformation of the United States into a suburban nation has had significant consequences for every aspect of American life. In terms of politics, the concentration of voters in various suburban enclaves has had the aggregate effect of focusing national political energies first and foremost on the concerns of suburbanites.[2] Social movements have similarly been affected, as the problems of central-city residents—poverty, deindustrialization, and the "urban crisis" writ large—have been edged out of the national consciousness by the agenda of suburbanites.[3] The suburban ascendancy has done more than simply shift the priorities of the nation as a whole; it has also fostered new patterns of localism and isolation that have also revolutionized relationships between individual communities within the nation.[4] Meanwhile, traditional categories for understanding the varieties of the American experience—race, class, and gender—have been thoroughly reshaped by the processes of suburbanization and reshuffled into newer, more complex arrangements.[5]

Perhaps most important, the resettlement of Americans across the suburban landscape has radically altered the basic political economy of the country, decentralizing wealth and power in places distant from their traditional locations in urban hubs.[6] Postwar suburbanization was fundamentally intertwined with the processes that reshaped postwar urban America, including capital flight, the concentration of African Americans in central cities, the hardening of racial divisions in housing markets, and the large-scale shift of governmental resources away from urban centers. Suburbs played a distinct role in the redrawing of racial and ethnic boundaries, in the reconfiguration of the role of the federal government, in the remapping of capital in America's geography, and in the rise of some of the most important postwar social movements, ranging from the New Right to modern environmentalism.[7] For all these reasons and more, suburbanization has come to affect all aspects of postwar life.[8] Any effort to understand modern America must put suburbs at the center. The two are inseparable.

The process of suburbanization long preceded the twentieth century. In its broad outlines, its history has been well told. The first generation of suburban historians offered synthetic accounts of the ways in which public policies, technological changes, culture, and individual desires combined to transform the geography of metropolitan America beginning in the nineteenth century. As these pioneering studies demonstrated, early suburbanization was shaped by the rise of a culture of domesticity that emphasized the separation of work and home, made possible by the ready availability of undeveloped land around central cities, and facilitated by transportation innovations beginning with commuter railways and streetcars and, later, the automobile. Middle-class movement out of central cities was also spurred by perceptions of urban disorder and fears of immigration. The scope, the scale, and form of suburbanization changed dramatically with the advent of the New Deal. Beginning in the 1930s, market-driven decisions were supported and strengthened by public policies that financed single-family home ownership and promoted residential segregation by race and class. Taken together, the government's approach on a wide array of issues led to explosive suburbanization. Federal loan policies encouraged the construction of new housing over the renovation of old. At the same time, tax laws favored homeowners over renters and rewarded construction on suburban "greenfields" rather than the rehabilitation of commercial and industrial properties in central cities. Public housing programs pinned low-income projects in racially isolated neighborhoods in central cities, while federal officials channeled transportation funds toward sprawling highway construction and away from centralized mass transit. "Because of public policies favoring the suburbs, only one possibility was economically feasible," concluded historian Kenneth Jackson.

"The result, if not the intent, of Washington programs has been to encourage decentralization."[9]

The first suburban historians offered comprehensive accounts of the origins and process of middle-class suburbanization. But they sketched out a vision of suburbia that was narrow in both demography and geography. To a great extent, suburban historians implicitly accepted the terms of 1950s-era cultural, social, and architectural critics who described suburbia as homogeneous, conformist, and bourgeois. In his classic critique, published in 1961, Lewis Mumford reviled suburbia as a crushing mass of conformity: "A multitude of uniform, unidentifiable houses, lined up inflexibly, at uniform distances, on uniform roads, in a treeless communal waste, inhabited by people of the same class, the same income, the same age group, witnessing the same television performances, eating the same tasteless pre-fabricated foods, from the same freezers, conforming in every outward and inward respect to a common mold. . . . The ultimate effect of the suburban escape in our own time is, ironically, a low-grade uniform environment from which escape is impossible." Seeing postwar suburbia through the eyes of postwar critics like Mumford, many observers painted a monochrome picture of the suburban world as white, affluent, and conformist.[10]

Indeed, many early suburban historians chose to study only those suburbs that fit that stereotype and, in so doing, reified it. In his seminal synthesis of American suburban history, for instance, Kenneth Jackson argued that there were "essential similarities in American suburbanization." In a single sentence, he offered a list of core suburban commonalities that echoed Mumford in content, if not condemnation: "Affluent and middle-class Americans live in suburban areas that are far from their work place, in homes that they own, and in the center of yards that by urban standards are enormous."[11] In a similar vein, Robert Fishman argued that, at heart, suburbia represented "the triumphant assertion of middle-class values." "Suburbia," in his telling, "expresses values so deeply embedded in bourgeois culture that it might be called a bourgeois utopia."[12] Many suburbs were indeed "bourgeois utopias," populated by affluent Americans who sought out white neighbors separated by ample green space. But an emphasis on bedroom suburbs as a haven for the middle and upper classes overlooked significant diversity by class and race in suburbia. Wealthy suburbanites, after all, depended on all sorts of unskilled and skilled laborers—stone masons and carpenters, groundskeepers and chauffeurs, household servants and laundry workers. Even the early, prototypical upper-class suburbs in places such as Philadelphia's Chestnut Hill and Main Line, Chicago's North Shore, and New York's Westchester County had blue-collar enclaves that were ethnically and, sometimes, racially heterogeneous. In addition, beginning in the late nineteenth century, many manufacturing industries chose suburban locations. By the mid-twentieth century, as the pace of retail, business, and industrial decentralization accelerated, suburban shopping malls, office campuses, and industrial parks employed an army of pink- and blue-collar suburbanites whose working-class world of modest houses, apartments, and trailer parks was central to suburbia, but nonetheless remained on the periphery of suburban historiography.[13]

As such scholars trained their sights on the suburbs, they largely accepted the standard tale of suburban homogeneity along racial and socioeconomic lines, addressing its consequences without ever calling into question the veracity of such claims. Typically, these observers have paid more attention to the suburban uniformity of class rather than race. This is not to say that they ignored the role of race and racism in shaping the bourgeois suburbs they studied. Quite the opposite. Jackson in particular has done much to expose the policies of discrimination and racism that excluded minorities from the suburbs. All too often, however, such scholars have assumed that public and private policies of racial exclusion worked flawlessly and, as a result, they have come to believe that suburbia was more or less the all-white environment that popular imagination and popular culture would have us believe. They have overlooked the real presence of racial minorities in the suburban environment and perpetuated an interpretation that assumes homogeneity of race as well as class. Indeed, as Andrew Wiese has noted, "historians have done a better job excluding African Americans from the suburbs than even white suburbanites." Likewise, other racial minorities have remained largely on the margins of suburban historiography, though certainly not suburbia itself. To be sure, many suburbs, like cities, were marked by patterns of racial exclusion and became battlegrounds in the struggle for racial equality in housing and education. But even such suburbs were shaped as much by the presence of racial minorities as by their absence.[14]

In terms of geography, many suburban histories replicated the shortcomings of an earlier generation of urban history. As sociologist Charles Tilly has observed, urban historians all too often "take city limits as boundaries for the analysis of ostensibly self-contained urban processes."[15] Indeed, most historians of twentieth-century suburbanization (Jackson being the noteworthy exception) wrote histories that inverted Tilly's observation, focusing disproportionately on what happened on the other side of city boundaries. Just as most urban histories left the suburbs out, few suburban histories discussed central cities at all, except through the rear-view mirror of those fleeing urban life. They produced rich accounts of the culture, architecture, politics, and institutions of suburbia with little attention to the interaction of suburbs and cities and, equally important, the relationships between suburbs and other suburbs. As important as the first generation of suburban community studies have been, their inward focus often obscures the larger social, political, and economic processes that reshaped modern America.[16]

One major current in suburban scholarship takes a different tack in explaining the relationship of cities and suburbs. Focusing on developments after the Second World War, many scholars came to see suburbanization as the most recent stage of urban development. Crafting an analytical framework that stressed "the urbanization of the suburbs," these observers increasingly proclaimed the suburb to be the "outer city," an "urban fringe," or a "suburban 'city.'"[17] The "new city" argument found its fullest expression in the writings of Robert Fishman and Joel Garreau. Taking stock of the decentralization of housing, industry, and employment, as well as the widening divisions between the central city and encircling suburbs, Fishman asserted that postwar suburbs represented "not suburbanization at all but the creation of a new kind of city."[18] Likewise, Garreau argued that the urbanization of suburban sites "smashed the very idea" of the suburb as a category separate from the city. "By moving the world of work and commerce out near the homes of the middle and upper-middle class," he asserted, postwar patterns of development and decentralization "knocked the pins out from under suburbia as a place apart."[19] As such scholars came to question the distinct nature of suburbs, they likewise came to doubt the need for a separate category of suburban history as well. Indeed, in Fishman's telling, the many similarities he found between the modern city and suburb meant that "the history of suburbia comes to an end." Historians of the "suburb as city" usefully undermined the tired stereotypes of suburbs as a leafy refuge of domesticity, but they downplayed the most salient feature of metropolitan America: the fragmentation and proliferation of local governments. In most of the United States, the difference between cities and suburbs is political. Suburbs might look more like cities now than ever before, but in most of the nation, they remain separate, usually competitive entities. Municipal boundaries separate and fragment metropolitan areas and govern the distribution of political goods and resources. Suburbs and cities, whatever their commonalities, remain places apart.[20]

The contributors to this collection build upon the path-breaking work of the first quarter century of suburban histories, but they push the field in new directions. As an important starting point, the authors in this collection do not confine their studies to isolated suburban enclaves.

Instead, they take a broader metropolitan perspective, paying attention to the place of suburbs in political and economic relationship with central cities, competing suburbs, and their regions as a whole. The essays in this collection challenge an older scholarship that looks at the history of suburbs largely internally and, instead, examine the ideological, political, and economic issues that bound city and suburb together in the postwar world. At the same time, they explore the tensions that divided suburbs as they competed for business, development, and investment in the politically and socioeconomically fragmented metropolis.[21]

At the core of this project is an argument that twentieth-century suburban history—and, indeed, twentieth-century American history—cannot be understood without close attention to the political and economic transformations that remade metropolitan America. The history of suburbanization and its consequences is, in large part, a question of power. The division of metropolitan America into central cities surrounded by fragmented, politically and economically competitive suburbs was shaped through politics and the law. Public policies, including federal housing and economic development subsidies, state and local land-use policies and environmental regulations, locally administered services and taxation policies, and locally controlled schools, all inexorably shaped the process of suburbanization in the postwar period. The division of metropolitan areas by race and class, a division that was reified and reinforced through the drawing of hard municipal boundaries, created a distinct form of spatialized inequality in the modern United States. This drawing of municipal boundaries represented a form of what Charles Tilly has called "opportunity hoarding," in this case the replication of inequalities through the creation of suburban municipalities that provide differential services to their citizens. Put simply, in postwar metropolitan America, where you lived has determined your access to goods and services and how much they cost in the form of your taxes.[22]

As the metropolitan approach makes clear, however, the histories of cities and suburbs are fundamentally intertwined, even as municipal boundaries kept them politically separate. In one form or another, all of the essays in this collection illustrate this point. Arnold Hirsch, for instance, demonstrates that policies that trapped the poor and minorities in central cities served as an essential precursor to letting more affluent whites create new homes in suburbia. And as David Freund makes clear, the federal financing of metropolitan segmentation along lines of race and class can only be understood from a perspective which considers the city, the suburb, and the nation as interconnected entities. The metropolitan approach not only illuminates the ways in which dividing lines were etched along the urban and suburban landscape, but also shows how such lines were blurred or contested. Andrew Wiese, for instance, investigates multiple metropolitan areas to track the movement of white-collar blacks across city limits and into the suburbs. Matthew Lassiter, meanwhile, discusses how disparate groups across metropolitan Charlotte forged alliances of race and class that transcended a simplistic urban-suburban division. Taking an even wider view, Michael Jones-Correa shows how new generations of immigrants have come together in richly diverse suburban environments to transform the racial and class compositions of the prototypical suburb. Other essays use the metropolitan approach to track struggles over money, growth, and power. Margaret O'Mara, for instance, discusses the ways in which the mobility of capital, assisted by federal policies that encouraged the decentralization of knowledge industries, encouraged sprawl and facilitated the division of metropolitan areas by education and class. Robert Self, in turn, shows how different suburbs could display as much hostility to each other as they might to the inner city, suggesting that competition and cooperation between suburbs needs to receive more attention. In a similar vein, Peter Siskind demonstrates that the combined impact of sprawl across suburbs and squabbling between them led to new alliances that transcended a single location.

Despite the overwhelming evidence of the fluidity of political, social and economic movement across the urban-suburban line, of course, such a line existed in the minds of many residents in the suburbs and cities alike. Once again, a metropolitan approach helps investigate the creation and persistence of divisions. In her essay, for example, Becky Nicolaides explores the ways in which a generation of influential urban scholars crafted a nightmarish image for the suburbs outside their cities, one which contrasted the two worlds as decidedly different places, with little in common save their mutual contempt. Such intellectually crafted divisions were, in turn, cemented as politics and law, as Gerald Frug makes clear. His study not only chronicles the creation of artificial barriers to movement between city and suburb, but also offers prescriptive measures for overcoming such divisions.

Adopting a metropolitan framework, the essays in this collection thus see the city and suburb in dialogue on a number of subjects neglected by the older scholarship. Issues of race and class, for instance, move to the forefront. Many earlier works on postwar suburbia addressed such categories only to note their supposed absence from the suburban scene. Focusing on stereotypical suburban enclaves, populated by overwhelmingly white and middle- or upper-middle-class residents, earlier scholarship assumed that race and class played little or no role in that world. Indeed, as the essay by Becky Nicolaides makes clear, for many early critics of postwar suburbs, the presumed absence of racial minorities and the poor from such locales was one reason for such critics' disdain. The contributors to this collection complicate our earlier understanding of suburban demography by thoroughly demonstrating the diversity of suburbanization. Andrew Wiese details the processes of African American suburbanization, for instance, while Michael Jones-Correa complicates the racial picture of suburbia even more with his attention to the influx of immigrants from Latin America, Asia, and the Middle East.[23]

Our contributors also build on recent revisionist historians who emphasize the class heterogeneity of suburbia. Several essays, for instance, explore the symbiotic relationships between middle-class and working-class suburbanization. Matthew Lassiter investigates how working-class whites came to rebel against the sheltered lives of bourgeois suburbanites and instead found common cause with African Americans in a campaign for "socioeconomic integration." In a similar vein, Robert Self explores the complex politics of middle-class homeowners and Gerald Frug analyzes the exclusionary tools employed by suburbs to maintain their homogeneity of class as well as race. Andrew Wiese's essay pays close attention to the middle-class aspirations of black suburbanites, demonstrating that class concerns shaped their experience of suburbia alongside the more obvious obstacles of racism.

Recognizing that struggles over race and class often overlapped, several of the essays address the intersection of the two, as in Margaret O'Mara's handling of the racial and class exclusivity in high-tech suburbs and Peter Siskind's discussion of the role of fair housing activists in suburban growth politics. Taken together, these studies demonstrate that suburbs came in countless varieties, not simply the affluent and white bedroom communities of the suburban cliché, but also blue-collar suburbs (such as Warren, Michigan; Cicero, Illinois; and Milpitas, California), minority suburbs (such as Freeport, New York; Chagrin Falls Park, Ohio; DeKalb County, Georgia; and Compton, California), and high-tech suburbs (such as Palo Alto, California; Redmond, Washington; Stamford, Connecticut; Bethesda, Maryland; and White Plains, New York).

While the demonstration of suburban diversity sets this volume apart from the standard suburban narrative, perhaps its most distinct contribution is its strong focus on the political economy of suburbanization. Such an emphasis is by no means new, but it still remains underdeveloped in the field. The contributors take as their starting point Kenneth Jackson's path-breaking work on federal housing policy and its role in creating the racially divided geography of postwar metropolitan areas.[24] In spite of its implications for suburban historians, however, Jackson's discussion of the role of the Home Owners' Loan Corporation, the Federal Housing Administration, and the Veterans Administration has had a much greater impact on the recent wave of books on the postwar urban crisis than it has on studies of postwar suburbanization.[25] Several of our contributors offer an in-depth discussion of the impact of New Deal and post–New Deal federal, state, and local public policies on the nature of postwar suburbanization. David Freund explores the impact of federal fiscal policy and the federal impetus to market homeownership on the ideology and practice of postwar suburbanization in metropolitan Detroit. Arnold Hirsch builds upon his previous work in the field with an exploration of federal housing policy in the late 1940s and early 1950s. Margaret O'Mara, meanwhile, traces the role of federal defense and scientific research and development spending on the creation of "cities of knowledge," particularly in the suburban Sunbelt. Peter Siskind explores the rise and troubled history of suburban land-use controls and housing regulations in the 1960s and 1970s, as critics of sprawl, environmental depredation, and exclusivity attempted to reshape suburbia throughout the Northeast Corridor, that broad metropolitan band that extended from Boston to Washington, D.C. Robert Self, through a study of the working-class and middle-class suburbs of Oakland's East Bay, shows how postwar efforts to lure industry and commerce to suburbia created a postwar suburban regime of expansive public services and low property taxes that came apart with deindustrialization and the rise of tax rebellions. Matthew Lassiter further explores the politics of suburbanization by focusing on the struggle over educational desegregation in Charlotte, a rapidly expanding metropolitan area whose consolidated school district encompassed both central city and suburbs. Finally, Gerald Frug, building on his work on home rule and court cases on municipal power, shows the role that state laws played in the perpetuation of suburban boundaries and the unequal distribution of resources and political power between municipalities. Each of these essays points to the centrality of suburbia in the contested politics of post–New Deal liberalism. Suburbs were battlegrounds over nearly every crucial postwar domestic issue, including civil rights, regulatory politics, environmentalism, the military-industrial complex, and the scope of government.

Taken together, these essays suggest a new way of understanding suburban history. The old categories—race and ethnicity, class and culture, even "urban" and "suburban"—are no longer preeminent. While such dividing lines served as convenient markers for an earlier generation of suburban historians, the scholarship represented in this volume finds a new locus in the struggle for power in metropolitan areas, a locus grounded in political economy. Mindful of the diversity of metropolitan America in terms of race, class, culture and politics, these new studies of the suburbs often find more compelling contests for power taking place in the struggles over policy, money, and the law. Such struggles lie at the heart of the suburban experience. Any effort to understand the suburbs—and the nation they have formed—must begin with an effort to understand them. *The New Suburban History* offers a starting point.

ONE

Marketing the Free Market

State Intervention and the Politics of Prosperity
in Metropolitan America

DAVID M. P. FREUND

The modern American suburb is heavily indebted to the federal government. For decades writers have chronicled this debt, documenting how state policy fueled the rapid suburban growth that has so decisively shaped U.S. politics and culture since World War II. Federal spending priorities, mortgage programs, tax incentives, urban renewal, and a host of other public initiatives fundamentally reshaped the metropolis. Most commentators agree, moreover, that those same interventions helped to secure the suburbs' most valuable resources—better housing and jobs, cheap consumer credit, safe and healthy neighborhoods, good public services and schools—almost exclusively for white people, and thus accentuated the nation's racial and class inequalities. The state's early postwar mortgage initiatives, for example, denied most racial minorities access not only to suburbia but also to the many benefits of homeownership. Meanwhile federal public housing, urban renewal, and highway programs undermined existing—often vibrant—minority communities in cities nationwide. By the 1950s and 1960s, the results were visible to most Americans. The fast-growing suburban fringe was becoming the center of postwar affluence, it was monopolizing the best public services and fastest-growing employment sectors, and it was populated primarily by whites who owned their homes. Meanwhile the nation's cities, and especially the minority populations concentrated within them, were left behind.[1]

The suburbs owe another important debt to the federal state, one that has received relatively little attention. In addition to creating wealth for some while helping to marginalize others, federal intervention also helped create and popularize a unique postwar political narrative that obscured the origins of race and class inequality in the modern metropolis. Paradoxically, the state helped popularize the myth that its policies did not facilitate suburban growth and did not contribute to new metropolitan patterns of inequality. Instead it insisted that "free market" forces, alone, were responsible for the gulf—economic and, increasingly, spatial—that separated the nation's haves from its have-nots. Not surprisingly this free-market story was embraced by the beneficiaries of federal largesse, most enthusiastically by an expanding, and increasingly suburban, white middle class. And their investment in this story holds special importance for our understanding of politics and culture after World War II, because suburban whites invoked the narrative and constantly elaborated upon it to justify racial exclusion.

Indeed whites' rationale for residential segregation changed quite dramatically during the years that saw more and more people of European descent attain the "suburban dream." Older, pseudo-scientific explanations for racial exclusion and inequality did not disappear. But beginning in the 1940s, with racial science discredited and a new antiracist, civil rights politics forcing whites, especially in the North, to at least acknowledge the *principle* of racial equality, those older racial narratives were quickly overshadowed by a powerful new defense of the residential color line. In metropolitan areas nationwide, whites increasingly argued that they opposed integration not because of race per se, but because it would disrupt the robust free market for housing that had produced so many thriving suburban communities. Whites began to defend racial exclusion by arguing that they were simply defending the rights and privileges that homeownership had afforded them. Suburban homeownership, in particular, became a powerful symbol of these rights. This subtle but decisive shift in whites' defense of segregation—from a discourse focusing on race and compatibility to one focusing on markets and rights—enabled white people to insist, quite earnestly, that the politics of suburban exclusion was not motivated by racism. As people of European descent mobilized nationwide to maintain the racial homogeneity of their neighborhoods, schools, and even public spaces, a new language of markets and rights helped unite whites that otherwise had few class, ethnic, or geographical ties to bind them.

Of course, this rights discourse—and whites' investment in a vision of purely market-driven metropolitan growth—was not simply the product of government storytelling. Excellent recent studies have helped us understand why so many northern whites came to view maintenance of the residential color line not necessarily as a racial matter but instead as a principled defense of white peoples' "rights"—as homeowners, working people, consumers, or citizens.[2] Quite often, though, scholars portray this rights talk, or even a new "investment" in whiteness itself, as an automatic, almost reflexive defense of postwar privileges in the face of black people's demands for access and political equality. In short this scholarship often portrays the defense of white privilege as a default strategy, rather than fully exploring how the definition of white privilege, itself, was transformed during these years. Moreover there has been very little investigation of the ways that institutional change—specific political and policy interventions—actively shaped whites' understanding of both privilege and inequality in the postwar United States. Institutional change was formative because state interventions taught very specific lessons about the nature of economic growth and patterns of metropolitan change. Most important, the postwar "free market" narrative—and its rationale for maintaining the color line—was popularized by many of the same federal interventions that were fueling economic growth and perpetuating inequality: namely, the banking, monetary, and credit programs that encouraged millions of Americans to finance new levels of consumption by going into debt.

This chapter focuses on one set of federal interventions: the New Deal–era selective credit programs that created the modern mortgage market. It argues that selective credit programs did not merely revolutionize the nation's housing and settlement patterns—a narrative familiar to urban historians—but that they also directly shaped whites' interpretation of postwar affluence, segregation, and inequality. It is well known that in the 1930s new federal credit programs—most famously those operated by the Federal Housing Administration (FHA)—standardized the long-term, low-interest home mortgage and facilitated its use nationwide, thus making homeownership affordable for most white people after World War II. Scholars have shown that by the 1940s, the state had created and begun to sustain an expansive, racially restricted market for the suburban single family home. But the state did much more, because it simultaneously assured the public that its interventions in no way disrupted American capitalism. Mortgage programs, officials insisted, merely "unleashed" existing, but latent, market forces. In short, public officials and policymakers claimed that it was simply the free market for property that produced suburban affluence, metropolitan segregation, and urban poverty. Suburban whites eagerly embraced this story and made it central to their defense of postwar prosperity and privilege.

To understand fully the politics of white flight and white backlash in postwar America, as well as the depth of resistance to redistributive public policies, it is important to examine why so many whites believed that postwar prosperity and racial segregation were simply the products of a free market for housing, one unfettered by government influence. Countless whites came to believe that the state had no right to intervene in the economy or in their local communities because the state helped convince them that it had not intervened in the past. Revisiting the FHA's operations and its political legacy suggests that countless Americans have vehemently rejected federal interventions designed to rectify patterns of class and racial inequality by tapping into a powerful myth about the "free market" for residence, a myth codified and promoted by the state itself.

The FHA, Postwar Suburban Growth, and the Legacy of New Deal Reform

Suburban histories generally pay little attention to banking, monetary, and credit policy because of a common assumption about New Deal reform and its postwar legacy: namely, that the state's most influential interventions were its socially progressive policies, the high-profile and often controversial efforts to create jobs, protect workers' rights, regulate prices, build public infrastructure, and provide social insurance or relief. We know a great deal about programs designed to arrest monopoly control or to distribute market resources more fairly. And scholars have shown that many of these programs were either compromised from the outset—not all deserving citizens could benefit—or undermined in the 1940s and 1950s. Scholars' approach to postwar state policy has often been shaped by a preoccupation with the "failure" of liberal reform, with the abandonment of radical experimentation in favor of policies encouraging unbridled economic growth. This focus, in turn, has led to an emphasis on a seismic shift in federal priorities in the late 1930s, when the Roosevelt administration abandoned efforts to build what Ira Katznelson has called the "developmental state"—one focused on promoting equity and social justice—in favor of a "fiscalist state," characterized by Keynesian, pump-priming interventions designed to promote unregulated growth. Many observers have joined Alan Brinkley in describing this shift in priorities as "the end of reform."[3]

The focus on opportunities lost has generally precluded careful consideration of the New Deal's less progressive reforms, many of which had equally decisive impacts on postwar politics and culture. Perhaps the most notable omission—especially among urban and suburban historians—has been the early monetary, banking, and credit policies that helped make the fantastic economic expansion of the postwar years possible. Historians generally date the emergence of the Keynesian state to the "Roosevelt recession" of 1937–38, when New Dealers, desperate to revive domestic markets, embraced both deficit spending and a compensatory fiscal policy.[4] Yet economists have long told a more complicated story, arguing that earlier federal initiatives, beginning in the Hoover administration and culminating with the Banking Act of 1935, created essential preconditions for postwar growth by revolutionizing the state's ability to manage the money supply and subsidize credit markets. Most important, it was during these years that the state began to regulate and provide capital for private banks and the savings and loan industry, transformed the Federal Reserve from a central bank into a federal regulatory body, and assumed control of discount rates and interest rates. By 1935, it had abolished the gold standard, was insuring a host of private lenders against loss, had expanded its ability to buy and sell Treasury securities as a means to supplement private bank reserves, and had greatly expanded its powers to provide emergency loans to institutional lenders.

The result was that by the mid-1930s, the federal government had set up the mechanisms to promote a new kind of national economic growth by creating and sustaining a very safe and flexible market for consumer credit. Put simply, the state made it easier—in many cases risk-free—for the private sector to lend and borrow, while simultaneously making the national currency more "elastic" so that it could meet producers' and consumers' changing needs. State actors were now poised to promote actively the expansion of credit markets and, by so doing, expand the nation's money supply, effectively creating new wealth.[5] The new system gave the state considerable control over both money creation and credit cycles, so it could strategically target chosen industries and consumer markets for subsidy. And, perhaps most important, the state's credit had now become the linchpin for both stabilizing the economy and fueling a debt-driven economic growth (a process that some economists call the "socialization" of the nation's debt). Taken together, economists argue, these early interventions fundamentally transformed the operations of American banking and credit markets, a transformation necessary to make possible both the fiscalist state and the stunning rates of postwar growth.[6]

Most historians, by contrast, treat monetary, banking, and credit policies not as interventions that transformed the workings of American capitalism, but rather as stopgap measures or concessions to vested interests, designed to "stabilize" existing markets and protect existing market structures. New Deal historians often describe the larger Keynesian revolution as simply reactive—a response "to the transformation of the United States from a producer-oriented to a consumer-oriented society." This analysis, however, threatens to minimize the state's role in facilitating that transformation. The disagreement here is not simply about the timing of the state's most decisive interventions, but rather about the impact of Depression-era legislation on the postwar economy. Many economists argue that state policy facilitated a monetary and credit revolution that created radically new kinds of market relationships, which both enabled and actively promoted a new kind of economic growth. Most general histories, by contrast, insist that these early reforms were designed not to alter the mechanics of the market, but rather to "prop . . . up the institutional foundations of capitalism."[7]

The selective credit initiatives that have received the most attention are the FHA's mortgage insurance programs established by the National Housing Act (NHA) in 1934 and the Veterans Administration's (VA) mortgage guarantee programs, established in 1944. By insuring[8] private lenders against loss, by standardizing appraisal practices, and by popularizing the use of long-term, amortized mortgages, the FHA and VA revived and dramatically expanded the markets for home-improvement and for privately owned homes, eventually making these markets the "bedrock" of the new consumer economy, as Lizabeth Cohen writes, and "central . . . [to] postwar prosperity." It is also well documented that FHA and VA operations systematically discriminated by race. Both agencies endorsed the use of race-restrictive covenants until 1950. And both followed the appraisal guidelines outlined in the FHA's *Underwriting Manual,* which prohibited realtors (and, by extension, lenders and builders) from introducing "incompatible" racial groups into white residential enclaves. "If a neighborhood is to retain stability," explained the first published edition, "it is necessary that properties shall continue to be occupied by the same social and racial classes," for a "change in social or racial occupancy generally leads to instability and a reduction in values."[9]

The FHA removed these explicit racial rules from its manual in the late 1940s, but both agencies actively supported these principles well into the 1960s and thus excluded most racial minorities from the robust new market for homeownership. That market was enormous. Together, the programs helped secure debt financing for millions of dollars of home-repair work and for nearly one-half of all new single-family home purchases between 1947 and 1958. By 1964, they had facilitated the purchase of more than 12 million mostly suburban housing units, almost exclusively for whites. Meanwhile most nonwhites were left to rent a home or apartment, usually in the oldest and traditionally segregated central-city neighborhoods, or to pay for their homes without the benefit of federal largesse.[10]

But calculations of the FHA's and VA's activity do not, by themselves, fully capture the government's impact on suburban growth and suburban politics, for two reasons. First, federal policy simultaneously restructured the "conventional," or noninsured, market for housing credit. Conventional mortgages financed most suburban home purchases after World War II and did so by obeying the segregationist principles outlined by the FHA. Second, federal selective credit programs decisively shaped countless Americans' interpretation of the new, racially segregated metropolis, because they helped convince white businesspeople and white consumers that the state was not meddling in the private market for residence.

The government's dramatic influence on the conventional mortgage market receives, at best, only cursory treatment in most suburban histories. State intervention began with Hoover's creation of the Federal Home Loan Bank system in 1932 and continued for decades. Powerful new federal programs—most important, the Federal Savings and Loan Insurance Corporation (1934) and the Federal National Mortgage Association (1938)— worked in concert with the FHA and VA to bring the terms of conventional lending in line with government-insured mortgages and, after World War II, to sustain the market's meteoric expansion. By standardizing appraisal practices in the noninsured market, insuring savings and loan accounts, and purchasing and reselling existing mortgages, federal programs attracted more institutional lenders into the home loan business and accelerated lending activity. The result was a steady increase in the flow of housing credit, both in the insured and conventional markets. By the late 1940s, the state's conventional market programs had dovetailed with FHA and VA activity to create a very flexible, lucrative, and fast-growing market for housing credit, one deemed safe by institutional lenders precisely because its operations were standardized, regulated, and in many cases directly insured by U.S. Treasury funds. Meanwhile federal oversight also meant that racial discrimination became a national standard because the interdependence of the insured and conventional markets required participating lenders to obey the appraisal guidelines codified by the FHA, including the principle that racial integration undermined property values in white neighborhoods. So, in the final analysis, federal intervention created and sustained powerful new markets for both insured and

conventional mortgage lending, while making racial segregation a constitutive element of both.[11]

In part because of their tendency to downplay the transformation of
conventional mortgage lending, historians have usually described the
FHA and VA as market-friendly interventions that "unleashed" pent-up
demand rather than components of a larger reform strategy designed
to create new wealth by subsidizing a market for debt. Indeed even the
scholarship that acknowledges the FHA's and VA's role in subsidizing
homeownership regularly portrays the larger mortgage revolution, and
the suburban housing market that it created, as the product of free market
forces, insisting that New Deal reformers relied on "unregulated private
markets" to revive construction and meet consumer demand. And they
conclude, accordingly, that the resulting racial segregation of neighborhoods and capital was an unfortunate—but unavoidable—result of policies that simply legitimized and institutionalized existing sentiments and
market practices. Since the federal government did not *create* the new market for private housing, many argue, it cannot be held responsible for the
discriminatory outcomes that this market produced.[12]

Again, housing economists have long understood the state's role very
differently. They have argued that selective credit operations created new
market structures and market relationships, which made possible new
kinds of economic activity and wealth creation. They describe the modern housing market, in other words, as highly regulated and unimaginable
without sustained federal involvement. Among these writers was Miles
Colean, co-author of the bill that created the FHA and later the agency's
chief economist. As early as 1950, Colean described the postwar housing
market as "more completely under [government] surveillance and control"
than it was during World War II. Colean's contemporaries then described
how New Deal and postwar credit programs "create[d] and [kept] in operation a greater number of banks and S&Ls than a purely competitive process
would have permitted," how the state "increased the flow of funds into
residential construction" by billions of dollars, and even how new financial
industries were born "to meet a need that was created when FHA and VA
operations [helped create] a national market for mortgages." James Gillies
explained quite simply in 1963 that "market forces do not set the return"
for investment in the modern mortgage market. Two years later Raymond
Goldsmith summarized the consensus among economists, writing that
"the effects of government participation in the residential mortgage market were so strong, pervasive, and intricate, that it is impossible to visu-
alize the form this market would have had in the absence of government
intervention." Starting with the assumption that government programs

gave birth to a new kind of postwar housing market, many of these writers simply debated whether or not selective credit policies—as opposed to, say, direct payments—offered what one author called the most "appropriate method of subsidization."[13]

A glimpse at the operations of the FHA further demonstrates how state policy created new market activity and wealth for specific businesses and consumers. Most notably, federal officials designed, promoted, staffed, and eventually managed credit agencies by working closely with the private sector, especially representatives from the building, home finance, and real estate industries. From the outset, the FHA enlisted private organizations to collect data for every metropolitan region on tenancy patterns, property values, building permits, the volume of housing sales, employment trends, payrolls, and the financial conditions of local lenders. Meanwhile in Washington, FHA administrators consulted with developers and bankers to assess the program's impact, propose legislative reforms, and lobby congressmen for their passage. And the FHA's technical staff organized educational conferences nationwide to introduce the insurance system to businesspeople and municipal officials and to coordinate local lending efforts.

Postwar planning began as early as August 1945, when FHA Administrator Raymond Foley appointed a committee to examine how the agency could "be of help to private enterprise in all broad phases of the post-war housing market" and specifically to determine "what further authorities may be necessary and desirable to put us fully in [that] market." Administrators continually met with bankers, mortgage lenders, builders, insurance executives, and realtors to discuss legislative adjustments to current FHA policy. Indeed, collaboration remained so integral to postwar operations that staff members repeatedly turned down offers of honorary membership in private building and financial institutions, insisting, as one official noted, that while it would not be "illegal," it could nonetheless be "embarrassing" and seen as a conflict of interest. Regardless, the FHA continued to work with business groups at the local and national levels to measure the programs' impact on business volume and to co-sponsor educational events. In fall 1948, for example, the FHA joined forces with the National Association of Home Builders to sponsor 110 meetings in 60 cities, at which 13,500 attendees were updated on the new liberalized terms of insured mortgages and the reauthorization of the government's secondary market operations.[14]

The need for such an intense public-private collaboration in the promotion and operation of the new mortgage market has two important implications for the history of suburbanization and postwar inequality.

First, it further demonstrates that the state did not merely revive and expand existing housing markets—or awaken "hibernating" capital, as many contemporaries liked to say—but rather was instrumental in creating new supply, new demand, and new wealth. Even the FHA's first administrator, James Moffett, admitted as much, at least in the early 1930s, telling business audiences that the agency was "creating a year-round market" for home improvement and "educating the banks to carry on indefinitely a tremendous amount of lending," activity that would "develop far more business than in the past." "There are billions of dollars to be taken out of" the mortgage insurance programs, he predicted, acknowledging that "no such market has ever before in all history been offered industry."[15]

Second, if the depth of public-private collaboration underscores the government's role in structuring postwar growth, it also helps explain the state's ability to popularize an alternative—and dominant—narrative: the claim that it was not federal policies, but rather the free market for homes, that was fueling both prosperity and new patterns of inequality. In addition to structuring and subsidizing the postwar housing economy, the state also helped shape whites' vision of that economy. And by doing so it helped fashion a language that enabled whites to support racial exclusion while insisting that they were not "racist."

Federal Housing Policy and the Marketing of a Myth

Given the postwar repudiation of pseudo-scientific racism and increasing support for the principle of racial equality, the public renunciation of racism by white suburbanites is hardly surprising. Whites in the North and West had long supported residential segregation, in cities and suburbs alike. But to do so in the wake of a war against fascism and in the midst of a national debate over civil rights required a new, race-neutral rationale. Whites fashioned a new rationale for housing segregation by tapping into the countless Cold War–era celebrations of consumption, the single family home, and the power of the free market to resolve economic conflicts. Above all else, homeownership became for countless whites a cornerstone of what Lizabeth Cohen calls the new "faith in a mass consumption postwar economy," which celebrated an "integrated ideal of economic abundance and democratic political freedom." In this context whites saw the protection of their homes—from any kind of supposed threat—as the right of any citizen who had held up his or her end of the economic compact.[16]

Still, in most histories of the postwar suburbs, the impact of housing policies on white racial politics is rather narrowly construed. Scholars describe government policy as doing little more than fueling growth and segregating housing resources, thereby creating the geographic, architectural, and economic settings in which countless local battles over neighborhoods, housing, jobs, and schools took place. In short they portray the state as helping to create the segregated metropolis, but then treat the fact of segregation simply as a stage for these (presumably) more politically formative struggles. Indeed, these histories typically depict the new language of rights as a "homegrown" phenomenon. They assume that whites simply ignored the state's role in perpetuating racial discrimination and then used local conditions and local events to construct rationales absolving them of responsibility for segregation and inequality. But structural transformations and local organizing do not, by themselves, explain whites' fundamental misunderstanding of postwar prosperity and inequality. A closer examination of selective credit programs reveals that the state was also instrumental in creating and popularizing a powerful narrative about metropolitan change, the story that it was impersonal and value-neutral markets—not white people—that made racial segregation necessary. Widely embraced by a new generation of suburban residents, this myth would have profound implications for racial politics in the postwar decades, because it enabled whites to support racial segregation openly while insisting, quite earnestly, that exclusion was not fueled by prejudice.

Government intervention promoted this story in two closely related ways. First, by entering the mortgage market in the 1930s, the state validated and disseminated a relatively new economic theory about the relationship between race and property: the claim that the laws of free markets required the racial segregation of residence. That theory quickly became conventional wisdom among white businesspeople and consumers, encouraging them to portray racial exclusion not as a byproduct of their racial preferences, but rather as an inexorable market imperative, one confirmed by the hard science of land-use economics. Second, and paradoxically, the state actively promoted the story that it was not interfering with the free market for homes.

The creation and operation of the new selective credit programs helped shift whites' thinking about the relationship between race and property. Put briefly, New Deal interventions created a new market for credit (and thus a new market for private residence) that explicitly disqualified minorities from participation, yet justified exclusion without invoking the principle of racial "difference"—a dramatic departure, indeed, from the common rationale for segregation invoked in the years before the Depression. Officials claimed quite explicitly that federal appraisal guidelines were *not* racially motivated, but rather tailored to respect the principles of real estate economics, which simply required racial separation. Put another way, federal intervention gave birth to a suburban housing market grounded in the principle that racial exclusion was solely an economic imperative, rather than a product of personal preference or a belief in racial difference. Accordingly the maintenance of segregation quickly became a prerequisite for assuring robust metropolitan growth. Federal officials did not invent this "market imperative" theory; it had its origins among a loose-knit coalition of realtors, planners, and housing economists, who led the movement to promote race-restrictive covenants and municipal zoning during the 1910s and 1920s. But their rationale for exclusion remained a minority view at the time and largely unnecessary given state sanction for racial discrimination and whites' deep investment in racial pseudo-science. During the 1930s and 1940s, the market imperative theory of segregation rapidly became the dominant and, in many settings, the sole rationale for segregating residential neighborhoods by race. This transformation occurred as the theory was codified by federal intervention and written into the operations that oversaw the new market for residence.

The means of dissemination were quite conventional. The theory was outlined in the *Underwriting Manual* and in the other professional publications that quickly set the standards for construction, appraisal, and real estate practices nationwide. Beginning in 1934, the rules that structured the suburban housing market explicitly described nonwhites as a calculable, actuarial risk to white-owned property. This meant that the market's day-to-day operations were now governed by the principle that racial exclusion was both necessary and not ideologically driven. This principle quickly became foundational to businesspeoples' and consumers' defense of racial exclusion, not coincidentally during the years that more and more whites were declaring their commitment to racial equality. By the 1940s, the state had helped create a new economic environment that defined nonwhites as a threat to property and markets for property—not, that is, as a personal threat. This encouraged a generation of whites to view racial exclusion not as an act of individual or group racism, but rather as a matter of sound land-use planning.[17]

Meanwhile the state shaped whites' ideas about metropolitan growth even more directly and self-consciously. Most important, it aggressively promoted the story that free markets and consumer demand alone enabled the nation to rebound from the Depression and later fueled suburban growth. During the years that its mortgage programs popularized the theory that it was not racial difference or prejudice, but rather the impersonal forces of the market, that required racial segregation, the state simultaneously assured consumers that its intervention was in no way distorting the natural market for residence.

Significantly it was not the race issue per se that produced this characterization of selective credit operations. Indeed most housing officials were unapologetic about the program's racial rules, seeing no conflict between promoting homeownership and excluding minorities from this new market.[18] Instead what most preoccupied New Dealers was the need to convince business groups and fiscally conservative congressmen—and, perhaps, even themselves—that the government's unprecedented interventions in the U.S. economy were not cutting a path toward "state control" of private enterprise. Policymakers feared, justifiably, that doubts about the economic soundness of the mortgage insurance experiment would keep people from lending, borrowing, and spending and thus undermine the program's potential to resuscitate the moribund economy.

So to calm a Depression-weary public and to ensure the requisite economic activity, the FHA aggressively marketed its programs, with a multifaceted promotional campaign designed to draw institutions and consumers into this new and largely untested market for credit. The agency sponsored speaking tours, produced radio and film advertisements, distributed promotional literature, hosted regional "home" fairs, and sent canvassers to millions of individual residences. The goal was to increase lending, borrowing, and spending on home construction, purchase, and repairs, by convincing Americans that the new, government-insured market for credit was safe. Yet the rhetorical refrain holding the campaign together was a celebration of the "free market for homes" and that market's untapped curative powers. Uniting the speeches, pamphlets, and other appeals in this ambitious public relations gambit was a consistent reminder that federal mortgage programs were wholly compatible with free enterprise, and that American consumers and businessmen held the keys both to national recovery and sustained economic growth.

The most visible PR efforts targeted consumers and businesspeople in local communities. They began on August 9, 1934, when the FHA kicked off its "Better-Housing Campaign," a multimillion dollar effort to stimulate borrowing and spending for both home improvement (under Title I of the NHA) and new home construction (under Title II). FHA Administrator James Moffett described the initiative as a "massive education campaign," even defining the "business of the Housing Administration" as "a vast, nation-wide selling job, an educational campaign to sell the public on Better Housing." The key to ensuring this new market's success, he believed, was informing businesses and consumers about federal insurance and the opportunities that it afforded them. Within a week, the agency supplied 28,000 financial institutions with copies of the rules and regulations for Title I insurance. By late October it had spent $1.3 million on the campaign and had mailed out over 52 million pieces of literature. Meanwhile its new "public relations division" initiated local Better Housing campaigns in thousands of communities, appointing regional, state, and district directors who supplied educational materials to businesspeople, chambers of commerce, and civic groups. By early December, the FHA had appointed 4,513 community chairmen, who in turn had initiated 3,245 community campaigns. And by then, house-to-house canvasses were underway in over 1,100 municipalities, where volunteers tried to "persuade property owners," Moffett explained, to get started on "the modernization and repair work they need." The campaign was enthusiastically embraced by municipal officials, local businesspeople, and average citizens, who often contributed novel promotional ideas of their own. For example, fifteen "church women" involved in the house-to-house canvass in Fairfax, Oklahoma, "decided to modernize their own homes as an example to the rest of the town."[19]

According to agency estimates, in just four months the campaign had already generated between $145 million and $210 million in business nationwide. Its rapid impact was attributable, in part, to the unique institutional environment created by the federal government's new stake in credit markets. Because the FHA's day-to-day operations involved constant public-private collaboration, on both the national and local levels, the agency had a ready-made platform for its promotional initiatives. The collaboration that made FHA operations possible (and cost-effective) also facilitated its efforts to promote lending, borrowing, and spending. And by year's end, those efforts had organized 4,000 communities and initiated 3 million household visits. By March 1935, campaigns were underway in 6,000 communities—which together contained about 65 percent of the country's population. House-to-house canvasses in over 2,000 locales had reached 5.6 million individuals. The canvassing, alone, secured pledges for over 1 million home improvement jobs.[20]

Meanwhile the agency enlisted the nation's newspapers and magazines, supplying them with "education copy" and inviting dailies and press associations to use the FHA's "spot news and feature service." By December 1934, over 1,000 newspapers—accounting for 55 percent of the nation's dailies—were running Better Housing sections or supplements, ranging in size from 1 to 33 pages, while more than half of the nation's 1,600 trade publications, according to Moffett, were "cooperating with [the FHA] in a fine spirit." Half of the nation's 2,000 dailies had already requested additional promotional materials—exclusive articles or features tailored to their communities—while another 2,500 weeklies, mostly from rural areas, had asked to be included in the campaign. Moffett called the press "a godsend to the Housing Administration," claiming that news coverage and advertising was providing "invaluable help in telling American industry and the public generally what we have to offer them."[21]

Other media and venues were equally influential. The agency prepared films, radio promotions, exhibits, and posters for distribution and broadcast. An FHA-produced weekly radio feature, "The Master Builder," was so popular that the agency drafted a form letter to expedite responses to fan mail. And in a particularly aggressive campaign, also initiated in August 1934, senior FHA officials spoke directly to the public over NBC and CBS affiliate stations, introducing listeners to the mechanics of the federal mortgage insurance system and assuring them that it was now safe to borrow. These programs were essentially primers in the new housing economics, literally teaching listeners how the new long-term mortgage worked and advising them how to take advantage of federal insurance. Yet the speeches were always bracketed by assurances that the market's revival was being driven solely by the forces of supply and demand. Audiences learned that FHA operations did not change or disrupt existing markets, but rather "invite[d] capital once more into the home-mortgage field," "restore[d] normal real estate values," and "permit[ted] new construction to proceed again." The new programs were "straight business proposition[s]," FHA spokesmen insisted, which meant that economic recovery would be achieved not through government spending but rather by "loosen[ing] up frozen credits in the form of existing mortgages."[22]

The message remained constant throughout the 1930s, altered only by increasingly aggressive appeals to spend ("every owner of home or business property [would] be wise to modernize and repair while present prices prevail," Moffett told one audience) and by increasingly detailed instructions for soliciting the agency's help. By 1938, Administrator Abner Ferguson was telling listeners over WCFL, a Chicago radio station, that the FHA was "prepared to see you all the way through your construction from the time that you first consider building a home until the last nail is driven and the final papers are signed." He also encouraged his audience to visit local agency offices, where they could obtain "a list of those private institutions which are lending FHA insured mortgage funds in your locality." And he assured qualified borrowers that the agency would not only "insure your mortgage" but also "guide you until you own your home outright." Such direct offers of agency stewardship, however, did not stop officials from insisting upon the program's compatibility with the free market for property. "Remember," Ferguson concluded, "the Federal Housing Administration has no money to lend. It is not competing with private capital, rather it is bringing private capital back into the mortgage field."[23]

Parallel to this public campaign was an extensive effort by FHA administrators to reach out to countless trade and municipal associations. By December 1934, Moffett had introduced the mortgage insurance system to meetings of the Chicago Association of Commerce, Pittsburgh's Duquesne Club, the New York Chapter of the American Institute of Banking, and to a builders' convention in Knoxville, Tennessee. The following spring, he spoke before the Advertising Club of New York, the Oklahoma Chamber of Commerce, and a meeting of the National Retail Lumber Dealers' Association in Washington, D.C. His successors toured the country throughout the 1930s, 1940s, and 1950s, addressing hundreds of audiences: real estate groups; chambers of commerce; local, state, and regional associations of bankers, mortgage bankers, and builders; and the national conferences of groups including the American Title Association, the National Association of Mutual Savings Banks, the Home Builders Institute, the American Bar Association, and the Institute of Cooking and Heating Appliance Manufacturers.[24]

The goal was to educate businesspeople about the new mortgage market, update them on amendments to the insurance programs and promote lending, advertising, building, and spending. FHA officials exhorted their audiences to encourage consumption, either by spreading the word about the new mortgage programs informally, or through direct participation in the agency's promotional campaign. In 1935, Moffett told a national conference of lumber dealers to "advertise more . . . [and to try] new methods of promotion," reminding them of their responsibility to "make every property owner in your community conscious of the program through which a responsible citizen can either improve an existing building or build a new home." Months earlier he told advertisers in New York City to "persuad[e] industry that it does a fine job for itself and for all business through liberal use of its advertising space to point out how and why its products can be used in modernizing and repairing buildings." These appeals were bracketed, without fail, by declarations of the programs' compatibility with private enterprise. Speaking before a Memphis meeting of the American Title Association in 1935, for example, Ferguson even outlined what he called the "fundamental premise" of FHA insurance operations:

1. That private capital operations in the housing field are both necessary and desirable.
2. That private capital in that field can and must be made effective upon a far wider scale than has ever been possible heretofore.

3. That the collapse of our real estate and mortgage market under the impact of the depression was not caused by any defect in the theory of private capital operation, as such, but by the unsound, unrealistic and disastrously short-sighted system of appraisal and finance [under] which those operations were conducted.

Ferguson added that he was "somewhat puzzled by talk, emanating from certain quarters," that the FHA represented "an unwarranted and competitive intrusion by the Federal Government into legitimate private business sphere." The program was in no way "an attempt by the government to infringe upon private businessmen," he insisted. "To private business it offers not a threat but an opportunity."[25]

After a wartime hiatus, the FHA responded to considerable pressure from the builders' lobby and resumed its multifaceted promotional efforts. In addition to launching an "economy housing" campaign in January 1949, designed to promote construction of smaller, more affordable single-family homes, FHA administrators made hundreds of appearances before industry groups, where they guided the private sector through the constant revisions of the National Housing Act (such as the liberalization of terms on Title II loans, and cutbacks in agency activity during the Korean War). On occasion FHA representatives literally reprimanded private organizations for not doing more to accelerate borrowing and building.[26]

Meanwhile the celebration of free market principles grew even more pronounced. Administrator Raymond Foley set the tone in a September 1945 speech before New York financial and building interests, noting that "never in recent years has there been a more generally expressed agreement that the housing task of this nation is one to be done for the most part by private enterprise." He confidently predicted that once government restrictions on building materials were lifted, the nation would quickly meet its citizens' housing needs solely "through the channels of private enterprise." Variations on this story provided a chorus for the FHA's postwar talks and publicity efforts. In 1948 and 1949, builders in Illinois, Oklahoma, and Texas learned that their industry's fate would be determined solely by "competitive supply and demand economics," and they heard predictions about a spike in residential construction that would be a testament to the "determination of private industry to surmount the current difficulties in . . . housing American families." Mortgage bankers in New York City and builders in Wisconsin and North Carolina learned that it was "up to private industry as a whole" to jump-start the housing economy and produce more affordable housing. And FHA spokesmen assured California mortgage bankers that "adequate funds [were] available" for the financing of new housing projects, so it was up to private industry to build. Once housing starts picked up considerably, by 1951, realtors in Georgia and mortgage bankers in Washington, D.C., were reminded that the surge in suburban development had "been accomplished with private funds by private investors," and that "every dollar" spent on government-guaranteed homes "is private capital and every property is privately owned." Reinforcing the message were repeated threats to introduce so-called nonmarket alternatives if necessary. Administrator Franklin D. Richards told builders and lenders in Tennessee, for example, that unless the nation's businesses met the needs of moderate-income families, they would have to acknowledge that "private enterprise is not equipped to do the job."[27]

This ambitious PR campaign represented only the agency's most self-conscious effort to cast federal mortgage programs as nothing more than incentives to healthy market activity. Since the earliest congressional debates over the selective credit initiatives, advocates portrayed them as means to "unleash" frozen markets and to "unloosen" existing funds—what one administration official memorably called "sleeping capital." National press coverage of New Deal reform dutifully repeated the message. This narrative accompanied policy debates throughout the postwar period, as well, both in legislative chambers and popular commentary on the suburban housing boom. Franklin Richards repeated the refrain in 1952, when he urged the House Banking Subcommittee to sustain the FHA mortgage insurance program by stressing that his agency "does not make loans and does not plan or build housing." "I want to emphasize the fact that every cent of money advanced under any FHA plan is private capital of private lenders. It is important, too, to take into consideration that this is a completely voluntary system. The $25 billion in loans that the FHA has insured is solely because of [sic] the confidence of lenders and borrowers in the system." Fittingly, the agency's self-published history, issued in 1960 to commemorate its twenty-fifth anniversary, described the FHA as a "do-it-yourself program." The FHA was "a helper only," the pamphlet explained, and its achievements were those of "the builders, lenders, realtors, and other members of industry with whom it has worked, and the American families whose enterprise and integrity have made the program succeed."[28]

Meanwhile this story about the market friendliness of federal credit operations and, crucially, the market imperative for racial segregation permeated local conversations about suburban growth, housing, race, and rights. In many cases the links between federal intervention and local discussions were quite concrete. Businesspeople requested copies of administrators' speeches, which they distributed to local lenders who were "not as yet converted"—as one mortgage banker wrote in 1939—or reproduced in trade publications and industry yearbooks. Others jumped wholeheartedly into the promotional efforts, including Albert Merrill, president of the Kroger Grocery and Baking Company, who promised to display FHA advertising in each of his 5,000 retail stores, to place FHA literature in the 700,000 grocery bags that left those stores daily, and to inform his 22,000 employees and 20,000 stockholders about federal programs. Suburban residents, realtors, and elected officials defended racial restrictions by pointing to the racial compatibility guidelines from FHA appraisal manuals. Private sector publications continued to reproduce those guidelines—if in a more muted form—well into the 1960s.[29]

In other cases the evidence of the state's impact is more indirect, as its arguments about markets and race were reproduced by whites in numerous local conversations and political mobilizations to protect their suburban neighborhoods. Residents read local news coverage describing the postwar housing boom as the fruit of free enterprise and describing public housing as an unwarranted strain on the market, no doubt unaware that these columns often originated as industry or government-produced press releases. Realtors, builders, lenders, and local FHA officials—long exposed to the government's promotional efforts and its appraisal guidelines—spoke regularly at meetings of homeowners' associations, zoning boards, and other groups debating development. In these venues they defended exclusion—of apartments, factories, or black people—solely by citing market imperatives and the principles of real estate economics, rules that required the separation of "incompatible" land uses. Indeed local businessmen and officials might return from regional meetings with FHA representatives to join with their neighbors and constituents in hard-fought battles against what they called "invasion"—be it by an individual black family, a federally subsidized, low-income housing project, or a terrace-style multifamily development.[30]

Most important, this story about postwar markets quickly became foundational to whites' defense of racial exclusion. The state originally promoted the free market narrative—its celebration of the economy's soundness and the pluck of the nation's producers and consumers—to deflect criticism of its new interventions in private financial markets. But in doing so it simultaneously told a story about the difference between those who had "made it" in postwar America and those left behind. Thus it provided white businesspeople and consumers with what seemed a sensible and specifically nonracial defense of racial exclusion. Indeed, FHA officials were among the first to invoke the free market narrative specifically for this purpose when challenged by civil rights activists to abandon the agency's discriminatory practices. Indignant at the charge that federal programs were discriminating by race, housing officials countered that they were merely respecting the demands of the free market for property.

One familiar statement of this defense was presented in 1941 by FHA Administrator Abner Ferguson, when he appeared before a meeting of the Negro Business Conference in Washington, D.C. To an audience waiting for some sign that the FHA would open all of its programs to minority businesspeople and consumers, Ferguson instead offered a refrain already familiar to black leaders, and one that they would hear repeatedly throughout the postwar decades.[31] "In any consideration of how the FHA program can benefit Negroes," he began, "certain things must be kept in mind." "The law is one providing insurance of loans made by private capital to property owners for the repair . . . [or] purchase . . . of homes . . . Nowhere in the law is there any compulsion upon financial institutions to make these loans. And, of course, in our form of Government the Federal authorities cannot dictate to whom a private financial institution shall or shall not lend its depositor's [sic] funds." His agency was "enjoined by the law," Ferguson continued, "to insure only those mortgages which are economically sound," and this required, among other things, that eligible properties be located in neighborhoods that are "desirabl[e] as a place of residence over a long period of years." Black occupancy, he explained, had been deemed undesirable by the market itself—not by the FHA.

Indeed, Ferguson repeatedly declared the agency's commitment to racial fairness, promising that it would give all qualified borrowers "the same consideration . . . regardless of race, color or creed." But he coupled this promise with an important qualification, the logic of which is vital for our understanding of postwar racial politics. When the FHA "appl[ied]" its programs "to Negroes," he explained, it encountered "two specific problems," the first of which he named "marketability." "FHA operations, of course, do *not create* the market. The national income, general business and industrial activity, the shortage or supply of materials and labor, local customs and many other conditions of a given moment are the barometers of the real estate market." And because of this, "the FHA can only follow the trends in the existing market and accept it as we find it, giving reasonable consideration to what changes may be expected in the future." The second problem, he continued, was "income," explaining that since most blacks were poor, they could only "be provided adequate housing . . . through Government subsidy." Ferguson concluded by reiterating that "what we *can* do for [Negroes] is limited by the law, and in no sense are those limits to be construed as discrimination because of race."[32]

FHA and other housing officials rehearsed a version of this defense throughout the 1940s, 1950s, and 1960s, while their programs, despite constant pressure from civil rights activists, continued both to subsidize suburban homeownership—for white people only—and to segregate public housing. Not even the Supreme Court's defense of the principle of equal protection, first in *Shelley v. Kraemer* (1948) and later in *Brown v. Board of Education* (1954), altered officials' stance. Within the FHA and the other programs reorganized under the Housing and Home Finance Agency (HHFA) in 1947, white officials steadfastly refused to interfere with what they portrayed as objective market considerations. Eisenhower's nominee to run the HHFA, Albert Cole, even announced during his 1953 confirmation hearing that he would not stop local authorities from maintaining racial segregation in federally funded programs. Then throughout his six-year term he obstructed enforcement of nondiscrimination, insisting that the government could not "legislat[e] acceptance of an idea." Meanwhile the FHA, while eventually disavowing its support for race restrictive covenants and removing the explicitly racial language from the *Underwriting Manual*, continued to encourage the use of privately published appraisal standards that identified racially "mixed" occupancy as an actuarial risk. Even during the 1960s, prominent white housing officials echoed Cole's position, despite the 1962 Executive Order banning discrimination in federally supported housing, despite passage of Title VI of the 1964 Civil Rights Act, and despite Robert Weaver's tireless efforts, both as HHFA administrator and secretary of the new Department of Housing and Urban Development, to enforce the new fair housing mandate. The height of the modern civil rights era saw most white housing officials repeatedly declare their commitment to racial equality, while insisting, in the same breath, that market dynamics and "local custom" nonetheless trumped the government's fair housing obligations.[33]

Two fallacies of this "free market" defense for discrimination deserve special note because both would figure prominently in whites' postwar efforts to exclude minorities from suburban neighborhoods. First, despite officials' claims, federal selective credit programs did, indeed, discriminate *because of race*. They never discriminated against blacks solely because of income differentials, as Ferguson and other FHA officials often insisted, or simply because inexorable market forces demanded it. Rather, they discriminated by asserting and enforcing the principle that the presence of a black resident posed a calculable threat to white economic interests, a principle that guided practices in both the insured and conventional mortgage markets.[34] Federal interventions set the rules for this new credit market and federal operations made its existence possible. Thus, to deflect responsibility for discrimination to the "market" is, in effect, an admission of federal culpability. Second, and equally important, public housing was not the only form of government subsidy in the postwar era. Selective credit programs actively subsidized the market for private housing, and thus suburban growth. And they did so almost exclusively to the benefit of whites.

The gap between the real impacts of federal intervention and the conventional wisdom about its role in shaping the postwar suburb helps explain a key paradox of suburban politics. Why did so many whites insist, so earnestly, that their preference for segregation was not racially motivated? And why did they see suburban growth and their own prosperity simply as products of fair competition in a free market for property and neighborhoods? Their investments in these claims turn out to be related. For most whites were encouraged to see racial and class segregation as the result of healthy competition in a robust market for private property. It followed quite naturally that defending the spoils of that market was not an ideologically motivated act. Supporting residential segregation, whites believed, need not have anything to do with racial preference.

Thus the state's deep involvement in the market for homes helps us understand why in local communities nationwide—and particularly in the fast-growing postwar suburbs—white people enthusiastically embraced a story about the free market origins of their prosperous, homogenous neighborhoods and the new lifestyle that economic growth had made possible. Of course government policy and its aggressive promotional efforts do not alone explain suburban whites' views on race, property, and homeownership. There was no shortage of paeans to free enterprise in Cold War America, while advocates of fair housing and public housing were regularly targeted for their un-American or socialist tendencies. Popular film, television programming, and print advertising also contributed to the pervasive celebration of market values and free enterprise. But the FHA's efforts suggest that the state itself, in concert with its private-sector allies, played a critical role in shaping whites' views about suburban growth and their insistence that minorities posed a calculable threat to the free market for residence. On the issues of homeownership, neighborhood integrity, and race, federal programs helped popularize the story that suburban growth and prosperity, as well as the racial segregation and poverty that accompanied it, owed nothing to the state's own efforts.

TWO

Less Than *Plessy*

The Inner City, Suburbs, and State-Sanctioned Residential Segregation in the Age of Brown

ARNOLD R. HIRSCH

On January 10, 1955, the National Committee against Discrimination in Housing (NCDH) launched a rhetorical assault on President Dwight D. Eisenhower's housing policies. Declaring the president's program "misguided," the committee asserted that it did little more than promote and finance "a vast program of intensified, enforced segregation." It was quite simply, in the committee's estimation, a policy of "incredible folly and recklessness." Writing a full decade before the "long, hot summers" of the 1960s, the NCDH presciently admonished that the housing initiatives of the 1950s would "fix" a "pattern of constrictive ghettos ... upon America" that would increase the "danger of violence."[1]

The target of this verbal broadside was the urban renewal program recommended by the President's Housing Advisory Committee in late 1953 and presented to Congress in January 1954. The occasion that called it forth was the firing of Frank S. Horne from government service. A nineteen-year career employee, Horne directed the Racial Relations Service (RRS), an agency given the mandate, within the various housing agencies, to protect minority interests. Created in 1938, largely as a result of Robert C. Weaver's vision and hard work, Horne served as Weaver's handpicked successor. Applying a policy based on the concept of "equity" through the 1930s and 1940s, Horne and a handful of black RRS staffers secured

33

a "fair share" of public housing units, construction jobs, and even management positions with the Public Housing Administration (PHA). Able to work within a framework of segregation, the "equity" policy, nonetheless, in the hands of Horne's RRS, generated new challenges by the early 1950s.[2]

The RRS thus found itself, at times, playing a contradictory role. Conscious of the desperate need to facilitate the construction of new housing for African Americans, Horne and company worked feverishly to open the private housing market. They especially pressured the Federal Housing Administration (FHA) and Veterans' Administration (VA) on behalf of an emerging, housing-starved black middle class. Despite such actions, however, they still tried to slam the bureaucratic brakes on those postwar developments launched by local authorities that seemed little more than exercises in "Negro removal." President Harry S. Truman's upset election in 1948 emboldened Horne to change his strategy from what he characterized as a "defensive 'holding operation'" to "an all-out offensive."[3] The final years of the Truman administration subsequently saw service officials encouraging local experiments in nondiscrimination and desegregation.

Horne continued, moreover, to indulge his penchant for writing lengthy, scathing, and incisive memoranda regarding the operations of the Housing and Home Finance Agency (HHFA) and its constituent agencies—the FHA, PHA, and (after the passage of the Housing Act of 1949) the Division of Slum Clearance and Urban Redevelopment (DSCUR)—detailing weaknesses in policy and practice. His actions had already compelled revisions in the process of project approval under the Housing Act of 1949 that were designed to give voice to (dis)affected minorities. And Horne's careful cultivation of allies outside the government, such as the NAACP and the NCDH, not only served to place additional pressure on his bureaucratic colleagues but also made him a symbol of policies that stressed equality of treatment.[4] He subsequently survived one attempted purge in 1953 only to succumb to a more concerted effort in 1955.

Personal and political reason abounded, therefore, to make Horne an obvious target for President Dwight D. Eisenhower's new HHFA administrator, Albert M. Cole. A defeated Republican congressman from Kansas, Cole could not avoid questioning the loyalty of such an outspoken Democrat and Adlai Stevenson supporter as Horne. More to the point, the patronage-starved Republicans, locked out of power through the long political winter known as the New Deal, desperately sought jobs for their own supporters and hoped to transform what had been a merit-based civil service slot into a patronage plum.

There was, however, a much larger significance, a greater structural determinant that lay beneath the surface of the Horne-Cole confrontation.

The Eisenhower administration inherited much more than a horde of job-seekers and a housing shortage. A festering urban crisis brewed as well—and the political dilemma was far more easily stated than addressed: How could the second Great Migration, increasing black militancy, and majoritarian racist sentiment be accommodated, the President might well have asked himself if given a moment to see the situation whole, within a single plan to revive decaying metropolitan cores, avoid another postwar depression, and strengthen the national economy? If enhancing the fortunes of the Republican Party while rolling back the influence of the New Deal were tacked on, Ike's "to do" list became more daunting still.

In short, the culmination of a demographic revolution that transformed African Americans from the nation's most rural population to its most urban, the budding of a civil rights revolution that invested such novel concentrations with new political power and voice, and an ongoing (though still largely invisible) process of deindustrialization that continued to eat away at already aged and frayed central cities, called forth a political response that contributed heavily to the rapid departure of whites to the relatively vacant suburban fringe and the anchoring of the poorest nonwhites in the central core. The rise of "second ghettos" in the postwar era and the suburban boom were thus organically linked. The appearance of a two-tiered federal housing policy represented, then, much more than the division of the market into public and private spheres.[5] Nor did that system's easy accommodation of an unprecedented degree of residential segregation sufficiently capture its social significance. It was, in the end, not the mere fact of racial separation that was important, but the population's decidedly less than random distribution between the core and periphery that enabled the Eisenhower administration to contain, if not resolve, its hydra-headed urban problem.

It would have been possible, theoretically, to have developed a middle-class black housing market far more extensively after World War II, even if it entailed the development of scattered, highly segregated enclaves situated on still vacant urban land. A growing black middle class could have entered the private market, become home and property owners, and provided a more variegated residential pattern (not to mention suburban experience) with untold future consequences. And if they had done so simply as scattered individuals vested with the same property rights as other citizens (as opposed to being tenants in planned, monoracial developments), the impact would have been greater still.

But they did not, and the cumulative effect of federal housing policies—ranging from urban renewal, slum clearance, and public housing to FHA/VA mortgage insurance (and a host of related programs that impacted housing)—was to produce a federally sponsored social centrifuge that not only separated black from white but increasingly linked the latter to placement on the economically dynamic fringe as opposed to the crumbling core, to equity-enhancing single-home ownership as opposed to means-tested, multigenerational tenancy, to the receipt of the hidden subsidies of the private market instead of the very public subsidies associated with PHA projects.

Obviously, such results represented tendencies, powerful though they were, and not absolutes. The suburbs were not, in fact, entirely white and the inner city, though increasingly identified as nonwhite, also held recent immigrants, the remnants of earlier waves of settlement, gentrifiers, and iconoclasts of all colors. But to the extent that location revealed race, class, and status, however, the popular image of a white suburban noose looping around a black-occupied core conveyed the Eisenhower administration's answer to the nascent urban crisis. A full-fledged construction boom that fueled a staggering expansion of the national economy, a laundry list of ready-to-go projects that could be taken "off-the-shelf" to prime the Keynesian pump in the event of a downturn, the expectation of home-ownership on a racially exclusive metropolitan periphery for whites, and more, new, and better housing for African Americans constituted the foundation upon which the new accommodation stood. That the housing intended for blacks was largely segregated, concentrated in an increasingly obsolescent central city, and provided little entre to the private, mainstream market was the price for being noticed at all. "Containment" seemed the operative principle, not simply as a Cold War foreign policy, but also in domestic, racial affairs. Contain as many African Americans as possible in the central city—especially if they are poor, the reasoning appeared to go—and provide housing for the mushrooming black middle class on the outer banks of the core settlements, on the vacant urban fringe beyond that, and, only to the extent necessary, in new suburban developments beyond municipal borders. If pushed to this final extreme, development would be undertaken on a segregated basis in isolated locations. Coincident economic and suburban booms sustained each other and proceeded without the fear that values and futures would be jeopardized by uncontrolled African American settlement.

Urban renewal, in other words, would be the underside of the process of suburbanization as it unfolded after World War II. This is not to say, of course, that policy or politics could be assigned the sole responsibility for articulating such goals and successfully reaching them. Stated objectives often appeared in the garb of social reform in the case of urban renewal and proved, not surprisingly therefore, elusive. And the suburbs appeared as just another success story to be attributed to the unfettered free market and natural law. But the degree of segregation, the degree of separation and isolation, as well as the functional connection between core and periphery, were deeply influenced and conditioned by political choices.

Postwar Redevelopment Under the Democrats

Two early examples of the process at work in Chicago and Baltimore set the tone, established precedents, and demonstrated how eager local authorities could seize the new federal tools to implement longstanding plans to shore up established barriers and, in fact, establish new ones. First, a set of remarkably durable beliefs misinformed both policymakers and the general public with regard to the construction and occupation of urban accommodations at the end of World War II. The racialization of property and the stereotypical images that rose from that fact remained powerful constraints capable of conditioning policy. The resurgence of migration, the massive overcrowding in already dilapidated neighborhoods, the lack of materials for repairs, and the lack of incentive to make them conspired to accelerate the urban aging process, particularly in African American neighborhoods. Such external realities meant little, however, to those who wedded the rush of urban difficulties to the personal characteristics of the city's newest inhabitants. The Hyde Park–Kenwood Association in Chicago, for example, in a letter to black civic leader Irene McCoy Gaines, assured her that the association's rejection of black neighbors was "based on behavior, not color." "The Negro has shown neither disposition or ability to maintain a decent American community," the association declared. A black "college graduate will live next door to a pickpocket and rent a room to a prostitute," the group complained. It was this "insistence on indiscriminate mixing" that has "contaminated with vice and crime" the local neighborhood, church, and schools. The answer, according to the Hyde Park group was to advise blacks to "try bathing and not belly-aching."[6]

The notion that African Americans lived under such segregated and dangerous conditions by choice or preference even gained currency among city officials and others whose experience should have taught them better. In trying to trace the whereabouts of those blacks forcibly displaced from a number of project sites, the Chicago Housing Authority (CHA) discovered that "higher income families" actually remained in the "slums" until forced to vacate their apartments by the onset of redevelopment. This was evidence, the CHA believed, not of the severity of the housing shortage or ubiquitous discrimination, but of the residents' preference for the "unusually low rentals in the slums" and their doubts that an "improved quality of housing" would be worth the "increased costs." Yet the real "enigma" for the authority was the number of families eligible for public housing who accepted instead the worst the private market had to offer in preference to the projects.[7] Unwilling to probe very deeply to get at the root of the problem, many whites seemed satisfied to believe a life under such conditions was freely chosen.

Whatever the cause of the lack of housing or the horrendous, overcrowded conditions, there was a consensus among whites—even those seen as "reformers"—about how to relieve the distress. One such detailed plan came to Holman D. Pettibone, president of the Chicago Title and Trust Company and a major force in the city's redevelopment, through the Chicago Association of Commerce and Industry's Leverett S. Lyon. The way to "solve the colored man's problems" was to completely rebuild the area between Twenty-second and Thirty-ninth "for colored occupancy," Lyon's missive suggested. Because it was obviously insufficient for Chicago's vast numbers, and unsuitable for much of the black community's middle class, the author also called for the development of two additional sections, both "suburban in character." In holding up the CHA's low-rent Altgeld Gardens as a model, however, it was clear that he was referring to its isolated, far southside location and not any imagined status as a well-to-do-community of detached, owner-occupied homes.[8]

To the extent that Pettibone pondered the plan to provide blacks "adequate housing" through redevelopment, however, he had his own notions of where it should be located. In communicating with investors, Pettibone acknowledged the need for private as well as public projects, the existence of a middle-class African American market, and the necessity for carefully selecting sites. Given the possibility of choosing among several plans and locations, he and his colleagues noted explicitly that if the neighborhood selected for redevelopment was "close in," it "would have to be a negro project."[9]

The notion that the city should be divided into racial sectors, explicitly or implicitly, was ubiquitous and took many forms. The scheme entertained by Pettibone was not even the only one coming out of Hyde Park. Where the first plan considered rebuilding a solid bloc of the near South Side, another emanating from the Hyde Park Property Owners' Association asserted that it was "absolutely essential" to recycle the "many thousands of vacant parcels of land" scattered throughout the central city. Proponents of both approaches, however, found themselves united in the belief that black mobility had to be controlled and the assumption that existing

African American communities had to be "improved within themselves to prevent the encroachment of blight."[10] Everyone had to realize, one of Pettibone's correspondents wrote, "that both whites and colored have acute problems which tend to develop dangerous fears." Whites needed only to provide "adequate housing through redevelopment" to solve the "colored man's problems," this observer theorized. In return, "the white man" should receive assurances that "certain areas coveted by colored will remain white until a better solution is found."[11] The great problem, however, was that the crushing housing shortage, combined with the dilapidation of the existing supply, meant that any degree of slum clearance or demolition necessitated at least *some* relocation of teeming inner city residents to the relatively sparsely populated urban fringe. The "inside-outside," "black-white" division could not be absolute.

Even the strongest political allies of the African American community recognized the explosive potential inherent in the situation and subsequently worked with that reality in mind. The U.S. senator from Illinois, liberal Democrat Paul H. Douglas, frankly acknowledged the inescapable necessity of relocating at least some "slum dwellers" to the "outskirts" of the city. But, needing to reassure constituents that he did not advocate the kind of social engineering that threatened the racial exclusivity or economic security of their new, suburban communities, Douglas released for public consumption a letter to HHFA Administrator Raymond M. Foley that announced his belief that the federal assistance used to pay for such vacant sites was nothing more than an "adjunct to the slum clearance operation." The acquisition of such sites at public expense was not a prelude to the dispersal of minority populations into outlying suburbs, the senator insisted. The real intent of such a program, in other words, was not to alter racial patterns, but to make the inner city a proper and desirable place to live. The acquisition and development of open sites should "at all times be subordinate to . . . the actual clearance of slums," Douglas wrote. Left between the lines was the clear implication that the provision of more and better housing in the inner city would relieve the pressure promoting racial succession. Reassuring Douglas that the program's "primary purpose" was, indeed, the augmentation and improvement of the central city's housing supply and the facilitation of an economic revival, Foley responded that it would "be my policy to administer that program in such a manner as to concentrate its benefits on local programs that will place maximum emphasis on the actual clearance of slums."[12] In short, the goal was to refurbish and increase the housing available in the core, while recognizing a minimal need for public relocation housing on vacant, peripheral sites. Holman Pettibone could not ask for more.

Chicago may have been a pacesetter in responding to the demographic, economic, social, and political multi-crisis that redefined urban America in the postwar era, but it was hardly idiosyncratic. Baltimore, a border city that put into place formal structures of segregation (such as a dual school system) represented characteristically Southern cities whose residents displayed perceptions and prescriptions that would be familiar in many Chicago neighborhoods. Enduring a postwar wave of neighborhood transition and racial succession, Baltimore experienced, as did Chicago, "blockbusting" at its worst. Playing on traditional fears and hostilities, unscrupulous real estate dealers stirred up a racial panic in those communities vulnerable to black expansion. Buying cheaply from whites and selling dearly to African Americans, they rode the attitudes expressed by the Hyde Park–Kenwood Association to the bank. Arguments may persist as to whether whites were victimized by stereotypes and myths, or whether they acted pragmatically in face of the real world choices placed before them. In any event, the results were the same.[13]

Similarly, the common racial perceptions and beliefs that attended the growing black presence in Chicago and Baltimore evoked comparable attempts at accommodation. If whites generally conceded (or, at least, understood) that blacks needed more and better housing, many questions remained unresolved. As indicated by Holman Pettibone, those in the private sector giving these problems the closest attention did not contemplate an integrated or nondiscriminatory society. The favored location for black urban redevelopment was "close in," in their view; and if suburbanlike, vacant fringe areas (whether within or beyond municipal boundaries) had to be considered out of necessity, such sites were to be situated in isolated, self-contained, and generally undesirable locations.

In Baltimore, not even the wartime emergency could dampen the angry protests and threats sparked by municipal and federal authorities when they sought shelter for nonwhite workers. City and national officials feared violence on the part of whites who had no trouble making their feelings known. Even temporary projects, slated to come down at war's end, called forth mobs of protestors. Selecting sites for a new permanent black presence thus seemed out of the question—in either city. In Chicago, even enlightened and empathetic thinkers such as community organizer Saul Alinsky and University of Chicago sociologist Louis Wirth engaged in a "heated discussion" over the issue. Pragmatist Alinsky supported a CHA resolution to build a project on the edge of the urban frontier at 130th and Langley just to get the units built and people housed. Wirth denounced it as an attempt to "foist" an "unfortunate" site on the black community and believed that "no housing" was better than what was being offered.

Indeed, the proposal took "no account of the real needs of the Negro community nor of their social problems," as Wirth complained. The attempt to whip up public support for the authority's position amounted to nothing more, the academic concluded, than a "whitewash" intended to make the CHA's "stupidity look like wisdom."[14] Lacking the "enlightened" component of the Chicago debate, Baltimore, by the end of 1943, had built no more than seven small projects for industrial workers to meet the wartime crisis. Whites occupied all of them.

The result was that, even before the war ended, the Housing Authority of Baltimore City (HABC) planned, through clearance and redevelopment, to increase the density of already identifiable black neighborhoods and thus stabilize the city by "arresting" the movement of minorities. As for the great difficulty in finding a suitable inner-city location to accommodate thousands of war workers, the city had no choice but to finally agree to an outlying, vacant site. After an "exhaustive study of all available sites," the HABC selected Cherry Hill, an area bounded by the polluted Patapsco River, marshlands, and a railroad right-of-way. Reminiscent of Chicago's Altgeld Gardens in its splendid isolation, the site selected likewise served more than one purpose. Once rejected as a potential recreational park, Cherry Hill contained a cemetery and an incinerator among its prominent features. Also among its attractions, however, were its postwar possibilities as the core of a new, spacious permanent black settlement. The site was large and contained enough low-rent public relocation units to facilitate the massive demolition program contemplated by the HABC. Indeed, one authority official noted its rough proximity to another African American enclave, Mt. Winans, and concluded that the "whole area might be developed . . . as a large colored section, which could house a large colored population without overcrowding." For its part, the FHA approved a private project for blacks in the shadow of Cherry Hill's public units sparking great enthusiasm among federal officials eager to cooperate with local authorities in creating "such a controlled and preplanned neighborhood."[15]

Such straws in the wartime wind were clear indicators of postwar problems. Chicago and Baltimore subsequently provided major headaches for the HHFA and Frank Horne's RRS when they pursued redevelopment projects under Titles I and III of the Housing Act of 1949. From the site selection for public housing to the issues of "Negro removal" and the reduction of living space for minorities, the Midwestern metropolis and the border city outside the nation's capitol served as troubling models for those projects that followed. In Chicago, slum clearance transformed public housing essentially into a "Negro program" that contributed to

African American containment and segregation, the RRS reported. Frank Horne, moreover, felt compelled to warn his superiors that federal approval of Chicago's plans, and the statistical legerdemain employed to bring them into technical compliance with the law, would only provide "sanction for the expansion of 'ghetto' living." Explicitly linking the exploitive character of inner city life to the willful refusal to consider outlying alternatives, Horne also noted that "the development of open land sites for private and public housing projects, open to Negroes, is the missing key" to a successful redevelopment program.[16]

In Baltimore, the seizure of black-owned and occupied property for whites and the use of redevelopment to achieve an unprecedented level of segregation could have put the Windy City to shame if it had any. Indeed, as was the case in Chicago, redevelopment plans depended upon racial succession "as white people move[d] out of certain neighborhoods" and the increased population density that accompanied racial transition. It also led to protests from the NAACP and an appeal from Frank Horne to "review and appraise" the city's loan application and grant contract "since fundamental questions of policy would appear to be involved." Anticipating the results of any such objective review, the NAACP's Clarence Mitchell declared that not only did the federal government have no obligation to assist Baltimore's redevelopment program, but that it had "no right" to do so under current circumstances. HHFA Administrator Foley assured Mitchell that federal discussions with local officials demonstrated the latter's awareness of the "necessity . . . to increase the supply of decent, safe, and sanitary housing for minority groups" and the former's "encouragement" for such a course. Beyond that, however, Foley claimed there was little he could do. "It should be borne in mind," he artfully reminded Mitchell, "that this agency does not have the authority to compel any local public agency to establish requirements governing the racial characteristics of the families to be rehoused in redevelopment projects."[17]

This was cold comfort, indeed, for the local agency's housing goals for black Baltimoreans were less than modest. Looking to the postwar period, the HABC acknowledged that the development of vacant, outlying tracts for African Americans seemed out of the question. According to the HABC, such sites were not only difficult to find, but they were "almost invariably contiguous to white residential developments" where "very violent neighborhood resistance" could be expected. The authority, like its counterpart in Chicago, subsequently settled upon a strategy of upgrading existing black communities. With little new housing built for blacks in Baltimore since the ante bellum era, however, the job proved overwhelming. The HABC ultimately conceded that the least it could do to "carry out its legal function is to use every effort to convert the obsolete and low rent areas from squalor to minimum decency, and to put such areas to their most complete and beneficial use." Where the *Plessy* standard of race relations spoke of "separate but equal" accommodations, those responsible for redevelopment in Chicago spoke only of providing undefined "decent living conditions," or, in Pettibone's case, "adequate" housing. Baltimore could get no further than to recognize the need for "minimum decency."[18]

If Chicago and Baltimore could be counted among the first cities to engage in a planned effort at ghetto renewal and economic revitalization, they soon had company as Detroit, Birmingham, and Savannah, among a handful of other cities, quickly fell into line, each asking for federal authority, sanction, money, and powers to implement locally devised redevelopment plans intended to contain the "threat" posed by the growing number of African Americans. By the summer of 1951, Horne complained bitterly to Foley that the Chicago experience merely highlighted a more general "surrender" to practices that "created and nurtured racial residential restriction" that were contained in "current proposals" from "Detroit, St. Louis, Baltimore, Norfolk, Tampa, New Orleans, Dallas, etc." "Surely," he stated plaintively, "the vast powers, funds, and prestige of the Federal Government are not to be utilized to underwrite official irresponsibility and community immorality."[19]

Frank Horne, the RRS, and a Push toward Nondiscrimination

Despite appearances, Horne had every right to be optimistic as the nation entered the second half of the twentieth century. In 1947, he had witnessed the emergence of a newfound, seemingly genuine concern for civil rights on the part of the president as evidenced by his unprecedented report on the subject, *To Secure These Rights.* The Supreme Court then weighed in with its decision in *Shelley v. Kraemer,* rendering racially restrictive covenants unenforceable in May 1948. Though there had been some bureaucratic foot-dragging in accepting that judgment, by early 1950 even the recalcitrant FHA stopped requiring such covenants as a condition for obtaining their approval. And the passage of the Housing Act of 1949 was a mixed bag that still held considerable grounds for hope. Congress had authorized the construction of 810,000 units of public housing in order to facilitate redevelopment, thus providing the possibility of an urban makeover that would address both questions of racial equality and the housing shortage. If, early on, Chicago's Lake Meadows project and Baltimore's Waverly and Johns Hopkins developments revealed an enormously destructive and discriminatory potential as well, Horne could still play "defense" by stalling approval of their plans and holding up the work.

Oddly enough, it was a portion of the Housing Act of 1949 that did *not* become law that was of the greatest significance for Horne and the other RRS staffers as they attempted to pull and tug the HHFA and its constituents in the direction of greater equality. Two conservative Republican U.S. senators, John Bricker of Ohio and Harry Cain of Washington, proposed an amendment to the Housing Act of 1949 that would have prohibited segregation in any project built with government assistance. Hostile to the enlarged role for public housing and hardly champions of racial equality, Bricker and Cain hoped their amendment would split Southern and Northern Democrats and compel liberal civil rights activists such as Illinois's Democrat, Senator Paul Douglas, to vote against integration. If the amendment were added, there was little doubt the housing bill would be defeated. If it were voted down, Congress would be on record as having considered and rejected a policy of nondiscrimination, with all that that implied for the bureaucrats charged with regulating and implementing the program. Any attempt to assault segregation administratively in the implementation of the act would be met by denials of authority and calls for explicit congressional reconsideration or an executive mandate. This was, in fact, the shield behind which Foley hunkered down in his response to Clarence Mitchell. Lacking, then, specific authorization from the legislative branch or a direct presidential order, those unwilling to challenge the status quo had a safe political haven. Horne and his allies had been placed in a box from which escape seemed impossible.[20]

The RRS, however, was not without resources, and it found a way to turn the stock HHFA rationales for inaction against themselves. In lieu of the specific micromanagement by Congress or the president, or the formal adoption of sure-to-be controversial racial policies, the HHFA simply *had* to develop its own bureaucratic guidelines and regulations—even if only implicitly through customary patterns of behavior that escaped daily scrutiny because they were so familiar. Among the HHFA constituents, perhaps the PHA's traditional deference to local housing authorities in the selection of sites for low-rent public housing projects stands out among these. The local tendency to pack, stack, and/or isolate those developments built with public money and federal sanction may have dismayed some officials beyond the fraternal bonds of the RRS, but the nearly universal reaction was to throw up one's hands and move on to the next project.

Customarily a way to avoid a national discussion on race while allowing states and cities to use federal aid to support the existing order, it now seemed possible, Horne believed, to turn that approach on its head.

If some saw an opportunity to enhance residential segregation through the application of newfound federal assistance, others were swept up in the movement toward nondiscrimination and chiseled some cracks in the wall of racial solidarity. On the eve of the Supreme Court's *Brown* decision, seven states had passed laws against segregation or discrimination in public housing; a few others had similar statutes governing redevelopment, and Illinois had a broader civil rights law that (according to liberal forces, at least) covered housing. Additionally, twenty-five cities and local housing authorities approved ordinances or passed formal resolutions prohibiting segregation in the implementation of the Housing Act of 1949. And, less formally, some two hundred local housing authorities issued statements favoring nondiscrimination while forty other localities could report some measure of integration in their projects even in the absence of any written policy. These facts, the RRS believed, documented significant local support for their agenda, and they moved to get the PHA to facilitate the removal of racial barriers in these places, just as it had sustained them everywhere else.[21]

The RRS staff's evolving strategy and intentions were sweeping and potentially subversive. By the spring of 1953, they sought a policy "reorientation" that would "place positive emphasis upon the principle that occupancy" in all federally assisted dwellings "be available to families of all races . . . on the same basis." The new policy could be promulgated immediately, they believed, with regard to defense housing and "all forms of public housing owned by the Government of the United States and operated by it or its local agents." It should, in short, not only compel a "reexamination" of occupancy policy under both Titles I and III of the 1949 Housing Act but apply to the permanent housing built for war workers under the Lanham Act and those private homes that fell back into government ownership when their occupants defaulted on FHA loans. As for federally aided but locally owned low-rent projects, the staff proposed "consideration of a policy that would indicate that the occupancy of these projects would be expected to adhere to pertinent local, state, and federal law." Field officers would be instructed, moreover, that local authorities would not be "permitted to enforce racial segregation in federally aided public housing projects" in the absence of such "legal restrictions on the use of public facilities."[22]

Among a slew of other proposals, these revealed, by themselves, a calculated strategy to contain and isolate pockets of segregation, much the same way abolitionists attacked slavery a century before. By proposing a ban on segregation where it was not mandated by state or local law, the RRS clearly targeted the North's brand of administrative apartheid. They sought, in short, to nationalize a policy of nondiscrimination, to make it a sort of default setting, and compel those who would deviate to make affirmative legislative statements to the contrary. Learning the lessons of the 1949 debate over the Bricker-Cain amendment to ban segregation, they wanted to remove the power to separate the races by regulation alone. They refused, simply, to accept segregation as an unquestioned, unproblematic part of some "natural" order. Nondiscrimination, in their view, should be the unthinking norm.

Not surprisingly, there is no evidence the Housing and Home Finance Agency administrator entertained their notions. The service subsequently swung into action in the early 1950s on the basis of two arguable assumptions. The first was a seemingly unbounded optimism that both time and history were on their side; its corollary was that a start could be made in those locales in the legislative vanguard of freedom. The second was that race relations was at least as much science as art, and that RRS officials were the "technicians" with the expertise and nearly two decades of experience who should be entrusted to lead the nation down the path to equality.[23] Underestimating the government's capacity for hypocrisy, they would learn that federal deference to local law and expressed sentiment was not absolute; indeed, it seemed one-dimensional, preserving the status quo or, in fact, enhancing segregation. Beyond that, they would have to confront the reality that laws, ordinances, and resolutions—particularly those favoring nondiscrimination—were often symbolic or political gestures that did not command the majority or committed support their adoption might imply.

After *Shelley* and the acceptance of the massive public housing program implicit in the Housing Act of 1949, however, the RRS goaded the PHA to accept the service's determination to "give aid in any way desired" to those localities that had "decided on integration." To that end, racial relations personnel produced two pamphlets—*Integration of Racial Minorities in Public Housing* and *Open Occupancy in Public Housing*—as "how-to" manuals. In what could only be labeled a split decision, PHA leadership shelved a third publication detailing local experiences with integration after it had already been produced and limited the distribution of the first two because it feared project managers might "misinterpret" them to be directives.[24]

The RRS pressed on despite the lack of official encouragement. In a confidential memorandum, the staff now attacked as "obviously unrealistic" the traditional practice of linking the racial composition of projects to the proportion of minorities in the "population as a whole or in the immediate neighborhood." "Conformance with neighborhood ratios," they declared, did not represent "sound planning," and, given the changing demographic scene, it failed "to recognize the basic need" of minorities for more living space. Finally, the service declared, denial of black access to large numbers of extant units violated the equity principle given the disproportionate African American demand for low-rent public housing. Racially integrated programs, they knew, had always "at least modified existing neighborhood patterns."[25]

Faced with the prospect, then, of introducing blacks into all-white enclaves, the RRS enumerated the "'special' techniques and principles" that would facilitate a peaceful transition. From the criteria for the selection of the first black families who would serve as pioneers crossing a contested racial frontier to the selection of their units, the timing of their occupancy, and the training of housing authority staff, racial relations advisors pored over every detail. Mindful of implacable opposition, the service nonetheless remained confident in moving forward in the belief that its careful handling would result in the application of objective, nondiscriminatory administrative policies and procedures that would "maintain the interracial character" of its projects and preclude the outbreak of violence. The threat of disorder was, the staff believed, "the least difficult of the problems involved" in integration; if trouble erupted, they concluded innocently, "it can be most decisively handled because it is illegal and subject to control by the forces of law and order."[26]

Eisenhower's Policy

There is little doubt about the rightward drift in the nation's basic housing programs that followed hard upon General Eisenhower's election. The process that produced Cole's appointment to head the HHFA was one indicator. His nomination as housing administrator followed a concerted lobbying effort by business and industry interests primarily concerned with reducing (if not eliminating) the nation's public housing program. A "roundtable" in Rye, New York, sponsored by *Time* and *Life* magazines—and one that included the newly sworn president's personal representatives—provided a venue for the discussion of a contemplated HHFA reorganization and further refined the criteria for its new leadership.[27]

Eisenhower's confidantes reported an emergent consensus on two points. First, the purpose behind initiating the shift from slum clearance to renewal was the general desire to emphasize rehabilitation over massive demolition. By redirecting resources away from the poorest areas and reducing the need to shelter those displaced by a scorched earth approach to urban revitalization, it would be possible to shrink the demand for public housing and ultimately, perhaps, eliminate the program altogether. Second, members of the roundtable agreed that the new housing administrator must keep public and private housing programs separate. As Aksel Nielsen, Eisenhower advisor and president of Denver's Title Guaranty Company, put it, the HHFA's leader should be "a man who has, first of all, a desire to separate the self-supporting agencies from the subsidized agencies."[28]

Nielsen obviously perceived the existence of the two-tier housing policy recently identified by historian Gail Radford.[29] Private sector programs, especially those of the FHA, occupied the upper, frequently suburban, tier and made available supports and incentives designed to ease the transition to homeownership for its virtually all-white clientele. The second tier consisted of means-tested, low-cost, low-rent public housing in the only program to offer benefits to African Americans from its inception. Special Assistant to the President Charles F. Willis, Jr., quickly detected an ideological compatibility between Nielsen and Cole and, after discussing the nomination with a handful of others, sent Cole's name forward with the support of the home-building lobby.[30]

A second indicator of a rightward drift in policy came with the appointment and report of the President's Advisory Committee on Government Housing Policies and Programs. Weighted heavily with representatives from the building, real estate, and loan industries, the committee generally ignored race—as did Cole and the president—in its deliberations and recommendations. This was not "color-blindness" of a nondiscriminatory sort; it was, instead, a willful ignorance more akin to a superstitious person's whistling past the graveyard than a referee's fair arbitration. In speaking of slum "prevention" rather than slum "clearance" and in eschewing a "piecemeal" attack on the problem by adopting a "broader" approach that would treat causes as well as symptoms, the committee once again redirected public resources away from the most decayed neighborhoods and announced that urban renewal was no targeted effort at social reform.[31]

Convening at the end of 1953, committee members could not avoid hearing from Frank Horne, who lobbied hard for a general policy of nondiscrimination in any transaction or development in which the government played a role. Not content to see that principle applied to urban renewal and public housing alone, Horne made the case for extending it to cover the FHA, the black middle class, and outlying, vacant land developments (that is, suburbs) as well.[32] Pursuing nondiscriminatory color-blindness as a default setting for all government involvement, Horne did not enjoy much success. Indeed, the committee dutifully reported at the end of 1953 that it was "deeply concerned with the housing problems of minorities" but promised only that it would deliver "substantial improvements" in their general housing conditions.[33]

The articulation of a "substantial improvements" standard for black housing is notable in that it logically could—and certainly did—fall far short of the then regnant, but already legally challenged, "separate but equal" guideline established in *Plessy*. In both cases, the "separate" part of the formula was simply taken for granted. The "equality" promised by *Plessy*, however, had always been honored in the breach. As an increasing number of cities now scrambled to provide "equal" services in the attempt to forestall the principle's legal demise, those devising a national plan for urban revitalization could neither see beyond nor aspire to more than "substantial improvements." And, given the state of minority housing in the 1950s, this was a low bar, indeed.

This should have come as no surprise, for the committee's blueprint for renewal was driven, according to *Business Week*, by the "twin objectives of satisfying the demand of the American people for good homes and the maintenance of a sound and growing economy." Hardly conceived as an aid package for minorities, urban renewal devolved responsibility back "on private business and local governments" and did so with the goal of "upgrading real estate and human values." The national press almost universally recognized and consequently praised the conservative principles that framed the program.[34]

Administrator Cole presented the advisory committee's urban renewal proposal to the President in a Cabinet meeting on December 9, 1953. Horne's detailed memorandum to Cole on racial policy and his personal briefing of the advisory committee notwithstanding, neither the report nor the Cabinet cared to discuss explicitly—at least on the record—the racial implications of the proposal. Eisenhower and Cole were certainly aware of the plan's racial impact, and the report only lingered over it long enough to deny the efficacy of a legislated solution. In preemptively asserting that urban renewal constituted a "well-rounded program" that would benefit "the entire country," the president acknowledged that the committee's legislative proposal emerged not as a laser beam pinpointing the neediest, but more as a measure highlighting the interconnectedness of all groups in a "trickle down" world.[35]

Much of what the president had to say to minorities subsequently focused on the housing problems that would be caused, not solved, by the administration's initiative. First, he offered assurances—important assurances given the recent experience in Chicago, Baltimore, and other cities—that he would prevent their dislocation by the misuse of slum clearance projects and that those who would necessarily be uprooted would have a "fair opportunity to acquire adequate housing." And for those who could afford market-rate housing, he promised "equal opportunity for all of our citizens to acquire within their means good and well-located homes." Again, the standard seemingly applied here is "separate and adequate" or, on the outside, "good and well-located" with the "separate" left unsaid.[36]

That the "separate" could be fairly read into the text, there could be no doubt. Indeed, in reading Cole's initial draft section on renewal, presidential advisor Gabriel Hauge had apparently scribbled a terse, two-word commentary in the margin: "condones segregation." Equally important, the portion of the speech eliciting that note seemed the only section to escape revision and appear in the spoken version as it had originally been written.[37] It is easy, of course, to read too much into such reactions. But, at the least, it is possible to say that the results of the Eisenhower proposals were hardly unpredictable or unforeseen. Whether intended as policy or merely accepted as a necessary evil, the dire outcome denounced by the NCDH should have been no surprise.

It must have been very difficult not to have noticed the danger in the intersection of race and housing in the year leading up to *Brown*. Bitter racial accusations swirled about plans for slum clearance in Birmingham, Alabama, and redevelopment proposals in Baltimore. Mob violence in the Chicago suburb of Cicero had shocked the world in 1951, and that city's seemingly endless disorders continued through 1953 with the reaction to the Chicago Housing Authority's attempt to desegregate the Trumbull Park Homes.[38] But Eisenhower's counselor on racial affairs, Max Rabb, registered the administration's apparently genuine surprise when it was accused of "giving aid to segregated housing." "This is a brand new problem that I haven't touched at all," the president's expert on minorities mused six months into Eisenhower's first term. It may, he concluded with a bit of understatement, "represent an area of some difficulty."[39]

Still, the administration showed little inclination to do anything about it. Indeed, as late as May 17, 1954—the very day the Supreme Court outlawed "separate but equal"—Max Rabb condescendingly dismissed Walter White's complaint on behalf of the NAACP that administration support for segregated, suburban Levittown developments constituted an "arrogant . . . abuse" of public resources and power. While the president voiced the opinion that the federal government should not discriminate "in its own acts" and believed it "highly improper" to lend public support to a development where "one man by himself could bar a race from a whole community," he "held a more reserved position in regard to 'indirect' activities such as loan guarantee programs for private housing."[40]

When the court finally rendered its judgment, then, the administration's considered reactions reveal that *Brown* became less a clarion call to end racial discrimination in housing as well as in education than it was a "firebell in the night" evoking the construction of new defenses. A flurry of self-examination subsequently consumed the housing agencies through the spring and summer of 1954.

Personal racial predilections aside for the moment (there is no reason to believe they would have worked in favor of liberalizing racial policy), the upper reaches of the administration found compelling economic and political arguments militating against an easy acceptance of *Brown*. A White House meeting subsequently produced no more than a call for a housing conference that offered a quota system for new construction and a site selection process Walter White compared to South Africa's.[41] Industry warnings that radical change would kill the postwar building boom and open the door for a new depression combined with the possibility of political gains in a panic-stricken South to suggest an abundance of caution in considering how to respond to the court's determination.[42]

The failure to embrace *Brown* shaded into resistance in some quarters, and the extension of the court's ruling to housing could nowhere be taken for granted. Indeed, starting with the HHFA and extending down through its major constituent agencies, the housing hierarchy's reticence in bringing their policies into line with the newly declared racial realities proved manifest. HHFA General Counsel B. T. Fitzpatrick took a narrow, hard line and advised Administrator Cole that the "Court expressly limited its overruling of the *Plessy v. Ferguson* 'separate but equal' rule to the field of public education." Where Fitzpatrick argued the law, the Associate General Counsel for the Division of Slum Clearance and Urban Redevelopment (DSCUR) argued the facts, claiming they were not "analogous" in the two instances and that a "major extension of Federal authority" remained unwarranted in the realm of housing. FHA Director Norman Mason took a practical stance. He simply ordered a halt to the gathering and reporting of racial data by his agency after questioning the "desirability" of possessing it. It was indeed difficult to find among HHFA leaders those willing to go as far as DSCUR Director J. W. Follin, who conceded the national government's power to desegregate publicly owned and operated developments, and even for him publicly assisted and subsidized private projects remained beyond *Brown*'s reach. Cole needed little urging or guidance in reaching similar conclusions. Serving as HHFA administrator through nearly all of Eisenhower's two terms, he denied, as late as November 1958, any federal government responsibility either in fostering residential segregation or in ending it.[43]

Ignoring, by that time, the existence of outside, independent studies by the new Commission on Civil Rights and the private Commission on Race and Housing that cast a harsh light on government housing policies and called for federal, especially executive, leadership in ending housing discrimination, Cole was especially insistent on the sanctity of the private market. If he was willing to leave localism unfettered with regard to public housing (making federal approval and subsidy for clearly discriminatory site- and tenant-selection policies automatic), he remained unwilling to concede that FHA operations or programs such as urban renewal in any way altered a pristine private market or brought federal responsibilities along with federal involvement. HHFA operations under the Housing Act of 1954 subsequently displayed a disregard for its own legal and professed requirements (including timely reviews of "workable plans" for their social impact, the failure to set up proper mechanisms for citizen/minority input, and—either before or after 1954—the provision of "equal" housing available across the color line). Vastly disproportionate effects of subsequent displacement and relocation not only enhanced segregation in the civil rights era but demonstrated the impact of policies that called for no more than "substantial improvements" in deplorable material conditions or "separate but adequate" housing. Striving to satisfy a less than *Plessy* standard before *Brown*, federal policy still could not even assert, let alone attain, that goal after it had been ruled constitutionally deficient.[44]

Conclusion

In 1952, Racial Relations Service officer George B. Nesbitt addressed the meeting of the National Association of Intergroup Relations Officials and warned that the programs then being implemented under the rubric of urban redevelopment would establish the spatial and psychological framework within which the civil rights struggle would take place in "decades to come." The racial implications of the program were awesome and could not be avoided, he added; and it was already clear, "given the bitter displacement experiences of racial minority groups," that "too many city officials . . . employ[ed] slum clearance projects . . . to preserve and extend" the "ghetto." A rare opportunity had presented itself to "expand the volume of racially unrestricted dwellings," he believed, but officials were no more inclined to do that than they were to take his suggestion that "vacant land sites" be used to house those soon to be displaced. Such available land, he suggested, should not be "geared altogether to luxury levels." The moment soon passed.[45]

The Metropolitan Housing Council of Chicago, perhaps the city's preeminent housing "reform" organization had a different perspective on redevelopment. Speaking for many such groups, the MHC believed its "primary purpose" was "the need to restore deteriorated areas to profitable uses." Redevelopment offered the central city "the first significant opportunity . . . to compete with outlying areas for new and expanding industry," the MHC wrote. Conversely, the city stood in fear of the acceleration of "decentralization, with further loss of jobs, business, families, and tax revenues." Citing plant growth in the suburbs, the MHC concluded the city needed "more than just housing" to "assure future growth and prosperity."[46]

Within five years, redevelopment "morphed" into renewal, and HHFA Administrator Cole sold the program to the people and the Congress on both social and economic grounds. As he put it in a speech before the Chamber of Commerce in St. Louis, urban renewal was a "policy of liberality in dealing with the welfare of the people, and of conservatism in the economics of method."[47] Cole's rhetorical balancing of these interests, however, hardly reflected an evenhanded policy. For all his talk of assisting cities to win their ongoing battle with the slums and improving living conditions, the administration's social agenda was always constrained, contingent, and in thrall to its economic program. It was precisely that ordering of priorities that left impoverished blacks behind to occupy the weakened hearts of aging cities and placed the more well-to-do in still segregated communities on the fringe of their old neighborhoods or in isolated newer ones. The administration raced through the racial crossroads described by Nesbitt without so much as slowing down. And, once past, it did not bother to look back.

Racial affairs advisor to the president, Max Rabb, tried to make it appear that such would not be the case. Urban renewal, he wrote, as embodied in the Housing Act of 1954, "shall be used for the advantage and opportunity of all citizens regardless of race." But, again, the program's benefits and burdens fell unequally on its participants. African Americans in the inner city soon found their role quite a specialized one. Once an unforgiving foe of public housing, Cole became its advocate with the advent of urban renewal. The president had recommended building 35,000 such units in each of four years (considerably less than the 810,000 authorized by Congress in 1949) for the sole purpose of relocating project site residents prior to demolition. Cole knew that the modest commitment to public housing was far "less than the . . . total need," but it was enough "to make possible major progress in clearing the slums and rehousing the lowest income groups." The only thing they needed to do was get out of the way—and not disperse across the urban landscape; that determined the limits of the assistance they might expect. With the law linking access to the new units to the renewal process and local politicians controlling site selection for both private and public housing projects, the latter quickly became overwhelmingly black and heavily concentrated in inner city neighborhoods. The provision of such new quarters merely proved the administration's "liberality" regarding the social needs of minorities in Cole's estimation and, at the same time, facilitated the implementation of renewal.[48]

The administrator acknowledged in a public address that "assisted public housing provides the only present means that most cities have for re-housing the lowest income families." It subsequently enjoyed elevated status as "an integral part of the administration's overall housing program." Indeed, the President's Advisory Committee hailed the 1954 renewal legislation as "a broadscale integrated campaign" that met the needs of all groups. Such a characterization made no sense absent larger plans to revitalize the city and stimulate the national economy through a massive construction program carried out on the vacant urban fringe and the suburbs that lay beyond.[49]

There is no doubt, moreover, that notions of social reform, nondiscrimination, and integration had little to do with administration plans. Cole tried to reassure critics and those who asked about social policy by stating it was the "desire of the President and the policy" of the HHFA to "encourage and assist" both public and private efforts to "expand and improve" housing supplies "available to all." Even that vague pronouncement, however, was weakened further by Cole's use of the back door constructed by Senators Bricker and Cain years before. His efforts would be constrained, he confessed, "by the limits of our authority," which did not extend—the Supreme Court's verdict in *Brown* notwithstanding—to a federally mandated nondiscrimination.[50]

FHA Commissioner Franklin Richards continued to employ the same defense to shield his agency from similar pressures, thus contributing significantly to the exclusion of nonwhites from the suburbs. He found nothing, he wrote to a complaining Thurgood Marshall, either in the housing legislation itself or in Supreme Court decisions "that would authorize this administration to refuse to insure mortgages" in order to impose a policy of nondiscrimination or desegregation.[51] Suburban racial exclusivity remained, howover, more than the product of a rogue agency that defied a definitive judicial ruling.

Indeed, symbolic of the Eisenhower administration's refusal to confront the race issue in the suburbs was its handling of developer William

Levitt. Levitt fought feverishly to keep both his FHA subsidy and the racial exclusivity of his massive developments against growing pressure. Frank Horne had made it a personal crusade to cut off such support ever since a clerk at the Bucks County, Pennsylvania, Levittown assured the fair-skinned black bureaucrat that they would "keep the colored out" if given FHA support.[52] And Eisenhower certainly had his own misgivings. He said more than once, after all, that the government should not, in its own actions, "differentiate" on the basis of color or race.[53] Neither the president's reservations, however, nor Horne's protests, or even a formal written request from Walter White and the NAACP could alter Levitt's behavior or subsidy.

The deep-rooted conservatism manifested in Eisenhower's housing program thus appeared in several different forms. As Cole noted, it was economically conservative. Public money and powers were needed to get renewal going, but the administration knew its success depended upon "much larger expenditures by private investors." The proper role of government, they believed, was to "assist" and "stimulate" the private investment that would "provide the long-term basis for stabilizing and maintaining a community."[54]

It also became evident very quickly that racial policy, whether formally adopted or simply permitted to emerge from day-to-day practice, would bear the same political hallmark. Having left the financial initiative with the private sector, federal officials also paid great deference to localism and tried to wash their hands of the racial issue. Whether site and tenant selection for public housing or approving dubious "workable plans," local authorities seemed to hold the power. To the extent federal officials looked the other way, that was so. But the national government not only had the power to shape the program, it had legal obligations not to sanction or support such abuses of the renewal process that did occur.

Finally, with the urban renewal legislation on the books, the administrator poised to set the massive program in motion, and local officials straining to complete applications for the federal assistance that would enable them to reconfigure the face of the postwar city without a disruptive breach in the racial status quo, Frank Horne and the RRS loomed as obstacles. Displaying a conservatism that was now institutional as well as economic and social, Cole dismissed Horne once again and made it stick this time despite another round of serious protest. With Horne gone, the RRS fell under a withering bureaucratic onslaught. Shunned in the renewal process, their mail routed to other offices, its officers were left with little to do other than fill requests for government publications.

No one could be surprised, then, when the HHFA ignored the policy implications of the *Brown* decision. Indeed, when it came to housing, for the rest of the 1950s, the Eisenhower administration had yet to embrace *Plessy*, let alone *Brown*. An assumption that all people should be treated equally and enjoy the "same" rights in property appeared as a dangerous novelty whose advocates had to be driven from public service. There was talk of "adequacy," improved conditions, and "minimum decency." But virtually the only new housing built for blacks in the immediate postwar period consisted of publicly owned and operated projects concentrated in the inner city. Given urban renewal's disproportionate displacement of African Americans, the laws tying relocation to publicly provided units, and the predilections of the administration, segregation emerged enhanced instead of reduced, reinforced instead of undermined. The burgeoning black middle class, by and large, expanded into older private housing that "trickled down" to them in previously exclusive neighborhoods that bordered the older black communities. A modicum of new housing (even some with FHA support) came to those nonwhites who accepted it in isolated fringe areas, but the suburbs remained overwhelmingly a white preserve. If it could be said that more and better housing eventually fell into black hands, it also had to be acknowledged that more low-income units were destroyed than built, that residential segregation reached a peak only after the implementation of renewal, and could not have reached its unprecedented level of intensity without government assistance. The pursuit of "substantial improvements" in providing shelter for African Americans in the context of a sustained construction boom addressed short-term logistical problems posed by the second Great Migration, white consumer and homeowner demands for suburban access and exclusivity, black calls for assistance, and the political needs of the party in power. It soon became apparent—as evidenced by the NCDH's grim (though accurate) prognostication—that a housing policy that supported white mobility in and to the metropolitan fringe, while demanding black settlement (especially of the poor) in the central city, lacked neither design nor danger. Buying a temporary peace, postwar federal housing policy, when measured against even weak contemporary standards of racial equity and justice, aimed low and fell short. Having paid a steep price for such shortcomings in the 1960s, we still live with that legacy.

THREE

Uncovering the City in the Suburb

Cold War Politics, Scientific Elites, and High-Tech Spaces

MARGARET PUGH O'MARA

By the close of the twentieth century, the American urban landscape had become low-density and decentralized, its older central cities surrounded by steadily spreading suburbs that were increasingly diverse in form and function. The era of mass suburbanization had not only given rise to the cul-de-sac, the shopping mall, and the residential subdivision but had also created another distinctive and influential metropolitan subspecies: the high-tech suburb. From California to Illinois to Massachusetts to North Carolina, these economically privileged communities at the suburban edge filled with gleaming low-rise buildings and meticulously landscaped research parks, becoming home to the high-tech flagships of the Information Age economy and to their white-collar managers, engineers, and financiers. These places were not simply suburban business centers but contained distinct concentrations of firms engaged in software development, electronics development and production, biotechnological research, and related fields. Mass media and popular culture celebrated the places that were particularly notable examples of the form—chief among them Northern California's

Silicon Valley and suburban Boston's Route 128—and politicians and business leaders in other cities, states, regions, and nations embarked upon repeated efforts to create "Silicon Somethings" of their own.

The emergence of suburban high-technology clusters was one strand in a greater decentralization of economic activity that blurred and complicated the distinctions between city and suburb at the close of the twentieth century. Journalist Joel Garreau called these kinds of settlements "edge cities"; more recently, geographer Robert Lang countered that such decentralization had created "edgeless cities" and termed this white-collar suburbanization "office sprawl."[1] Historian Robert Fishman labeled the clusters "technoburbs" not simply because of the preponderance of high-tech industry within them but also because "the very existence of the decentralized city is made possible only through the advanced communications technology which has so completely superseded the face-to-face contact of the traditional city."[2]

Despite emerging within a larger context of rapid metropolitan decentralization, however, the development of high-tech clusters attested to the enduring power of *place*—even for industries that were themselves in the business of developing the technologies of the placeless, "virtual" workplace. While the mobility of information and capital allowed a dramatic globalization of production, the rules of economic agglomeration still applied: physical proximity to other, similar firms and to sources of capital provided entrepreneurs with an immeasurable competitive advantage. Spiraling real estate prices in high-tech centers during the heyday of the 1990s Internet boom showed the economic importance of location in the new economy. Many studies of Silicon Valley have noted the importance of face-to-face contact in developing distinctive networks among professionals who lived, socialized, and worked in close proximity to one another; such connections turned the Valley into what one observer called a "remarkable petri dish of industrial innovation."[3] As many of the would-be imitators of Silicon Valley and Route 128 discovered, a high-tech suburb did not come about merely because of the presence of a few research parks at the urban fringe, but resulted from a complex bundle of spatial, social, institutional, and economic characteristics that only a few places possessed.

Terms like "edge city" and "technoburb" thus do not fully capture the distinctive—and difficult-to-replicate—urban ecosystem on display in high-tech capitals, nor do they explain why high technology has gravitated so overwhelmingly to suburban environments. The literature on the history of these clusters has illuminated why certain individuals and companies thrived, where particular technologies evolved, and how formal and informal networks between firms and workers played a crucial role in cluster development. Yet the history of the U.S. high-technology industry remains strangely distanced from that of mass suburbanization.[4] To capture the significance of space in the story of high-tech growth (and postindustrial economic change in general), we must address the subtle interplay between public policy, markets, and institutions as well as the larger historical context in which this technological explosion was happening: mass suburbanization; industrial realignment; demographic shifts along lines of race, class, age, and gender.

The suburban office- and research-park phenomenon stands as more than simply a phase in a serial process of metropolitan decentralization. It is neither purely the product of top-down public policy incentives, nor is it an accidental market creation resulting from the spontaneous combustion of technological innovation and entrepreneurial energy. It is the physical manifestation of a particular historical moment, shaped by the relationship between the state and civil society in late twentieth-century America. The high-tech suburb holds a special place within the larger narrative of postwar political and economic history and is in fact a distinct and influential urban type: the city of knowledge. Like the suburbs of which it was a part, the city of knowledge came into being because of a complex interaction between public and private, in which the federal government used the politics of private-sector persuasion to attain broader economic and strategic ends. And like many other affluent American suburbs, cities of knowledge have been spaces populated by white-collar professionals that rarely were home to working-class families, even though these groups made up a large and hidden part of the high-tech industrial workforce. However, the city of knowledge was distinguished from the suburbs that surrounded it by being a community specifically designed to foster a certain type of postindustrial production—research-intensive high technology—and in which an important institutional creation of the postwar political economy—the research university—played a key economic and cultural role.

This strand of suburban history forces a further reconsideration of the postwar suburb in three respects. First, it demonstrates the intricate interconnection between Cold War politics, from civil defense to the structure of federal scientific research programs and the growth of the Cold War research university, and the shape of urban space in the postwar United States. Second, it provides further evidence that spatial arrangements sometimes derided as inchoate suburban "sprawl" are actually the result of careful orchestration of policies and markets toward specific social and economic ends. Third, it raises some important questions about the connection between educational attainment, economic class, and the shape of urban space in twentieth-century America. This is a story of sub-urbanization that has less to do with white flight and more to do with the deliberate creation of enclaves for a rarified upper stratum of the white-collar class: the professor, the scientist, the engineer.

The Cold War and Urban Decentralization

Between 1945 and 1970, the urban United States experienced two simul-taneous transformations: the mass suburbanization of people and jobs, and the growth of a massive industrial complex built around Cold War military spending. Both of these transformations fundamentally realigned the nation's economic geography. Responding to strategic military con-cerns, economic development needs, and intense congressional pressure, federal officials concentrated military spending in Sunbelt regions of the South and West. Heavy military spending served as an economic stimulus in these regions (most dramatically in the underindustrialized South), and accelerated the flight of people and jobs from the Northeast and Midwest to the Sunbelt states.[5] Meanwhile, federal programs subsidizing middle-class home ownership, new commercial construction, and the develop-ment of an interstate highway system played a central role in the move-ment from cities to suburbs.[6] While plenty of attention has been paid to the larger regional economic shifts precipitated by Cold War spending patterns, historians have tended to examine the growth of what President Dwight Eisenhower famously labeled the "military-industrial complex" and the rise of suburban America separately from one another. Yet the political economy of the Cold War defense complex laid the foundation for the latter-day patterns of high-tech suburbanization in a number of ways.

One connection is quite straightforward: the regions where defense money was going during the early Cold War years happened to be the parts of the country where suburbs were spreading the most rapidly. The Sunbelt states receiving the bulk of defense research and development (R&D) contracts were places experiencing particularly rapid, and largely untrammeled, suburban growth. Southern and western defense centers also had major metropolitan regions that were polycentric, low density, and sprawling. The relatively modest downtown skyline and giant urban footprint of many Sunbelt cities attested to the fact that these were places that came of age during the era of the automobile and the highway, where

Figure 3.1. The progrowth sentiments found in Sunbelt metropolises like Atlanta, Georgia, helped drive the construction of highways and other infrastructure that encouraged people and jobs to decentralize to the outer suburbs. Tracy O'Neal Photographic Collection, Special Collections Department, Georgia State University.

a significant portion of the regional economic activity took place well beyond downtown.

Yet even more significant, the regions most favored by Cold War defense spending were often places with state and local political institutional structures that placed few curbs on suburban growth and with leaders who actively supported economic development at the urban fringe.[7] Atlanta, Georgia, provides a compelling case. Georgia enjoyed considerable federal largesse as a result of its powerful representatives in Congress, Senator Richard B. Russell and Representative Carl Vinson, who chaired the Senate and House Armed Services Committees during many of the years in which Cold War defense spending was at its peak. Atlanta, the state's capital and largest city, was like many of its southern peers in that its greatest growth spurt occurred after 1940. Unlike such northern cities as Detroit, Chicago, or Philadelphia, where urban renewal–minded city planning professionals dominated local politics during the immediate postwar period, Atlanta had a relatively weak city planning tradition as well as a highly fragmented local governance structure. Whereas the city limits served as a powerful demarcation line for political allegiances in Rustbelt metropolises, cities like Atlanta adopted what might be called a "metropolitan mindset" when it came to economic development during the 1950s and early 1960s. Atlanta's city fathers—like many of their progrowth peers in other Sunbelt metropolises during the immediate postwar era—considered it an economic development victory when any new business moved to the region, regardless of whether the firm located downtown or at the sub-urban fringe.[8] As in other southern cities during this period, of course, the progrowth and prodecentralization sentiments of the city's business and political elite were inseparable from concerns about racial integra-tion and civil rights. By encouraging development in suburban areas, Atlanta's leadership (then all-white) not only made the metropolis better able to compete with other states and cities for new industrial fa-cilities and middle-class migrants, but also shored up its own political position in a time of great racial change by shifting economic and com-mercial activity away from African American city neighborhoods. Patterns of defense spending created opportunities for the region to build a new research-intensive manufacturing and business sector, but the leaders of Cold War–era Atlanta made little effort to recruit such scientific firms to the city itself, instead steering these industries and their professional workers to the affluent (and all-white) areas of the region's northern suburbs.[9]

The Pacific West, another fast-growing area of defense spending, ex-hibited similar patterns. In the San Francisco Bay Area, postwar industrial development schemes, created in the corporate boardrooms of downtown San Francisco with the support of the city's elected officials, mapped out an ambitious and geographically far-flung plan for the next several decades of industrial growth. Immediately after the end of the Second World War, the city's business leaders established the San Francisco Bay Area Council, an organization that promoted an aggressive prodecentralization strategy "dedicated to the proposition that the San Francisco Bay Area is an inte-grated economic unit" and predicated on the conclusion that because "San Francisco has reached its peak in residence and industrial sites—this city must now have an areawide viewpoint."[10] The Bay Area Council looked toward the less-developed areas at the suburban fringe as logical homes for industry and, in doing so, built upon a century-old pattern of cen-trifugal development in the Bay Area that had been facilitated by the absence of state or local political restraints on land development, the vestiges of the Spanish colonial land-grant system, which had placed large tracts of land under single ownership, and by the abundance of still-unincorporated suburban acreage.[11] While race was not as pervasive a subtext of San Francisco's industrial decentralization plans as it was Atlanta's, the effort betrayed some presumptions about segregation by economic class—specifically, the separation of blue- and white-collar workers and corresponding industrial activities. Some places were appropriate for heavy manufacturing, others (like the San Francisco Peninsula, where Silicon Valley would later grow) were better-suited for the "clean" and research-intensive industries such as electronics.[12] By mapping out this industrial geography at the beginning of a period of explosive growth in California, the business leaders of San Francisco helped set in place a pattern in which some of the region's fastest-growing industrial sectors would be located at least thirty miles from the city limits.

Yet the regional allocation of defense spending is only one part of the story. Federal defense contracting regulations and guidelines themselves contained incentives that endorsed the idea that suburban locations were more logical, and economically feasible, for private-sector firms.[13] The civil defense concerns of the earliest years of the Cold War drove these policy choices. In the doomsday scenarios outlined by military planners, downtown business districts became ground zero for Soviet nuclear attack; as the nation enlarged its military research and production capacity, strategists argued, it needed to ensure that these laboratories and factories were outside these target areas. This concern prompted the U.S. Congress and the Truman and Eisenhower administrations to build in a number of incentives into military contracting and tax policy during the late 1940s and early 1950s that aimed to encourage contractors to choose suburban locations over urban ones. A quiet effort that operated largely below the political radar screen, the "industrial dispersion" campaign focused its attention on the decentralization of defense contractors and other customers of the military—firms that made up the most defense-critical sectors of the economy and that had the most financial dependence on the federal government.

Industrial dispersion was in part a marketing campaign, producing a flurry of government publications darkly asking its corporate audience questions like: "Is your plant a target?"[14] But, in a manner similar to the postwar tax and land-use policies that supported mass suburbanization, the dispersion effort instituted small but significant changes to regulatory and tax policy that encouraged federal contractors to decentralize. In August 1951, amid escalating conflict in Korea, President Truman issued an executive memorandum that instituted a broad-based dispersion

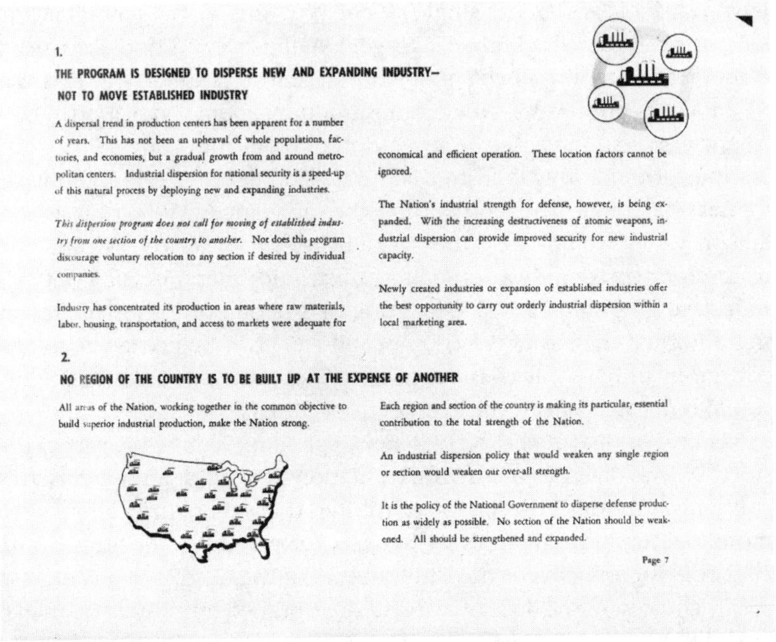

1.

THE PROGRAM IS DESIGNED TO DISPERSE NEW AND EXPANDING INDUSTRY—NOT TO MOVE ESTABLISHED INDUSTRY

A dispersal trend in production centers has been apparent for a number of years. This has not been an upheaval of whole populations, factories, and economies, but a gradual growth from and around metropolitan centers. Industrial dispersion for national security is a speed-up of this natural process by deploying new and expanding industries.

This dispersion program does not call for moving of established industry from one section of the country to another. Nor does this program discourage voluntary relocation to any section if desired by individual companies.

Industry has concentrated its production in areas where raw materials, labor, housing, transportation, and access to markets were adequate for

economical and efficient operation. These location factors cannot be ignored.

The Nation's industrial strength for defense, however, is being expanded. With the increasing destructiveness of atomic weapons, industrial dispersion can provide improved security for new industrial capacity.

Newly created industries or expansion of established industries offer the best opportunity to carry out orderly industrial dispersion within a local marketing area.

2.

NO REGION OF THE COUNTRY IS TO BE BUILT UP AT THE EXPENSE OF ANOTHER

All areas of the Nation, working together in the common objective to build superior industrial production, make the Nation strong.

Each region and section of the country is making its particular, essential contribution to the total strength of the Nation.

An industrial dispersion policy that would weaken any single region or section would weaken our over-all strength.

It is the policy of the National Government to disperse defense production as widely as possible. No section of the Nation should be weakened. All should be strengthened and expanded.

Page 7

Figure 3.2. Government brochures sought to convince American business owners of the economic and strategic usefulness of industrial dispersion. National Security Resources Board, "Is Your Plant a Target?" (Washington, D.C.: U.S. Government Printing Office, 1951), 2.

policy and asked all contracting agencies to embed provisions into their bidding competitions to encourage firms to move out of high-threat central city areas.[15] Adequate distance from nuclear ground zeroes—central cities—became a criterion for consideration in awarding defense contracts to a particular firm. Contractors won generous tax breaks for the construction of new facilities in dispersed areas. Despite the fact that metropolitan areas were rapidly expanding in physical size during this period, the definition of "adequate dispersion" was quite generous, ranging from ten to twenty miles outside the city center. A "dispersed" area was, in actuality, a suburb.[16]

Like many other persuasive policies of the American welfare state, the spatial consequences of dispersion policy are difficult to quantify. Standing alone, the dispersion campaign seems like something of a blip on the national political screen, another byproduct of a civil defense campaign now embedded in the popular imagination as little more than senseless "duck-and-cover" drills for schoolchildren. Its provisions gained minimal public attention and government investment relative to other policies, and its effects are hard to isolate because it not only occurred during a moment in which businesses were suburbanizing anyway but also when federal housing and highway programs were, indirectly or deliberately, encouraging the decentralization of industry and residence.

However, the dispersion policy of the late 1940s and 1950s increases in significance when we consider its effect on the research side of R&D. Research-intensive activities made up a minority of the federal contracts going to private-sector firms during this period, but they were the sectors of the defense complex from which the late twentieth-century high-tech economy grew. Whether new entrepreneurial start-ups or the research arms of established manufacturers, these enterprises usually lacked a significant commercial market for their products in the 1940s and 1950s and needed government contracts to stay in business. And these were the kinds of firms to which dispersion policy was specifically targeted. While dispersion was ostensibly a strategic policy, the reasons for this targeting were both economic and political. Large manufacturers often had more invested in their physical plants and were less able to move to a lightly settled area, and, as one government report noted, a program that placed tax-generating activities outside city limits "would not be wholeheartedly accepted by the potential target cities."[17] Thus dispersion policy targeted "new or expanded" facilities, a category that encompassed sectors like computers and electronics as well as the research laboratories of larger companies. If a dispersed location gave these firms a leg up in grant competitions, federal officials reasoned, then these sorts of enterprises would be more likely to decentralize. In order to ensure that the process worked smoothly at the local level, federal officials got help from more than 100 "local citizen committees" in cities small to large, who surveyed local industrial patterns to assess the risk of their regions being "attractive enemy targets" and actually helped firms fill out the necessary forms and access beneficial dispersion tax breaks and other incentives.[18] These committees were, by and large, made up of business leaders, and in many cases were offshoots of the same progrowth coalitions—like the San Francisco Bay Area Council—that were spearheading decentralized industrial development.[19]

While failing to gather broad-based statistical evidence indicating that dispersion policy had a decisive effect upon firm location, Truman- and Eisenhower-era executive branch officials were quick to draw a causal connection between the two. A 1956 Commerce Department report noted that the traditional geographic concentration of the electronic industry in a few large cities began to break down after 1950 and disperse over wider geographic areas. "Governmental policy on industrial dispersion has undoubtedly encouraged this move," the report noted. "All other things being essentially equal, a firm with welldispersed facilities has a definite advantage in securing military electronic business over competitors whose facilities are in critical target areas."[20]

––––––

Politics, economics, and military strategy all contributed to the geographic unevenness of federal defense spending, a pattern that played out at both regional and metropolitan levels. Sunbelt growth politics and federal industrial dispersion policies help explain why high technology tended to decentralize. Yet they do not explain how and why these industries and workers clustered in certain places, not merely dispersing to suburban areas but in fact creating new and influential kinds of urban ecosystems. To understand this part of the story, we must turn our attention to how these patterns of Cold War spending not only privileged certain places but also favored certain types of institutions and certain classes of workers. While the United States had long valued science and technology for its important role in industrial production and contributions to intellectual life, the Cold War made science more important than ever before. The military buildup, the new emphasis on educational excellence, and the desire for significant economic growth all worked to privilege—to an unprecedented degree—American scientists and the institutions that trained them. Enriched by federal money and politically empowered by Cold War policy priorities, universities became agents of the state, carrying out activities seen as critical to winning the Cold War and fundamental to maintaining global economic competitiveness.

The new economic and political prominence of universities and scientists during this period had important and lasting spatial implications. For the government-university relationship that emerged as a result of Cold War politics was not one simply affecting the "inside game"—the internal workings and research priorities of large American research universities—but also the "outside game" of land management and economic development in the communities in which these institutions were located. And the Cold War R&D effort not only spurred a high market demand for skilled scientists and engineers, but refocused local, state, and regional economic development efforts upon creating living and working environments attractive to this newly desirable type of white-collar professional. The confluence of these forces brought the high-tech city to the suburb.

Scientific Elites and the High-Tech Suburb

The unprecedented federal expenditures on scientific research and technological development during the early Cold War created a huge demand for trained scientists and engineers who could work on rapidly proliferating defense contracts, both at universities and in private-sector manufacturing and research firms. Because Ph.D. and M.A. programs in science and engineering existed at relatively few, top universities and technical schools during the 1940s and early 1950s, talented and experienced scientists and engineers were in short supply and thus in great demand by potential employers. Changes on the development and production sides of the military-industrial complex only increased the demand for highly trained professionals as the Cold War wore on. During the early 1950s, the large-scale production of conventional armaments to fight the war in Korea and build up military capacity at home had given the Cold War effort a predominantly blue-collar cast. Over the course of the decade, while defense workers remained more likely to work on an assembly line than in a laboratory, increased technological sophistication in weaponry and the new emphasis on space exploration intensified the need for a higher-skilled workforce, and the ranks of scientists and engineers grew.[21]

The rapturous media attention afforded scientists and their activities during this period bolstered their visibility and their credibility. As one observer noted in 1964, "media treatments were almost uniformly on the side of the 'expert' who was depicted as 'objective, disinterested, uncorruptible [sic],' and an 'impartial searcher for the truth.'" The general public, in turn, tended to think very highly of scientists and "most polls designed to rate professional prestige put the scientist close to the top."[22] Public enthusiasm about science had not waned by the mid-1960s, when a National Science Foundation (NSF) report to Congress noted, "the adult population of the United States has increased by approximately 5 percent in the past 4 years. In the same period of time, subscriptions to the magazine *Science* have increased by 45 percent, to *Scientific American* by 60 percent, to *National Geographic* by 44 percent."[23] By the early 1960s, producing and attracting skilled scientific workers had become a near-obsession for private employers and public economic development authorities alike. One observer noted that high-technology firms' "one critical requirement . . . is brain power, which they must attract to keep ahead of competition."[24] Industrial research laboratories and high-technology manufacturers directly competed with universities for physicists, engineers, chemists, and other trained personnel.

The rising demand for white-collar scientific manpower coincided with a new federal emphasis on university research after the launch of the Soviet Sputnik satellites in late 1957. Eisenhower administration officials, who had previously derided the "academic boondoggle" of basic university research, now saw scientific excellence as key to winning the Cold War and recognized research universities as the chief producers of scientific innovation and talent.[25] A 1960 report by Eisenhower's chief science advisors provided an eloquent summary of the new attitude of the federal government toward the university. "With all their irritating faults," the science advisors wrote, "universities are essential agencies of our national hopes, and they must be treated accordingly."[26]

Universities became agents of, and partners with, not only the national government but state and local ones as well. As Cold War investments in scientific R&D grew, state and local economic development policies began increasingly to orient themselves toward science and technology. Elected officials, bureaucrats, and business leaders alike seemed to agree that a university was a key ingredient in the economic development schemes to attract scientific industry and educated workers. Universities themselves became powerful voices in the design and implementation of these kinds of regional development strategies. The engagement of the university community planning with early corporate partnerships is an important, and underexplored, element in the political history of the military-industrial complex, and it demonstrates the full extent to which postwar universities became—in the famous words of former University of California Chancellor Clark Kerr—true "multiversities," with political and economic influence far beyond campus borders. As Kerr wrote in 1961, "universities have become 'bait' to be dangled in front of industry, with drawing power greater than low taxes or cheap labor."[27] Part of these institutions' power stemmed from their attractiveness to the newly desirable scientific workforce. Survey after survey revealed that scientific workers wanted to locate in the same neighborhood, city, or metropolitan area where there were prestigious scientific research universities, for proximity to a research university gave high-tech firms a competitive advantage in that they could have access to the latest research as well as a pool of well-trained graduates in the sciences and engineering. Nearness to a university functioned as an important amenity, even if the actual interaction between private worker and university was not very extensive. One 1963 survey of high-tech firms near Boston noted: "We were surprised to find that the frequency of direct contact between industrial research operations and MIT, Harvard, or the other universities is actually very low. . . . Yet these same people insist that they would not consider living and working anywhere but in the major scientific centers in the nation. In explanation, they cite the vital intellectual environment which makes them feel a part of an elite scientific community—a community whose influence extends to the schools, the arts, and a whole variety of social institutions which they deem essential to their way of life."[28] Whether proximity to a university provided a measurable economic advantage for firms or not, by the early 1960s universities had become the new magic ingredient for regional economic development. Yet this focus—and the accompanying interest in creating working environments for scientific professionals that were aesthetically compatible with university campuses—had profound spatial implications. American colleges and universities were institutions with a long tradition of physical disengagement from the heterogeneous and disorderly urban landscape beyond their gates. The prevailing design and architecture choices of American colleges and universities reflected the deep-seated cultural presumption that the urban environment was no place for intellectual discovery. Students needed peaceful, natural settings that would uplift them intellectually and morally. Henry David Thoreau once commented that "it would be not a small advantage if every college were . . . located at the base of a mountain."[29]

Rather than building institutions of higher education in the centers of cities, as continental Europeans did, Americans instead imitated the English models of Oxford and Cambridge and tended to locate colleges and universities in the country, in small towns, or on the sparsely populated outskirts of cities.[30] At the time of their founding, the most prominent twentieth-century "urban" universities deliberately sited themselves in places that were accessible to the commercial center of the city, but at a certain remove from it. Harvard was in suburban Cambridge rather than the heart of Boston; the University of Pennsylvania's original campus was a scant half-mile from the heart of mercantile Philadelphia, but in this "walking city" such a distance placed the campus on the urban fringe. More than a century later, Columbia University was founded in a lightly settled, suburban part of upper Manhattan, and Penn had left its too-urban location for a new campus in an upper-middle-class suburban neighborhood in the western part of the city.

Even prior to the Cold War, the influence of campus planning traditions—and the notion that pastoral environments fostered intellectual creativity—extended well beyond academia. From the late nineteenth century on, there were examples in both the United States and in Western Europe of factory towns and industrial facilities that had created carefully planned, geographically decentralized, and distinctively campuslike environments. This connection was particularly strong in the case of industrial laboratories employing white-collar scientists, and there existed a number of well-publicized examples of "industrial campuses" that deliberately mirrored the look and feel of the college campus. General Electric was one of the first major American corporations to develop a facility of this kind when it built its Nela Park campus outside of Cleveland in 1913. Half a century later, planners continued to praise Nela Park for "its spacious and beautifully landscaped lawns [that] give it the appearance of a university campus rather than an industrial district." Bell Laboratories in New Jersey was another well-known prewar example, a suburban research facility that blended architectural modernism and abundant green space in a manner that foreshadowed the new university campuses of the postwar decades.[31]

The pastoralism and separation that characterized the design of both university and industrial campuses fit very comfortably with larger industrial trends by the time the United States embarked upon the Cold War. Mass suburbanization after 1945 spurred a proliferation of low-density new "industrial parks" in outer neighborhoods or suburbs of major cities; the 33 parks in existence in the United States in 1940 had swelled to 302 by 1957.[32] Often owned and developed by large landholders like railroads and utility districts, the parks tried to increase their attractiveness to employers—and their attractiveness to the suburban communities in which they were situated—by incorporating abundant green space, pleasant low-rise buildings, and disguising less-pleasing elements like parking lots behind shrubs and trees. These amenity-rich developments were particularly appealing to smaller firms that lacked the resources to build these sorts of facilities on their own. As one Eisenhower administration official phrased it, "the controls exercised by well-planned and well-supervised districts, often embodied in protective covenants which run with the land, assure the property buyer of a desirable address, considerate neighbors and security against deterioration."[33]

Not all of the industrial parks were truly parklike, however. And their tenants could vary greatly, from old-style manufacturing plants to ordinary office buildings. Real estate developers still could find them to be a hard sell in some areas, particularly affluent white-collar suburbs that approached industrial activity warily, however much it might enrich the community's tax revenues. The university-centered economic development process of the early Cold War provided a remedy to this shortcoming. In its emphasis on high-tech production—a sector characterized without fail as being "clean" and "smokeless" even though many of its activities could have toxic byproducts—and its recruitment of white-collar professionals was an economic development approach about which even the most affluent suburb could have little complaint.[34] Capitalizing on the trend toward decentralized industry, the public- and private-sector pro-moters of science-based economic development created a new and even more alluring variant on the form: the research park. The research park took the architectural and planning restrictions of the industrial park to a new level, creating an environment that had the look and feel of a col-lege campus, filled with carefully selected tenants and their white-collar workers. Real estate developers and other research park promoters took pains to distinguish these places from the industrial districts and fac-tory towns that had come before; a research park was, in the words of one observer, "an environment characterized by greenery, culture, and scholarship."[35]

Because of its new wealth, new research capacity, and its ability to act as a magnet for high-tech industries and workers, the research university became the crucial ingredient to making an industrial park into a research park. Yet politicians, pundits, and even university administrators them-selves often overlooked one of the crucial realities of the new economic and political order, which was that "research university" was a monolithic term that applied to a widely divergent group of institutions. Federal research spending created one of the most important distinctions among this group, as the Cold War research bounty reached only a small and select number of universities. The government research spending of the first two decades of the Cold War had followed well-established patterns of scientific capacity. In 1939 and 1965, exactly the same group of 25 uni-versities (fifteen private and ten public) was responsible for producing two-thirds of the nation's Ph.D.'s in science. Not surprisingly, the top 25 institutions received 60 percent of all funds spent by the federal gov-ernment on university science, and "an even greater percentage of the research grants and contracts of mission-oriented agencies."[36] Because of this selectivity, only a few communities had institutions in their midst of enough size and reputation to serve as catalysts of high-tech economic activity.

The institutional favoritism of federal spending patterns often under-mined efforts to generate high-tech clusters in regions that did not have one of these favored institutions in their midst. And achieving success in this endeavor not only depended on the ability to create attractive environments for scientific industry but also depended on the degree of active participation of the university itself in development of research parks. By the mid-1960s it seemed clear that, in the words of one Depart-ment of Commerce pamphlet, "the most successful parks have been those where the local university has a national technical reputation and also has a substantial proprietary position in the park development."[37]

Figure 3.3. Cold War investments in scientific research and technology created new alliances between university and industry beginning in the late 1950s, and these alliances helped spur the development of many low-density research parks. Here, a Stanford official shows two Lockheed representatives the location of the Stanford Industrial Park on an area map. Courtesy Stanford University Archives.

In outlining these criteria, the Commerce Department clearly had in mind the two most successful of the nation's high-tech regions, Silicon Valley and Route 128. The case of Silicon Valley and its anchoring research institution, Stanford University, provides a particularly illuminating window into the way high-tech cities of knowledge emerged from a confluence of broader economic and political changes, local political conditions, and luck. Unlike Harvard and MIT, the top-ranked institutions that fueled the growth of suburban Boston's Route 128, Stanford entered the Cold War era as one in a pool of respected but by no means top-tier research universities that needed to work a little harder to tap into the bounty of the federal science complex by establishing Washington offices, adjusting their academic missions and becoming more entrepreneurial and political in their approach. Stanford and its counterparts in Cambridge also differed dramatically when it came to land development. Route 128 was built by private real estate developers who capitalized on the metropolitan proximity to these institutions to lure tenants, but prior to the 1970s Harvard and MIT did not see real estate development as a central part of their institutional missions. When trying to go about building their own cities of knowledge during the 1950s and 1960s, other localities looked West: to Stanford, a place that had built itself up from seemingly nothing into a high-tech powerhouse. Would-be cities of knowledge deliberately imitated Silicon Valley's low-rise, heavily landscaped, and distinctively suburban and western look and feel, an aesthetic and arrangements of space on which Stanford had a profound influence.

However, Stanford came into the high-tech economic development game with advantages that few other universities possessed. Founded in Palo Alto, California, by a Gilded Age railroad baron, the university's founding grant had included nearly nine thousand acres of surrounding land to own in perpetuity, land that it could lease but never sell. As the towns surrounding the university turned into booming and desirable suburbs in the postwar era (a process encouraged by the industrial decentralization plans of regional leaders like the San Francisco Bay Area Council), Stanford's property turned into a gold mine. University administrators decided against merely developing the land into hundreds of acres of more subdivisions, but instead built a research park that, through careful tenant selection and very high architectural and planning standards, could become a model for suburban industrial growth. In mandating such standards, the school violated nearly every cardinal rule of economic development; one official remarked later, "We didn't know what the hell we were doing. If we knew how hard it was to get industry, that you've got to give tax exemptions, cheap labor and free buildings, we probably wouldn't have tried." But in a new Cold War environment where scientific activity and proximity to a university were such desirable things, the rules of the game had changed. "We were as tough as we could be," the official said, "and we couldn't discourage them."[38]

Research parks elsewhere had already demonstrated the effectiveness that pleasant landscaping and high architectural standards could have on the ability of real estate developers to find tenants, and on the willingness of wealthy communities to accept industry in their midst. What the Stanford example provided was a model showing university and industry how they could work together toward mutually beneficial ends. The businesses that leased land in the park gained access to Stanford faculty and laboratory facilities through specially created cooperative programs. They gained well-designed facilities in a prime real estate location that carried the cachet of the Stanford name. This was real estate development as conscientious community planning, an effort to create an industrial landscape that was highly compatible with the elite institution at its heart. As the Stanford Board of Trustees declared at the outset of the land development process, the exercise aimed "to produce in the ultimate a community of which the University Trustees and all those who have its welfare at heart can be proud and that will, by reason of the fact that it is a University project, serve in an important way as an educational example in the field of community development."[39]

To the hundreds of other cities and regions in the United States who were seeking potent and fast-acting economic development strategies, Stanford University and its surrounding area seemed to have stumbled upon the perfect and easy solution: parklike industrial real estate, located near good housing and quality schools, whose tenants could take advantage of the resources of a world-class university. As other local economic development authorities embarked upon their own schemes for industrial development—high-tech and otherwise—they often invoked Stanford as a model. Newspapers from Oregon and Idaho to Texas, Kansas, and Mississippi gave glowing reports of local initiatives inspired by the Stanford development. The park was a feature in the American exhibit at the 1958 Worlds' Fair in Brussels. During a visit to the United States in 1960, Charles DeGaulle specifically asked to see the park; other foreign dignitaries followed.[40]

In their enthusiasm to develop high-tech centers of their own, however, these imitators often focused on aesthetics without recognizing the tremendous political, economic, and demographic advantages that formed the underpinning of the success of the Stanford Research Park. The university's many admirers, as well as the more dispassionate observers of the research park phenomenon in government and industry, failed to note that a location in an *affluent suburb* had been a crucial element in the park's success. Stanford not only benefited from being located in the booming Cold War economy of the Pacific West, but it also possessed a tremendous and unique advantage in owning open land surrounded by rapidly growing, majority-white, and markedly well-off residential areas.

The degree to which wealth and suburban location functioned as an advantage becomes clear by comparing Stanford's case with those of peer institutions located in economically declining city neighborhoods. A good number of elite research universities had urban campuses and embarked upon science-focused economic development efforts as a means by which to "save" their surrounding neighborhoods from economic deterioration and racial change. Yet in doing so these institutions met with what one observer described as "frustration after frustration."[41] The research park form, with its low density and functional exclusivity, was ill suited to denser and more diverse urban neighborhoods. Unlike the ease with which Stanford and postwar developers could build on unoccupied and relatively unregulated suburban greenfields, establishing a research park on already occupied urban land often involved significant regulatory hurdles and daunting, racially charged political problems.

One case in point is the University of Pennsylvania, a major federal research grantee whose Philadelphia campus neighborhood was, by the 1950s, undergoing significant economic and racial change.[42] Penn administrators and their allies in city government engaged in a broad-based urban renewal and community planning effort that sought a redefinition of the area to such an extent that it renamed its West Philadelphia neighborhood "University City." The plan's high-profile industrial centerpiece was the University City Science Center, first announced in 1961. Planned along the main commercial artery of Market Street, considered the epicenter of urban blight in the University City area, local officials and university administrators saw the Science Center as a solution for both urban renewal and economic development needs, replacing run-down houses and shops with gleaming modern facilities full of jobs for scientists and engineers. The center's placement also happened to create a massive physical barrier between working-class black neighborhoods to the north and the Penn campus to the south. Although a higher-density development than the Stanford Industrial Park, the Science Center paid similarly close attention to architectural detail, the inclusion of green spaces, and the need to attract an exclusive group of tenants engaged in scientific research. With the Science Center, one contemporary newspaper account noted, Penn's neighborhood was poised to become "Brainsville, U.S.A."[43]

Despite glowing editorials and glossy promotional materials, almost as soon as the plans were announced for this development, protest began. While University City was being marketed to academic and professional families as a place of progressive racial integration, its urban redevelopment efforts were causing painful—and class-conscious—racial conflict. The fact that a place that in the 1960s was probably one of the more racially progressive neighborhoods in Philadelphia became the site for such bitter community protest reflected the class distinctions scientists and researchers sometimes drew when considering integration with their black neighbors. Certain white professional families might have had little problem with minorities of their class and background, particularly educated immigrants who may well have been their academic colleagues, but had less tolerance for working-class African American culture and values. The builders of West Philadelphia's city of knowledge adhered to this distinction as well. Certain kinds of integration were to be celebrated, but the presence of large numbers of poor blacks was incompatible with the "new" community of scientific production. This created a recipe for political conflict, spurring community outrage on the part of those displaced, and little enthusiasm among those recruited as their replacements.

The difficulties faced by urban universities like Penn illuminate the complicated undercurrents of class and of race that underlay the university-centered economic development efforts of the 1950s and 1960s and the high-tech suburbs that emerged afterwards. The political discourse around university-centered economic development emphasized gathering educated people in one place and excluding (or removing) the less-educated, effectively creating class homogeneity. During the early decades of the Cold War, the corollary outcome of this homogenization was that racial minorities were usually left out, because in the pre–Civil Rights Act, pre-affirmative action United States, people of color almost never obtained the opportunities to join the scientific elite. The dilemma of urban universities also illuminates what might be called the "means-not-ends problem" when it came to building cities of knowledge. Places that embarked upon high-tech development as an end in itself—and, more pointedly, did not have economic, social, or environmental factors distracting them from their goal of building a well-designed community of scientific production—were more successful at it than those that saw high tech as a means of meeting other economic or social goals like urban renewal, demographic change, or economic revival.

The Twenty-First Century City

Born of Cold War geopolitics and midcentury economic and social change, the city of knowledge outlasted both the U.S.–Soviet conflict and the Levittown-style subdivision. After 1970, a slowing rate of federal research spending and a growing commercial market for high-tech products shifted the political matrix somewhat, making private capital an increasingly important sponsor of this kind of production. While public spending continued to matter a great deal, the most visible public-sector involvement in generating regional high-tech economies during the 1970s and 1980s became that of state and local governments. In North Carolina, a vigorous state-directed effort to draw research facilities to an underindustrialized rural area near the Duke University campus and the flagship state university campus at Chapel Hill resulted in the Research Triangle Park. In Texas, state leaders played an instrumental role in wooing two large semiconductor research projects to Austin, seeding a high-tech economy around the

University of Texas that became another of the more prominent American cities of knowledge by the end of the twentieth century.[44]

In both cases, the lessons of earlier university-centered economic development initiatives held firm. A Sunbelt location, availability of undeveloped land away from big-city problems and near places that educated workers wanted to live, and effective state- and local-level leadership gave tremendous advantages in the high-tech economic game. Unsurprisingly, the builders of research parks in the Research Triangle and Austin looked to Stanford for inspiration. Landscaped and low density, convenient to freeways and affluent neighborhoods, these were places where scientific and technical workers could spend their days in environments that looked much like the university campuses a few miles away. Their success further solidified the association between research park facilities and certain kinds of "knowledge work," a category that expanded in the postindustrial era well beyond computer engineering and biotechnological research to include a vast array of white-collar service and management industries.

At the outset of the Cold War, the notion that more Americans would go to work in the suburbs than in the central city by the year 2000 would have seemed somewhat unbelievable. The decentralized landscape of production, where millions of Americans work in office parks and lush "campuses" at the fringe of metropolitan areas, has become so normal that most people do not deeply question how it came about. The historical and spatial dynamics underlying the development of the cities of knowledge help explain this. In this chapter I have sought to provide a brief glimpse into the complex interactions of policy, economics, and culture that spurred postindustrial suburbanization and to show that the process was far more complicated and more deliberately planned than might be commonly supposed. The relevance of local political approaches to industrial decentralization and the influence of certain university-centered land developments as an economic development model also provides additional evidence of the profound influence of the Sunbelt and Pacific West in twentieth-century urban development patterns and lends support to the argument that influence and imitation in postwar American city planning and development radiated from west to east rather than vice versa.[45]

No longer adjuncts to the central cities around which they grew, the high-tech suburbs of the early twenty-first century evidenced a new, and influential, kind of urbanism. Suburban communities of scientific production have been magnets for people and industries outside the high-tech arena, home to a range of related and complementary production activities, cultural amenities, and services. In metropolitan areas with high concentrations of science-based industry, the rise of the high-tech suburb over the course of the late twentieth century served to shift the focus of economic activity away from the central cities that previously dominated the regional economy and turned sleepy agricultural areas and bedroom suburbs into internationally influential concentrations of industrial production and commercial capital. By placing the history of these cities of knowledge back within the broader history of postwar American cities and suburbs, we can see how much politics and policy had to do in shaping this economic geography—not only the policies related to taxes, housing, and road-building, but also ones having to do with civil defense, scientific research, and higher education.

As an urban phenomenon, the city of knowledge has not only had a profound spatial influence but a social one as well. High technology flourished in the postwar suburbs because the midcentury political economy helped make suburbs into the most desirable sort of environment for the white-collar professional. Placing a city of knowledge in a suburban, white, middle-class setting eased the development process and reduced community opposition to these projects in the short term, and in the long term the high-tech clusters that have thrived have been ones in suburban (or similarly decentralized and functionally segregated) environments.

Despite the strong overlap between class and race in the geographic sorting of the high technology workforce, it is perhaps more accurate to think of the defining criterion for a city of knowledge being one that has more to do with class (which in this instance is usually synonymous with education levels) than with race. It is telling that, during the 1990s Internet boom, high-tech activity tended to move back to cities—populating districts like South of Market in San Francisco and Silicon Alley in Manhattan—at the same time that the professional classes began to move back. As the early twenty-first century racial makeup of the workforce in places like Silicon Valley attests, education and training, not gender or skin color, now determines entry into the city of knowledge, places that continue to remain in or near the most affluent places in America.

The white-collar homogeneity becomes more striking when we consider the fact that the vast majority of the high-tech workforce was not made up of professional scientists and technicians but instead consisted of blue-collar assembly-line workers. In a high-tech world whose managers and technicians have, to an overwhelming degree, been white men, these workers are often minority and female.[46] The research park has housed high technology's professional class and its knowledge work; the production of silicon chips and motherboards has taken place elsewhere, often on other continents. The story of the city of knowledge is thus one of *disguise* on a number of levels—where polluting industrial activities were billed as "clean" by economic development advocates, where race and class homogeneity was a largely unspoken but crucial criterion of research park design, whose public face was the white-collar scientist and whose hidden workforce was often working class and nonwhite.[47]

Spatial and social segregation itself was what made American cities of knowledge the productive and innovative places they became. This reality may make some uncomfortable, but the growth of high technology in the United States has never been a democratic or egalitarian process. It is a system that worked because it concentrated money, power, and privilege among certain groups, certain institutions, and certain places. Yet just as cities and suburbs have changed since the 1950s and 1960s, so might cities of knowledge also change. The suburbanization of science, and the association of high-tech activity with low-density and exclusive landscapes, may no longer be the only tactic to create "desirability" and foster innovation and entrepreneurship. Not only was the design of the city of knowledge intended to give scientists an ideal environment in which to live and work, but it also was seen as an ideal hybrid of urban and suburban life, and put forth as a model for other communities to imitate. Perhaps the future development of the city of knowledge will build upon this idea of a hybridization of urban and suburban life, yet reconstitute the community of high-tech production in ways that better reflect the democratization of technology.

FOUR

How Hell Moved from the City to the Suburbs

Urban Scholars and Changing Perceptions of Authentic Community

BECKY NICOLAIDES

Over the course of the twentieth century, a funny thing happened in the thinking of scholars observing life in American cities. The environment that seemed most harmful to authentic community—most likely to kill off any chance for meaningful human interaction—that environment moved from the city to the suburbs. I first noticed this perceptual migration when I developed an undergraduate course on the history of urban community, a course that explores changing experiences of community, changes in the urban environment, and how these two relate over the course of American history. By the twentieth century, a fascinating discourse had emerged among scholars deeply concerned about how the urban environment was shaping social life. Writers like Louis Wirth, Lewis Mumford, Jane Jacobs, and William Whyte conveyed ideas with profound impact on public understanding of what both city and suburban life were doing to the health of American community. The city started out as the culprit. But by the postwar era, the suburbs had elbowed their way into that maligned position—the site of social dysfunction and pathology. Hell, it seemed, was moving from the city to the suburbs—like everyone else.

In this chapter, I offer a brief sketch of these perceptions as they were carried forward into the 1960s . It is by no means exhaustive; it focuses on a few key figures and leaves many out. They represent a small subset of a larger group of suburban critics in the postwar years. The 1950s and 1960s, in fact, were a period when a veritable "culture war" over suburbia broke out between its supporters and its critics; their opinions reached wide audiences via the mass media. Those who celebrated the virtues of suburbia included developer-builders, advertisers, and television shows (which were dependent on advertisers), while the critics included academics, novelists, filmmakers, and urban scholars.[1] The writers highlighted here represented some of the more important voices among urban scholars who were weighing in on the issue. Their ideas attracted wide notice, helped shape the thinking of cultural producers, and assumed a key place in an impassioned national discourse about the health and fate of American metropolitan areas.[2]

All of these writers shared certain assumptions about the relationship of community to place. Most important, they generally embraced the concept of environmental determinism, that is, the notion that spatial form had a direct impact on social relations. This belief infused a passion in their writings. They felt that if the "right" physical environment could be created, a healthy community might come out of it. Second, despite their deep cognizance of how advances in communication and transportation were changing the ways that people related to each other, they maintained a keen interest in social relations at the local level. To some degree, they *expected* that community would manifest in a place rather than in a more amorphous web of dispersed relationships. So when place-based community was not present, they perceived it as a social failure rather than a sign that community might be manifesting in other, nonlocal ways. This way of thinking surely reflected the first point, their interests in exploring the impact of the built environment. But it also stands as a rather rigid way of thinking about community.[3]

Wirth, Mumford, Jacobs, and Whyte were all urban-based intellectuals who cared deeply about the American city. From the 1920s to the early 1960s, the years when these writers published their seminal works, the general public discourse on cities was undergoing a crucial transition, as Robert Beauregard has shown. Up to the 1920s and 1930s, commentators held great optimism about the future of the metropolis. Yes, cities suffered numerous ills, but these problems stemmed from the excesses of growth. The city itself was still perceived as a locus of innovation, progress, and creativity; it was just growing too quickly and wildly. Proper reforms and good planning could solve this. Even decentralization was looked upon favorably, as a kind of safety valve that would allow the city to grow manageably without imploding. City and suburb were seen as compatible partners in a metropolitan vision that embraced the importance and vitality of the city itself. By the 1940s and through the 1960s, this discursive optimism about cities gave way to pessimism. Cities were no longer on a growth swing, but rather on a decline, even on their way to crisis. Urban racial transformations played a large role in this perceptual shift. And so did the exploding suburban trend. Suburbs were no longer the city's benevolent partners but their destroyers. As Beauregard writes, "Ultimately, suburban growth and urban decline became locked in a discursive opposition that framed the postwar discourse on cities."[4] This was the general frame of reference for these writers, all based in the city and deeply concerned about its future. Although they maintained a faith in the superiority of urban life and even some optimism about the urban future, they approached their social analysis of cities and suburbs from within this oppositional framework.[5]

Beauregard has astutely suggested another critical transformation during these years, in the perceived relationship between city, suburb, and modernism. From the mid-nineteenth century on, many commentators believed the city embodied modernity itself, that cities sat "at the center of modernist sensibility." If modernity signified economic growth, social and technological advances, and bounteous opportunity on the one hand, and oppression, alienation, and a depersonalized existence on the other, indeed the city contained it all. By the 1940s and 1950s, as millions of Americans flocked to the suburbs, modernity itself seemed to join in this mass exodus. The progress and the alienation, the growth and the oppression—the fundamental polarities that signified modernity—were also relocating to suburbia. This perception was especially strong among those who spoke of an "urban crisis."[6] The critics explored in this article did not see such a sweeping shifting of the winds. Their work proposed that modernity's canvass may have expanded to metropolitan proportions, but its goodness and strength stayed in the city; its angst moved to the 'burbs. They maintained a hope for the city, a passionate faith that cities—not suburbs—held the greatest potential for progress and human civilization itself.

––––––––

The Chicago school of urban sociology set the stage in this progression of ideas. Led by Robert Park and Ernest Burgess, the Chicago school scholars intended first and foremost to collect objective information about the city. "The urban sociologists' purposes," writes Andrew Lees, "were scholarly, not polemical." They were neither urban champions nor reformers, seeking instead to amass an empirical base of knowledge about life in the American city. As Lees observes, their collective works reflected deep ambivalence about the city; while they emphasized the pathological aspects of urban life, they also held fundamental faith in the city as the locus of "the fulfilling and meaningful life," in Louis Wirth's words. The Chicago school was quite influential, generating long-lived theories about the city, as well as spawning urban sociology programs nationally that followed their lead.[7] As practitioners of "human ecology," these scholars firmly embraced an analytical paradigm that emphasized environmental factors. Their very definition of "human ecology" reflected this assumption: "a study of the spatial and temporal relations of human beings as affected by the selective, distributive, and accommodative forces of the environment."[8]

Robert Park initially expressed the problem of city and community in his seminal 1925 essay, "The City." Here, he argued that city living destroyed the possibilities for face-to-face primary relationships essential to genuine community, replacing them instead with indirect, secondary associations. This more impersonal existence was further diluted by the depersonalizing influences of a pecuniary culture. In the end, authentic community deteriorated. He wrote, "Cities, and particularly the great cities, are in unstable equilibrium. The result is that the vast casual and mobile aggregations which constitute our urban populations are in a state of perpetual agitation, swept by every new wind of doctrine, subject to constant alarms, and in consequence the community is in a chronic condition of crisis." Here, then, was a critique of modernization. Newcomers to the city were on their own, freed from the moral constraints of the "peasant community" but also lacking the social nurturing and wisdom of that same community. Park drew on the social theory rooted in Ferdinand Tönnies' *Gemeinschaft-Gesellschaft* dichotomy, in forecasting the dire social consequences of this change—the dissolution of moral order, a rise in vice and crime, and the substitution of social mores with laws, advertising, and the press as the more impersonal agents of order. The large-scale, commercial nature of cities, Park thus argued, devastated the chances for authentic community.[9]

Louis Wirth, another Chicago school sociologist, amplified these ideas in his 1938 essay, "Urbanism as a Way of Life." Wirth saw the urban environment—what he defined fundamentally as large, dense, permanent, and diverse—as the root cause of social difficulty and community deterioration. As cities grew, urban social life evolved in a linear fashion from primary to secondary relationships, from community to society. Though people connected face to face in cities, he observed, those contacts were "impersonal, superficial, transitory, and segmental."[10] The results were loneliness, weakened bonds of kinship, a decline in family importance, and disappearing neighborhoods—all in all, a highly impersonal, isolated existence.

While Wirth mostly implicated "the city" in this process, he too indicted urban consumer culture, echoing Tönnies and Park and foreshadowing suburban critiques two decades later.[11] Wirth wrote, "The pecuniary nexus which implies the purchasability of services and things has displaced personal relations as the basis of associations. Individuality under these circumstances must be replaced by categories."[12] The pressures of mass production and mass consumption in cities caused city people to lose their sense of individuality and, in turn, their ability to relate in authentic ways. To compensate for this "virtual impotence as an individual," the urbanite joined groups, resulting in "the enormous multiplication of voluntary organizations."[13] Wirth's portrait of urban man thus came into view: he was lonely, cut off from kin, losing his sense of self, a voracious joiner to compensate, and a creature of consumer culture. This picture bears uncanny resemblance to the Organization Man living in postwar suburbia, but Wirth held the *urban* environment largely responsible for this state of social dysfunction.

It is important to recognize that Chicago school scholars brought nuances and some complexity to their work. Andrew Lees emphasizes the fundamental faith these scholars held in cities. Despite the tremendous social stresses and problems of big city life, cities, they believed, still offered important social benefits—individual freedom, a milieu for creative expression, and the advantages of great diversity. In its "big, booming confusion and excitement," the city represented a hotbed of innovation and ambition, a view that reflected an essentially nineteenth-century liberal sense of optimism about urban life, as Lees points out. Even on the community issue, there was some acknowledgement of community survival in the urban milieu. Wirth, for example, recognized the presence of communal solidarity in Chicago's Jewish ghetto. Yet he concluded that the more overpowering urban force of mobility would eventually weaken those traditional loyalties, and urbanization—marching along that linear path—would eventually eradicate local neighborhoods as a locus of meaningful community.[14] The community declension theme thus continued to resonate.

At the same time these sociologists were gathering data and formulating theories in Chicago, Lewis Mumford was in New York developing his own ideas about how community and city interconnected. A brilliant, deliberate "generalist" with strong philosophical convictions, Mumford wrote on a wide array of topics—the city and suburb among them.[15] He was skeptical of urban sociology, dismissing it as "throw[ing] no important light upon the problem," and was no doubt critical of its rational detachment, lack of historicism, and blindness to the link between city and civilization.[16] In the 1920s and 1930s, Mumford was a central figure in the Regional Planning Association of America; by the 1960s, he had published prodigiously and brought together many of his ideas about urban life in his monumental *The City in History*. By this point, Mumford had become part of a diverse, growing group of critics of postwar sprawl.

A brief description of Mumford's philosophy about history, cities, and the human condition helps establish a context for his ideas about cities, suburbs, and community.[17] Mumford believed the city was a historical force tied intimately to the rise of civilization. Cities did not rise for purely economic reasons; they were expressions of the human spirit and existed to contribute to the ever-evolving human personality. Related to this, Mumford embraced the idea of "organicism," the notion that humans are organisms and "their behavior and arts are best understood as the outcome of organic processes."[18] History, in Mumford's view, embodied an elemental tension between organic and mechanical ways of thinking.[19] Organic systems displayed "qualitative richness, amplitude, spaciousness, free from quantitative pressure and crowding." "Mechanical" systems—which he nicknamed the "megamachine"—embodied "power, speed, motion, standardization, mass production, quantification, regimentation, precision, uniformity, astronomical regularity, control, above all control."[20] Whereas organicism in artifacts and ways of living facilitated healthy, meaningful societies and individual lives, mechanistic values snuffed out a humane existence.[21] The conflict between these tendencies began well before the modern era, first appearing in ancient Egypt with "megamachines" that drove the earliest urban formation.[22] This mechanistic tendency continued to manifest itself in the emergence of "megalopolis"—from imperial Rome, to the baroque city, to the twentieth-century sprawling metropolis.[23] Dangerously stifled in the process were designs for life based fundamentally on human need. Yet Mumford also found examples in urban history when organicism reigned, such as the medieval city, the Greek polis, and in Ebenezer Howard's garden city ideal. He perceived the city historically as a "two faced institution," embodying "both heaven and hell," as he put it. The city represented "the source of the most rewarding intercourse that civilization makes possible; it is a place where the arts and sciences have been pushed to a higher pitch." Yet at the same time, it could be "a place of dominance, of control, of the mastery of the large part of the population by a dominant minority."[24]

By the time *The City in History* came out in 1961, Mumford saw the pendulum swung closer toward hell. The excesses of megalopolis were everywhere, manifest even in Mumford's own beloved New York City. Both central cities and outlying suburbs—as a conurbation—embodied the problem. The trend of metropolitanism was a latter-day manifestation of the megamachine. In a 1961 interview, Mumford explained, "I think we have to distinguish between the necessity for urban life and the over-concentration that has taken place in our big cities, like London and New York, Chicago and Paris, by the desire on the part of those who created the big city to monopolize the resources of civilization. Giantism is usually in the organic world a sign of some abnormality. And I think one can say the same thing of the overgrowth of the great city; it is the sign of an over-concentration of political and economic power. And we have both those things today."[25] This problem of giantism not only obliterated regional distinctiveness and cultural variety, but it also ravaged the internal social life of cities. Large-scale projects like urban renewal, highways, and high-rise buildings were products of the megamachine. Instead, Mumford preferred small-scale plans that fostered neighborhood life, where people could walk and mingle easily. "We really have to make the city so good to live in that you will not feel it desperately necessary to escape every week-end," he stressed. "The resources of a pleasant environment and a little space to move around should be much closer at hand than they are now."[26] For Mumford, the small scale allowed authentic community to thrive and ultimately was an expression of organicism: a humane existence of primary bonds, communal concern, and life-affirming relationships. Metropolitanism was destroying this, symptomatic of a bigger social malaise: "the increasing pathology of the whole mode of life in the great metropolis.... a pathology connected to its vast size, materialism, congestion, and disorder."[27]

Now, to the question of community. Mumford believed that community and city had the innate capacity—and need—to coexist. As he wrote in 1937, "The city is a related collection of primary groups and purposive association: the first, like family and neighborhood, are common to all communities, while the second are especially characteristic of city life." In the spark of this convergence, the city created its very human richness: "As indirect forms of association ... supplement direct-face-to-face intercourse, the personalities of the citizens themselves become many-faceted.... Here lies the possibility of personal disintegration; and here lies the need for reintegration through wider participation in a concrete and visible collective whole." Mumford believed a moderate-sized, balanced city held the greatest potential for this symbiosis.[28] At this level, not only would human-scale intimacy and community thrive but urbanites would also benefit from the cultural richness of city life. Mumford, indeed, enthusiastically embraced the idea of "regional cities," based on Ebenezer Howard's Garden City model. This design, he believed, best reflected an organic approach, in its moderate size and density, its balance, its decentralized functions, and its embrace of nature. In Mumford's eyes, this moderate-sized city allowed for the best aspects of urbanity to flourish—the diversity and complexity—but within a context of "organic limitation and controlled growth." He wrote of Howard's vision, "What was significant about the garden city was not the mere presence of gardens and open spaces: what was radically new was a rational and orderly method for dealing with complexity, through an organization capable of establishing balance and autonomy, and of maintaining order despite differentiation, and coherence and unity despite the need for growth. This was the transformative idea."[29] This was not a suburban vision but an urban one, softened around the edges.

American suburbs, in Mumford's mind, epitomized the problem of megalopolis. While he admired the earliest suburbs as organic communities—he praised their individuality, flexibility, communion with nature, symbiotic connection to the city, and human scale[30]—by the twentieth century, suburbs had become a "dissolute landscape." Mumford aired this critique as early as 1921, when he described Brooklyn as a "no-man's land which was neither town nor country," but rather a "twilight zone of an essentially suburban civilization." In their dull and dreary designs, their dormitory nature, and their rejection of urban culture, suburbs were a negation of everything that was good about cities. This suburban rejection of city life—"the flower of a well-developed civilization"—was a misguided trend. "The commuter, who spends a good part of his day, from an hour and a half to three hours, in wandering, like Tomlinson, between Heaven and Hell, presents a spectacle much more humiliating than a man without a country: he is a man without a city—in short, a barbarian." He continued, "Suburbia—that vast and aimless drift of human beings, spreading in every direction about our cities, large and small—demonstrates the incapacity of our civilization to foster concrete ways and means for living well. Having failed to create a common life in our modern cities, we have builded Suburbia, which is a common refuge from life, and the remedy is an aggravation of the disease!"[31]

By the post–World War II era, American suburbs had devolved to an even lower form, Mumford believed. As suburbia gained popularity, reaching its ugly climax in the mass-produced Levittowns of postwar America, what emerged was "a life that was not even a cheap counterfeit, but rather the grim antithesis" of the early organic vision. In the early 1960s, Mumford unleashed a trenchant critique of the postwar suburb as a supersized, standardized, diffuse, car-dependent mess. In a famous passage from *The City in History*, he wrote, "In the mass movement into suburban areas a new kind of community was produced, which caricatured both the historic city and the archetypal suburban refuge: a multitude of uniform, unidentifiable houses, lined up inflexibly, at uniform distances, on uniform roads, in a treeless communal waste, inhabited by people of the same class, the same income, the same age group, witnessing the same television performances, eating the same tasteless pre-fabricated foods, from the same freezers, conforming in every outward and inward respect to a common mold, manufactured in the central metropolis."[32] In Mumford's eyes, the mega-machine created the postwar suburb, which was spitting out people who had become the machine itself.

While these repercussions were pretty bad in themselves, Mumford pushed his critique further. For one, suburbia fostered isolation. In the city, people were forced into contact with the poor, with workers, with the diversity of humanity, ultimately encouraging a humane response by the whole community to improve the conditions of all. Suburbs isolated residents from this diversity. "In the suburb," he wrote, "one might live and die without marring the image of an innocent world.... Thus the suburb served as an asylum for the preservation of illusion. Here domesticity could flourish, forgetful of the exploitation on which so much of it was based." He expanded this idea into another theme, the childishness of suburban culture. Not only was suburbia a child-centered place, but its adult inhabitants took on childish ways of thinking. The flight from reality was one aspect of this—he called it a childish view of the world. But he also saw the postwar culture of consumption and leisure as a kind of childish impulse to play. He wrote of the suburb, "in breaking away from the city, the part became a substitute for the whole, even as a single phase of life, that of childhood, became the pattern for all the seven ages of man. As leisure generally increased, play became the serious business of life; and the golf course, the country club, the swimming pool, and the cocktail party became the frivolous counterfeits of a more varied and significant life." Notably, he saw the same shallow tendencies also infecting city life.[33] Finally, community itself was emaciated by suburbia. The low-density form, scattering people farther and farther from each other, exacerbated the isolation of individual households. People were cut off from face-to-face contact, holed up in their homes and cars, detached, alone, housewives finding their only companions on the television screen. "Untouched by human hand at one end; untouched by human spirit at the other," he wrote. The result was a tremendous, dangerous vulnerability of the people to media manipulation. "Each member of Suburbia becomes imprisoned by the very separation that he has prized; he is fed through a narrow opening: a telephone line, a radio band, a television circuit. This is not, it goes without saying, the result of a conscious conspiracy by a cunning minority; it is an organic by-product of an economy that sacrifices human development to mechanical processing."[34] Here, we come back full circle to Mumford's philosophical touchstone. In Mumford's eyes, hell had moved to both city and suburb—they were mutually constitutive parts of the megalopolis, a latter-day spatial manifestation of the megamachine.

Jane Jacobs emerges next. Jacobs began a career in journalism in 1958 at age 42, without a college degree and while raising a family in Greenwich Village.[35] She served as associate editor of *Architectural Forum*. Her first book, *The Death and Life of Great American Cities* (1961), became an "instant classic" in the words of sociologist Herbert Gans.[36] This work thrust her front and center in a spirited public debate over city form and planning, in a period of exploding metropolitan sprawl and massive federal urban renewal. She joined Lewis Mumford, Frank Lloyd Wright, Victor Gruen, and Constantinos Doxiadis, among others, in fierce arguments over the relative merits of centralization versus decentralization, active planning versus unfettered urban evolution.[37] Jacobs and Mumford were particularly at odds over these issues. Yet while they quarreled fiercely over many things about the city, they could agree on one thing: postwar suburbanization was a destructive trend and a failed social environment.

Jane Jacobs' critique of suburbia rested on an inversion of her ideas about the city. Jacobs used an ecological model as her paradigm for understanding cities; she likened the evolution of cities and societies to developing ecosystems. The strongest, most long-lived ecosystems survive because they have diverse, mutually reinforcing species and are spatially well organized. Likewise, successful cities are like a mature forest ecosystem. They thrive when there are diverse "species" (i.e., social groups) and when there is a logical spatial organization. For cities, the payoffs are a resilient and even creative milieu, successful communities, and economic vitality.[38]

She believed that true social vitality in a city began on its streets and sidewalks. Neighborhoods were most lively and successful when they possessed high density, mixed land use (both spatially and temporally), a variation in the age of buildings, and a diverse population. She wrote vividly about the life of the street, and how an active, pedestrian-oriented streetlife promoted satisfying social contacts, safe play areas for kids, and low crime because people were out and watching. The result was neighborhoods of "close-grained intricacy and compact mutual support," based on a perfected balance between public and private life that happened in a natural, casual way. The very urban qualities that Louis Wirth believed snuffed out community—bigness, density, diversity—in Jacobs's view breathed life into community.[39] She was thus a strong believer in the capacity of the built environment to shape social life and in the importance of public life to a community's health. Jacobs loathed big projects, preferring that city neighborhoods be allowed to evolve and flourish without the meddling interference of large-scale planning.[40] She hated big highway projects, big public housing projects, federal urban renewal, and mass-produced suburbs. She especially hated Los Angeles, which became a kind of surrogate for "suburban" in Jacobs' mind.[41] (As a sidenote, Mumford hated L.A. just about as much.)

By setting up a kind of Manichean conception of urban space—dense, mixed, and diverse were good, and the opposite traits bad—Jacobs constructed a potent critique of suburbia and a "decentrist" approach to planning. She called the problem "The Great Blight of Dullness." A section of a city was dull if it was uniform in its inhabitants, land use, and the built environment. When a section of a city suffered this way, it was destined to decline. All-residential suburbs, like Queens and the Bronx, embodied the definition of dull.[42] Jacobs also criticized the decentrist city planning approach—which she located especially in Howard's Garden City [43] and LeCorbusier's Radiant City—for destroying public space and the chance for spontaneous sociability. An overemphasis on privatism in these planning schemes meant "nobody, presumably, was going to have to be his brother's keeper." Jacobs stuck firm to a belief that true community was place-bound, and when space was functionally differentiated, true community as well as economic vitality were destroyed. Bedroom suburbs lacked the diversity and density needed to create "a great and exuberant richness of differences and possibilities," so fundamental to community health.[44] Jacobs even wondered how suburban housewives could raise their children in such a privatized environment, so antithetical to the streetlife she prized. "Sometimes, on Hudson Street," she wrote, "we are tempted to believe the suburbs must be a difficult place to bring up children."[45] Here, Jacobs questioned the very raison d'être of suburban homeseekers, based on her conception of authentic community in urban space.[46]

Neither Jacobs nor Mumford, it seems, actually observed the suburbs firsthand, with the kind of keen eye they trained on Manhattan's

Greenwich Village or West Side. Maybe they couldn't bear the thought of spending that much time in a place like Levittown. This did, however, leave their suburban critiques open to criticism, exactly on these grounds—of being too generalized, inferred, and out of touch with real trends. They also seemed to overlook several famous social analyses of suburbia that appeared in the 1950s, which emphasized a much different impulse than isolation in the suburbs.[47]

William H. Whyte's *Organization Man* (1956) was central among them.[48] Whyte, an editor at *Fortune* magazine, actually entered the trenches of suburbia and lived to write about it. His book profiled a new pervasive ethic he believed had taken over America, and was graphically expressed in the "package suburb." He used Park Forest, Illinois, as his laboratory for analysis. And while his conclusions were starkly different from those of Jacobs and Mumford, the subtext of condemnation was similar. Whyte agreed that suburbia had become a kind of hell, but it was a hell of a different shade—not of social isolation but of oppressive community. As he put it, suburbanites had become "imprisoned in brotherhood."[49]

Whyte's well-known thesis centered on a concept he called the Social Ethic. He charted the decline of the Protestant Ethic, which prized individualism and salvation through hard work, thrift, and competitive struggle. As corporate capitalism grew, the Social Ethic emerged in its place. This belief-system placed utmost value on *the group*: "a belief in the group as the source of creativity; a belief in 'belongingness' as the ultimate need of the individual." Under this system, ambition was not about personal achievement; rather, he wrote, "It is an ambition directed outward, to the satisfactions of making others happy." What was most powerful (and dangerous) about this ethic, in Whyte's view, was the extent to which it had become internalized and accepted as a "moral imperative." "The fault is not in organization, in short; it is in our worship of it," he wrote.[50] And it pervaded society: education, corporate life, academia, science, and, of course, suburbia.

Whyte devoted nearly one-third of his book to the postwar "package suburbs," which he called Organization Man's dormitories and "communities made in his image."[51] Because Organization Man could express himself more freely here than in the Organization itself, suburbia became the site where one could observe the Social Ethic in its purest form. What did he find? In short, an intensely vibrant community life, or as he put it, "a social atmosphere of striking vigor." It was a place where neighbors dropped in without knocking, where "coffeepots bubble all day long," where neighbors held communal notions of property (like lawnmowers) and labor (like babysitting). Some joked it was "a Russia, only with money." Suburbanites also joined groups voraciously: hobby clubs, the PTA, the League of Women Voters, reading groups, a church, and on and on. Whyte called Park Forest a "hotbed of Participation."[52]

How did he explain this intense urge to belong? He identified several factors. First and foremost, of course, was the Social Ethic itself. Another factor was the transience of Organization Man. Job transfers were endemic to corporate life. Organization Man knew this and accepted it, partly because transfers usually signified upward mobility. Rootlessness thus became an expected fact of life. Whyte recognized that this context of instability created a deep need in Organization Man for a sense of connection, a sense of recognizable community wherever he found himself. He needed to sink down roots—even if shallow—to provide the social support he desperately craved. These floating junior executives transferred this ideal to each new destination, spreading their generic sense of community across the national landscape a little like McDonalds propagating its golden arches. People and suburbs became interchangeable. "In the externals of existence we are united by a culture increasingly national. And this is part of the momentum of mobility. The more people move about, the more similar the American environments become, and the more similar they become, the easier it is to move about. More and more, the young couples who move do so only physically. With each transfer the *décor*, the architecture, the faces, and the names may change; the people, the conversation, and the values do not—and sometimes the *décor* and the architecture don't either."[53] Here, Whyte joined a broader postwar critique of "mass society."

Yet his portrait of postwar suburban community had nuances, which lent it more credibility than, say, Mumford's image of mass man being churned out of the megamachine of mass suburbia.[54] One example was Whyte's discussion of how the environment shaped behavior. He was a strong believer in environmental determinism, going so far as to claim that "it is possible deliberately to plan a layout which will produce a close-knit social group." He went on to map out "the webs of friendship" in Park Forest, concluding that the layout of homes had immense impact on how people connected. For example, neighbors with adjacent driveways or front stoops were most likely to form friendships: "where they join makes a natural sitting, baby-watching, and gossip center, and friendship is more apt to flower there than across the unbroken stretch of lawn on the other sides of the houses." This is vaguely reminiscent of the kind of social surveillance Jacobs described on the urban street. Whyte also observed that street width and traffic determined whether people could make friends across the street. He asserted that the "tightest-knit groups are those in which no home is isolated from the others." Finally, he concluded confidently: "it would appear that certain kinds of physical layouts can virtually produce the 'happy' group."[55]

But Whyte's analysis ultimately extended into a deep critique of this communal way of life—and of the Social Ethic itself. Whyte recognized the vexing paradox of this community spirit, whose very strengths also posed its most dangerous threats. "The group is a tyrant," he wrote, "so also is it a friend, and *it is both at once*. The two qualities cannot easily be separated, for what gives the group its power over the man is the same cohesion that gives it its warmth. This is the duality that confuses choice." This was the central dilemma of the Organization Man. The Social Ethic had become so internalized and so accepted as a moral imperative, that man now found himself "imprisoned in brotherhood."[56] The costs of this, as Whyte saw it, were legion: the loss of individuality, of the creative spirit, of depth, and even of privacy. Man had become a mediocre creature of the middle, afraid to question and think deeply, for fear of destroying consensus. In suburbia, this manifested as a loss of privacy, a ruthless intolerance of outliers, and even little outbursts of individuality that bordered on the pathological—like housewives caught shoplifting—simply because there were so few outlets for individual expression. Here, hyperactive community—as a kind of disfigured artifact of mass society—had itself become hell.[57]

In future writings, Whyte continued to voice trenchant criticisms of the suburban trend. The year after *Organization Man* was published, he wrote a piece for *Fortune*, predicting that people would eventually tire of the suburbs and move back to the city. High taxes, high maintenance, long commutes, and the sheer blandness of social life, he believed, would drive suburbanites back to the city. He also waged an impassioned critique of suburban sprawl on environmental grounds, decrying its tendency to destroy open space and exhaust natural resources. It was a message he delivered in *Fortune*, *Life*, Senate hearings, planning symposia, and his book *The Last Landscape* (1968). Like the other writers discussed, Whyte held a deep, abiding interest in the city and its wellbeing. He was a passionate defender of high density, believing it absolutely necessary to vibrant social life. He applied this principle not only to his planning ideas for cities, but also for suburban cluster developments.[58]

Among the writers I've considered here, Whyte was really the first one to question the value of community itself, and to explore the darker side of its excesses. This put Whyte (and others writers like him who perpetuated what came be known as the "suburban myth") at odds with writers like Jacobs and Mumford, who saw the problem of suburbia stemming more from an excess of privatism and isolation. Somehow, all of these writers saw the same physical environment but extrapolated two very different social milieus. Yet the common denominator was still *hell*. Whether it was a hell of isolation or a hell of hyperactive sociability, suburbia retained its place of dishonor.

––––––

Each of these scholars expressed broader strands of social criticism, in the sense that city and suburb became surrogates for (or at least symptomatic of) broader concerns: modernization, mass society, the "megamachine," an oppressive corporate ethos, the excesses of conformity in the context of the Cold War, the destructive impact of big government. In each case, the built environment was "read" as an agent of these larger forces. As we all do, these writers brought a potent set of values to their interpretations of space. Similarly, they brought strong value judgments to their definitions of community. It wasn't enough that people knew their neighbors, joined groups, and socialized regularly—something deeper, more civically-minded, and more inclusive had to be present for it to count as *authentic* community.[59]

One result is a murky picture of exactly how the built environment produced social outcomes. Take, for example, Wirth and Whyte. Both described a "way of life" that was superficial, transitory, consumption oriented, and lacking in kinship ties, where man had lost a sense of individuality so he joined groups to compensate. Yet each implicated a completely different environment. Wirth blamed the city—its enormity and diversity. Whyte focused on suburbia—its small scale and homogeneity. If they had it right—which is open to question—then it was likely that something besides the environment was at work.[60] Similarly, both Jacobs and Whyte described neighborhoods of great social vitality, where people knew one another, interacted on a daily basis, and forged community. Yet Jacobs attributed this to the urban life of the street; Whyte documented it in the rambling streets and cul de sacs of Park Forest. Shaded by the vigorous arguments these writers were waging, the relationship between built environment and social life was obscured more than revealed. While these works certainly failed to resolve the question of social causality, collectively they do point to one striking fact: different types of communities could survive and even thrive in very disparate settings. Taken together, they offer an inadvertent reminder that we need to think flexibility when we approach the question of community.

Despite their many differences, Wirth, Mumford, Jacobs, and Whyte all shared a deep, abiding interest in the built environment and a faith in its capacity to solve urban problems. At times, this perspective could lead them into an analytical trap; they tended to place blame for the city's problems on its spatial form and the planning principles upon which it rested. Sociologist Herbert Gans called this "the physical fallacy."[61] Its weakness was a fixation on environmental forces, at the expense of considering how economic, political, cultural, or even social forces could make or break a city. If cities could just be built—or even left alone—in the right way, then cities would prosper and humans might enjoy fulfilling, authentic modes of life and community. All of the authors fell back on this "physical fix" in one way or another. In the process, they had a tendency to underplay issues of politics, power, and inequality, and especially to overlook the ways that racial divisions were shaping the postwar metropolitan landscape.[62]

When it came to their analyses of suburbia, this environmental paradigm yielded some curious results. For one, it focused attention on how this distinctive built environment was impacting, above all, its own residents. White suburbanites became the victims in this story. They suffered from oppressive conformity, landscapes of monotony, and a culture of shallowness. This narrow framework obscured a broader picture of who was truly being victimized in the suburbanization process. People of color who were shut out of white subdivisions, denied federal assistance in home buying, and confined to inferior, costly urban neighborhoods, were bearing a much heavier burden than, say, the white home owner worried about his neighbor's opinion. As much as the 1950s was the decade of postwar suburbanization, it was also the decade of civil rights activism; indeed, as work by Thomas Sugrue, Robert Self, and others suggests, they were deeply intertwined. But if one juxtaposes the suburban analyses of Mumford, Jacobs, and Whyte, against the civil rights struggles for open housing in suburbia, the images do not easily comport. On one level, why would African Americans want to move into the suburbs at all, if they were such social wastelands? On another, would good city planning be enough to solve the problems that civil rights activists were seeking to redress, like better housing and access to all-white suburban neighborhoods? Would a "physical fix" be enough? Many postwar suburbs were deliberately all-white, made so by legal covenants, real estate practices, federal housing policies, private lending practices, and violent intimidation, detailed in several essays in this volume. A multifaceted structure of discrimination shaped the social life of Park Forest and Levittown, as much as its mass produced housing did. It would take much more than thoughtful city planning to solve this problem. It would take a critical reassessment of the entire metropolitan polity and political economy.

A virulent desire for racial exclusivity dwelled deep in the hearts and minds of white suburbanites. This reality offered another devastating counterpoint to the vision of someone like Jane Jacobs, who believed urban vitality rested on diversity. She assumed people desired diversity, that they wanted communities that mixed it up. Indeed, she even believed that people were moving to suburbia because they were repulsed by dull central cities, made so by poor planning. Here, Jacobs misjudged the depth of popular enmity for landscapes of diversity.[63] On this count, Whyte had captured a truth. He called it the "social ethic," the desire to fit in with the group, to find comfort in sameness, and to reject outsiders.[64] Yet even his work stopped short of a racial analysis.

The approaches taken by Jacobs, Mumford, and Whyte reflected the main currents of both urban and cultural analysis of their time. In the 1950s and early 1960s, an age of anti-communist anxiety, intellectuals were more prone to critique mass culture, conformity, and consumerism, rather than basic structural flaws in the American liberal state. The focus was more on cultural form, less on politics and political economy. Essentially an apolitical critique, their ideas gained wide currency at the time.[65] Mumford and Whyte were central in this intellectual movement, seeing the aesthetic and social failure of suburbs as emblematic of these postwar trends. Likewise, as we have seen, urban analysis of the period fixated more on form, less on structure. In one sense, this was a testament to the tremendous longevity of the Chicago school's urban ecology approach. By the 1970s, the political economy approach came to dominate urban analysis and, indeed, continues a long, fruitful run, as evidenced by the work of this volume. Yet even despite the revisionism of the political economists and of the postmodern urbanists who followed, the critical assessments of Mumford, Jacobs, and Whyte still shape certain deeply-held assumption we retain about postwar suburbia.

The collective verdict of these works reviewed here, in the end, leaves a gaping void in our understanding of postwar suburbia. One is left to ponder some basic questions. If the suburbs offered only social anguish and failure, why did Americans keep moving to them in ever-rising numbers? And more pointedly, why was the civil rights movement passionately fighting for access to this suburban life? Why would African Americans be willing to risk vandalism, cross burnings, and violence, for the opportunity to live in these social wastelands?

One explanation is that these writers had it wrong, that meaningful community could—and did—exist in the suburbs. There's certainly sporadic evidence to show this: from a second wave of sociological studies in the 1960s that aimed to tear down the "suburban myth"[66] to the "new suburban history" that is expanding the definition of suburbia beyond a simplistic white, conservative middle-class model.[67] The essays by Andrew Wiese, Michael Jones-Correa, and Matthew Lassiter are fine examples of the latter. Collectively, this literature has revealed a more nuanced portrait of suburban social life, with tremendous variation in residents, their outlooks, politics, and experiences. And then there's Robert Putnam's *Bowling Alone,* which takes the image of postwar suburban hell-on-earth and transforms it into the good old days. He argues that Americans' civic engagement and social connectedness reached a peak from 1945–1965, then declined precipitously thereafter.[68] All of these works are valuable for questioning the too-easy conclusions of people like Mumford, Jacobs, and Whyte. However, I also believe that much work remains to be done on postwar suburbs, if only to untangle certain contradictory images.[69] On the one hand, we imagine suburbia as a place of nosy neighbors, kaffeklatches, PTAs, and block parties. On the other hand, are images of families locked behind doors and gates, neighbors unknown to each other, and empty sidewalks. Perhaps these images are historically contingent, predominant at different stages since 1945. Perhaps they are linked to issues of class, ethnicity, race, age, and gender. These social realities still need sorting out.

A second explanation might point to another dynamic. Perhaps the ways some postwar suburbanites deployed community precipitated a kind of destructive redefinition of the concept. Yes they had community. But they tipped the scales so far away from inclusive, bridging communities to exclusive, bonding communities, that community no longer represents a social good. In producing racial and economic inequality and doing so in a context of *community vitality*, suburbia has transformed the community ideal from a positive source of human fulfillment and acceptance into a destructive tool of exclusivity and inequality. Suburbia has thus corrupted a benevolent community ideal.

Or possibly another dynamic is at work. If we assume people crave and need community, yet they continue moving to these suburban social wastelands, then maybe they're getting their community elsewhere. It has been well understood for some time that community is no longer a place-bound phenomenon, that it can be experienced in many different places by individuals.[70] For suburban dwellers, the possibility exists that community has become completely divorced from place.

For all of the scholarship that has both deepened and complicated our understanding of postwar suburbia, the writings of Mumford, Jacobs, and Whyte still resonate powerfully in the public imagination. This derives partly from the nature of public discourse about suburbia in the 1950s and 1960s: the ideas of the critics were adapted by cultural producers of the era, who gave them even wider public reach through novels, short stories, and films.[71] Their collective message created a recognizable cultural icon that lives on even in popular culture of own day. In several recent films, *American Beauty, Pleasantville, The Truman Show, Far From Heaven*, and even the television series *Desperate Housewives*, suburbia continues to come across as a place of oppressive conformity and shallow lives, a place that stifles creativity and individual human expression and where community is contrived at best. These cultural references owe a debt to writers like Mumford, Whyte, and Jacobs, who saw in suburbs a vision of social hell with little chance for redemption.

FIVE

"The House I Live In"

Race, Class, and African American Suburban
Dreams in the Postwar United States

ANDREW WIESE

It took Jim and Ann Braithewaite two years to find a home
in the suburbs. After transferring to Philadelphia in 1957,
the family began looking for a house almost immediately.
Meanwhile, they rented in "a predominantly Negro neighborhood" in the city. They dreamed of owning a detached,
split-level house with a big yard in the suburbs, which
was common enough for couples with children in postwar
Philadelphia, yet like thousands of African Americans, they
searched in vain while white families moved to new suburban
homes with relative ease.[1]

The Braithewaites' struggle exemplified the experience
of many African Americans after World War II. Although
they were plainly middle class—she was a school teacher,
he a mechanical engineer—with a combined income well
above the metropolitan average, their race made them out-
casts in the suburban housing market. They answered newspaper ads, contacted real estate brokers, attended auctions
and made an estimated 300 phone calls, but they met a
"stone wall" of resistance. "We don't have any split-levels,"
or "That's already spoken for," brokers told them. Others
were straightforward: "You're colored, aren't you? I can't
do anything for you," said one.[2] Whatever the reaction,

the results were the same. As African Americans, they were not welcome in any part of Philadelphia's white suburbia.

In "desperation," the Braithewaites recalled, they shifted strategies. With the help of a local fair housing organization, they found a vacant lot whose owner was open to selling. Though they had reservations about the location because it was "very close to a public school" and near an existing "Negro neighborhood," they hired a contractor and built a new home, inspecting progress at night, "hoping to prevent the accumulation of resentment" among their new neighbors. The family took occupancy in October 1959, remaining fearful that "something cataclysmic" might happen. For "some time" they even avoided standing in front of the picture window, but the neighborhood remained quiet, thanks in part to the efforts of local Quakers who hosted a meeting to calm the neighbors and stayed with the family on their first night in the house. After months of frustration, the Braithewaites were suburbanites at last.

As a white-collar family, the Braithewaites exemplified a new wave of black suburbanization after World War II. During the 1940s and 1950s, the number of black suburbanites rose from one and a half to two and a half million.[3] Whereas working-class families had dominated the prewar migration, middle-class African Americans—wealthier, better educated, and more likely to hold white-collar jobs than earlier suburbanites—began moving to suburbs in growing numbers after the war. Bolstered by national economic expansion and the opening of new occupations, black family incomes rose. By the mid-fifties, the United States was home to a growing black bourgeoisie and a cohort of economically stable industrial workers whose members had the means to purchase comfortable suburban housing on a greater scale than ever before. As their numbers increased, middle-class families became the predominant suburban migrants by the mid-1950s. These decades represented a period of transition in a century-long process of black suburbanization. Working-class households remained a majority through the mid-1960s, but the momentum had shifted perceptibly toward the nascent middle class.[4]

The Braithewaites' struggle for a suburban home also points to the links between black suburbanization and the making of race and class in the postwar United States. As upwardly mobile blacks achieved middle-class incomes, occupations, and education, they also expressed a sense of class status through choices about how and where to live. Like millions of postwar Americans, many sought to own modern homes in recognizably middle-class neighborhoods. Their suburban dreams emphasized leisure-time pursuits, opportunities for children, proximity to jobs and services, and architecturally uniform residential landscapes. Contrasting in subtle and not so subtle ways with the ethic of prewar suburbanites, postwar suburbanization became a means for members of a rising middle class to express and reinforce their newly won social position.

Nonetheless, changes in the palette of black suburban preferences did not connote a lessening of racial distinctions or a "whitening" of the middle class. As racial outsiders in a predominantly white society, families like the Braithewaites could not be ordinary suburbanites even if they had wanted to be. Their distinctive public experience indelibly shaped the meaning of private places, such as homes and neighborhoods, and it nurtured a distinctive politics related to housing. By achieving widespread suburban living patterns, African Americans asserted their equality and consciously minimized the social distance that whites sought to maintain as a privilege of race. In so doing, they challenged and subverted a central element of the dominant suburban ethos, which was white supremacy.[5] In these ways, suburbanization tended to strengthen migrants' identities as black people even as it reinforced patterns of class stratification among African Americans themselves.

Images of Home

A closer look at African Americans' ideas about housing and landscape after World War II reveals evidence of both persistence and change in black suburbanization. The clearest indication of continuity between pre- and postwar suburban values was the unswerving appeal of homeownership among African Americans of every social class. Attitude surveys uncovered a widespread inclination among African Americans to own homes of their own, and for many it included the wish to buy in the suburbs. A nationwide survey of black veterans in 1947 disclosed that between one-third and one-half of veterans in cities such as Philadelphia, Detroit, Indianapolis, Atlanta, Houston, and Baton Rouge hoped to buy or build a home of their own within the next twelve months.[6] A 1948 study of 600 "middle-income Negro families" in New York City revealed that three-quarters "would like to move to suburban areas and nine-tenths of them preferred to buy their own homes."[7] Approaching the question from a different angle, researchers in Philadelphia asked some 1,500 African Americans in 1960 how they would spend a "windfall" of $5,000. More than half reported that they would use the money to buy a new house or pay off an existing mortgage.[8]

Evidence of African Americans' tenacious "demand for homeownership" was apparent in everyday behavior as well.[9] Supported by gains in income and civil liberties as well as marginal assistance from the federal government, rates of nonfarm homeownership among African Americans climbed from 24 to 39 percent between 1940 and 1960. In the most populous suburban areas, however, the proportion of owners rose from 32 to 51 percent. Homeownership, which had long been a goal among African Americans, remained a fundamental aspiration among black suburbanites after the war.[10]

What homeownership meant to suburbanites, of course, remained a complex matter. As was common before the war, many suburbanites viewed homeownership as the basis for economic security through thrift and domestic production. Older patterns of suburban life endured in a range of working-class suburbs. Suburbanites relished their gardens and fruit trees, and many insisted on keeping livestock. In places like Chagrin Falls Park, Ohio, the war did little to change the disposition of residents like Clydie Smith, who fondly remembered gardens, lush with "pinto beans and collards and black-eyed peas and cabbage and beets and squash and peppers" as well as the sow, called "Sookie," that her father kept.[11] Across the continent in Pasadena, California, city officials fought a running battle with black householders who raised chickens and ducks in violation of a local ordinance.[12] In Mt. Vernon, New York, David Doles, who had prospered as a laundry owner in Harlem before moving to the suburbs, extolled self-provisioning as part of an ethic of thrift that included other productive uses of property as well. Recalling that "we used to eat off our place down home" in Virginia, Doles boasted that he planted "more fruit right here in my place in the back yard than some people with a great big place."[13]

This vision was also evident in the popular culture of the period. In her 1958 drama, *A Raisin in the Sun*, playwright Lorraine Hansberry used this rustic ethic to symbolize both the endurance and violation of African Americans' hopes for the urban North. The character, Mama, a southerner living in a Chicago tenement dreams of buying "a little place" with "a patch of dirt" out back, explaining "[I] always wanted me a garden like I used to see sometimes at the back of the houses down home." The sun-starved plant on her windowsill is as close as she was able to come.[14] In fiction and real life, the echoes of rural and working-class upbringings reverberated in the choices that migrants made. For as long as they lived, lifeways such as these would shape the environment of hundreds of suburban communities.

Many postwar suburbanites also used their homes as a source of income and an anchor for continued migration by renting rooms to recent migrants and sharing space with kin. Older suburbs in particular witnessed intensified multifamily occupancy during the period. In Evanston, Illinois, scores of homeowners converted houses to include rental units. In the streets off Emerson Avenue on the suburb's west side, the number of owners and renters rose simultaneously despite little new construction, indicating that African Americans were buying and converting their own homes to multifamily use. Similar practices affected neighborhoods in East Orange, New Jersey, New Rochelle, New York, and Pasadena and Berkeley, California, where black homeowners capitalized on continued migration by becoming landlords.[15] Though some residents expressed a more restrictive view of domestic space, charging that "overcrowding" would lead to "possible neighborhood deterioration," old settlers offered a foothold for migrants in established communities, while newcomers provided rental incomes that supported homeownership and upward mobility for a rising class of black proprietors.[16]

Advertisements in the black press indicate that a vision of economic independence through productive use of property remained a marketable option in urban communities through at least the late forties. As the war ended, realty companies in Detroit, New York, Chicago, and other cities dusted off old subdivisions and began selling low-cost building lots much as they had before the war. The Chicago *Defender* advertised home sites for as little as "$10 down" in suburbs such as Robbins, Phoenix, East Chicago Heights, and Maywood, Illinois, as well as in predominantly black subdivisions within the city such as Morgan Park and Lilydale. Ads in New York's *Amsterdam News* pitched building lots in Westbury, Hempstead, Amityville, and Hauppauge, New York, and other suburbs where African Americans had lived since the nineteenth century.[17] A 1947 advertisement for "Farm Homesites" in Farmingdale, Long Island, for instance, depicted a small house and outbuildings surrounded by tilled fields and fruit trees, while the text stressed links to the urban economy, highlighting "easy commuting, close to large airplane factory, plenty of employment."[18] Like advertisements published during the Great Migration, these appealed to a working-class, southern aesthetic, describing semirural landscapes, open space and low-cost property ownership plus "the opportunity to grow your own food" within proximity to established communities and urban jobs.[19]

Owner construction and other informal building practices also persisted in blue-collar subdivisions. In Chagrin Falls Park, Ohio, Clydie Smith, William Hagler, and George Adams built homes after the war.[20] So, too, did families in suburbs such as Inkster, Michigan, the American Addition near Columbus, Ohio, and North Richmond, California, where lot owners went "to the lumberyard and bought what they could without access to mortgage loans, and . . . put up what they called their home."[21] Advertisements for do-it-yourself house kits, quonset buildings and other

Figure 5.1. Advertisements for building lots on Long Island, New York. Like their counterparts during the Great Migration, real estate agents in the 1940s marketed subdivisions that promised urban African Americans a vision of rustic self-sufficiency in a borderland between rural and urban life. Mass suburbanization and the proliferation of suburban land-use regulations sharply curtailed this avenue to suburbia. *Amsterdam News,* May 24, 1947.

nontraditional shelters, such as the prefabricated "Port-o-Cottage, the house you have been waiting for," were common fare in the black press through the late 1940s.[22] As this evidence indicates, homeownership for many black families remained a productive enterprise rooted in the working-class experience, and to the extent that middle-class status was fleeting or uncertain, such practices remained attractive, representing continuity in African American values and lifeways in the postwar suburbs.

In contrast to the thrift-oriented ethos that prevailed in older suburban areas, an increasing number of new suburbanites articulated preferences for housing that reflected norms prevalent across the wider middle class. In a study of black professionals and technical employees in upstate New York, Eunice and George Grier concluded that "little if any-thing . . . distinguishes the requirements of these Negro home seekers from criteria one would expect to find among their middle-class white counterparts." They sought "adequate play space for children, good schools, safety and quiet, good property maintenance, and congenial neighbors of roughly equivalent income and educational background." Not surprisingly, most were "looking for a house of post–World War II vintage in a suburban area."[23] Researcher Dorothy Jayne encountered similar attitudes among pioneer families in suburban Philadelphia. Two-thirds of her respondents hoped to buy a single-family home in a "desirable" suburban neighborhood; a third were looking for ranch or split-level models. They described their ideal neighborhoods as "quiet, clean, with well-kept properties," convenient to shopping, with good schools and services and an abundance of "fresh air and green grass." Many indicated that they were willing to pay more to attain these amenities.[24]

Among the attractions of suburban life that many middle-class African Americans shared with their white counterparts was an emphasis on a materially abundant family life in a residential setting removed from the "grind" of paid labor.[25] A glimpse of the ideal lifestyle circulating among middle-class blacks after the war can be seen in the pages of *Ebony* magazine, which appeared on newsstands in 1945 and targeted readers in the aspirant black bourgeoisie. During its first few years, *Ebony* ran regular features publicizing the housing and domestic lifestyles of the nation's black elite. Reporters fawned over "big impressive home[s]," "sumptuous" furnishings, stylish house parties, and the financial success and style that these implied. Many stories featured families who lived in elegant central city apartments, reflecting the continued concentration of black elites in neighborhoods such as Harlem's "Sugar Hill," but an equal number highlighted the owners of detached, single-family homes in suburban or suburban-style neighborhoods.[26]

An *Ebony* feature on the Addisleigh Park neighborhood of Queens, New York, reveals the physical and social environment that many middle-class African Americans idealized in the postwar decades. With its two-story, Tudor and colonial revival houses, green lawns and canopy of mature trees, the place merited its description as a "swank suburban neighborhood" or a "suburban Sugar Hill" even though it was located inside the municipal limits of New York City.[27]

Reflecting the importance of landscape as a status marker, the writer highlighted residents' richly appointed housing and abundant greenery. The essay featured more than twenty photographs of tree-shaded homes belonging to such celebrities as Ella Fitzgerald, Roy Campanella, Billie Holiday, Jackie Robinson, and Count Basie, underscoring the affluent surroundings and amenities that they enjoyed. "Many home owners have two cars," including "more Cadillacs per block . . . than any other like community in the country," the reporter enthused. Meanwhile captions listed the dollar value of almost every home pictured, suggesting none too subtly the connection between homeownership and wealth, not to mention good taste.

If few *Ebony* readers could afford such luxuries, the article took pains to emphasize Addisleigh Park's down-to-earth social life, which the writer described as "swank without snobbery." According to the reporter, Mercer Ellington mowed his own grass and preferred to "romp with his children on the front lawn," while Illinois Jacquet spent his leisure time in "bull sessions with famous neighbors." When Count Basie wasn't getting his "kicks" playing the organ in his living room, he could be found engaged in "marathon poker games . . . famed . . . for their high stakes and salty talk."

Though residents were household names in black America, the writer pictured Addisleigh Park as a "typical . . . suburban community, with its civic association, women's clubs, Boy Scout troops and Saturday night pinochle games . . . lavish lawn parties and hearty cocktail sessions in pine-walled rumpus rooms."[28] Thus, *Ebony* portrayed a vision of suburban life that many middle-class African Americans could appreciate and to which they might aspire. In its emphasis on comfort and an expressive, consumption-oriented social life, the magazine impressed upon, and no doubt reinforced among its readers, a distinctly middle or upper-middle-class vision of suburban life. In a suburbanizing nation, *Ebony* signaled, middle-class African Americans were gaining equality as citizens through equality in their tastes and acquisitions as consumers, not least of which was their consumption of housing.[29]

Advertisements for new tract homes aimed at black home buyers appealed to a cluster of similar values, further suggesting the strength of this vision among the new black middle class as well as the pressures for conformity that shaped it. A 1947 ad for the Hempstead Park subdivision in West Hempstead, Long Island, was typical. It pictured a modest, saltbox-style home in a background of trees, while the text extolled the virtues of the house and neighborhood. For just $9,900, no cash down, black veterans and their families could own "4 1/2 spacious, sun-filled rooms" with "large picture windows," on a "large landscaped plot" just a "short walk" from schools, shopping, and Hempstead Lake State Park. With the exception of the ad's placement in a black newspaper, there was nothing to distinguish it from hundreds of advertisements aimed at white veterans. Hempstead Park's amenities, emphasizing children, leisure, homeownership, and a picturesque residential setting, fit squarely within the mass suburban ethos of the period.[30]

Ten years later, an advertisement for three subdivisions in the San Fernando Valley, north of Los Angeles, appealed to the same suburban imagery. The ad in the black-owned *Crown City Press* of Pasadena

Figure 5.2. Through its coverage of housing issues, *Ebony* reflected as well as promoted a consumer-oriented vision of suburban living among the nation's growing black middle class. *Ebony*, September 1951.

featured a sleek, garage-dominant ranch house framed by tall trees and written text: "Give your family the pleasure of living in Pacoima's Quality Circle." A map indicated the "desirable San Fernando Valley location," marking such features as Hansen Dam recreation area, the San Gabriel

Figure 5.3. Advertisement for suburban housing near Los Angeles. By the 1950s, mass-produced suburban imagery predominated in the real estate pages of the nation's black press. Like *Ebony*'s reportage, ads for new homes emphasized a vision of suburbia that had wide appeal in the nation's middle class. *Pasadena Crown City Press*, February 7, 1957.

Mountains, a school, public park, and pool as well as the highway to downtown Los Angeles. In addition to situating these developments in a recreation-filled landscape that had already become synonymous with middle-class suburban living, the ad emphasized the "exquisitely modern" but cozy amenities of the houses themselves, including "sliding-glass walls," "large, cheerful kitchens," and "brick fireplaces," plus a choice of nine "exciting exteriors."[31] Like advertisements for thousands of white subdivisions after World War II, these ads could not have evoked a more distant imagery from the chicken coops, second-hand lumber, and upstairs renters that characterized working-class suburban life at the time.[32] They marketed modern, affordable comfort in an environment oriented toward nuclear families and leisure just a short commute from the central city, a suburban dream firmly anchored in the post-war mainstream.

As these examples indicate, another important feature of postwar black suburbia was an emphasis on the suburbs as a "better place for children" to live.[33] In the early years of the baby boom, children gained prominence in suburban advertising for African Americans much as they did in ads designed for middle-class whites. "Here is the safety of suburban living for your children," boasted the developer of Ronek Park, a thousand-home subdivision in North Amityville, New York. "Yes, here, the entire family can enjoy the pleasures and advantages of a wonderful new community offering everything you ever dreamed of." Another broker, who specialized in "high class neighborhoods" of Westchester County, New York, encouraged urbanites to "bring up your children in this suburban paradise."[34] Developers increasingly incorporated images of children in their advertisements, which also reflected a shift in the class composition of black suburban migration after the war. Though prewar ads often mentioned schools and parks among a list of community facilities, subdividers rarely mentioned children directly—certainly less often than they referred to chickens or vegetable gardens.

Even ads for homes in unplanned suburbs such as Robbins, Illinois, which had attracted working-class blacks since World War I, were not exempt from the national celebration of childrearing that succeeded the war. A 1946 campaign for "homesites" in the Lincoln Manor subdivision depicted children playing in the front yard of a new home while a woman sat on the front steps watching and perhaps waiting for a bread-winning father to return up the front walk. Blending elements of old and new, the ad portrayed a square, brick-faced bungalow typical of Chicago's southwest suburbs, plus a large garden plot—tilled for row crops, no less—at the back of the lot.[35] The image of a stay-at-home mother belied economic reality for millions of African American families, but through such advertisements suburban developers reinforced a vision of middle-class domesticity even in suburbs that had long been home to the black working class.

Suburbanites themselves were also more likely to mention children as the basis for residential choice, often doing so in class-specific ways. Discussing his search for housing, a black professional from upstate New York reported, "locality would take precedence over price for me because I have a family to bring up and want them to grow up in an area which will aid in their development." Another described his preferred place of residence as "an area where the schools provide opportunities to give my children a good education, and where they could skate, bike ride, and keep pets."[36] The musician Milt Hinton explained that he and his wife moved to the leafy environs of St. Albans from an apartment in Manhattan because they were expecting a baby and "we wanted a nice, clean place to raise a child."[37] In contrast to the emphasis that working-class suburbanites had placed on extended families, children and nuclear families loomed large for the middle class, and suburbs appeared the ideal place to raise them.[38]

The centrality of children in middle-class ideology emerged in discussions of other preferences as well. For African Americans who valued racial integration as the antithesis of segregation, children were an important justification. Celebrity couples such as Jackie and Rachel Robinson and Sidney and Juanita Poitier justified their decisions to look for housing in mostly-white neighborhoods in just such terms. "We feel if our children have an opportunity to know people of all races and creeds at a very early age, their opportunities in life will be greater," Jackie Robinson explained.[39] For the Poitiers, it was the lack of such opportunities in Los Angeles that caused them to rethink their move to that city in 1960. After having difficulty finding a house in West Los Angeles, Mr. Poitier stated, "Our children are established in a multi-racial community in Mount Vernon [New York]. They attend multi-racial schools. The difference in color is no longer a curiosity to our children. We don't want to barter that kind of atmosphere for something that is hostile."[40] Likewise, Winston Richie, a dentist who moved to Shaker Heights, Ohio, in 1956, explained that he wanted his children to learn they "could compete with all people at all levels if they are prepared themselves. Living in an all-black community," he argued, "makes this lesson a bit harder to learn, or at best, it comes later in life."[41] For parents such as these, selecting suburban neighborhoods rested heavily on the opportunity they perceived for their children to grow up as equal citizens.

Race, Class, and Suburbanization

If many new suburbanites aspired to goals and amenities that they shared with middle-class whites, they also approached homes and neighborhoods as people with a distinct history and with experiences that distinguished them from whites. As sociologist Mary Patillo-McCoy notes, "Being middle class did not annul the fact of being black."[42] Discrimination blocked African Americans' most ordinary aspirations, forging from their individual choices a politics of housing linked to the quest for racial equality. Suburbanization underlined racial cohesion in a practical sense, too, by forcing house hunters to rely on black social and institutional networks, especially if they sought housing beyond established black areas.

Direct confrontations with racism also shaped the experience and understanding of suburban life. For thousands of families, the search for housing was a struggle that left economic as well as emotional scars. Legal activist Loren Miller explained, "Those who cannot buy in the open market in a free-enterprise economy are subject to obvious disadvantages. The special market to which they are forced to resort tends to become and remain a seller's market. Supply is limited. In the ordinary situation that supply will consist of those items that cannot be sold or will not bring satisfactory prices for one reason or another in the open market. The disadvantaged buyer is in no position to reject shoddy merchandise or haggle over prices. He must take what he can get and pay what he is asked."[43]

The struggle for housing could be emotionally trying as well. Black home-seekers described their experiences in the housing market as "difficult," "degrading," "nerve-racking," or "like knocking your head against a wall."[44] After numerous unsuccessful attempts to find a home in upstate New York, a black engineer admitted to researchers that "in all my life I have never felt so completely shut out." A doctor's wife in San Francisco suggested that repeated rejection in the housing market had left her feeling "like a leper and a criminal." A psychologist recalled the search for housing with equal poignancy: "Having worked my way up to a responsible position, I had gained a certain amount of self respect. Then I moved to this town and had to find housing, and once again found myself viewed as something less than human. This problem is more than economic—there's a great deal more involved." A black physician concluded: "any kind of move for a Negro family today is expensive in terms of dollars and ruinous in terms of mental happiness."[45]

Jim and Ann Braithewaite's experience in suburban Philadelphia illustrates the emotional repercussions that many couples felt in trying to move to the suburbs. Repeated encounters with racism put a strain on their marriage and family, affecting how they viewed themselves and the people around them. When discrimination "happens to *you* it hurts more," Mr. Braithewaite explained. He had difficulty sleeping. His mind wandered at work. Resentments welled up inside. "I just kept thinking about it," he said. "I was tired twenty-four hours of the day." Moreover, he felt bitter, alienated, and prone to "explosion," all of which "made for a very unhappy family life."[46]

In addition, the experience led him to focus his anger outward, questioning his job with a Cold War defense contractor and even his "allegiance to society." He asked himself, "Why am I defending this kind of people—people who have so great a desire for personal satisfaction that they place this above all other convictions they may have—religious, national, and sociological?" A year after their move, the Braithewaites' three children were adapting well to their new schools, and they counted white friends among their circle of playmates, yet the scars remained. "What does it cost me to be a Negro?" Braithewaite asked rhetorically.[47] For upwardly mobile African Americans, such questions perhaps never seemed so real nor the answers so disheartening as during the search for suburban homes.

African American suburbanites were also more likely than whites to express ambivalence about their present home. Many families moved where they did because it was the only place available. More than half of families in Dorothy Jayne's study "had no choice" in the home they selected, and a number expressed dissatisfaction with their neighborhoods ranging from the proximity of taverns or busy thoroughfares to poor transportation and shopping, distance from schools and subsequent changes in the racial and socioeconomic character of the neighborhood. In several instances, the family's arrival touched off panic selling by whites. "It's like the black plague," said one couple, "everyone wants to escape." Others felt isolated or intensely scrutinized like "goldfish in a bowl." One woman reported poignantly, "I don't want to be intimate with my neighbors, but I had hoped they would be friendly." Another lamented that the neighbors "are killing us with silence."[48]

For black pioneers, especially, the desire for equal amenities and opportunities for children often ran at cross purposes with their desires for safety and a sense of belonging. For those who moved to mostly white areas, moving day was often the prelude to hostility, vandalism, and even violence. The William Myers family, which broke the color bar in Levittown, Pennsylvania, endured two months of organized harassment. Whites paraded in cars at all hours, the phone rang constantly, and a white group rented an adjoining house from which they blared songs such as "Dixie" and "Old Black Joe" throughout the day. With the help of a group of supportive white neighbors, the family was able to hang on. Nonetheless, the Myers family longed for black company. "They used to say about Levittown, 'You never have to live in Levittown and look at a black face,'" Mr. Myers said. "I'd like to look out and see a black face."[49] Even under the best circumstances, many pioneers found it difficult to "feel completely comfortable" or to escape the gnawing awareness that "there are people within a quarter mile who don't want me here." If suburbanization reflected a fruition of black economic success and civil rights activism, it was an uncertain and often painful harvest.[50]

As these examples suggest, the meaning and experience of suburbanization was bound up in African Americans' experience as racial outsiders in white-dominated space and society. In a world where public places were routinely hostile and whites behaved as though the greater part of metropolitan territory belonged to them, private spaces such as homes and neighborhoods became places of refuge from and sites of resistance to the wider white world.

In many suburbs, black pioneers sought to create racial communities that transcended place by maintaining and reinforcing contacts with other African Americans. Suburban pioneers often worshipped, shopped, and purchased services such as hair styling in black neighborhoods "back in the city" or in black communities nearby. They maintained ties with black peers through active involvement in sororities, fraternities, and other social or civic organizations, and they made special efforts to find black peers for their children. One family in southern New Jersey recounted the miles they and other parents logged in order to maintain a black peer group for their teenaged children via "the biggest car pool you ever saw."[51]

In addition to reaching outward for social contacts, African Americans also turned inward on their homes to create safe, private places that shielded them from the worst abuses of public space. Though many pioneers were joiners by nature, participating in community activities such as parent-teacher and neighborhood associations, most nurtured what sociologists St. Clair Drake and Horace Cayton described as "home-centered" social lives based on family, relatives, and close friends.[52] A family who designed their own house "planned this living room with the idea of entertaining church groups here." One suburbanite remarked archly that he hadn't moved to Westchester County, New York, to "eat and drink" with his white neighbors. Families entertained "professional groups, church groups, wives' clubs, bridge clubs," as well as "children's and international groups."[53]

The largest number of postwar suburbanites avoided the hazards of racial isolation altogether by settling in neighborhoods where a significant number of blacks already lived. Racial discrimination and fears of "having a cross burned on my lawn," acted as weighty constraints on choice, but African Americans also made decisions that magnified racial concentration, as a respondent told researchers in Philadelphia, because they simply "[felt] more at home" with other black people.[54] The actress Ruby Dee gave voice to this sentiment, recalling why she and her husband, the actor Ossie Davis, selected an "already well integrated" neighborhood in

New Rochelle, New York, when they moved from a smaller house in nearby Mount Vernon. Though a white acquaintance urged them to strike a blow for open housing by buying in one of the suburb's all white areas, they declined. "I want my children to feel safe," she said. "I want to feel safe. I'm away so much, I want to be friends with my neighbors. I don't want to be tolerated, on my best behavior, always seeking my neighbor's approval. I want to be able to knock on a door, assured that my neighbor would more likely welcome any one of the family. Or if I should need help. . . . I admire the pioneers who risk so much in the process of integration, but I cannot break that ice. . . . Thanks, but no thanks. We just don't choose to struggle on this front."[55]

Surveys suggest that the Dee-Davises were in good company. In the late 1950s, anywhere from 45 to 65 percent of African American home-seekers expressed a preference for neighborhoods that were at least one-half black.[56] For the majority of African Americans who indicated preferences for interracial living, racial isolation was apparently something they hoped to avoid. Most upwardly mobile African Americans—black people with the greatest latitude of personal choice—simply preferred areas where an appreciable number of black families already lived.

Suburban racial congregation also reflected the conduits of information and association available to African American families. Like most Americans, blacks trusted their social networks—friends, neighbors, relatives, church members, co-workers, and other associates—for information and assistance in finding places to live.[57] Because of their exclusion from conventional real estate channels, however, the legacy of past segregation reinforced the concentration of home seekers in just a handful of suburban areas. One study of middle-class families in Philadelphia, for example, revealed that 80 percent of respondents had "no Negro friends who lived in predominantly white areas outside the city limits."[58] In such circumstances, media reports of white resistance and stories of racial hostility passed through the grapevine gained weight in black perceptions of suburban opportunity. Lacking firsthand knowledge or positive experiences with white suburban areas, many families preferred to avoid the unknown, a fact that tended to funnel black suburban migrants to just a handful of already integrated or mostly-black suburbs.

Emphasis on homes and neighborhoods as safe space was not unique to African Americans, of course. As historian Elaine Tyler May demonstrates, many postwar parents perceived suburban homes as "a secure private nest removed from the dangers of the outside world," a "warm hearth" in the midst of a Cold War.[59] But for African Americans, who experienced not only the international anxieties of the era but the palpable dangers of domestic racism, the vision of home as a refuge had special resonance. As sociologist Bart Landry points out, because middle-class blacks were "denied ready access to the recreational and cultural facilities in the community," they "developed a lifestyle centered around home and clubs. The home grew in importance not only as a comfortable, secure place that shielded them from the stings of white society but was also the center of their social life."[60]

Black-oriented publications reinforced this connection, celebrating hospitality and conviviality focused on black homes and neighborhoods. *Ebony*'s "home" columns dwelled on such features as "pine-walled rumpus rooms," "informal redwood den[s]" "spacious" patios "fac[ing] a big swimming pool," "expensive oak wood" bars "with matching chairs, phonograph radio combination and two large sofas," "lavish lawn parties," and "expensively equipped kitchen[s]."[61] To be sure, tasteful entertaining was a staple of home-oriented magazines targeted at whites, but this emphasis had special resonance among African Americans, who were excluded from or faced harassment in public spaces frequented by middle-class whites. In the postwar era, *Ebony* portrayed an idealized domestic life, reflecting the exceptional value that middle-class blacks placed on their ability to entertain well at home. Not surprisingly, *Ebony*'s article on St. Alban's evoked an image of the neighborhood as "self contained," a "refuge" and a "happy haven," applauding it as a place where residents found "comfort, relaxation, and breathing space." Early residents had overcome white attempts to restrict the area, the writer pointed out, but by the 1950s the neighborhood was the site not of racial activism but "placid privacy" where celebrities "come home to rest."[62] Just as many working-class black suburbanites had used their homes as shelter from the insecurities of wage labor under industrial capitalism, members of the rising middle class valued their homes and neighborhoods as places of shelter from the racial hostility they experienced in public life. Whether they created spatially separate black enclaves or dispersed racial communities centered on private homes, they sought safe black spaces in the suburbs.

In these ways, race shaped the process of suburbanization, even as growing numbers of African Americans entered the middle class. These markers were not primarily governmental nor imprints of "the state" but were rooted in localized struggles between black families and communities and the white people around them. By the same token, African Americans' attempts to attain and control suburban space contributed to a continuing conversation about class in black communities. Given the pervasiveness of racial distinction in postwar society, however, even the process of class stratification tended to reinforce a sense of racial solidarity among African Americans.

"A Better Class of People"

Since the nineteenth century, class had been an important feature of African American social life, but within the racialized society of the United States, class strata in black communities rested largely on distinctions that African Americans drew "relative to other blacks."[63] Based in part on objective characteristics such as occupation, income, and wealth, which situate people within the wider political economy, class distinctions also reflect values and behavior related to work, education, leisure, consumption, and place of residence. Just as important, class implies a relationship among differently situated individuals and groups in a given society. For African Americans, who were barred from the achievement of stable occupational and income markers that were essential to class standing among whites, class distinctions had traditionally relied on patterns of behavior—what historian Willard Gatewood describes as "performance"—that people developed as a means of identifying their peers and distinguishing themselves from others.[64] Even as a growing cohort of African Americans attained economic positions comparable to middle-class whites in the postwar period, class remained a distinction that African Americans drew largely with reference to other blacks.

Of course, class was a spatial as well as social distinction. For the urban black middle class, in particular, physical separation from poor and working-class blacks was an important emblem of class status. Writing in the 1940s, St. Clair Drake and Horace Cayton argued that socioeconomic divisions within black communities produced a process of "sifting and sorting" by neighborhood.[65] More recently, Mary Patillo-McCoy concluded that "like other groups, African Americans . . . always tried to translate upward class mobility into geographic mobility."[66] In this view, class was not merely a measure of what one did for a living or how one behaved, but also how and where one chose to live. In the postwar period, suburbanization represented a continuation of this process across the city limits.

The comments of middle-class suburbanites reveal that concerns about class and distance from poorer blacks were thoroughly intertwined with other residential preferences. In various contexts, middle-class blacks drew implicit contrasts between the types of neighborhoods to which they aspired and those in which they had been "bottled up" with other African

Americans. As the housing activists George and Eunice Grier reported, middle-class blacks sought the "freedom to choose an environment in accord with middle-class standards, instead of housing restricted to the overcrowded, run-down neighborhoods generally available to Negroes." However, the contrasts that families drew focused as often on the social as the physical environment. "I would be very satisfied with an all-Negro neighborhood if it were a decent neighborhood," one black professional told the Griers. "I do not see why I, because I am a Negro, should be forced to live in a neighborhood where I have nothing in common with others around me."[67] A black attorney in San Francisco expressed a similar recognition of class difference when he commented that the "thing that struck me when I moved out of the ghetto was that for the first time I was friendly with my immediate neighbors. They have the same interests that we do."[68] Reinforcing this impression, leading black real estate brokers in Westchester County, New York, reported screening clients on the basis of their "social and cultural qualifications" in order to protect the "character" of suburban neighborhoods and ensure that their customers were a "credit . . . to the race." Referring to people he called "Negro trash," one broker exclaimed, "I wouldn't damage a neighborhood with people who don't know how to live in it. I put them in their place."[69]

The same emphasis on class separation was evident in suburbanites' descriptions of their ideal neighborhood. Middle-class respondents said that they preferred environments "where the neighborhood would be congenial and stimulating—a middle-middle neighborhood," "an area where the general income level was equal to my own," "an area which will aid in [children's] training and development . . . where people are interested in the surroundings they live in," or simply, "a quiet, well-kept middle-class neighborhood."[70] Correspondingly, middle-class references to "respectable," "clean," "quiet," "well-kept," or "decent" neighborhoods betrayed an obvious class consciousness if not antagonism toward working-class and poor blacks. The musician Nat "King" Cole made the point as clearly as anyone. When white neighbors opposed his purchase of a house in 1948, on the grounds that "we don't want any undesirable people moving into the neighborhood," Cole shot back: "Neither do I. If I see anybody undesirable coming in, I'll be the first to complain."[71]

Several studies of upwardly mobile African Americans in metropolitan Philadelphia during the 1950s revealed that the desire to live among a "higher" or "better class of people" played a role in families' choice of neighborhoods. Dorothy Jayne's study of black pioneers found that over half had initiated their search for new housing when "a poorer class moved in[to]" the neighborhoods where they were living. Class concerns also surfaced in respondents' observations about their new neighborhoods. One couple expressed disdain for their "small-time snobbish" white neighbors, lamenting that they had "underbought." Another, recalling harassment by whites, pointed to their class status vis-à-vis other African Americans as well their new neighbors. They were "annoyed," they said, because "We're not trash. . . . our status is so much above theirs."[72] By implication, it was not their citizenship nor humanity that earned them the right to move where they pleased, but their membership in a particular social class, a status they had achieved and learned to express through everyday behavior. Having drawn boundaries between themselves and other blacks, moreover, they resented their neighbors' inability or unwillingness to recognize the distinction. Another couple declared their "philosophy" as the ability of "decent folks to be able to live decently without regard to religion or race."[73] In the view of these pioneers, class made a difference not only in who was "decent" and who was not but in the rights that each group should enjoy.

By emphasizing their rights as citizens and their membership in a particular socioeconomic class, middle-class black suburbanites articulated a vision of racial equality that largely ignored or evaded class inequalities. Political scientist Preston Smith points out that most approached the problem of race with a class bias, defending a brand of "racial democracy" in which, "affluent blacks should have access to the same housing as affluent whites. Likewise working-class and poor blacks would have the same quality of housing as working-class and poor whites." Hence, open housing advocates such as Carl Fuqua, the executive secretary of the Chicago NAACP could argue that, "the goal is to let a man live where he wants to live, if he can assume the proper responsibilities." In Smith's view, "embracing racial democracy meant black civic elites accepted class privileges and the distribution of social goods according to conventional political economy." This adequately summarized their vision of space as well.[74]

African Americans' expressed preferences for racially mixed neighborhoods also reflected concerns rooted in class as much as race. Quite unlike the majority of white suburbanites, many middle-class African Americans said they were willing to live in racially integrated settings.[75] For most, integrated neighborhoods were a means to an end: better schools and services, proximity to work, and other environmental factors. As George and Eunice Grier noted, "racial composition was not in itself an essential criterion, however, most felt that areas generally open to Negroes . . . did not meet their standards of a 'good neighborhood.'"[76] For these families, living in integrated neighborhoods was not only a means to a higher living standard but also an assertion of their right to share equally in the benefits of suburban location. Just as well, some "Negro professionals insist[ed] on looking outside 'Negro areas'" as a means of distinguishing themselves from poorer blacks. The San Francisco Council for Civic Unity spoke for many when it asserted that "individual people of Negro . . . or other non-white ancestry may feel more at home with people not of their own race but of their socio-economic level." For many middle-class African Americans, the desire to live in integrated settings may have been as much a means of achieving social distance from the black working class as securing social intimacy with middle-class whites.[77]

By the 1950s, a new generation of middle-class blacks began moving to suburbs in greater numbers than ever before. Their efforts, prefaced by the struggles of working-class black suburbanites and firmly resisted by whites, reinforced the salience of both race and class in postwar life. By transgressing racial boundaries, they redefined the racial ownership of suburban space and also extended the geographic continuity of black residential areas across a wider terrain. Despite spatial continuity with older settlements, new suburbanites affirmed their class position through achievements in income, occupation, and education as well as in decisions about how and where to live. Growing numbers expressed residential preferences that they shared with a broad spectrum of middle-class Americans. The dream of improved life in the suburbs, reflecting both the history and contemporary circumstances of the new suburbanites, remained a potent force, and they sought to give life to these dreams in spite of whites' best efforts to stop them. In these ways, the history of black suburbanization offers a window into the interwoven processes of making race, class, and space in the midcentury United States.

SIX

"Socioeconomic Integration" in the Suburbs

From Reactionary Populism to Class Fairness
in Metropolitan Charlotte

MATTHEW D. LASSITER

"Let us listen now to . . . the voice of the great majority of Americans, the forgotten Americans, the non-shouters, the non-demonstrators," Richard Nixon proclaimed in his acceptance speech at the 1968 Republican convention. "They are not racists or sick. They are not guilty of the crime that plagues the land. They are black and they are white. . . . They work in America's factories. . . . They run America's businesses. . . . They work, they save, they pay their taxes, they care." Praising the essential decency and quiet heroism of Middle America has always been a shrewd electoral tactic, but Nixon's affirmation of the moral innocence of the "great majority" also represented a carefully calibrated response to the civil rights movement. Only months earlier, the Kerner Report issued by the National Advisory Commission on Civil Disorders asked the residents of the segregated suburbs to ponder an unpopular interpretation of postwar metropolitan history: "What white Americans have never fully understood—but what the Negro can never forget—is that white society is deeply implicated in the ghetto. White institutions created it, white institutions maintain it, and white society condones it." Richard Nixon instead repeatedly assured "the great silent majority of Americans" that "there is no reason to feel guilty about wanting to enjoy what you get and get what you earn, about wanting your children in good schools close to home, or about wanting to be judged fairly on your ability." These populist appeals to the Silent Majority represented a suburban strategy designed to obscure class divisions among white voters and take advantage of the increasing convergence of southern and national politics. Racial segregation "isn't just a southern problem," Nixon told the audience at a campaign rally in Charlotte, North Carolina, in the fall of 1968. The Republican candidate endorsed the *Brown* decision but promised that his administration would oppose "forced busing" between the ghettoes and the suburbs and defend the right of all families to send their children to neighborhood schools.[1]

In the spring of 1969, Charlotte became the first large city in the South to face court-ordered busing to overcome state-sponsored residential segregation. Although political fragmentation of municipal govern-ments emerged as a dominant trend in the twentieth-century American metropolis, civic leaders in Charlotte and other "elastic" Sunbelt regions followed an alternative path of aggressively annexing new suburbs and advocating the merger of city and county school systems. Since the con-solidated school district in Charlotte included the surrounding county of Mecklenburg, affluent neighborhoods outside the city limits could not evade the integration decree and white flight to the outer-ring suburbs did not destroy the busing formula. The judicial mandate galvanized a powerful revolt by the Concerned Parents Association (CPA), a grassroots insurgency that mobilized under the populist banner of the Silent Majority and enlisted tens of thousands of white families throughout the suburbs. Based in the upper-middle-class and residentially segregated sub-divisions of southeast Charlotte-Mecklenburg, the CPA adopted a scrupu-lously "color-blind" discourse that demanded race-neutral assignments to neighborhood schools and portrayed housing patterns as the class-based outcome of free-market meritocracy. The white-collar professionals who dominated the organization insisted that Charlotte's metropolitan landscape corresponded to the "de facto" segregation of northern cities and not the "de jure" segregation of the Jim Crow South. During a year and a half of grassroots resistance, the suburban antibusing movement polarized a city regarded as one of the most progressive bastions of the New South and played a leading role in the mobilization of the Silent Majority in national politics. But in the fall of 1970, the school system finally implemented a comprehensive desegregation plan, ordered by District Judge James B. McMillan and affirmed by the Supreme Court in the land-mark case of *Swann v. Charlotte-Mecklenburg*. During the next half-decade, Charlotte's metropolitan school district became a national test case for two-way busing between the black neighborhoods of the central city and the white subdivisions on the suburban fringe.[2]

The antibusing movement in Charlotte claimed to represent a suburban consensus, but the actual implementation of two-way integration shattered the grassroots coalition assembled by the Concerned Parents Association and ushered in an era of bitter class conflict among white neighborhoods throughout the metropolis. The CPA leaders from the upper-middle-class suburbs of southeast Charlotte initially recruited thousands of working-class white families who lived in the areas located to the north and west of the downtown business district. The racially mixed sectors of north and west Charlotte included older textile mill towns, newer blue-collar and middle-income suburbs, almost all of the city's public housing projects, and about 96 percent of the African American population. Interracial tensions often flared on the northside and westside, where many white families lived in transitional neighborhoods and many white students already attended integrated schools before the arrival of busing. But after municipal leaders devised an inequitable desegregation plan that exempted the affluent suburbs from two-way busing and extensively burdened the black and white families of the northwest sector, fierce resentment emerged in the blue-collar neighborhoods toward the privileged status of their former allies from southeast Charlotte. On the eve of the busing program, a white mother from north Charlotte announced that her side of town had "borne the full burden of integration for several years.... I'm ready to share 'social progress' with all the citizens of Mecklenburg." In a private letter to the lead NAACP attorney, another working-class mother confessed her initial opposition to desegregation but then endorsed a comprehensive busing plan that would spread the burdens of social change fairly across the metropolis. The former antibusing activist concluded with the observation that she had now experienced an awakening of what it meant not to be wealthy, a feeling that must be similar to the moment when black people discovered the consequences of not being white.[3]

During 1969–70, the antibusing revolt in suburban Charlotte paralleled the national discovery of a racial backlash by the "great silent majority" that culminated in *Time* magazine's designation of Middle Americans as the "Man and Woman of the Year." The editors of *Time* defined the no-longer Silent Majority in the language of whiteness and populism, rather than partisan ideology or social class: a broad cross-section of white-collar professionals and blue-collar laborers that occupied a radicalized political center through a "contradictory mixture of liberal and conservative impulses." *Newsweek*'s extensive examination of the "Troubled American" discovered a similar "vast white middle-class majority," from the tract homes outside Atlanta and Los Angeles to the industrial suburbs of the Midwest and the ethnic enclaves of the Northeast, in full-scale rebellion against the redistributive agenda of racial liberalism. This mainstream validation of the populist formulations of the Nixon administration obscured some basic political facts about the so-called Silent Majority and about American suburbia more generally: white-collar professionals and blue-collar laborers do not have the same class interests, do not generally live in the same neighborhoods, and have never fit comfortably into a cohesive political coalition. The full trajectory of Charlotte's busing saga demonstrates the internal class contradictions within the legendary Silent Majority of the Nixon era and the potential for metropolitan and socioeconomic integration remedies to defuse "reactionary populism" at the grassroots level. Between 1971 and 1974, as class consciousness assumed a decidedly spatial orientation in Charlotte-Mecklenburg, an extraordinary alliance between black and white neighborhoods forged a desegregation resolution based on the twin pillars of socioeconomic fairness and racial stability.[4]

––––––––

At the height of Charlotte's antibusing revolt, a civil rights activist named Paul Leonard circulated a grassroots manifesto calling for an interracial movement to challenge the domination of local affairs by the corporate elite and the white-collar suburbs. "The present and past political and business leadership is dedicated to the (unwritten) goal of a racially and economically segregated city," Leonard charged. The "development and protection of the southeast has been and is the controlling factor in every decision affecting the life of this city." Residents of the inner-ring "garden suburbs" of southeast Charlotte "maintain a liberal façade," he explained, "because of their physical and social distance from the problems of race and poverty." In north and west Charlotte, "the problems of law and order, housing, and schools are very real to these people [working-class and middle-income white families] because of the physical nearness of blacks." The manifesto concluded by outlining a new vision of neighborhood politics based on class solidarity and interracial cooperation, in order to spread municipal resources throughout the metropolis on an equitable basis and halt the ongoing conversion of northwest Charlotte into an impoverished ghetto. Leonard observed that "what has happened to the west side of Charlotte has happened to whites and blacks alike who live there, and it will continue to happen until they stand together on common issues."[5]

During the postwar decades, as Charlotte experienced the economic boom and population surge spreading across the Sunbelt, the city's civic and political leadership pursued a development agenda of suburban sprawl and urban containment. Following the pattern found throughout America's major metropolitan regions, municipal planning policies combined with massive federal subsidies to construct a spatial landscape of stark residential segregation. Charlotte-Mecklenburg tapped federal funds for urban renewal and highway construction projects that displaced about ten thousand in-town black residents during the 1960s alone, and official planning procedures combined with pervasive real estate discrimination to relocate almost all of these families in the northwest quadrant. At the same time, generous federal and local government investments facilitated the rapid expansion of outer-ring suburbs in the southeast section of Mecklenburg County, which became the primary destination of middle-class white families drawn into the corporate economy of the Sunbelt metropolis. Reports by the Charlotte-Mecklenburg Planning Commission revealed the intentional placement of highways and industrial belts to create physical buffers between the heavily black westside neighborhoods and the overwhelmingly white southeast suburbs. The deliberate concentration of more than 90 percent of the black population in the northwest sector created the conditions for a horizontal ghetto and deeply antagonized the white residents of the blue-collar neighborhoods clustered nearby, which began to undergo the predictable process of racial transition. But despite steady white flight from north and west Charlotte, the prompt incorporation of new suburban developments under North Carolina's automatic annexation laws proved to be the critical element in the city's demographic stability, which remained approximately two-thirds white and one-third black throughout the postwar era.[6]

The annexed suburbs of southeast Charlotte controlled municipal politics through an at-large voting system that systematically disfranchised the black and white neighborhoods of the northwest sector. The inner-ring suburbs of the Myers Park area represented the unquestioned center of wealth and power, home to almost all leading corporate executives and almost every elected and appointed official in city and county government. During the civil rights era, the presidency of the Chamber of Commerce served as the routine stepping-stone to the mayor's office, and the corporate leadership of the booming metropolis preached the New South gospel of economic prosperity through racial harmony. The business executives who dominated the planning commission placed the most desirable developments—golf courses, parks, hospitals, shopping malls—in the white-collar suburbs of southeast Charlotte, where

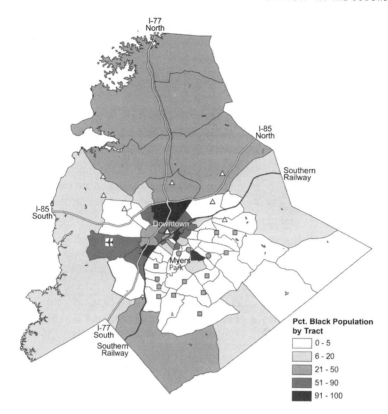

Figure 6.1. Distribution of the Black Population of the City of Charlotte and Mecklenburg County, 1970, by Census Tract. The northwest quadrant contained about 96 percent of Charlotte's black population, while ten census tracts in the southeast suburbs included no black residents at all. The circles indicate the most affluent annexed suburbs of the Myers Park region, including older neighborhoods developed before the postwar growth boom. The squares denote the outer-ring southeast suburbs, constructed during the 1950s and 1960s, that formed the base of the antibusing movement of the Concerned Parents Association. The small triangles represent white suburbs and school zones on the northside and westside that initially supported the CPA but later defected from the antibusing coalition and began to experience racial turnover during the battles over busing equalization. Source: U.S. Census Bureau, 1970 Census of Population and Housing.

exclusionary zoning policies maintained residential segregation by a fusion of race and income. Municipal leaders methodically located the noxious industrial zones, intrusive interstate highways, and public housing projects in the northwest sector implicitly designated for the minority population. In 1970, as the growing backlash against these growth policies threatened to jeopardize the city's reputation as a progressive center of the New South, the *Charlotte Observer* acknowledged that local citizens were "governed by an elite minority" and called upon corporate leaders to share power with the disfranchised sections of the metropolis. Neighborhood activists from north and west Charlotte warned of an explosive situation because working-class families "feel the Chamber of Commerce is running the city" and were no longer willing to be "neglected and ruled by a few people" from Myers Park.[7]

Before the busing crisis, the most volatile conflict in municipal politics revolved around the site selection of low-income housing systematically located in northwest Charlotte. "Location of public housing," a civil rights report concluded, "represents [the] city's official stamp that particular neighborhoods have gone down and will never come back." In the late 1960s and early 1970s, white homeowners' groups on the westside repeatedly protested the "planned segregation of the poor" and accused municipal leaders of an open conspiracy to trigger white flight and transform their part of the city into an all-black ghetto. An umbrella organization of homeowners' associations called the Citizens for Orderly Development reached out to middle-class black families who also denounced the destabilization of their neighborhoods by public housing projects, and both groups predicted that failure to scatter low-income housing would accelerate white flight from the schools and neighborhoods in the northwest quadrant. Black and white neighborhood activists in north and west Charlotte also joined forces in a bitter struggle to force the county commission to build a hospital on their side of town, an ultimately unsuccessful endeavor that served as the catalyst for a broader taxpayers revolt against the growth policies championed by the Chamber of Commerce. An interracial coalition from the northside and westside simultaneously battled the business leadership of southeast Charlotte over a referendum to replace the at-large electoral system with district representation, culminating in a 1971 defeat that convinced grassroots activists that "the way things are now we don't have a democracy."[8]

Although the black and white neighborhoods on the northside and westside shared many grievances, the racial friction caused by geographic proximity prevented the emergence of an effective class alliance against the hegemony of southeast Charlotte until the mid-1970s climax of the busing saga. In the outer-ring suburbs of southeast Mecklenburg, where large majorities of white-collar voters supported Richard Nixon in the 1968 election, the leaders of the antibusing movement carefully framed their crusade in a color-blind language of middle-class respectability grounded in complete residential security. In the blue-collar precincts of north and west Charlotte, where a substantial percentage of white voters cast their ballots for the reactionary populism of George Wallace, the more frequent expressions of overt racism reflected deep anxieties about the stability of white neighborhoods and the fragility of class status. "No, I don't want to live with the blacks, I'll be honest!" a white mother from the westside admitted in a letter to her congressman. "I do not want my teen-age daughter socializing with blacks. . . . I'll go down fighting! So will millions of us whites." "We worked hard to be where we are," explained a mother from a westside suburb that bordered a fading textile town. "I don't want my kid coming down here between niggertown and the mill village to go to school." Another westside mother declared that she and her husband had saved and struggled to move into a middle-income subdivision for nothing: "It appears we would be better off to quit work, sit down do nothing, draw welfare and live in a low income housing development. . . . Then our daughter would be bussed into a good neighborhood school!"[9]

During the initial phase of the desegregation showdown, the antibusing coalition assembled by the Concerned Parents Association turned out to be a temporary exception to the prevailing pattern of class conflict over the metropolitan distribution of political power and economic resources. The CPA first emerged during the spring of 1969, after District Judge James McMillan ordered two-way busing to achieve comprehensive integration of every school in Charlotte-Mecklenburg, in rough approximation of the district's overall ratio of 70 percent white and 30 percent black. The leadership and the grassroots strength of the antibusing movement came from the outer-ring suburbs of southeast Mecklenburg County, where young professional couples lived in exclusively white subdivisions developed during the previous decade. From the beginning, the CPA insisted that opposition to busing had nothing to do with racial prejudice or anti-integration sentiment, but instead merely reflected the color-blind desire of suburban families to send their children to the neighborhood school of their choice. Two thousand parents attended the first major protest conducted by the CPA, held at a junior high school located south of the city limits. The upscale crowd applauded a speaker who insisted: "I am not opposed to integration in any way. . . . But I was 'affluent' enough to buy a home near the school where I wanted my children to go. And I pay taxes to pay for it. They can bring in anybody they like to that school, but I don't want my children taken away from there." Another member of the group explained that she would not complain if black parents wanted to work hard and buy a house in her subdivision in order to send their children to the nearby school, but "if anyone thinks they're going to bus my children across town . . . without a fight, they're dreaming."[10]

The one theme that never appeared in the CPA's defense of neighborhood schools was any acknowledgment of the finding at the heart of Judge McMillan's decision: that government policies had shaped the stark patterns of residential segregation that produced school segregation in Charlotte-Mecklenburg. The white parents who joined the antibusing movement thought of the locations of their homes and the proximity of excellent public schools as nothing more and nothing less than the consumer rewards for their willingness to work hard and make sacrifices for their children's futures. This pervasive philosophy of middle-class accomplishment naturalized the glaring metropolitan inequalities in educational opportunity and finessed the internal contradictions in the meritocratic ethos through an unapologetic defense of the rights of children to enjoy the fruits of their parents' success. The spatial landscape of the white-collar suburbs shaped a fundamental approval of the status quo, grounded in a historical narrative of color-blind individualism that emphasized the family privileges of class and consumerism rather than collective remedies for past discrimination. This suburban ideology of racial innocence underlay a predisposition to reject—or more often to fail even to consider—the abstract proposition that the government's culpability in concentrating black residents in a certain part of the city should have any personal impact on middle-class lifestyles. The "anti-bus hysteria" of the CPA seemed "more mistaken than racist," observed liberal activist Pat Watters, in the context of decades of municipal development and federal policy based on the "hypocrisy of blinding itself to the 'de jure' nature of most 'de facto' segregation."[11]

The grassroots mobilization of the CPA quickly reached the national stage as a color-blind revolt of the center by the suburban families in the Silent Majority. One Republican activist in Charlotte's antibusing movement warned that the CPA represented "a majority that has been pushed around for the last five years by a militant minority and an aggressive bureaucracy, a majority whose chafing has been restrained only by its good manners, but also a majority which is reaching the end of its tether, and is going to bring forth its own revolution when pushed too far." In a letter to President Nixon, a pastor from southeast Charlotte explained that "I love my country and I do not want to be a party of participating in a movement that would show disrespect to the principles of our great country, but . . . [the court order] is not fair and I do not believe that it is morally right." "As a member of the silent majority," a white father from the southeast suburbs declared, "I have never asked what anyone in government or this country could do for me, but rather have kept my mouth shut, paid my taxes, and basically asked to be left alone. . . . I think it is time the law abiding, tax paying white middle class started looking to the federal government for something besides oppression." Yet another parent from an all-white subdivision informed the president that "if my child is refused admittance to the school she has been attending because she is white then she will be being excluded illegally because of her race." He demanded that the White House "come to the rescue of the silent majority who may not be silent much longer. The silent majority has been pushed about as far as it will tolerate."[12]

Richard Nixon responded with a major policy statement on school desegregation confirming that suburban protectionism represented the official civil rights policy of his administration. In the spring of 1970, the White House effectively endorsed the color-blind platform of the suburban antibusing movement and explicitly defended the constitutionality of neighborhood schools even when they reflected segregated housing patterns. "There is a constitutional mandate that dual school systems and other forms of *de jure* segregation be eliminated totally," the president explained. But "*de facto* segregation, which exists in many [metropolitan] areas both North and South," resulted from forces in the private housing market and remained beyond the proper jurisdiction of the federal courts. This stance simply evaded Judge McMillan's finding in the Charlotte case that the artificial distinction between de jure and de facto obscured the official policies that produced educational and residential segregation. In addition to declaring that court-ordered busing in metropolitan regions exceeded the Constitution, the president adopted the conservative mantra that public schools should not be used for liberal social experimentation. The White House statement closely echoed the color-blind stance of the Concerned Parents Association and clearly represented a direct response to the mobilized members of the Silent Majority. While civil rights groups responded with outrage, the Nixon administration promised to support the legal appeals undertaken by the Charlotte-Mecklenburg school board.[13]

The CPA uprising also reshaped the local political landscape, especially after the southeast leadership of the organization forged a crosstown alliance with the white neighborhoods on the northside and westside. In the late winter of 1970, following almost a year of legal maneuvering, the district court unveiled a two-way busing formula that paired schools in the inner city and the outer-ring suburbs. CPA chapters organized seven major rallies during the next week, and for the first time the antibusing network established a formal presence in the white areas of north and west Charlotte. At a protest in the westside suburb of Paw Creek, two thousand parents heard the CPA leadership call for a mass boycott of the public schools as soon as the busing order became operational. The association adopted the slogan "United We Stand, Divided We Fall" to publicize its grassroots outreach to homeowners throughout the metropolis. "A STRUGGLE FOR

Figure 6.2. Protesters from an affluent suburb picketed Judge James McMillan's home, in south-east Charlotte, during the antibusing backlash of 1970. The leader of this neighborhood schools demonstration explained that white families were "taking a page from the book of our black friends." Reprinted with permission of the *Charlotte Observer*. © by the *Charlotte Observer*.

FREEDOM IS COMING," the CPA's literature proclaimed. "WHERE WILL YOU STAND?" Fliers distributed at the antibusing rallies explained that taking freedom of choice "away from the child solely because of his race is grievously wrong. It is morally indefensible. It puts force in the place of freedom. It creates dictatorial power and undermines the American Constitution. It destroys individual liberty in an area that is close to the hearts of us all!" By the summer of 1970, more than 104,000 people had signed the antibusing petitions that CPA activists circulated at shopping malls and in door-to-door membership drives, representing more than half of the white adults in Charlotte-Mecklenburg.[14]

The CPA's crosstown coalition enabled the antibusing movement to take control of the Charlotte-Mecklenburg school board and execute a strategy of resistance to the federal courts. In the spring of 1970, the sub-urban alliance targeted three incumbent board members who supported compliance with the desegregation mandate. The CPA slate employed an extensive network of volunteers behind a campaign that promised to defend color-blind assignments to neighborhood schools. The antibusing candidates won the election with overwhelming support in the white working-class and lower-middle-class precincts of north and west Charlotte, but they failed to carry the wealthy inner-ring suburbs of the Myers Park area and managed to secure only narrow margins of victory in the outer-ring southeast subdivisions that formed the CPA base. The election returns empowered the antibusing movement in municipal politics but also revealed the absence of political consensus in southeast Charlotte and the broader geographic instability of the suburban alliance. Future events would illustrate the inability of the CPA to maintain a confederation with two disparate groups: blue-collar families from north and west Charlotte that had placed their hopes in an organization dominated by white-collar professionals from the other side of town and upper-middle-class moderates from southeast Charlotte who disapproved of busing but refused to support an organization that pledged to boycott the public schools. As legal developments brought the situation to a climax in the fall of 1970, the white parents in the broad but diverse antibusing majority found that they could no longer avoid the choice between maintaining their traditionally deep commitment to public education and resisting through a self-destructive boycott or a self-interested retreat to private schools.[15]

The Concerned Parents Association touted the mass boycott as a weapon of political unity, but the arrival of the day of reckoning divided rather than strengthened the suburban coalition. In the weeks before the deadline, the CPA conducted nightly rallies throughout the white suburbs and advised parents to keep their children at home in order to demonstrate the unworkability of busing to the Supreme Court. But once it became clear that appeals for a stay would not succeed, the socioeconomic and geographic fissures within the CPA quickly rose to the surface. After several white-collar leaders of the organization announced that they were placing their children in private schools, working-class members complained bitterly about the sanctuaries available only "on the rich side of town." On the evening before schools reopened, the CPA sponsored a huge rally of ten thousand people at the county fairgrounds north of Charlotte. William Booe, an attorney from southeast Charlotte and an incoming member of the school board, urged the audience to unite behind the boycott, but resentful members in the largely blue-collar crowd shouted "out of the private school or off the platform." When the buses finally rolled both ways in Charlotte, the vast majority of white students showed up at their assigned schools, although about two thousand families from the southeast suburbs chose private education for children scheduled to be transported to facilities in black residential areas. The defection of affluent students from southeast Charlotte created a "tipping" phenomenon in the northwest schools, and working-class white families who suddenly found themselves in majority-black institutions began accusing education officials of sacrificing their children in order to present a showcase of failure to the Supreme Court. A common refrain—"they wouldn't do

Figure 6.3. The Concerned Parents Association organized a massive rally at the county fairgrounds in northern Mecklenburg County, September 8, 1970. On the eve of the busing deadline, thousands of working-class white families promised to boycott the public schools, but schisms within the suburban antibusing movement quickly surfaced. During the next four years, many parents from north and west Charlotte in attendance at this rally joined the Citizens United for Fairness. Reprinted with permission of the *Charlotte Observer*. © by the *Charlotte Observer*.

it to Myers Park"—captured the fusion of racial anxiety and class anger spreading across north and west Charlotte.[16]

The Supreme Court upheld the two-way busing program in Charlotte-Mecklenburg in the *Swann* decision released in the spring of 1971. Judge McMillan promptly reaffirmed his original mandate to achieve stable desegregation—defined as the supervision of racial ratios to maintain a majority-white enrollment—in every school in the countywide district. The liberal editorial page of the *Charlotte Observer* called on education officials to adopt a new busing plan that would broker a compromise by evenly distributing the "burdens and opportunities of desegregation" to all sections of the metropolis. Although the CPA rapidly faded as an organized movement after the legal defeat, the legacies of the antibusing uprising continued to shape the recalcitrant stance of the school board, which refused to accept the explicit court order to devise an assignment formula that would prevent resegregation in the formerly all-black schools. As the community awaited the new desegregation approach, a profound dispute emerged over two competing narratives of the dangers of white flight. The antibusing majority on the school board believed that two-way busing would drive affluent families to private education, and the arrival of the three CPA leaders reinforced the resolve to keep students from southeast Charlotte in their neighborhood schools. The NAACP warned that unless the board sent upper-middle-class students from secure suburban areas to the schools located in northwest Charlotte, the unstable educational situation would accelerate residential flight from nearby neighborhoods. "I'm surprised there are even a few on the school board who even know where the westside is," remarked one white neighborhood activist who demanded the redress of severe imbalances such as the 508 black students and 68 white students at one inner-city elementary school.[17]

After losing its appeal to the Supreme Court, the school board implemented a new formula that shifted the busing burden on white students from the outer-ring suburbs of southeast Charlotte to the blue-collar neighborhoods of the northside and westside. The revised desegregation plan in the fall of 1971 assigned white students from north and west Charlotte to historically black schools for either six or eight years, while busing black students to suburban schools for an average of ten out of twelve years. Most children from the powerful Myers Park area and the outer-ring southeast suburbs that had launched the CPA would remain in neighborhood schools throughout their academic careers. Judge McMillan acknowledged that the approach revolved around "class discrimination" and created neighborhood schooling "protectorates" throughout southeast Charlotte-Mecklenburg. The judge nevertheless adopted a wait-and-see attitude toward the question of whether obvious socioeconomic inequality would produce unconstitutional racial resegregation. Desperate white families from the blue-collar suburbs of north and west Charlotte immediately made it clear that the class-based discrimination inherent in the busing plan encouraged migration to the safe havens on the metropolitan fringe. "To sell out and move is a whole lot cheaper than sending a child to a private school," one white father exclaimed during a speech warning the school board that its policies would turn the westside into an all-black ghetto. On the northside, residents who moved away from a formerly all-white suburb candidly acknowledged their motives in a media survey: "We just had to go. . . . We were the only white family left on the block"; "We had some neighbors moving in that we did not particularly like, and we have a teenage daughter [so] we had to get out of there"; "I moved out here [to the outer-ring suburbs] because my kids were being bused."[18]

In the summer of 1971, one thousand parents from five predominantly white subdivisions in north and west Charlotte formed a coalition called the Citizens United for Fairness (CUFF), cementing an informal alliance that had emerged during the recent battles over planning policies and electoral representation. Many of the same families had joined the Concerned Parents Association a year earlier, but now the southeast-based majority on the school board had assigned their children to formerly all-black institutions throughout the junior and senior high years. Instead of adopting an antibusing platform, CUFF announced that "we are willing to bear a fair portion of school assignment burdens" if all white neighborhoods in the county were placed "in the same boat." Wilson Bryan, the leader of the group, explained that "we have been told by some black people that this is a similar type of discrimination to what they experienced over a period of years." When the board refused to alter its formula, CUFF filed a class-action lawsuit asking the district court to invalidate the busing plan on equal protection grounds. As the five suburban neighborhoods represented by CUFF began to undergo the classic signs of racial transition, white activists on the northside and westside pleaded with the judge tointercede before the inequitable desegregation approach destabilized itself. In an important sign of an emerging interracial groundswell for busing equalization, the NAACP plaintiffs expressed solidarity with CUFF by denouncing the pupil assignment formula as an unconstitutional scheme "designed by southeast Charlotte" and a transparent blueprint for resegregation that "discriminat[es] against both blacks and whites."[19]

The neighborhood-based populism of the Citizens United for Fairness demonstrated the potential but also the powerful obstacles facing an interracial coalition between the white and black families of north and west Charlotte. The same geographic landscape that created a shared resentment of the privileges and power of southeast Charlotte inflamed racial tensions that hampered an alliance of class interests. Both of the fairness policies demanded by the parents in CUFF—the equalization of the busing burden among white neighborhoods and the prevention of school resegregation in northwest Charlotte—revolved around fears that the integration formula would cause the complete racial turnover of their once fully segregated subdivisions. CUFF simultaneously represented a reactionary crusade against the reassignment of white children to facilities in black areas, a progressive demand for stable school desegregation through class fairness, and a desperate effort by white homeowners to stick together to maintain the racial integrity of their neighborhoods. One white liberal who observed the chain reaction in the suburb of Hidden Valley blamed the class discrimination in the busing formula for the white flight from north Charlotte: "After a year of patience, whites began to leave to escape [busing] and some blacks moved in.... Most of the people here had a tolerance level, the number of blacks that would have to be on their block before they would move.... Shady real estate operators were going from door to door soliciting business.... Only when the influx of blacks was sudden did real problems arise."[20]

The steady resegregation of the facilities in northwest Charlotte placed the district in direct violation of the court order, and the eruption of racial brawls in several high schools during the fall of 1971 contributed to the widespread sense of a city caught in a permanent crisis. In response, prominent civic leaders asked the local Community Relations Committee to hold hearings to explore the root causes of citizen anger in order to discover a peaceful solution to the impasse. Hundreds of parents seized the opportunity to castigate the Concerned Parents Association, the board of education, the Chamber of Commerce, and the wealthy suburbs. "A lot of white people in Charlotte would like to do something in relation to their better instincts," maintained one father from a northside suburb who formerly supported the CPA but now expressed anger about the favoritism extended toward southeast Charlotte. "They don't quite know what to do and they are resentful and alienated from the traditional leadership.... They feel that the busing system that we now have is unjust and inequitable. That some neighborhoods where the rich and powerful live you don't have to be bused at all." A white westsider active in CUFF explained that his neighborhood was "willing to bear our part of the burden, our part of the opportunity, but we're just not going to take the present situation. We'll just move away or form private schools." Another white father described how his initial opposition to busing had evolved into an appreciation of the need for compliance with the law and an awareness of the discrimination faced by the black community. "I can't afford private schools," he admitted. "It's this or nothing else.... I'm not asking everybody to love my child or my child to love everybody, but he can respect their life and they can respect his. Usually as you get to know people, you do begin to like them better and respect them more. I don't know what else I can contribute, but I am trying. I may be against it, but I am trying."[21]

The heartfelt responses revealed the existence of a local silent majority in a community in transition, still deeply divided in many respects but largely united in the desire to end the constant political battles over the schools. The 1972 report by the Community Relations Committee acknowledged the fundamental obstacle to peaceful and stable desegregation: many black and white families from north and west Charlotte believed that they "are somehow less favored as citizens in this community and that citizens in other neighborhoods are better treated because of personal favoritism by those in power." The commission forcefully concluded that "we need to involve the total community in a radical rethinking of what our schools are all about and what we expect of them." In the biannual school board election held a few months later, voters elected three political moderates who pledged to return the focus to quality education for all students, although the majority faction still remained under the control of members from southeast Charlotte. Taking advantage of the conciliatory climate, the professional educators in the superintendent's office released a Pupil Assignment Study that blamed the "self-destroying" busing plan for the residential transition in north and west Charlotte. The report warned that an "equitable and stable assignment plan is hardly possible as long as school assignments are based on residence," because the location of suburban havens from two-way busing had become the primary determinant of neighborhood selection for new arrivals and local migrants. The study concluded with a warning that the time had come to stabilize the schools in the northwest quadrant by busing in students from the symbolically powerful and residentially secure neighborhoods of southeast Charlotte.[22]

During 1973, after three years of residential turnover and school resegregation in north and west Charlotte, black and white neighborhood activists finally forged an effective grassroots alliance that demanded geographic fairness through the elimination of the "no busing" sanctuaries in the southeast suburbs. The breakthrough came after the school board proposed the reassignment of students from two additional suburbs north of Charlotte to make up for the departure of white families that had moved away from the areas represented by CUFF. As residents of the newly targeted neighborhoods began to place their homes on the market, a supporter of integration named Julian Mason reported that "feeling is running high and growing in this section that it is being unfairly discriminated against in these matters in favor of the more affluent.... Ugly, overt racism has begun to show itself again, and the feeling of having been treated unfairly gives it too fertile ground to grow in." To rechannel this reactionary populism, Mason joined a liberal cadre of white ministers and professors from nearby UNC-Charlotte who urged their neighbors to organize an interracial protest movement around the themes of racial and class fairness rather than antibusing hostility. The ad hoc group circulated fliers calling on residents to "Stand up and be counted before it's too late.... Since we cannot all move to the southeast, ... we must try to influence this board to create stability for us all." In May, white parents in the fairness movement turned out in force for a school board meeting where Mason warned that "until all of the community is involved in busing there will be no stability in our school system.... The black community and the northern part of the community have done their share." The turning point came when civil rights leader Kathleen Crosby criticized the heavy busing burden on black students sent to overcrowded suburban schools, and the white families from north Charlotte responded with rousing applause. "I said to myself, 'Honey, this can't be happening,'" Crosby told the news media afterward, as black and white parents huddled to formalize the geographic alliance.[23]

The interracial coalition represented an extraordinary development in Charlotte's four-year saga, as suburban neighborhoods that had recently joined the CPA's antibusing crusade now demanded comprehensive integration based on class and racial fairness. At the next school board meeting, a blue-collar leader of the northside parents held up a map demonstrating that two-thirds of board members and three-fourths of the officials on the city council and county commission lived in southeast Charlotte neighborhoods that enjoyed complete immunity from two-way busing. Adopting the interracial discourse of the equalization movement, construction worker Bruce Patterson declared that he was "not asking, not pleading, . . . I am demanding that the board take immediate action to insure fair busing for all citizens—black and white." In an informal conference with board members, Judge McMillan announced that he would not approve the reassignment of any more white students from north Charlotte, and instead he recommended that all additional transfers come from the neighborhoods surrounding Myers Park. "There is an unconscious assumption on the part of a lot of people on the board that folks with big lawns and spreading houses are more intolerant," the judge remarked. "I don't think that's true." But the busing of students from southeast Charlotte remained anathema to William Poe, the longtime chairman of the school board, who promised another appeal and forecast a doomsday scenario in which affluent families abandoned the public schools en masse. "Originally, the judge was talking about racial integration," Poe told the press. "Now he is talking about socioeconomic integration, and the law says nothing about that. . . . It's just the judge's idea of how society ought to be."[24]

McMillan struck back with a remarkable appeal to the collective conscience of southeast Charlotte, tapping into a growing refrain that white families in the affluent inner-ring suburbs were "limousine liberals" unwilling to accept their fair share of social change. For two years, the judge had resisted the class discrimination charges by the NAACP plaintiffs and the CUFF interveners, but now he found as a matter of law that the unequal treatment of white neighborhoods thwarted the constitutional mandate to achieve racial integration. In the summer of 1973, McMillan directed the school board to stabilize the racial enrollment in the northwest quadrant with white students from southeast suburbs that "continue to enjoy substantial immunity from having children transported to 'black' schools."

The judge rejected predictions of upper-middle-class flight as an "apparent assumption that the people who live in south and east Mecklenburg are more self-centered or racially intolerant than the people who are already experiencing 'bussing'.... I can not and will not make such a gloomy and defeatist and uncomplimentary presumption about such a large number of progressive citizens." McMillan also ordered the district to develop a completely new integration formula, based on class fairness and racial stability, in time for the 1974/75 academic year. The school board filed another appeal, with the three former CPA leaders providing the decisive votes, but by this time many ordinary citizens and civic leaders alike had decided that the long crisis must come to an end. Supporters of integration launched a "fairness and stability" campaign that eventually drew support from a broad cross-section of the metropolis: black parents who demanded a reduction in their children's transportation burdens, northside and westside white families mobilized for busing equalization, suburban moderates and liberals who endorsed full compliance, and business leaders who simply wanted the uncertainty to end.[25]

The participants in the fairness and stability movement joined forces as the Citizens Advisory Group (CAG), based on the belief that only an ad hoc committee that represented the many competing factions within the community could break the impasse between the school board and the district court. CAG's membership included white liberals from the League of Women Voters, northside and westside leaders of CUFF, ministers and civil rights activists, and delegates from each of the assignment zones in the school district. From one end of the spectrum, a longtime antibusing leader admitted that participation in CAG had convinced him that "we'll have a better society if we assure everyone an equal education." From the other, a black parent from north Charlotte reported that after "yelling at each other for the first couple of meetings, we discovered ... we wanted the same things for our children—good education at the closest school possible, a minimum of time spent on the bus, an end to these constant changes and tipping schools." In the spring of 1974, CAG unveiled a new assignment formula that roughly equalized the busing burdens among white neighborhoods throughout the county, substantially reduced the transportation requirements for black students, and promised aggressive oversight to guard against resegregation in the northwest schools. To supply the white enrollment at West Charlotte High, one of the chronic sources of racial instability, CAG selected five of the most prestigious inner-ring suburbs of southeast Charlotte. More than anything else, these measures represented political solutions, designed to address the concerns of black parents about the survival of community institutions and to defuse the charges of class discrimination from the white neighborhoods of north and west Charlotte. When the school board rejected the fairness and stability plan, Judge McMillan declared the elected officials to be in default and empowered CAG to submit its formula directly to the district court, paving the way for a resolution at last.[26]

In the spring of 1974, three candidates who supported the CAG plan defeated a slate of antibusing challengers in a school board election that confirmed the new spirit of compliance in the community. When the public schools reopened that fall under the revised formula, every facility in Charlotte-Mecklenburg remained within the court-mandated racial ratios, and most of the reassigned students from the southeast suburbs showed up for classes. "I really think this is a more fair plan, but I don't like it," one mother from a wealthy Myers Park neighborhood conceded. "I didn't think it was fair that the youngest black children got most of the busing in the past, while ours haven't been bused. . . . My son, I guess, has accepted it more than I have." Board chairman William Poe, a racial moderate who led the resistance against "socioeconomic integration," remarked: "we have frankly sought stability by consciously giving to every neighborhood some reason to be unhappy about its school assignment at some point between kindergarten and graduation. It's an odd way to gain stability, but it does show some promise." A white neighborhood activist from north Charlotte offered his own assessment of the metropolitan climate: "Fair-minded people will not abandon the school system just because everything isn't favorable to their special interests. I believe most people are fair if given the chance, and that our leaders have failed in their responsibility to encourage the best of our instincts and have sometimes inflamed the worst." Charlotte-Mecklenburg soon emerged as the national model of a successfully integrated urban school system, thanks to an expansive metropolitan remedy that included the white-collar suburbs, the district court's refusal to accept white flight as inevitable, the revolt of a desperate neighborhood movement that lacked formal political power, and the grassroots momentum behind the twin pillars of racial stability and class fairness.[27]

––––––––

On the national stage, the mobilization of the Silent Majority depended upon a populist discourse designed to mask the divisions between working-class and middle-class white voters by defining Middle America through an identity politics based on taxpayer and homeowner status, consumer rights, and meritocratic individualism. In both the political and judicial arenas, the busing battles of the 1970s appeared to represent a clear con-frontation between color-blind conservatism and race-based liberalism. But at the metropolitan level, the links between social class and residential geography largely determined the success or failure of public policies to achieve racial integration. The most perceptive investigations of the back-lash of Middle America have placed the racial resentments of blue-collar families within a broader story of the structural limitations of Great Society liberalism and the class-based inequality that animated reactionary populism. In a 1969 essay on the "Forgotten American," Peter Schrag warned of the anger among lower-middle-class white families that lived in the psychological and physical spaces in-between the affluent suburbs and the impoverished ghettoes, who believed that their neighborhoods were bearing the full burden of racial integration while the limousine liberals and the country-club conservatives watched from the sidelines. In her provocative reassessment of the racial backlash thesis, the social critic Bar-bara Ehrenreich concluded that "working-class anger should have shown that middle-class liberalism had not gone far enough," but instead the pop-ular narrative of blue-collar racism allowed "middle-class observers . . . to seek legitimation for their own more conservative impulses." "To under-stand reactionary populism," Ronald Formisano found in his study of busing in the urban North, "we must recognize the role of class and its con-sequences in the formation of public policy, particularly policies designed to alleviate racial injustice. If class is ignored, as it . . . consistently tends to be in dealing with desegregation, then those policies have little chance of success."[28]

The Charlotte case reveals that the long-term viability of urban school systems undergoing court-ordered desegregation depended upon spatial and socioeconomic remedies that encompassed the entire metropolitan region and pursued racial stability through policies sensitive to the demands of class fairness. In most metropolitan regions, the exemption of affluent white suburbs from the consequences of racial integration, com-bined with the concentration of social change in struggling working-class neighborhoods, accelerated white flight and ushered in an apparent po-litical consensus that busing represented a disastrous liberal experiment. In Charlotte-Mecklenburg, Judge McMillan's mandate to prevent racial resegregation by removing the class-based inequalities among white neighborhoods represented a legal doctrine even more innovative than his original order to overcome state-sponsored residential segregation by employing two-way busing throughout the countywide school district. By eliminating "no busing" sanctuaries through the "socioeconomic integration" of the suburbs, the equalization decree demonstrated that

TABLE 6.1 **Decline in white enrollment, 1968–1986, and desegregation levels for black students, 1986, in large city-suburban consolidated (countywide) school districts in the South**

City, County	White in 1968 (%)	White in 1986 (%)	Black in majority white schools in 1986 (%)	Black in racially isolated schools in 1986 (%)
Greenville, Greenville Co., SC	78	72	87.4	1.8
Raleigh, Wake Co., NC	74[a]	71	N/A	N/A
Tampa, Hillsborough Co., FL	74	69	80.8	1.5
Louisville, Jefferson Co., KY	80[b]	69	93.3	0
Orlando, Orange Co., FL	83	67	53.2	7.4
Ft. Lauderdale, Broward Co., FL	75	65	41.6	23.9
Nashville, Davidson Co., TN	76	63	62.0	2.1
W. Palm Beach, Palm Beach Co., FL	70	62	36.4	27.9
Jacksonville, Duval Co., FL	72	60	50.9	14.9
Charlotte, Mecklenburg Co., NC	71	58	65.2	3.2
Mobile, Mobile Co., AL	58	55	34.0	43.1
Miami, Dade Co., FL	58	24	8.2	59.2

Sources: Gary Orfield and Franklin Monfort, *Racial Change and Desegregation in Large School Districts* (Alexandria, NSBA, 1988), 7–9, 11–13, 20–23; *Raleigh News and Observer,* Aug. 7, 1970.

a. City schools only (consolidated by administrative policy in 1976).
b. City schools only (consolidated by court order in 1975).

a class-based approach could desegregate the public schools of an entire metropolitan region without producing a crippling degree of white flight. The retrospective political consensus that blames court-ordered busing for the destruction of urban school systems ignores the necessity of metropolitan strategies to stabilize racial integration, an approach undertaken in a small number of countywide districts in the South but foreclosed in most of the country after the Supreme Court's landmark decision in *Milliken v. Bradley* (1974). The *Milliken* case, which overturned a busing plan that would have consolidated the city school district of Detroit with three surrounding counties, immunized most politically autonomous suburbs throughout the nation from meaningful integration and sentenced most minority students in urban centers to attend public schools hypersegregated by a fusion of race and class.[29]

The divergence of Charlotte-Mecklenburg's public school system from the prevailing national trends of metropolitan fragmentation and urban crisis turned out to be exceptional but not unique. During the era of court-ordered busing, the South's consolidated city-suburban school systems displayed much higher levels of racial integration and suffered much lower degrees of white flight than almost all urban districts inside or outside the region. Three interrelated factors decisively shaped the outcome of successful cases of court-ordered school desegregation in the metropolitan

South: the prior existence of a consolidated countywide school system, the presence of a substantial white majority in the overall district enrollment, and the implementation of an expansive busing formula that achieved class as well as racial integration. Most of these metropolitan school systems were located in three states—North Carolina, Tennessee, and Florida—where public policies and land-use laws facilitated suburban annexation and encouraged city-county consolidation. In Raleigh, which pushed through the consolidation of city and suburban schools in the mid-1970s in order to minimize white flight by following the Charlotte model, working-class white neighborhoods also joined forces with nearby black areas to demand racial stability through busing equalization. The leader of Raleigh's blue-collar parents announced that "we understand the black man's problems for the first time," and the interracial coalition successfully demanded the inclusion of the affluent suburbs in the busing plan. In contrasting southern cities such as Atlanta and Richmond, where the NAACP's pursuit of city-suburban consolidation failed in the federal courts, the middle-class flight of families of all races resulted in hypersegregated urban schools that reflected the dominant national pattern and mocked the elusive promise of *Brown*.[30]

Metropolitan problems require metropolitan solutions. "For integration to really work," an African American principal at an inner-city Charlotte school observed in the summer of 1974, "you've got to have a good socioeconomic mix as well as a black and white mix." For the next decade, black and white supporters of comprehensive integration maintained control of the Charlotte-Mecklenburg school board and championed busing as the necessary remedy for persistent patterns of residential segregation. Charlotte garnered national attention as the "city that made busing work," including a CBS-TV special report portraying the southern metropolis as the antithesis of the Boston disaster and a glowing *New York Times Magazine* profile featuring numerous black and white students who praised the racial diversity of their educational experiences. But metropolitan Charlotte never implemented a collective housing remedy that addressed the causes instead of the symptoms of residential segregation: the public policies that simultaneously constructed the southeast suburbs and created the northwest ghetto. Over time, the steady suburbanization of the black middle class increased the hypersegregation of poor minority families in the urban core, while the explosive growth of the outer-ring suburbs gave rise to a revitalized antibusing movement that demanded a return to neighborhood schools. Resegregation trends began to reemerge in the early 1990s, when Charlotte-Mecklenburg shifted to a magnet school approach designed to make busing voluntary rather than mandatory. Then in 1999, in response

TABLE 6.2 **Decline in white enrollment, 1968–86, and desegregation levels for black students, 1986, in large urban school districts in the South and non-South without metropolitan integration plans**

City	White in 1968 (%)	White in 1986 (%)	Black in majority white schools in 1986 (%)	Black in racially isolated schools in 1986 (%)
South				
Atlanta	38	7	1.6	90.8
New Orleans	31	8	0.7	84.2
Richmond	36	13.6	0.1	56.6
Houston	53	17	3.4	69.6
Dallas	61	21	4.6	65.7
El Paso	42	23	9.8	3.1
Memphis	46	24	12.0	66.0
Ft. Worth	67	37	22.1	36.4
Austin	81	47	21.8	6.9
Non-South				
Washington	6	4	0.5	94.1
Detroit	39	9	0.6	76.1
Newark	18	9	1.0	96.6
Chicago	38	14	2.4	81.3
San Francisco	41	15	0	49.3
Los Angeles	54	18	4.9	70.0
Baltimore	35	19	5.1	68.3
New York	44	22	6.8	74.1
Cleveland	43	25	0.9	5.2
Philadelphia	39	25	10.6	73.7
Boston	68	26	4.0	13.3
Milwaukee	73	36	11.8	23.6
Denver	66	37	19.0	0
San Diego	76	44	26.5	8.5

Source: Gary Orfield and Franklin Monfort, *Racial Change and Desegregation in Large School Districts* (Alexandria: NSBA, 1988), 7–9, 11–13, 19–21.

to a reverse discrimination lawsuit filed by white suburban parents, a federal judge appointed by Ronald Reagan issued a "color-blind" mandate that forbade Charlotte-Mecklenburg from employing any race-conscious remedies to achieve school integration. Thirty years after the initial antibusing revolt of the Silent Majority, the metropolis that once boasted of being "the premier integrated urban school system in the nation" returned to neighborhood schools now segregated by class as much as by race.[31]

SEVEN

Prelude to the Tax Revolt

The Politics of the "Tax Dollar" in Postwar California

ROBERT O. SELF

It has become commonplace in academic and political circles to observe that at key moments in the last quarter of the twentieth century California modeled to the nation a particular kind of American populist revanchism. Indeed, since the so-called tax revolt of 1978—or perhaps since California voters famously repealed the state's fair housing law in 1964 and elected Ronald Reagan governor in 1966—the academic and popular commentariat has cast California as both a weird political hothouse of fanatical extremism *and* the most reliable barometer of emerging national political trends. There has been good reason for this. California politics since 1945 have distilled to an essence what has been at stake in the nation: distribution of the assets and costs of postwar affluence; the triumph of growth liberalism and the vast inequalities it created and left unresolved; the possibilities of a progressive welfare state and the retrenchment of the tax revolt; the bonanza of Keynesian mass consumption and its social and environmental fallout. The tax revolt was preceded by two decades of liberal experimentation that made California a very different kind of model between the 1940s and the late 1960s: of state-subsidized social policy that democratized health care and higher education, undertook a massive public works project to build dams and canals, erected one of the nation's most generous welfare safety nets, and supported (mostly) organized labor, backed by the votes of the nearly 50 percent of California workers who were unionized in the 1950s. The pace of the turnaround in a generation was astonishing.[1]

No single event has more prominently marked the interpretive dividing line between one California and the other as the passage of Proposition 13 in June 1978. Immediately identified not as *a* tax revolt but *the* Tax Revolt, Proposition 13's property tax–reduction formula, along with the antistatist (and antipolitician) political groundswell that underwrote it, was quickly exported around the nation in a wave of imitative ballot measures and state legislation from Massachusetts to Oregon. That wave swelled in the early 1980s, overlapping with and lending legitimacy to President Reagan's campaign to dismantle parts of the national welfare state. As many historians have noted, the political tide had turned against the New Deal and Great Society state as local tax limitation movements became the leading edge of a much larger project to reduce the power, scope, and credibility of regulatory, social-wage public policy at state and national levels. Whether they dub the post-1978 period in California "paradise lost," the tax revolt constituency a "homegrown revolution," or tax revolt politics an effort to get "something for nothing," commentators agree that after 1978 California and the nation were forever changed.[2]

The California tax revolt nonetheless awaits its first in-depth historical treatment. A series of studies in the immediate aftermath of the 1978 election, along with a handful of five- and twenty-year anniversary publications, still constitute the bulk of the scholarly work on Proposition 13. As may be expected, studies of Proposition 13 have generally developed along three axes: (1) the economic environment of the 1970s, especially the extraordinary inflation of 1973–77 that gave tax reform such immediacy, (2) the political campaign on behalf of Proposition 13, carried forward by the now legendary figures Howard Jarvis and Paul Gann and the United Organization of Taxpayers, and (3) the public policy and public services implications of property tax limitation for state and local governments. Despite the burgeoning interest of historians in the confluence of rights discourse, white racial backlash, and tax limitation at the core of New Right political doctrine, no one has to date placed Proposition 13 in the longer postwar history of California liberalism or national urban and metropolitan political economy. The horizons of analysis have tended to be shorter and more constrained, limited usually to the period between the late 1960s and the early 1980s and confined to tax policy alone. This is unfortunate, because the politics of the "tax dollar" were integral to postwar city building and the public policies that advanced and sustained it. Furthermore, growth liberalism itself, about which I will have more to say below, was

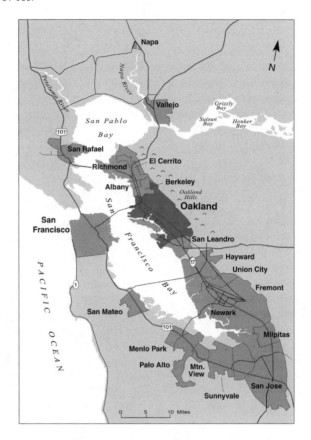

Figure 7.1. Map of San Francisco Bay Area, in the 1960s. University of Wisconsin Cartography Lab.

intimately linked to tax policy, even at the most local level, across the whole of the postwar period.[3]

While not a systematic historical analysis of the tax revolt in the manner I call for above, my own contribution here is an effort to push the scholarship in that direction. Looking at the politics of suburbanization in San Francisco's East Bay between the late 1940s and the late 1960s, I make two sets of arguments, neither of which should strike the reader as entirely surprising. My hope, however, is that, taken together, they advance us modestly toward a deeper understanding of the relationship between consumption, political economy, and public policy in the postwar suburb. In particular, they offer for consideration one of the essential but neglected contexts in which Proposition 13 and tax revolt politics must be understood. The first set of arguments begins with the premise that property taxes were the central political issue in postwar suburban city building and that the origins of the state's celebrated tax revolt in 1978 lay partly in the breakdown of a decades-old "compact" between home-owners, industry, and city governments that dated to the 1940s. Because tax policy is at base a mechanism for distributing social costs, local tax structures are particularly susceptible to mutable ideas of "fairness." Tax reform became a central tenet of modern California conservatism in part because the suburban development strategies of postwar growth liberal-ism and the political compromises that undergirded them had begun to weaken and fail.[4]

The second, related set of arguments has to do with how suburban places were mobilized into political units to capture capital flows. Let me give this abstraction real historical purchase. Since Kenneth Jackson's *Crabgrass Frontier,* historians have understood postwar suburbanization primarily as a consolidated form of consumption driven by the broad subsidizing of the nation's middle class by the federal government. But to date historians have not adequately studied and theorized local municipal governments as important state actors in this process. One of the stickiest paradoxes of postwar urban/suburban history is the extraordinary power of local po-litical arenas on the one hand and the vast reach of federal power across jurisdiction and distance on the other. One way to think about the postwar California suburb in terms of this paradox is through the lens of the clas-sic conflict between "use value" and "exchange value" identified by John Logan and Harvey Molotch.[5] In the tempestuous politics of the "growth machine" business elites and their political patrons seek constant growth while neighborhood residents seek to minimize costs and preserve qual-ity of life. This classic political tension was temporarily quelled in the postwar California suburb through the judicious combination of federal subsidy and local tax policy. In short, federal subsidy on the one hand and local political strategy on the other created the conditions for a subur-ban grand compromise. When that combination could no longer mollify competing local interests—in the late 1960s and especially in the 1970s—homeowners rebelled against "politicians" in both the statehouse and in local suburban communities. The tax revolt was thus one manifestation of a return in suburban California to a classic growth machine politics that postwar liberalism had temporarily displaced.[6]

With these two contentions in mind, we may begin with a broad view. The pace and reach of postwar suburbanization transformed California in a single generation. Between 1950 and 1970, the state's population doubled, from just over ten million to just under twenty. Men and women from every state, Mexico, and, after 1965, Southeast Asia, poured into California in these two decades, dwarfing even the enormous World War II migration. To accommodate them, three and a half million new housing units were built—double the number that existed in 1950—in a twenty-year construction bonanza of enormous scope. The new population was overwhelmingly young. As the median age in the state dropped from 32 to 27, the percentage of people over 65 years of age fell from eight to three, and the percentage of school-age children shot up from seventeen to twenty-five. Population growth and development fed a real estate boom in which the median home price jumped by 50 percent ahead of inflation. Capital in a variety of forms and industrial sectors poured into the state, entering markets wholly or partially subsidized by the Federal Housing Administration (FHA), the Veterans Administration (VA), the G.I. Bill, the federal Highway Act, the military-industrial and military-educational complexes, and a huge range of state-level subsidies and spending. In the space of twenty years, California became the nation's economic engine and population magnet—and the national epitome of growth liberalism.[7]

A good deal of what follows concerns the politics and policies of postwar *growth liberalism,* a broad term under which an enormous range of governmental activity is collected, including, for instance, both the social-wage welfare state and the military-industrial complex and its defense-based research and development. But the concept usefully describes a key orientation of both the federal government and many state and local governments in the three decades after World War II: the use of state power to create, subsidize, and stabilize private markets. These markets, along with trade unions and a moderate social welfare policy, helped to expand the size and economic power of the U.S. middle class. Indeed, between the middle 1930s and the 1970s, the activist state profoundly shaped the direction of private sector economic growth in the United States, from the international arena to the California suburb. But it is important to understand that growth liberalism was always racialized in this period and that within metropolitan political economies always had differential spatial expressions. Growth liberalism shaped racial and class segregation as local communities across the nation were sorted into winners and losers. In particular, the subsidizing of suburbanization and capital flight from central cities in the Northeast, Midwest, and select parts of the West set in motion three decades of urban underdevelopment that produced what many commentators have called an "urban crisis."[8]

The enormous transfer of capital and people from other regions of the country to California, underwritten by growth liberalism, did not occur in a static metropolitan context. It occurred within, and profoundly shaped, a metropolitan world in which cities competed with one another to capture investment. They competed to intercept these massive flows of public and private capital and redirect them into their communities. This process represented the crucial interface between broad national and state-level policies and the tax structure of local communities. More investment meant more property tax revenue; conversely, the lower a city's tax rate, the greater the incentive to invest in that city. But a low tax rate also threatened desired public services—schools, fire protection, police, libraries, and the like. It was (and remains) a delicate balance. Postwar city-builders viewed this competition as a zero-sum game. To fail to recruit new industrial plants, shopping malls, freeways, rapid transit lines, and the like was to lose them to another city. To succeed in such recruitment was to guarantee a city's "progress" and to ensure, in the market-driven logic of American city-building, "future growth." In 1964, when the mayor of Fremont, thirty miles south of Oakland, announced the opening of a new General Motors plant, he told the press, simply, "Fremont has arrived."[9]

How did suburban cities like Fremont "arrive"? What did it mean in the era of ascendant growth liberalism and this vast national investment in California to "arrive"? An enormous array of suburban forms emerged in postwar California, as in the nation. It would be impossible in this limited space to account for all of them. But we can look at one major type, one classic representative of a very important kind of metropolitan formation in this period: the industrial suburb. To "arrive" meant three things for this kind of postwar California city. It meant, first, that the FHA and VA would underwrite home mortgages for middle-class residents; second, that various types of restrictive measures would guarantee racial and class homogeneity; and third, that new industry (often "branch plants" of eastern firms) would provide enough tax revenue (through taxes assessed on property holdings) that the homeowner property tax rate could be kept reasonably low. Through the judicious combination of these factors, the city would pursue homeowner consensus. As postwar city-builders saw it, all three components were essential. Absent one, their fate was not assured. This local opportunism was itself a synthesis of three core traditions within American political culture: antitax conservatism, white racial nationalism, and booster promotion.[10] In much of postwar California, the suburban "compact" briefly described here between industry, city-builders, and homeowners cemented a set of expectations and ideologies that could be mobilized politically. It also cemented in place a kind of political *space* that could be effectively mobilized to capture ever larger shares of postwar capital flows.[11]

I would like to turn now to two specific examples to illustrate how public policy, commercial development, homeowner consumption, and the politics of the "tax dollar" combined in the emergence of the postwar California suburb. Two medium-sized cities (each with a population between 65,000 and 100,000) in the East Bay together help to narrate the prelude to the tax revolt. We may begin with the city of San Leandro, just southeast of Oakland's city line, which entered the national iconography of suburban industrial growth in 1966 when it was named a "model municipality" by the *Wall Street Journal*. "Since 1947 some 600 companies have moved to town," cooed the *Journal*, "adding some $200 million in property to the tax roles." San Leandro, the *Journal*'s enthusiastic reporter continued, "managed to get all the benefits of lavish public spending while putting a surprisingly small bite on the local taxpayers." Indeed, between 1948 and 1957 alone, the city added 15,000 industrial jobs and over $130 million in capital investment in property and facilities. Caterpillar Tractor, Chrysler and Dodge parts and assembly divisions, Frieden Calculators, General Foods, Pacific Can Co., Peterson Tractor and Equipment Co., California Packing Corporation, Kaiser-Frazer Aircraft, and Crown-Zellerbach all had new or expanded factories or processing plants in San Leandro by the end of the 1950s. By the early 1960s, industry in San Leandro paid more than one-third of the cost of city government.[12]

All of this was by design. In 1948, San Leandro voters had elected a reform mayor and city council who had pledged in the election to "let the people decide and know where their tax dollar is spent." The relationship between property taxes and local industry had been crucial to that election. One neighborhood activist had asked her constituents on the eve of the election if they "know how much of the city taxes come from your neighborhood?" and "how much of that is spent in your neighborhood?" Indeed, the 1948 election had shaped up as a classic confrontation between a "growth machine" business coalition and a tax-conscious group of homeowners who were concerned that runaway growth would burden them with excessive taxes and would bring unwanted "smoke-stack" industrial development into their garden communities. The election brought a resolution of this paradigmatic conflict. The new administration would appease the homeowner constituency by setting the property tax rate deliberately low (indeed, San Leandro's property tax rate was among the lowest in the state for decades). Industry would bear the extra cost, but if the city could recruit new businesses successfully that cost would be distributed widely and no single employer would feel unduly burdened. At its heart was the philosophy of growth liberalism: a larger economic development pie meant that everyone's slice was bigger and no one was unduly burdened in the distribution of social costs—as long as the frame of reference remained in San Leandro alone.[13]

Beginning in 1949, the Chamber of Commerce developed a program designed to convince homeowners of "their stake in terms of personal benefits and in the continued growth and expansion of industrial and business firms in San Leandro." With declarations like "San Leandro industry helps pay your taxes!" and "San Leandro industry puts money in everyone's pocket!" a series of chamber pamphlets and advertisements blanketed the city in the late forties and early fifties. Addressed to homeowners, this supercharged booster literature translated the city's industrial strategy into easy bites of colloquial economic wisdom. San Leandro's homeowners did not subscribe to anti-industry, redistributive politics of a radical stripe, but the chamber nevertheless understood that the sorts of nitty-gritty concerns residents did have about taxes, city services, and quality of life amenities could lead them to oppose certain kinds of industrial development in the future, especially so-called "smokestack" growth. Here was the antidote: constant messages that industry is on the homeowners' side, keeping taxes low, schools good, and jobs local. Cutting the tax rate was both an economic incentive to attract industry and a sociopolitical tactic designed to incorporate local homeowners into an ideological and political consensus about the benefits of growth.[14]

San Leandrans developed a parallel racial strategy. Immediately after the war, residents erected a figurative white wall along the city's border with Oakland. In 1947 a major real estate firm developed a plan to place as much of San Leandro's residential property under restrictive covenants as possible, limiting future property sales to "members of the Caucasian race." Such restrictions had been used in San Francisco and parts of the East Bay for decades to contain the mobility of Chinese and Japanese residents, and while the postwar covenants perpetuated such exclusions the 1947 tactics were aimed at newly arrived African Americans. The *San Leandro News-Observer* reported in the autumn of 1947 that a real estate representative had outlined his "plan for protecting property values" in an address "before the board of directors of the Chamber of Commerce," which concluded with "the board giving its approval of the program and authorizing that a letter of approval of his program be furnished [him]." In undisguised language the *News-Observer* announced that the "sudden increase in the East Bay Negro population" meant that "local neighborhoods are spontaneously moving to protect their property values and calling upon Friel's company to assist them." The U.S. Supreme Court's ruling against covenants in 1948 (*Shelley v. Kramer*) slowed but did not halt the process, as real estate representatives created "neighborhood protective

Figure 7.2. The San Leandro Chamber of Commerce encouraged local homeowners to see industry as a community asset. Industry, the chamber's argument went, helps keep property taxes low.

associations," pseudo-corporations of homeowners that could legally se-lect acceptable homebuyers through "corporation contract agreements" as long as "race and creed" were not taken into account.[15]

In its glowing report on San Leandro in 1966, the *Wall Street Journal* took note of the city's whiteness. The low-tax industrial strategy had been a suc-cess, the *Journal* observed, because San Leandro "hasn't been forced to ab-sorb a heavy influx of minority groups and unskilled workers." "Minority groups" were understood as inherently bad for business, perhaps because their class status (presumably as "unskilled workers") invited greater social service costs, perhaps simply because diversity was understood ipso facto as a potential brake on local prosperity. Either way, the *Journal*'s equation was a telling example of growth liberalism's racial rulebook. Together, by the 1960s the FHA and VA had guaranteed more than $3 million in home loans in San Leandro, all on a restricted basis. In San Leandro, industry paid the taxes, the federal government guaranteed the mortgages, and racial exclusion opened the city to whites only.[16]

City-building in San Leandro yielded one version of the California suburban dream. A related but still distinct version emerged in Fremont, southern Alameda County's largest suburban community and eventual home of northern California's biggest automobile plant, a 6000-employee General Motors factory that opened in 1965. Incorporated a decade earlier, in 1956, Fremont became the county's most elaborately planned city. It lay 25 miles southwest of Oakland, on the bay, just north of San Jose. Its founders, an eclectic group of political entrepreneurs and landholders, envisioned a coordinated series of neighborhoods linked by broad boulevards and ample green space. As in San Leandro, industry was expected to provide the tax base and support city services. But Fremont's homeowner politics were not the progrowth industry-friendly, tax-savvy white populism found in San Leandro. Fremont's founders decried "runaway growth," kept local developers in close check, and designed a community that for many years was affordable only for the region's managerial and professional classes. Imagined as a planned community of controlled growth, the Chambers of Commerce of five small rural communities organized local homeowners, landowners, and businesses into an incorporation movement. By 1955 the Fremont Citizens' Committee had neatly encapsulated their philosophy in a question printed on their campaign flyers: "Home rule? Or high taxes dictated by non-residents?" Proponents of incorporation cast themselves as modern day American revolutionaries who sought to protect their communities from unjust taxation by establishing "home rule." It was to be, literally, the rule of the *home*.[17]

Homeowner politics in Fremont combined low taxes with disdain for "runaway growth," a potent political mix. A small group of petty bourgeois entrepreneurs and professionals managed Fremont's incorporation campaign. Local ranchers were prominent in the effort, as were small businessmen (the chairman of the Committee for the Incorporation of Fremont, Wally Pond, was a local druggist), but the various incorporation committees included judges, insurance agents, orchardists, newspaper editors, and engineers. Some among the founders had clear speculative economic interests in incorporation—a few ranchers and orchardists, for instance, could expect to receive high prices for land once the city was established— but the majority identified themselves as "homeowners" or "taxpayers" and articulated vague and idealistic notions of what was "best for the community." Still, incorporation finally came down to a more specific issue— taxes. "We want to see you aren't taxed one cent more than you need to be," a representative of the Alameda County Taxpayers Association told Wally Pond and the Committee for the Incorporation of Fremont.[18]

Chamber boosters claimed that the city's stringent zoning and careful planning made possible Fremont's selection in late 1960 as the site of a new General Motors production plant. In December of that year, GM promised the massive facility to Fremont, jilting its cross-bay rival, Sunnyvale. Local planners had long known that the city would require an industrial tax base. The original 1956 general plan estimated that an industrial payroll of 16,000 workers was necessary for a city the size of Fremont, with a projected population of 100,000. A year later, the *News Register* warned that only "intelligent planning" and "the importation of industry, to provide jobs and balance the assessment roll with factories" would safeguard the city's future. When GM announced its decision to build a state-of-the-art production plant employing more than 4,000 workers in the southern industrial zone of the city, plan loyalists could rightly point to their rational approach to growth as reason for the coup. The Southern Pacific Railroad Company, which owned the land and sold it to GM, benefited enormously when Fremont incorporated and the Planning Commission zoned hundreds of acres of property along SP tracks, former farmland, for heavy industry.[19]

Fremont's "arrival," however, produced a spatial landscape in which the idealized proximities and homeowner consensus found in San Leandro went unrealized. Rapid property speculation within the vast new city (it was larger in land area than Oakland) drove land and housing prices up, as did strict enforcement of the general plan. Developers built enormous subdivisions and sold thousands of homes to a narrow range of middle-class families. Residents of these tracts, especially Glenmore Gardens and Mission Ranch, where homes sold for between $19,000 and $29,000, formed the backbone of the city's political class. In the general plan's prescriptions for ample green space, parks, and controls on growth and development, these homeowners found their values reflected and protected. But as the city's population increased through the 1960s (from 43,000 to just over 100,000 in 1970) and as the General Motors workforce grew apace (from about 4,000 in 1964 to 6,100 in 1969), observers and critics noted that surprisingly few workers seemed to live in the city. Commuting from East Oakland, San Jose, Milpitas, East Palo Alto, Santa Clara, Redwood City, Hayward, and other communities within the Bay Area, GM workers streamed in and out of the plant's massive parking lot at each shift change. "We're creating a beautiful city where most of our workers cannot afford to live," Jack Brooks told the *Fremont News Register* in 1967. By 1970, out of a total population of just over 100,000, not even 400 African Americans lived in the city; the median income ($11,933) was higher than in any other city in Alameda County and almost twice that in Oakland; and median housing prices were the highest in the county.[20]

By the 1970s, Fremont's critics did not lack for evidence that the bloom on the suburban dream had begun to wilt. Fremont more than doubled both its population and its production workforce between 1960 and 1970. During that decade the city sustained a working-class population, with half of its residents employed in trades, clerical work, and as operatives or laborers. Nevertheless, in relation to other East Bay cities, especially San Leandro, Fremont was a more expensive place to live and had fewer industrial jobs and industrial establishments. With a median income somewhere in the middle among Alameda County suburbs in 1960, by 1970 the median and average incomes in Fremont were higher than in any East Bay city save the professional suburban enclave of Castro Valley. Housing prices, too, were higher. By 1970, families paid more for homes in Fremont than in *any* East Bay city. Moreover, while the city had grown, it lagged behind the region's model industrial community, San Leandro, by a considerable margin. Despite its notable success in acquiring the General Motors facility, Fremont in 1972 still had one-third the total number of production plants of San Leandro and about half the number of production jobs—all of this in a city with a population one and a half times that of San Leandro. Most important, Fremont's relative lack of industrial property translated into higher property taxes for homeowners. By the early 1970s, Fremont homeowners were paying local property taxes at a rate 40 percent higher than in San Leandro. Indeed, in 1970 Fremont's total combined tax burden was higher than Oakland's, a negative advertisement for the industrial California suburb if there ever was one.[21]

San Leandro and Fremont illustrated in different ways how the contradictions within the postwar development strategies of growth liberalism were laid bare in the 1970s. In the 1950s and 1960s, cheap land, federal mortgage subsidies, a booming industrial economy, and racial segregation combined to permit San Leandro's leaders the luxury of manipulating property taxes both to attract industrial investment and to maintain a political consensus among homeowners. Though successful for a time, this strategy always contained within it two regressive tendencies. First, suburbanization of this kind had the affect of segregating wealth and development by race and class. Second, keeping property taxes low as a development tool, especially taxes imposed on business property, placed a constant pressure on local municipalities to redistribute the tax burden away from businesses. In a competitive capitalist marketplace in which cities across the state were competing for business investment, this pressure on individual urban governments had the cumulative effect of increasing the regressive nature of the tax structure. In the case of Fremont, this was obvious from the beginning. There was no low-tax golden age as in San Leandro. Property taxes were high relative to other cities for the aforementioned reasons: property speculation and a relatively low industrial-residential property ratio.

These contradictions came dramatically to public consciousness between the late 1960s and the middle 1970s. During those years, property taxes increased in two ways in California. Tax *rates* went up as municipalities, counties, and school districts faced rising costs, and property value *assessments* rose in a real estate boom tied to the state's extraordinary postwar growth and the nationwide accelerating inflation. In different ways, each contributed to a steady escalation of the tax load on individual homes. In the two decades between 1950 and 1970, as California's population doubled and the number of school-age children quadrupled, the number of people living in poverty rose to over one and a half million. These jumps were dramatically ahead of the nation at large. New populations placed heavier demands on government services, and local leaders responded by raising tax rates—for cities, counties, school and hospital districts, junior colleges, municipal utilities, flood control, and transit districts, to name the most common. At the same time, California's booming real estate market made for higher and higher home valuations, and those, too, translated into a higher tax bill for homeowners. Median housing prices in Fremont, for instance, increased by 19 percent between 1960 and 1970, and then jumped a phenomenal 79 percent between 1970 and 1980. Overall, East Bay suburban homes increased in value far ahead of inflation in the 1960s, then exploded during the 1970s.[22]

California's spectacular property market inflation during the 1970s amplified the state's already regressive tax structure. Until the early 1970s, property values in California consistently rose between 4 and 5 percent annually. By the late 1970s, however, inflation was as high as 14 percent. This translated into as much as a tripling of an individual homeowners' tax bill. Two additional developments combined to make matters worse. First, in response to a series of county assessor scandals the state legislature enacted reforms in 1968 that had the unintended effect of raising assessments on individual homes. Second, between 1967 and the late 1970s, California had gradually increased its reliance on income taxes as a source of state revenue. By the later years of the decade, the per capita state collection of income taxes was rising at a rate of about 20 percent annually. Inflation combined with a state tax structure that burdened homeowners more than business and industry meant that individual Californians experienced dramatic increases in virtually every form of taxation across the decade of the 1970s. The fabulous land price increases that boosters and developers had so praised in the 1950s and 1960s as the key to California's prosperity had now boomeranged to strike back at homeowners.[23]

In this political economic context, antistatist conservatives, rather than liberal or left leaders and activists, emerged to set the tax reform agenda. Proposition 13 was conceived by two conservative political activists from southern California, Howard Jarvis and Paul Gann. In his post–tax revolt memoir, entitled *I'm Mad as Hell*, Jarvis cast himself in the mold of the American populist. "The brains and capacity of the citizens of the United States are invariably greater than the brains and capacity of the bureaucracy," he rhapsodized. Jarvis, an apartment house owner and longtime anti–New Deal Republican, loudly and passionately proclaimed Proposition 13 to be the "people's" revolt against incompetent spendthrift politicians and their profligate welfare state. Gann was a former realtor and also a longtime political entrepreneur on tax reform initiatives. Though he shared neither Jarvis's crusaderlike voluntarism nor his quest for the spotlight, he was nonetheless a staunch political opponent of liberal social policy. Jarvis and Gann's political orientation and the alliances on which they drew were important because they framed tax reform as an oblique attack on the liberal state. Rather than arguing for tax reform as an effort to correct the regressive nature of the state's tax system—as the Black Panther Party and other groups on California's left had done—Jarvis and Gann approached the tax question from the right. They thus combined two political positions that did not necessarily converge: tax reform and antiliberalism. It was, however, a powerful combination that gained appeal month after month in the first half of 1978 as Jarvis and Gann shaped the state's political discourse around a broad rejection of the political establishment and government "bureaucracy."[24]

The populist appeals issued by Jarvis and Gann resonated among Californians for a variety of reasons. But in places like San Leandro and Fremont, where the development logic of growth liberalism collapsed on itself in the 1970s, these appeals had special potency. Industry had begun to leave the East Bay during the recession of the early 1970s, and suburban deindustrialization proceeded even more quickly as the decade progressed. Meanwhile, housing prices—and thus the homeowner property tax burden—continued to climb steadily upward, shooting skyward late in the decade. What remained? What remained were reified political-spatial suburban communities that would respond to the postwar boom's limits and contradictions by attacking local and state politicians and through them the liberal state—the very state, of course, that had made the rise of such suburbs possible. As that development logic collapsed, so did the political compromises that had undergirded the rise of the suburban growth machine. The tax revolt politics of the late 1970s, then, were less an entirely new phenomenon than an older political standoff that the conservative right repackaged in 1978—repackaged within an updated populism that blended an attack on the liberal state with a nostalgic American agrarianism and property-rights discourse. No observer of Alameda County in the decade before 1978 could deny that the tax burden on small homeowners had increased—indeed, opponents of the Jarvis initiative often rushed to make this admission in order not to seem insensitive—but the ferocity and scale of attacks on state government shifted debate from how best to correct an uneven tax structure to the broader social legitimacy of liberalism and state social policy.[25]

Proposition 13 proposed an enticing, superficially simple resolution: limit the taxes levied on any piece of real property and require a two-thirds vote of the state legislature to increase any other tax. Coming on the heels of failed property tax limitation measures in 1968 and 1973, the Jarvis initiative purposefully streamlined its formula—property taxes could never exceed 1 percent of the "real cash value" of the property, and market-value reassessments for taxing purposes could only occur when property changed hands. Furthermore, Proposition 13's rules were placed outside the control of the state legislature: they could be altered only by another popular referendum. The measure mandated a two-thirds vote for all future state tax increases and a two-thirds vote for local increases as well. Finally, the measure did not include a provision prescribing how the state and local governments were to replace lost revenue: the hope was that they would simply cut.[26]

The Proposition 13 debate in Fremont offers a window on the political currents contending over tax reform. The Fremont chapter of the Alameda YES on Proposition 13 Committee was led by a local apartment building owner and a developer. They cast themselves and Proposition 13 as victims of a relentless campaign waged by government employees, cities, and school districts. "People who don't have time [for such a campaign] pay the taxes," Bob Reeder, vice chairman of the YES on 13 Committee told the *Fremont Argus*. The Fremont city manager, projecting budget cuts of up to $4 million, proposed to raise taxes on local businesses to compensate partially for such losses. Before the city council, and an audience of hundreds of the city's business representatives, the city manager explained that while homeowner property valuation had increased by 129 percent, business property valuation had done so by only 8 percent. Increasing business taxes was simply a way to correct these dramatic imbalances.

The council was not swayed, nor were those business interests who testified, many of whom according to the *Argus* attacked the city for "wasteful spending." When the council turned back the tax increase, the city manager lamented that "there doesn't seem to be any distinction in the public mind between this government and any other."[27]

The 1978 campaign was contested primarily in two arenas: local ones like San Leandro and Fremont and statewide, primarily through vast media coverage. Many opponents of Proposition 13 insisted that Californians were not prepared to reject the welfare state or liberalism outright but were worked into a voting frenzy by the extraordinary media coverage of Proposition 13 and its most vocal supporters. "The meanness and ugliness presently emerging throughout the State of California has largely been encouraged by television and radio," wrote one commentator on "the morning after" Proposition 13. Indeed, Jarvis and Gann proved to be adept, if duplicitous, strategists who forced political opponents onto their terrain. Jarvis frequently made outlandish accusations, as when he claimed that property taxes paid for politicians to travel to Paris and London. Gann would then counter with homilies that softened Jarvis's sharp edge. Proposition 13 will "let us dream the American dream of being safe and secure in our homes," Gann told a television audience during a debate in June. Jarvis and Gann's greatest success came in placing legislators on the defensive. The California legislature had done little to reform the state's tax structure. Democratic Governor Jerry Brown had even allowed the state to run unprecedented surpluses, largely a product of inflation. And Jarvis and Gann camouflaged Proposition 13 with broad populist, antiwaste political strokes. In this context, legislators often came across exactly as Jarvis and Gann hoped they would, speaking in bureaucratic language about budget numbers and feasibility studies, while Proposition 13 proponents spoke in the easy tones of populist everymen.[28]

California voters passed Proposition 13 by the extraordinary margin of 2 to 1, despite the opposition of nearly the entire state political establishment, both Democrat and Republican. In Alameda County, only the vote in Oakland and Berkeley kept the tallies close. In San Leandro and Fremont, voters approved Proposition 13 by 72 percent and 76 percent, respectively. South County as a whole represented a Proposition 13 stronghold. The tax revolt was engineered and led by political forces primarily from Southern California, Los Angeles and Orange County in particular. But voters in Southern Alameda County responded aggressively and with near unanimity. Alameda County residents made much less rhetorical noise in the months leading up to the election, but their votes spoke volumes in June. The contentious growth politics that had been so evident in

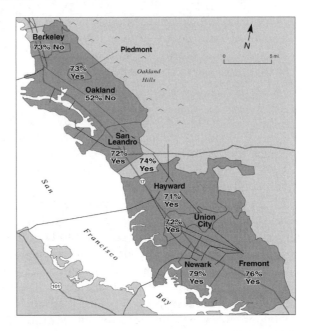

Figure 7.3. Voting results on Proposition 13 in 1978 in major Alameda County cities. University of Wisconsin Cartography Lab.

1948—and had been so thoroughly diffused for three decades—returned with a vengeance.

In diffusing the "growth machine's" political opposition in the late 1940s, postwar San Leandran leaders had helped to cement expectations among homeowners of low taxes and relatively inexpensive public services. Fremont's political leaders had hoped to forge the same consensus, but they were less successful and faced contentious homeowner and developer politics throughout the postwar decades. Capital mobility and the extraordinary growth of California's population during and after World War II propelled the process of suburban formation in San Francisco's East Bay, but homeowner expectations were the glue that held the new cities together during the long postwar economic expansion. When economic restructuring (deindustrialization), inflation, and rising social service costs began to wear away at the suburban "compact" in the 1970s, the conservative right in California mobilized with populist arguments about "fairness" and "government waste" linked to an antiliberal political project that sought tax limitation as a wedge for a large-scale assault on the welfare state, in California and the nation. In the process, they helped to make tax reform a central feature of modern conservatism.

EIGHT

Suburban Growth and Its Discontents

The Logic and Limits of Reform on the Postwar Northeast Corridor

PETER SISKIND

The mass migration of millions of Americans to suburbs in the decades following World War II generated an intense political debate about growth, land use, economic development, and reform. Newcomers and long-standing suburbanites alike discovered much that they wanted to change about the places where they chose to live, work, and play. On the Northeast Corridor (the region stretching from metropolitan Boston to greater Washington, D.C.) discontents with suburban growth grew markedly over the course of the 1960s and reached a peak in the early and mid-1970s. During these years, ever-expanding numbers of voters, activists, neighborhood organizations, and politicians, especially in the corridor's relatively affluent, faster-growing suburbs, decried suburban growth and sought solutions to the problems associated with it. A variety of environmental issues rose to the fore. Should land use be regulated in a region where farmland, marsh, and forest were disappearing? Fiscal worries took on heightened importance. How would new suburbs pay for the public services their constituents had come to expect? Frustrations with sprawl, traffic congestion, and inadequate public services came to dominate political discourse. Should suburban growth continue unchecked? Concerns about government corruption and development decision-making processes sparked demands for increased public participation. Should citizens have a greater voice in local governance? Efforts to increase the economic diversity of suburbs by building affordable housing gained new prominence. Should suburbs remain homogeneous enclaves or should they provide a range of housing options? Never before or since in the postwar era have such a variety of discontents emerged simultaneously from so many sources nor has the sense of political possibility and the potential for reform been greater.

"There is a new mood in America," began a much-publicized book-length report on land use and metropolitan growth, sponsored by the Rockefeller Brothers Fund in 1973. The report, drafted by a task force of twelve urban experts (eight of whom lived on the Northeast Corridor) offered a forthright assessment of widespread discontent in the rapidly growing region. "Increasingly, citizens are asking what urban growth will add to the quality of their lives. They are questioning the way relatively unconstrained, piecemeal urbanization is changing their communities and are rebelling against the traditional processes of government and the marketplace which, they believe, have inadequately guided development in the past.... [T]oday, the repeated questioning of what was once generally unquestioned—that growth is good, that growth is inevitable—is so widespread that it seems to us to signal a remarkable change in attitudes in this nation."[1] Just two years later, responding to the same concerns, the Urban Land Institute published the three-volume *Management and Control of Growth: Issues—Techniques—Problems—Trends*, a reference work that included over 140 authors who wrote overwhelmingly about suburban development issues. The collection's introduction aptly summarized the corridor's suburban development climate when it explained: "The ethic of growth . . . is increasingly being challenged; no longer is it being accepted unquestionably as a premise of progress. Its effects on the quality of life are widely debated, and its management and control are seen by many as essential elements of modern land use policy."[2]

From the late 1960s to the mid-1970s, critics of suburban growth were more vocal and prominent than ever before. Their challenge to unrestricted growth and their demands for "management and control" resonated with Great Society Democrats and moderate Rockefeller Republicans alike. However, despite the dramatically transformed "political mood" in the late 1960s and early to mid-1970s, growth critics ultimately achieved only modest success in reshaping suburban development patterns and processes on the Northeast Corridor. The process of suburban sprawl remained largely unchecked. Why did the "new mood" about suburban growth on the corridor only occasionally translate into substantive, long-term growth policy reforms? In this chapter, I assess the logic and limits of reform by exploring suburban discontents in two different contexts—suburban growth controls and the politics of affordable housing.

The history of suburban growth and its discontents complicates the conventional narratives of the role of postwar suburbs in the travails of liberalism and the emergence of a new conservative politics. So much of recent work on postwar suburbs focuses on western and southern locales and emphasizes the origins of New Right activism and a less ideological but nonetheless increasingly conservative "silent majority." Historians of liberalism have, by contrast, disproportionately focused on the federal government and social policy, with special attention to central cities.[3] On the Northeast Corridor, however, from the 1960s through the mid-1970s, suburban politics and liberalism were fundamentally intertwined. The two were inseparable, yet remained in real tension. Efforts to reform suburban development on the corridor at once emerged from and sought to recast post–New Deal growth liberalism; their politics cannot be confined in the simple categories of backlash, antistatism, or conservatism that dominate our understanding of suburban politics.

The Politics of Suburban Growth Controls

By the late 1960s, the suburban growth control movement had emerged as a powerful political force on the Northeast Corridor. Rapid postwar population gains and large-scale housing, infrastructural, and commercial development put real social, fiscal, and environmental strains on suburban communities and generated widespread popular discontent. Concern about the costs and risks of unchecked growth spawned many novel attempts to reform suburban development. Growth was, however, easier to criticize than it was to reform. Growth's critics offered compelling critiques of land-use policies and economic development, but they often did not have clear or coherent goals. What exactly did citizens, politicians, and planners want? Was it slower growth? Cheaper growth? More environmentally friendly growth? More socially equitable growth? More honest and participatory growth-related decision making? The answers to these questions varied widely both within and between suburbs in the region. Critics of growth sometimes fused together to form effective political movements, but just as often, they could not find any common ground beyond their shared discontent. In addition, the new discontents of the 1960s and early

163

1970s joined rather than replaced existing popular political impulses such as those seeking to resist racial and economic integration, protect property values, and preserve local home rule—impulses that further muddied the logic of reform.

The fragmented structure of metropolitan government also profoundly limited the possibilities of initiating new suburban growth policies. Local, state, and federal governments, the courts, and other public entities like regional transportation and sewer and water authorities all helped shape corridor suburban development. As a result, none of these governmental units had the influence—over each other or over the private developers that still initiated the vast majority of projects—necessary to carry out coherent reform. The amorphousness of discontents was due in part to the lack of an adequate political vessel to contain and give shape to them.

Three of the most prominent and path-breaking reform efforts on the corridor emerged in Montgomery County, Maryland; Fairfax County, Virginia; and Ramapo, New York, in the late 1960s and early 1970s. In each place, suburbanites elected public officials who had campaigned to reform the development process and then once in office launched ambitious reform efforts that would have been unthinkable just a few years earlier. But differences between the three jurisdictions' politics of growth controls proved at least as important as their similarities. Ultimately, varying visions of what new policies should consist of and divergent political experiences in implementing those visions demonstrated the logic and limits of suburban growth reform.

Montgomery County, Maryland, provides an example of a suburban area both where various popular discontents with growth fused coherently together and where those discontents were relatively successfully translated into policy reforms. At the end of World War II, Montgomery County was a largely rural area. Most of its population—barely over 100,000 in 1945—lived in a ring of suburbs that bordered Washington, D.C. By 1970, just a quarter century later, over half a million people populated the sprawling suburban county. Open space disappeared, air and water quality declined, and residents complained of rapidly increasing local taxes and traffic congestion. In the postwar years, Montgomery County officials encouraged explosive suburban growth. From the mid-1940s through the mid-1960s, both the Montgomery County Council and an independent regional water and sewer authority championed explicit progrowth policies. Yet over the next decade, growing popular discontent with suburban growth created a dramatically new political landscape. The 1974 Montgomery County Planning Board's first annual Growth Policy Report provided one indicator of the transformation. Written at the behest of the

County Council, it confirmed that "most of those seriously concerned with growth and its effects now concede that growth does not necessarily equal progress; and, therefore, various kinds and amounts of growth should be carefully controlled."[4] By the mid-1970s Montgomery County had become renowned nationally for its innovative and ambitious growth controls policies.

What contributed to such a political transformation? First, local activists, drawing from the rhetoric of "good government," challenged the county's land-use decision-making process. In the early 1960s, reform groups like the Montgomery Civic Federation and the Montgomery County League of Women Voters targeted local government corruption. The exploits of the 1962–66 County Council thoroughly aroused county reformers' ire. As one critic remembered later, council members during that term "were outrageously devoted to granting favors to the developers and landowners." Ties between councilors and developers appeared so close that both a grand jury and the Internal Revenue Service launched probes that found "shocking situations" of unethical practices and conflicts of interest. In response, voters turned out the incumbents in 1966. The only County Council member to win reelection that year was the lone, consistent critic of the council's land-use decision making; the member most closely identified with the developers' feeding frenzy finished a distant fourteenth. The new council, in turn, initiated a host of reform initiatives designed to make county government more professional, ethical, and transparent. It created the Office of Hearing Examiners to preside over rezoning applications in order to depoliticize and regularize that government-developer relationship. In addition, the new council encouraged citizen involvement in local development issues and created a climate of citizen participation that infused county political life through (and indeed beyond) the 1970s.[5]

Concerns about the environmental impact of growth moved dramatically to the forefront of Montgomery County growth politics next, when in April 1970 a vastly overloaded sewer system began releasing hundreds of thousands of gallons of raw sewage into the major creeks of two county watersheds. Residents living near these overflowing pipelines and the many others who found sewage backing-up into their homes received a quick education on the consequences of rapid and mismanaged suburban development. The next month, the Maryland Department of Health imposed a moratorium on new sewer authorizations in those watersheds until additional capacity could be created, and over the next several years the state, the regional sewer authority, and the county all imposed new sewer moratoria eventually covering the entire county. Far from an obscure political item of interest only to policymakers, the sewer crisis affected all aspects of county politics and development.[6]

In addition to the raw sewage that polluted creeks and rivers and the scores of bulldozers that transformed vast tracts of farmland, Montgomery County residents expressed growing concern about the county's air quality. As increases in car registrations consistently outpaced even the steep rise in total households in the county in these years, the resulting air pollution and congestion escaped few people's notice. As one member of the County Council wrote in 1973: "We always cared about air pollution but now, in the wake of air pollution alerts and high air pollution readings in some areas, air pollution has become a full-blown concern." The production and disposal of garbage also entered the county's political consciousness in a new way in the early 1970s. New state and federal environmental laws required both the county's primary incinerator and landfill to close, and the difficult search for acceptable disposal alternatives stimulated widespread debate.[7]

Rising tax bills and an ongoing fiscal crisis in the county in the 1970s constituted a third suburban discontent and directly precipitated calls for new growth policies. Financial issues dominated county politics throughout the decade. At the end of 1973, one county councilor opined, "there has not been any single issue in recent years that has so irritated the citizens of Montgomery County as have recent property tax assessments." And in 1976 an otherwise technical public information report on the county's finances began by declaring what even the most casual observer would have already been aware: "Montgomery County is facing a severe fiscal crisis this year." County residents struggled with tax equity issues, spiraling reassessments as the result of similarly growing housing values, and the forces of national inflation. The political spotlight on household and county government finances created enormous pressures to respond.[8]

Far from being independent political phenomena merely born out of common circumstances, in Montgomery County discontents with the government decision-making process and with environmental and fiscal crises fused together inseparably. The concerns and career of County Council member Neal Potter both reflected and helped precipitate this dovetailing of discontents. An economist by training and profession, Potter had, as he recalled later, "always been something of a conservative, financially and fiscally." In 1960 he organized the local Citizens Committee for Fair Taxation. On staff of the nationally renowned Resources for the Future, Inc., for fifteen years, he wrote or co-wrote three books on natural resources and in the late 1960s served as co-chairman of the Metropolitan Coalition for Clean Air. His interest in local land-use and planning issues was particularly stimulated when the Montgomery County farm he grew up on along the Potomac River was taken by eminent domain for the right-of-way for the Capital Beltway and his parents were displaced. In response, in the early 1960s he joined and later became president of the Montgomery Citizens Planning Association, and he also maintained close links with the county's political reform movement, serving as a member of such groups as the Alliance for Democratic Reform.[9]

Potter brought these concerns to the table when he was elected to the Montgomery County Council in 1970. Potter and his council colleagues rapidly transformed the growth process in Montgomery County in the early and mid-1970s. With the goal of slower, more rational, and more fiscally and environmentally friendly growth, the county developed new capital improvement plans, water and sewer plans, and was among the first jurisdictions in the county to pass an Adequate Public Facilities Ordinance. Together these measures provided a clear blueprint for citizens and developers alike of the location, timing, and type of building that would be allowed, and they required that such things as roads, public transportation, schools, and police had to be in place in order for private development plans to be approved. In conjunction with citizens groups, the county created detailed new land-use maps that included central business districts to encourage high-density commercial and residential building in particular locations (especially around future sites of subway stations planned for the Washington Metro system). Complementing high-density districts, a new "rural zone," with minimum lot sizes of five acres, was adopted for large sections of the county that were still largely undeveloped. The council also adopted new tax laws that explicitly sought to provide disincentives to sprawl-producing land speculation. In addition, in 1973 the County Council adopted a ground-breaking regulation requiring private developers building projects with fifty housing units or more to include a set proportion of them for those with moderate incomes.[10]

This collection of development reforms in Montgomery County represented the far-reaching extent on the corridor to which discontents with suburban growth combined to transform the political landscape. Throughout the 1970s and beyond, county politicians endorsing growth reforms remained popular, and the energy that policymakers devoted to devising new growth-control measures endured and even increased. Even in Montgomery County, however, there were problems; implementing new growth policies proved a vexing, uneven process. For example, untested new land-use techniques brought with them steep learning curves. The County Council, the county executive, and the County Planning Board experienced both structural and personality clashes that reduced the effectiveness of land-use reforms. County officials periodically fought about growth issues with both the state legislature and federal regulators. And the new hyperactive level of citizen participation delayed and encumbered decision-making and exhausted decision-makers. Yet where such obstacles somewhat inhibited the implementation of new growth policies in Montgomery County, reform there was remarkably coherent and directed compared with other suburban locales on the corridor.

One locale where the politics of suburban growth control proved less tidy was Fairfax County, Virginia, just across the Potomac River from Montgomery County. In many respects the two counties shared a great deal. In Fairfax County, the conditions inspiring popular discontents were similar to those in Montgomery County. Fairfax County's population grew even faster than its neighbor's—153 percent in the 1950s and another 83 percent in the 1960s—and as a result experienced accompanying environmental problems including loss of open space and declining air and water quality. Fairfax County also endured fiscal strains. In order to build the infrastructure and operate the public services for so many new people, local government budgets and taxes skyrocketed. Between 1961 and 1974 local spending in the county increased almost ninefold for schools, about eightfold for police, and twelvefold for fire departments. In addition, Fairfax County public officials during the boom years of the 1950s and 1960s had championed an explicit progrowth ideology that blurred into subtle conflicts of interests and outright corruption; in the mid-1960s several Fairfax County supervisors were indicted and convicted in rezoning bribery cases.[11]

These common suburban growth discontents in the two counties also produced similar political initiatives. In 1971, Fairfax County voters defeated a majority of the incumbent Board of Supervisors that ran the county and put into office in their place candidates whose campaigns had been based explicitly on promises to reform the pace and process of suburban growth. This new Board of Supervisors then spent its entire four-year term devising and attempting to implement a variety of new growth policies, culminating in an ambitious and comprehensive growth management program, the Planning and Land Use System (PLUS). But it was there that the similarities ended. For, in contrast with Montgomery County, the growth controls movement in Fairfax County produced neither sufficient political momentum nor a unified vision of reform for transforming the growth process. As a result, by the late 1970s the visionary heart of the uncompleted PLUS had been removed, some key supporters of PLUS on the Board of Supervisors were out of office, and the county continued to develop in a rapid and dispersed fashion much as it had in prior decades.[12]

Why did growth management evolve so differently in Fairfax County? One key factor that shaped the contrasting outcomes was the role that state courts played in validating or disallowing growth policies. Whereas the Maryland judiciary rarely intervened in Montgomery County's policy decision-making, the Virginia courts emerged as a source of constant frustration and impediment to Fairfax County policymakers. Faced with a backlog of more than 300 unexamined zoning cases before them after their election in 1971, one of the first actions that the new Board of Supervisors took was to impose a temporary zoning moratorium while they got their bearings and initiated a replanning for the county. But the Circuit Court of Fairfax County struck down this moratorium. The courts overturned Fairfax County's regulation requiring private developers to provide a set percentage of moderate-income housing in new projects of fifty or more units. The board tried rezoning certain land to reduce density and turned down numerous rezoning applications, but many of these actions, too, were overturned in court. The core of several court opinions focused on the board's decisions as being "arbitrary and capricious" and therefore illegal. In response, the board attempted to move beyond piecemeal growth management policies and began initiating a comprehensive program that they hoped would satisfy legal as well as political hurdles. After creating a task force to devise guidelines for creating a comprehensive growth management system, in January 1974 the board simultaneously embarked on an eighteen-month program to flesh out these guidelines and imposed an emergency moratorium on the entire development process until the details of the new PLUS regulations could be determined and implemented. But this set of actions fared little better in court. Elements of the moratorium were struck down, and the county and developers compromised on other elements in an out-of-court settlement. Finally, in 1975 the Virginia Supreme Court ruled so as to make the timed development system that comprised the regulatory centerpiece of the county's comprehensive growth controls program—a system which Montgomery County also employed without judicial interference—all but impossible to implement legally in Virginia.[13]

The judicial rulings handed down by Virginia courts played an essential role in preventing Fairfax County from reshaping the pace and patterns of suburban growth. One Fairfax County commentator, disappointed with the course of legal events, opined in 1979 that the "steady state of rebuffs" by the courts had "made it difficult for growth management advocates to retain their fervor." Similarly, a Fairfax County development lawyer supportive of the decisions approvingly concluded in 1976 that as a result of court decisions the "approach to land use which became a keystone of Fairfax policy in the 1969–1975 period is over."[14]

In addition to the legal constraints, a second important factor leading to the demise of growth management efforts was the form and endurance of Fairfax County citizens' dissatisfactions with growth. Popular discontents about growth did not automatically translate into support for county officials' proposed solutions. As in Montgomery County, Fairfax planners hoped to reduce density and delay development in many outlying and environmentally sensitive areas while rezoning for increased density in locations where public facilities, natural carrying capacity and transportation could support it. In numerous, rancorous public meetings about the master plan redrawing process, however, many organized and unorganized citizens frequently fought off attempts to plan for higher density development. According to a witness and close observer of the public participation process in Fairfax County: "Ironically, the considerable citizen involvement was the major factor in the county's failure to channel growth. . . . [D]espite the alleged desires of the citizens to control growth and preserve the environment, an effect of their input was to perpetuate the low-density sprawl pattern of development."[15] Further hindering Fairfax County's growth management efforts were the results of the 1975 district supervisor elections. The two Fairfax County supervisors who were most supportive of growth control lost by narrow margins, one by only eight votes out of 13,000 cast. As a result, what had been a somewhat consistent six-to-three voting block in favor of strong new growth management policies became a five-to-four majority much more favorable to a return to the status quo.[16] Although discontent with rapid growth and its effects remained pervasive in Fairfax County, deep divisions over what to do about it and a state legal climate chilly to the practice of local government initiative effectively ended the active search for alternatives to suburban sprawl.

While Montgomery County and Fairfax County followed divergent paths of development reform, the politics of growth controls that played out simultaneously in Ramapo, New York, revealed still another alternative. In Ramapo, a Rockland County town thirty miles from New York City, local officials elected on the promise to control growth largely succeeded in implementing their reform vision: the New York state courts upheld a timed development system created in Ramapo nearly identical to that which Fairfax County sought and the Virginia courts rejected. But if Ramapo's implementation story paralleled that of Montgomery County, the growth reforms sought turned out to resemble neither Montgomery nor Fairfax planners' goals. Rather, the growth controls that Ramapo policymakers worked toward ultimately proved more narrowly conceived—geared primarily to appeasing one rather than multiple suburban discontents. In Ramapo, a focus on easing rapidly growing local tax burdens translated into reforms that delayed rather than reshaped the patterns of suburban development.

On the surface, Ramapo's political reactions to explosive postwar suburban growth seemed to resemble closely those in Montgomery and Fairfax counties. In the 1950s and 1960s, Ramapo underwent a massive building boom, stimulated by the completion of major highway projects like the New York State Thruway, the Tappan Zee Bridge, and an extension of the Garden State Parkway. Population in Ramapo grew 70 percent during the 1950s and another 78 percent between 1960 and 1966. As a result, many local residents complained about the dramatic changes in their town's character, and with the rapid growth in the number of school-age children, local property taxes skyrocketed.[17] In response, Ramapo's changing electorate—newcomers to the town caused a steep increase in Democratic Party registration from 38 to 57 percent between 1957 and 1965—ushered in a new political era. Voters swept out the long-entrenched local Republican establishment and in 1965 elected as town supervisor John F. McAlevey, a Brooklyn-born lawyer and self-described liberal Democrat who campaigned almost exclusively on a growth controls platform.[18]

As promised, over the next eight years the McAlevey administration dramatically reshaped the political culture and development policies in Ramapo. Finding that "builders were running the town," upon coming into office McAlevey lambasted developer "fat cats" and initiated a series of growth control reforms in his first years including a new master plan, interim development controls, and new zoning maps and ordinances. Most controversially, in 1969 the town enacted a series of new amendments to the zoning law that created a then-novel timed development system. Under the new system—which a group of local developers and landowners immediately challenged in court—private housing proposals would only receive approval if they earned enough points as rated by the project's proximity to existing public facilities including sewers, drainage capacity, public parks, recreation and school sites, roads, and firehouses. Over the next eighteen years, Ramapo promised to provide such services over the entire undeveloped area of the town, but in the meantime developers could only build where the town did not yet encourage it if they were prepared to pay for the expensive public services themselves.[19] The legal contest over this timed development system proved a back-and-forth affair: the town prevailed at the initial, trial court and lost on appeal in 1971; then in 1972 the Court of Appeals of New York—the state's highest court—overturned the appellate ruling and upheld the town's land-use regulations. Observers in New York and around the nation viewed the Ramapo precedent as a striking alteration of the suburban growth process. As Ramapo's lead attorney in the case wrote in *Zoning Digest*: "What we have fought for and won was the right of a community to chart its own destiny within a framework of reasonable planning. Until we initiated the program . . . the pattern was for the developers and speculators to make the decisions as to where growth would take place."[20]

While Ramapo won the right to "chart its own destiny," what it chose for itself generated controversy. By far the most prominent public discontent that town officials sought to relieve was the fiscal burden of rapid growth. As Supervisor McAlevey explained: "The basic problem of the community when I came into office was the uncontrolled and too rapid growth and an increase in taxes far greater than anyone had anticipated." As a result, McAlevey's pledge to the town focused on giving citizens "relief from the rising burden of total tax load." This chief priority translated into specific land-use reforms that less envisioned creating an alternative model for suburbanization than simply ensuring more financially beneficial growth. Ramapo's entire timed development system applied only to residential development—not to commercial and industrial development, both of which would be expected to produce net fiscal gains for the town. In addition, unlike planners in Montgomery County (and planners' unsuccessful attempts in Fairfax County), those in Ramapo did not create new designated districts for denser, clustered housing, retail, and employment uses. In fact, they removed locations for multifamily housing and apartments from the zoning map. Ramapo, in other words, sought to delay rather than prevent suburban sprawl. As one land-use expert concluded: the town's "plan thus contemplates a continuation of expensive and exclusionary 'sprawl' which in all probability would have occurred—although somewhat faster—without the plan."[21]

The McAlevey administration did address problems associated with suburban growth other than fiscal concerns. Environmental standards shaped several criteria in the town's complicated development points system, and the socially exclusionary nature of single-family home building was at least modestly addressed by Ramapo's creation of a housing authority that in 1971 voluntarily built 198 units of public housing. But fiscal concerns in Ramapo took priority because that was what residents cared most about and because that was what private development pressures exacerbated most obviously. Regarding the construction of affordable housing, for example, Supervisor McAlevey pushed the issue as far as popular and market pressures would allow. Explaining that "I've believed in public housing from way back and I want to demonstrate that there can be beautiful projects in every community," McAlevey successfully fended off at least two citizen-initiated lawsuits protesting the public housing, squeaked through to reelection in a 1971 campaign focused primarily on his support for public housing, and in 1972 authored an article for the *New York Times* suggesting innovative methods for securing more suburban affordable housing. Ramapo's construction of public housing became the most divisive issue in local politics. Although the Court of Appeals of New York explicitly determined that Ramapo's development controls were not "efforts at immunization or exclusion," overflowing public hearings on the matter demonstrated widespread social and fiscal objections to any further subsidized housing.[22] Regional fair housing advocates were unimpressed with the town's mere 198 public housing units (three-quarters of which were reserved for the elderly). They demanded additional multifamily apartment zoning so that private developers might construct more affordable housing. McAlevey responded that it was not likely that such zoning would create affordable housing, given rapidly escalating building costs and declining federal housing subsidies during the early and mid-1970s. Instead, he argued that developers would simply build denser market-rate housing, further burdening the town with demands on public services, schools, and, ultimately, its taxpayers. "Ramapo will relax its zoning ordinance to admit various types of apartments," McAlevey wrote, "only if a social purpose beyond the enrichment of the builders is achieved." Ultimately, fiscal concerns in Ramapo trumped social and environmental ones not because of any fundamental incompatibility but because of the local political imperatives and extra-local market forces that circumscribed town policymakers' realistic options.[23]

The Politics of Suburban Affordable Housing

While suburban reformers were struggling to manage growth and reform land use, another set of issues simultaneously moved to the center of the debates over the future of the Northeast Corridor's suburbs. They focused on questions about whether suburban development should continue to reinforce patterns of segregation by race and class or whether growth should take a new, more equitable form. In the late 1960s and early 1970s the affordable housing issue gained unprecedented public attention, and arguments in favor of breaking down the walls of suburban exclusion gained many new and significantly more powerful supporters. Not only did some local jurisdictions—as we have seen in Montgomery County,

Fairfax County, and the Town of Ramapo—show a willingness to increase their stock of affordable housing, but regional political actors, including governors, state courts, a state legislature, and the corridor's most capable public development agency also joined the cause. Yet few issues proved more contentious. Politicians, local advocacy organizations, and citizens divided on the issue, and prominent efforts to construct affordable housing in this period usually touched off firestorms of protest that tapped into both explicit and unspoken concerns about taxes, race, property values, home rule, and the environment. These confrontations over affordable housing—like the battles over land-use management and growth controls—offer another revealing glimpse into the limits and opportunities of suburban reform. That advocates for affordable housing lost so much more often than they won during these years reveals a great deal about how clashing discontents and the practical impact of suburban political fragmentation combined to reinforce the suburban growth status quo.

New Jersey—the nation's most suburban state—provides a particularly prominent example of the new politics of affordable housing. The Garden State witnessed an outpouring of high-level political support for increasing affordable housing in the suburbs during the late 1960s and 1970s. To varying degrees, three different governors supported fair housing during this period, and the New Jersey Supreme Court issued a ground-breaking ruling in 1975 requiring localities to alter their exclusionary zoning policies. But despite these significant endorsements of affordable housing, by the end of the decade virtually nothing had changed in terms of actual housing built.

The succession of New Jersey gubernatorial administrations addressing fair housing issues in the suburbs began with that of Democratic Governor Richard Hughes, who served from 1966 through 1970, and the efforts of Hughes's Department of Community Affairs commissioner, Paul Ylvisaker. Previously a key figure at the Ford Foundation, where he helped develop programs that became models for the federal war on poverty, Ylvisaker introduced legislation in 1969 that reflected his beliefs that suburbs' local zoning authority "is a dangerous thing" when used for exclusionary purposes. Suburbs, Ylvisaker argued, needed "to rejoin the American Union." His Land Use Planning and Development Law, which Governor Hughes endorsed, explicitly sought to provide housing in each state locality for all economic and social groups and placed the legal burden on local governments to prove that their zoning was not exclusionary. Republican Governor William Cahill, who served from 1970 to 1973, endorsed a somewhat less bold approach, but as part of a series of proposed housing laws introduced in 1971, he advocated the introduction of state-determined low-cost housing quotas for every county, which would then be responsible for working with their localities to achieve these goals. In the mid-1970s, Cahill's successor, Democratic Governor Brendan Byrne, further pursued legislation that would create state housing quotas and voluntary housing allocations. But despite consistent executive support, every fair housing proposal met a similar fate in the state legislature: Ylvisaker's and Cahill's bills never made it out of the relevant legislative committees and Byrne backed away from even introducing his first piece of housing legislation in 1975 because of staunch opposition. Stated objections usually centered on home rule issues. Referring to "the czar in Trenton," one typical suburban opponent of Ylvisaker and his bill decried the "definite encroachment on home rule." Passing Cahill's laws, another opponent argued, would be to let "Big Brother step on the little guy." No matter whether under Democratic or Republican control during these years, a large majority of the state legislature rejected any and all state fair housing plans, and thus governors' prominent support ultimately meant little.[24]

Much more famously, the New Jersey Supreme Court's 1975 ruling in *Southern Burlington County NAACP v. Township of Mount Laurel* established a judicial beachhead in the fair housing fight. Originally filed in a lower court in 1971, the case arose out of an attempt by the Springville Action Council, a group of mostly rural blacks who were long-time Mount Laurel residents, to win a zoning change that would allow it to build thirty-six garden apartments for low-income tenants. The township of Mount Laurel—a then semirural area fifteen miles away from Philadelphia in the midst of rapid suburban growth—rejected the application, refusing to reconsider its minimum half-acre zoning code that effectively banned the construction of all apartments. With the assistance of the federally financed Camden Regional Legal Services, the Springville Action Council sued and won the lower court case in 1972. On appeal, the New Jersey Supreme Court used the case to establish its then-novel doctrine in support of "fair share" housing. Utilizing legally expansive notions of "equal protection" and "general welfare," the court ruled that localities must affirmatively make preparations for low- and moderate-income housing "at least to the extent of the municipality's fair share of the present and prospective regional need therefore." For the first time on the corridor and in the nation, it seemed that suburbs would be legally required to allow a much wider price range of housing within their borders.[25]

But even the clear intent of the state Supreme Court would not so easily translate into substantive changes in housing policies. While the 1975 *Mount Laurel* decision expressed an unambiguous vision of the ends that the court required, it dealt with the means much less clearly. Specifically, the state Supreme Court ruled that a given locality "should first have full opportunity to itself act without judicial supervision" and that the plaintiff and defendant should together figure out what regional fair share actually meant. Such a vague court-ordered remedy ensured years more of legal wrangling that thwarted the construction of affordable housing projects in Mount Laurel and throughout New Jersey. In the case of Mount Laurel, the township responded to the decision by rezoning three small parcels of land for apartments containing a total of twenty acres, but none of the parcels—for either financial, availability, or environmental reasons— offered a realistic opportunity to develop low-income housing. Townships all over the state reacted in similar ways, and as a result the mid- and late 1970s ended up witnessing a new avalanche of lawsuits rather affordable housing units built. As the legal scholar Charles Haar concluded, "municipal resistance . . . made a near mockery of [the court's] much-heralded ruling in *Mount Laurel I*." Ultimately, not until subsequent state Supreme Court rulings commonly referred to as *Mount Laurel II* (1983) and *Mount Laurel III* (1986) that took much more active remedy approaches were significant numbers of low- and moderate-income housing units finally built in New Jersey's suburbs.[26]

The politics of fair housing in Massachusetts during these years provides additional lessons about the suburban development process. In Massachusetts, the state legislature did what New Jersey and other corridor states resisted: in 1969 it passed a law giving prospective developers of low-income housing recourse when localities' exclusionary zoning decisions denied them the chance to build. In what became widely known as the Anti-Snob Zoning Act, the law created a state Housing Appeals Committee that was empowered to overrule local zoning decisions and grant qualified housing developers comprehensive permits to proceed with the construction of low- and moderate-income housing. Localities with less than their fair share of affordable housing—defined as less than 10 percent of total units—would be unable, it seemed, to prevent such development from being built in their communities.[27]

However, just as the effectiveness of attempted executive and judicial policymaking ran into stubborn obstacles in New Jersey, so too did the limits of legislative policymaking soon become apparent in Massachusetts. Putting this novel legislation into practice proved much more difficult than the law's authors—a collection of liberal state legislators—had hoped. On the one hand, by 1975 the Housing Appeals Committee had successfully withstood constitutional challenges and gone on to overrule twenty-two of the twenty-four local zoning decisions brought before it. On the other hand, of these twenty-two cases, only two projects had so far made it to the ground-breaking stage. While the Housing Appeals Commit-tee added a new legal avenue to alter exclusionary zoning, it did little or nothing to remove other practical hurdles to building in the suburbs such as stalling tactics by localities, environmental laws, and the insti-tutional weakness of so many low-income housing developers. All three factors came into play in the case of Concord, Massachusetts. There the newly formed Concord Home Owning Corporation sought to build a small mixed-income development and eventually won its case before the Hous-ing Appeals Committee. But the state Department of Natural Resources then ruled the swampy land, which the town had previously sought to buy for conservation purposes, unfit for such intensive uses. Meanwhile, after already experiencing years of delays, the novice developers lacked the money to purchase an option on new land that it would have to hold onto while starting the entire local and state zoning process over again. Such inexperience and financial precariousness handicapped the efforts of many groups seeking to build affordable housing in the suburbs, but even organizations better prepared encountered often debilitating obsta-cles. In the relatively liberal, older Boston suburb of Newton, the Newton Community Development Foundation (NCDF) had the financial support of more than 700 local residents and had on its staff and board of direc-tors a wealth of expertise in local and state politics, nonprofit housing, design, construction, and financing. Initially, many town officials were supportive too. But once NCDF announced a plan to build 508 low- and moderate-income units on ten sites in the spring of 1970, significant public outcry created a familiar, tortuous process: lengthy hearings, tactical com-promises, and determined opposition by critical town officials. When its conciliatory strategy had failed by 1971, NCDF switched to confrontation and took its case to the state Housing Appeals Committee. Yet largely as a result of town stalling, two years later the committee had yet to rule on the case and NCDF's once healthy bank account had dried up. The group was forced because of financial pressures to give up its options on most of its planned sites, effectively ending its once grand plans even before the legal issues had been settled.[28]

The 1969 Anti-Snob Zoning Act, therefore, ultimately put only a modest dent in the armor of suburban economic exclusivity in the state. Housing Appeals Committee decisions led directly to only a small addition of low- and mixed-income units in Massachusetts' suburbs through the mid-1970s. The Massachusetts Department of Community Affairs estimated in 1974 that the state had a total need for 400,000 low- and moderate-income units, yet the relatively effective Massachusetts Housing Finance Agency had funded only about 25,000 mixed-income units by 1975, just a third of these in suburban communities. And the vast majority of subsidized units in suburban Boston were reserved for the elderly. Twenty years after the law's passage, 95 Massachusetts towns still had yet to build their first unit of subsidized housing and only a handful of suburbs were anywhere near the law's original goal, which had called for 10 percent of each community's housing stock to be subsidized.[29]

Given the lessons simultaneously being learned in New Jersey and Massachusetts, the New York State Urban Development Corporation (UDC) inspired particular optimism among suburban fair housing activists up and down the corridor and throughout the nation. Created in 1968 after a legendary bout of legislative arm-twisting by Governor Nelson Rockefeller, the UDC possessed more extensive and wide-ranging development authorities than any other state government entity in modern American history. It operated as an independent public corporation, one empowered to plan, build, and manage various types of residential, commercial, and civic projects. It was given the ability to float its own bonds and—most controversially—to override local building regulations, including local zoning ordinances. And, finally, Rockefeller brought in a politically savvy, nationally known policymaker to head the UDC: Edward J. Logue—the experienced, combative former head of both New Haven's and Boston's huge redevelopment programs. Right away, Logue pledged to build affordable housing in the suburbs. Writing in an early UDC report, Logue stated: "It is my personal conviction that a modest amount of such housing in a large number of suburban communities will ensure decent living conditions for many of the inner city poor, and yet preserve the character and strengths which have made the suburban communities so appealing. It may be that a society which builds the kinds of walls we too often find around us can endure. But surely that is not the kind of America we should strive to build."[30] The UDC seemed to have it all: development powers and expertise, institutional capacity, money, political backing, and the desire to address suburban fair housing issues. That by 1973 the UDC's efforts to build affordable housing in the suburbs outside of New York City had collapsed for good provides a final, revealing window on the politics of fair housing.

How and why did this precipitous fall take place? The first answer lay in how suburban political opinion often expressed itself. In affluent Westchester County just north of New York City, where the UDC's suburban housing efforts were focused, both significant support and opposition to the plans existed, but opponents' better organization and their headline-gathering alacrity drowned out or intimidated supporters. No stranger to controversy, the politically crafty Logue assessed the situation and thought sufficient political backing existed. First and foremost, Westchester was the home base for much of the Rockefeller family and its vast holdings. Nelson Rockefeller, obviously the county's most important political figure, backed Logue's suburban plans. "It seems reasonable and proper to me," Rockefeller wrote, "that a fair share of new housing in a suburban town should be within the price reach of average income families." Westchester County Executive Ed Michaelian actively supported the UDC, and Logue expected local builders (who would receive construction contracts) and major locally based corporations (who often complained about the difficulty in attracting back-office employees to work in a place they could not afford to live) to come out in favor as well. Not surprisingly, local liberal interest groups concerned about housing issues like the League of Women Voters and the county branch of the Urban League backed the plans for subsidized housing in the county's affluent suburbs, as did metropolitan-focused organizations like the Regional Plan Association. Furthermore, a public opinion survey commissioned by the UDC in 1972 indicated the existence of significant support for affordable housing throughout the county. And a majority of local town supervisors in the jurisdictions to be built in expressed in private meetings with Logue and his UDC staff a willingness to cooperate.[31]

But once Logue announced the details of the UDC's housing plans at a meeting of the Westchester Association of Town Supervisors in January 1972, opponents dominated the political debate. Despite the modesty of the proposal—the UDC's "fair share" program called for the construction of only 100 units of mixed-income housing in each of nine relatively affluent northern and central Westchester towns—alarmed detractors swiftly and strongly organized themselves. Within days of the announcement, they created United Towns for Home Rule, and tens of thousands of dollars were raised to mount the fight. 3,000 people flocked to one public hearing, and bumper stickers, posters and petitions appeared everywhere.[32]

At least as important as the strident opposition that United Towns for Home Rule both reflected and created, however, was the fact that virtually no local politicians from the nine towns proved willing to ally themselves publicly with the plan. A few of these local politicians explicitly rejected the premise that their towns should play any role in providing affordable housing that other parts of the county clearly needed, and some others earnestly opposed all instances of home rule curtailment. But far more of them publicly opposed the UDC because no political incentive existed to support it. After the January 1972 meeting with town supervisors at which the UDC first revealed its "fair share" plans, Logue reported to Rockefeller that "most of them seemed to be willing to cooperate, although they may not be willing to do so very publicly." A year later, Logue again reported: "it has been our frequent experience that local officials, understanding the need for housing, will not object to our proposals but equally refuse to support them positively." And innumerable meeting memos and correspondence recording private relations between the UDC and the nine towns during this period indicated both a far more cordial tone and a greater willingness to compromise than existed in most local politicians' public stances.[33]

In suburban Westchester, however, there was simply nothing to be gained politically by actively supporting the UDC. No projects or patronage with which Logue regularly rewarded supporters in fractious urban settings possessed any appeal in the affluent suburbs. And given that the opponents of the "fair share" plan inevitably remained more outspoken than supporters—even the most liberal suburbanites, after all, were likely merely to accept rather than embrace the social obligation to provide the affordable housing the region needed—virtually no local leaders saw any advantage in positioning themselves with Logue and the UDC. With elections approaching in November 1972, criticizing the UDC and its housing plans became a staple of local campaigns. As one town supervisor commented at the time: "It would be political suicide for me in an election year to support UDC openly."[34]

The way that the Westchester opponents of subsidized housing shaped and overwhelmed the debate disproportionate to their numbers combined with a second factor in determining the fate of the UDC plans—the near immovability of the suburban development status quo. It required a rare alignment of political forces to accomplish something as unusual as the construction of subsidized suburban housing, and while the UDC with its rare supralocal authority seemed to wield sufficient power even after the outbreak of public opposition, such power did not last long. As in so many cases of plans that ran counter to the suburban status quo, delayed development projects often turned into defeated projects. In the hopes of creating political support, Logue had taken over three years since the UDC's creation in 1968 to go public with his Westchester affordable housing plans, and after the explosion of public opposition in 1972 further delays ensued. Timed to calm the political waters before voters cast their ballots in November, in September 1972 Governor Rockefeller imposed a four-month moratorium in which the towns would have an opportunity to come up with their owns plans for subsidized housing. When the moratorium ended in January 1973, Logue proclaimed his intention to go ahead and use his zoning override powers to build in the nine towns. But the delay had proven fatal: by then, financial and political circumstances had dramatically changed, and the window of opportunity for the UDC to attempt launching ambitious new projects in the suburbs had effectively closed. Earlier in January, the Nixon administration halted all federal housing subsidies, without which the UDC did not have the funds to build the suburban Westchester housing. The nine towns well understood this, and—recognizing the UDC's sudden weakness—as a result even the two towns that previously had been most accepting of the "fair share" plan reversed their relatively accommodating positions.[35]

The Nixon administration's cutoff of housing subsidies not only jeopardized Logue's suburban plans, but it dramatically reduced the financial viability of the entire UDC enterprise, which included dozens of active projects around the state. Within months, the UDC desperately needed increased state bonding authority merely to survive. As Rockefeller lost his will to stand in the way of mounting suburban opposition, he cut a deal: in exchange for granting the new bonding authority that would keep the UDC in business, the state legislature both stripped away its zoning override powers and gave localities a veto over all UDC projects in their jurisdictions. Divested of its unique powers, the UDC lost whatever chance it might once have had to fulfill its promise of breaking suburban housing barriers. The Westchester suburban housing plans stalled permanently, and elsewhere in the New York metropolitan area its other suburban subsidized housing projects failed as well. The UDC was now just like any other developer—one with no recourse when town boards rejected their proposals.[36]

The Logic and Limits of Reform

The politics of suburban growth controls and the politics of affordable housing provide two complementary perspectives on the logic and limits of reform on the postwar corridor. In response to the rapid physical growth that transformed so many woods and fields into freshly bulldozed suburbs of homes, offices, and retail establishments, the volume of public outcry increased dramatically as the web of discontents grew more complex. By the late 1960s and 1970s, the markedly increased depth and breadth of popular concerns about development helped stimulate unprecedented efforts to reshape the pace, type, and quality of suburban growth. Ultimately, however, the whole turned out to be less than the sum of its parts. Discontents with growth collided at least as frequently as they combined with one another, and the fragmented political structures of suburban government vastly reduced the possibilities for shaping disparate discontents into coherent policy reform. That such a mixed outcome emerged even in a region and an era when both Democrats and Republicans generally approved of the active use of government to solve social and economic problems teaches important lessons about the internal tensions within postwar American liberalism and the ways that suburban growth helped reveal and bring them to prominence.

The clash of ideas and institutions that the discontents with suburban growth precipitated left an ambiguous legacy. Critics of suburban development succeeded in discrediting many of the growth orthodoxies of the early postwar period. But the substantive concerns these critics raised were satisfied only in very partial ways and thinly scattered locations. As a result, subsequent decades have witnessed a familiar combination of festering popular frustrations and unresolved political divisions over sprawl, environmental degradation, and the lack of affordable housing. What has been lost, however, is the earlier optimism about the possibilities of reform—hope that was dashed on the rocks of fragmented local government and confused public wants.

NINE

Reshaping the American Dream

Immigrants, Ethnic Minorities, and the Politics of the New Suburbs

MICHAEL JONES-CORREA

Over the last generation, America's metropolitan areas have been transformed. More than half of all Americans now live in "suburbia," urban areas outside of what the U.S. Census defines as "central cities." The stereotypical view of suburbs is that they are overwhelmingly white,[1] characterized by unexciting and largely conservative politics. These generalizations, however, are faulty. Even during the postwar suburban boom, commentators were already noting the growing incidence of minority (mostly black) suburbanization.[2] The increase in the numbers of the black middle class has only accelerated African American migration to the suburbs.[3]

Immigration, already on the upswing after World War II, has also played a key role in the changing demographics of suburbia. The 1965 Hart-Cellar Act abolished national origin quota systems that had particularly favored immigrants of Northern European origin and instead placed a new emphasis on family reunification. These two provisions radically changed the nature of immigration to the United States: the abolition of national origin quotas allowed large-scale immigration from Asia, while the family reunification preferences contributed to the surge of immigration from Latin America and elsewhere. By 2000 there were 28.4 million

TABLE 9.1 **Population by area of residence, in percent**

	Urban	Suburban	Rural
Immigrants	47	48	5
Native-born	28	51	21
Non-Hispanic white	22	53	22
Black	55	31	14
Hispanic	48	44	8
Asian American	45	51	4

Source: U.S. Census, 1999 Current Population Survey.

first-generation immigrants in the United States, making up 10.4 percent of the nation's total population. Whereas previously most immigration had come from Europe, 80 percent of immigrants arriving in the United States between 1970 and 2000 were from Latin America and Asia, with only 15 percent hailing from Europe. These immigrants settled overwhelmingly in urban areas in the United States, and increasingly in the suburbia surrounding central cities.

So as immigration increased through the last decades of the twentieth century, suburbia rapidly became even more multiethnic.[4] After 1965, immigrants, having become economically and socially established, have been moving, as had previous waves of immigrants before them, out of central city areas and settling in outlying suburban areas. Indeed, one of the more interesting and understudied phenomena of the recent immigration is that a substantial portion has been skipping settlement in cities entirely, moving directly into suburban neighborhoods.[5] Much of the recent literature on immigrants and ethnic minorities, however, still maintains a traditional focus on the urban core.[6] For both researchers and policymakers, immigrants and other ethnic minorities in suburbia are, in many respects, an unknown quantity.

To give a sense of the scale of the phenomenon, a few statistics will suffice: In the 1990s, 94 percent of the foreign-born settled in metropolitan areas; over 40 percent lived in the New York and Los Angeles metro areas alone. Forty-eight percent of immigrants resided in suburbs.[7] Thanks in large part to the suburbanization of immigrants, the percentages of minorities in suburbs increased dramatically as well: in 1999, 31 percent of blacks, 44 percent of Latinos, and 51 percent of Asian Americans lived in suburbs.[8] These figures, confirmed by the initial releases from the 2000 Census, indicate that the suburbanization of immigrants, as well as that of ethnic and racial minorities more generally, is approaching, and in some cases has surpassed, that of the population as a whole.[9]

Suburban residents are now also a majority of American voters, and, by highlighting issues like gun control or tax cuts, both the Democratic and Republican parties have shaped their messages in response. Clearly suburbs have an increasingly important place in American politics. Yet the literature on suburban politics, which still sees suburbia as overwhelmingly dominated by the concerns of the white middle class, has not caught up with the demographic reality. Because suburbs are often thought to be still homogeneously white and middle-class, the politics of suburbs are generally assumed to be more conservative than those of urban areas and to deal largely with allocative issues rather than distributive ones (that is, providing basic "housekeeping" services rather than shifting resources from the most well off to the least well off). The arguments for the ethnic and racial homogeneity of suburbs and their conservative politics go hand in hand. Some commentators have pointed out that racial homogeneity may reinforce residents' sense of community, leading to higher rates of participation in local organizations and politics.[10] This sense of community is heightened by local self-reliance, since the needs of homogeneous middle-class suburbs can often be met through their own resources. As a result of their similarities in race and class, the argument goes, suburbanites become inward looking and defensive of their perquisites, increasingly dissatisfied with federal programs and the national tax policies that sustain those programs (which, as far as they see, do little to benefit suburban residents).[11]

If suburbia's low-key, fiscally conservative politics rely on the absence of any racial and class differences, what happens, then, to suburban politics as suburbia becomes more diverse? And as ethnic and racial minorities, both native and foreign-born, move into suburbs, how does this experience change both their politics and opportunities for political mobilization? Some scholars have hypothesized that less homogeneous suburbs become more "citylike" as they grapple with problems ranging from low-income housing to crime and that this inevitably leads to shifts away from conservative politics[12] and to the rise of a more contentious, albeit more actively engaged, citizenry.[13] But whatever racial and ethnic changes take place in suburbia, the shape of suburban politics will never match that of the urban core. The political fragmentation of suburbia, the design of its institutions, and its use of physical space will ensure that the dynamics of suburban politics will remain, to some extent, distinctive.

In this chapter I explore the changing nature of suburban politics as the result of rapidly increasing racial and ethnic diversification, much of it due to immigration; in it I set out new and emerging themes in the politics of suburbia, not only as indication of how suburbia is changing, but to set out both an agenda for research and to make an argument for an appropriate methodological approach to this kind of research. The section that follows poses some general questions for the study of the new suburban politics: how are ethnic and racial minorities incorporated into suburban politics? How do they change suburban politics, and, in turn, how are they changed by it? Next I focus the discussion on one particular metropolitan area: Washington, D.C. As described in greater detail below, suburban D.C., like other major immigrant gateway areas, has undergone a rapid transformation as the result of African American middle-class flight from the city, and large-scale immigration. These changing demographics trigger corresponding changes in the nature of suburban politics through issue areas. As a result of its great ethnic and racial diversity, suburban D.C. politics has changed in four significant areas: growth, education, quality of life, and representation. Drawing from this overview of changes in the D.C. metropolitan area, I argue that the study of immigration and ethnic and racial politics in suburbs requires some careful thinking about research strategies. The study of immigrants and immigrant mobilization in suburbia, for instance, cannot simply replicate the form of the classic urban ethnography: something new is needed. Finally, I conclude by summarizing what we know now and what we have yet to learn about immigrants and other minorities in suburbia.

Some General Questions

The locus of this chapter lies at the unexplored intersection of suburban politics and racial and ethnic relations in the United States. The unfamiliarity of the terrain means that there are a number of unanswered questions still to be investigated. Three of these are explored briefly here: the incorporation of new political actors in suburbia, the impact of new actors on suburban politics, and the effects of suburbia on these new actors—immigrants and minorities—themselves.

What are the effects of suburban political institutions on the participation of new immigrant and minority political actors that have moved to suburbia? Do the institutional and structural settings of suburbs trump or enable the particular concerns of new ethnic actors in suburban areas? It may be, for instance, that the institutional design of suburbia—a "weak government" ethos, nonpartisan politics, multiple specialized governments (water districts, school districts) with little centralization or coordination—proves murky and opaque to new arrivals. Rather than try to decipher the tangled schema of suburban politics, new arrivals may shift their focus to national or transnational politics, or perhaps decide to opt out of politics altogether. It may also be, however, that the layering of politics in suburbs (of city and county governments, school districts, water boards, etc.) actually provides multiple avenues for the entry and participation of new arrivals in political life. There is some indication that the more intimate nature of politics in the smaller cities and municipalities that make up American suburbia leads to higher rates of civic and political participation.[14] There is also ample anecdotal evidence suggesting that immigrants and minorities have an easier time getting elected to political office in smaller cities on the peripheries of metropolitan areas than they do in larger urban cores (the Los Angeles and Miami metro areas are both good examples). How, in the end, do immigrants and minorities respond to institutional settings in suburbia?

Given the plurality of policy arenas available to new political actors, do different institutional arenas provide distinct entrées into politics (for example, schools boards versus zoning committees; city councils versus county-level governments)? There may be ways that some arenas might allow for the participation of groups and individuals who might not have mobilized before—immigrant women might choose to take leading roles in parent-teacher associations and school boards, for instance. How might different institutional arenas affect political outcomes for newcomers? Differences might occur, for instance, between arenas dominated by elected officials versus those dominated by political appointees or civil service bureaucrats.

The Impact of New Actors on Suburban Politics

The politics of suburbia, some have argued, is based on the principle of exclusion, with much of the energy of suburban political actors spent shoring up and defending exclusionary barriers.[15] These barriers are meant to preserve the class and racial homogeneity prized by white middle-class suburban homeowners. The increasing racial and ethnic diversity within suburbs, however, signals that either these exclusionary tactics are working less well or perhaps are now targeted more at protecting property interests than in maintaining racial segregation. If the new suburban population is more ethnically diverse, is it still just as homogeneous along class lines, with new residents self-selecting to match the characteristics of present middle-class suburban residents? If so, then suburban politics may change little, if at all. Or is it the case that with the infusion of ethnic and racial minorities, suburban politics is also becoming more diverse along class lines and, by implication, less fiscally conservative?

The evidence is mixed, suggesting that while there is a good deal of self-selection along class lines for minorities in suburbs, this may be truer for some ethnic groups than others.[16] Also, minorities in suburbia still, by and large, have fewer resources than white residents do. African Americans in suburbia, for instance, have higher rates of education and income than their counterparts in central cities, but at the same time their average socioeconomic attainment is still below that of white suburban residents.[17]

If new minorities in suburbia have different socioeconomic backgrounds, does class overshadow ethnicity? For instance, if middle-class and poorer immigrant Latinos live in the same metropolitan area, will ethnic similarities lead to organizational links and common political mobilization, or will middle-class Latinos find more in common with other middle-class homeowners, regardless of ethnicity or race? If ethnicity links individuals together despite class differences, then this may lead to changes in the nature and tone of suburban politics, even if suburbia remains largely middle class.

With the introduction of new immigrants and other racial and ethnic minorities, does politics in suburbia remain allocative rather than distributive? Indeed, are these terms themselves still apt? It may be that issues that were once thought of as allocative (school funding, waste disposal, the placement of new roads, the provision of an adequate water supply) now take on distributive dimensions, for instance, moving tax revenue from property owners (disproportionately non-Hispanic whites) to schools (where the students are often the children of new immigrant and ethnic minorities). A sign of shifting suburban politics may be the rising resistance among older, largely white, residents to the demands and pressures placed on goods and services by newer arrivals, so that issues that were previously considered neutral become highly contested or issues that were contested (slow growth versus growth, for instance) take on ethnic overtones.

Are class differences reflected in variations across suburbs? On the one hand, it may be that newer ethnic and racial minorities are moving into suburbs that are largely older, more densely populated, and adjacent to central cities and thus share many of the central urban core's problems in infrastructure, resources, and social ills.[18] If so, analysis by age of suburb (say, by average age of housing) might reveal significant differences in the way new ethnic and racial minorities encounter and address social problems across suburban municipalities. On the other hand, there may be enough commonality across suburbs so that the physical layout of suburbs shapes political outcomes regardless of the ethnic and racial makeup of suburban neighborhoods. Several commentators have noted, for instance, that the physical characteristics of suburbia (dispersed residential communities with low population densities highly dependent on the automobile for transportation) have social and even political effects.[19] Are these effects present across all suburbs, regardless of the socioeconomic or ethnic characteristics of their residents?

The Effects of Suburbia on New Political Actors

What is the role of ethnic organizations in the suburbs? Much of the social science literature on urban ethnic organization focuses on place-based neighborhood organizations in central cities, built around a sense of compact geographic "community." But "community" in suburbia may not refer to a resident's immediate geographic surroundings at all. Instead, it might be situated around a place of worship miles away from an individual's place of residence or at an ethnic grocery store or restaurant that serves as a gathering place more miles away or at a place of work owned by ethnic compatriots. Does ethnic organization in suburbs still follow neighborhood lines, or does it draw its members across a region along functional lines? In the suburbs, for instance, where an ethnic group might be widely scattered, an organization might attract members from far beyond its immediate vicinity. What implications does this have for ethnic mobilization and politics? For one, it may be that the spatial organization of ethnic groups does not intersect with the geography of political jurisdictions. What happens then? How do ethnic organizations adapt to suburban settings? If new technologies such as the Internet allow organizations to surpass some of the barriers of physical distance, what are the implications of unequal access to computers and other means of communication?

For immigrants and other racial or ethnic groups residing in suburbs, does the experience of being a minority in suburbia reinforce ethnic or racial identities? Do these become more pronounced, serving as an additional impetus to political mobilization? It could be the case, for instance, that being a highly visible minority, however well-off, in a largely white suburban community might lead to a defensive ethnic mobilization on the part of new arrivals, if only to preserve a sense of social and cultural distinctiveness. Note the attempts of relatively well-off South Asian immigrants to preserve patterns of arranged marriages for their offspring, with video, Internet, and e-mail used to broker and cement betrothals. Ethnic mobilization might also occur as the result of discrimination by members of the larger white population, like the targeting of South Asian immigrants by "dot buster" teenage gangs in New Jersey or the beating of Central American day workers on Long Island.

However, even if racial and ethnic identities become salient in suburbia, this may not translate into political mobilization. Ethnic and racial minorities, placed in a context dominated by whites, may feel they have little chance to make any impact and so choose not to participate in civic and political life. Again, there is some evidence to suggest that while whites in a largely white suburban setting are more likely to participate, blacks living in a largely white setting are less likely to participate in any way. This may not be true, however, for Latinos and Asian Americans.[20] Why these differences among ethnic and racial groups might manifest themselves merits further exploration.

In general, is there variance across ethnic groups? For instance, the much lower segregation rates of Asians and Latinos (as opposed to African Americans) in suburbs[21] likely have very different consequences for their social and political accommodation. Because blacks in suburbia are more likely to be concentrated, this will likely facilitate their ability to elect African American representatives. Latinos, and particularly Asian Americans, who are more dispersed, might have to seek political influence in other ways.

———

These questions center around three themes: (1) the incorporation of new actors in suburbia, (2) the impact of these new actors on suburban politics, and (3) the effect of suburbia on new actors. The first will likely see variation across policy arenas: that is, new actors may experience politics and political incorporation differently depending on the political arena they are engaged in, whether it is education through the school board, zoning through the planning board, and the like. The second theme may well see variation across different suburbs. If suburban politics changes in response to new ethnic and racial minorities, these changes should be felt differently by suburban location (suburbs in "home-rule" versus "Dillon's rule" states, or older, "inner-ring" suburbs versus newer "outer-ring" suburbs, for instance).[22] Finally, the third theme suggests variation across and within ethnic groups (between African Americans and Asian Americans or Latinos, for example).

The Case of Metropolitan Washington, D.C.

Metropolitan Washington, D.C., like many of the nation's metro areas, has experienced rapid demographic change over the last twenty years. Its population grew by 16 percent over ten years (a larger increase than any other comparable metropolitan area, outstripping growth in Los Angeles, New York, and Chicago, for instance). In 2000 the metropolitan area numbered 5.4 million people, up from 4.7 million in 1990, making it among the dozen largest in the United States, but not nearly as large as the two behemoths of New York and Los Angeles. The D.C. metropolitan area is also overwhelmingly suburban; Washington, D.C., accounts for only 10 percent of the region's population. While the population of the District of Columbia itself has continued to shrink (by 6 percent between 1990 and 2000), the Northern Virginia suburbs grew by 25 percent, and those in Maryland by 17 percent.

The metro region is often thought of as composed of three distinct locales: the slow-growth "urban core" (the District of Columbia, Arlington County, and the City of Alexandria); the "inner suburbs" (Montgomery and Prince George's counties in Maryland, and Fairfax County in Virginia); and the fast-growing "outer counties" to the west (Virginia's Loudoun and Maryland's Frederick County). Though growth is most evident on the margins of the metro area, the largest employment sectors, and hence populations, are in the inner suburbs.

Much of the growth of the region's population over the last decade has been due to the increase of immigrants and minorities (African Americans, Asian Americans, and Latinos) in the greater Washington area. The D.C. metro region has ranked in the top ten immigrant recipient areas of the country since the early 1980s, and the D.C. suburbs have ranked high among the residential preferences of the nation's burgeoning black middle class. African Americans are the largest minority group in the metro area, making up 22 percent of the population. Asian and Latin American immigrants and their descendants make up approximately 15 percent of the population. Salvadorans are the single largest immigrant group, but make up only 10.5 percent of the total immigrant population. The top ten immigrant nationality groups (from El Salvador, Vietnam, India, China, the Philippines, South Korea, Ethiopia, Iran, Pakistan, and Peru) account for only half of all immigrants to the area. The other half are accounted for by immigrants from over 183 countries, none of which contributes more than 3 percent of the metro area's foreign-born population. The immigrant population in the D.C. metropolitan area is somewhat more diverse than that of other major metro areas, but it is not atypical of suburban immigrant populations along the eastern seaboard.

Ethnic and racial minorities now make up more then 75 percent of the population in Prince George's County, and 40 percent of that in neighboring Montgomery County. In Northern Virginia, minorities make up almost half of the population in Arlington and Alexandria (44 and 46 percent, respectively) and a third of Fairfax County's population (32 percent). Minority populations vary considerably by municipality, but are present in substantial numbers even in the outlying suburbs in areas like Loudoun County (17 percent minorities). The variety of ethnic and racial groups in the D.C. metropolitan area allows for comparison across immigrant groups and between foreign- and native-born (both black and white).

Unlike some of the other "melting pot" metropolitan areas that share its demographic characteristics, publicly contested issues in the Washington metro area are primarily adjudicated by county governments, not by counties together with a scattershot of independent municipalities. The Metropolitan Washington Council of Governments, the umbrella organization of the region's governments, has only 19 members, including the governments of Washington, D.C., itself and its surrounding counties. Though county governments are arguably equally important in other "melting pot" metros like New York, Los Angeles, or Miami, a comparable organization in the Los Angeles metro area would have close to a hundred member governments, while one in Miami–Ft. Lauderdale would have over sixty. On the one hand, then, political arenas in Washington are relatively uncomplicated, facilitating comparisons among them. On the other hand, although the number of relevant political arenas is relatively small for a metro area of its size, because the D.C. metro area extends into two quite different states, comparisons among political arenas inevitably highlight state-level differences as well in a way other metro areas generally do not.[23]

Like other "melting pot" metros, the Washington area has received a lot of immigration in a relatively short time; within a period of twenty years, the suburban counties have become significantly ethnically and racially diverse. Like other metro areas on the eastern seaboard, but unlike its counterparts to the west, the immigrant population in the D.C. metro area is not dominated by any single ethnic group. Again, like many metro areas in the East (as well as Midwest and South), African Americans are still the single largest minority group, but they are being eclipsed demographically by the increase in the immigrant population. The shifting demographics of the various minority populations make ethnic and racial politics in Washington's suburbs all the more complex.

Suburban Political Issues

What follows is a preliminary description and analysis of ethnic and racial issues in suburbia, as they have been playing out in the Washington metropolitan area. Table 9.2 is a first approximation of the set of salient issues from news stories in which race, ethnicity, and/or immigration play a role, stories that appeared in the local news or "Metro" section of the *Washington Post* from 1998–2003.[24] The issues are listed together with the "issue arena" in which they first appeared—that is, with the set of bureaucratic actors dealing with the issue most directly.

I outline some of the debates around four of these issues—growth, education, quality of life, and political incorporation—in greater detail below.

TABLE 9.2 **Issue areas and arenas, Washington, D.C., Metropolitan Area**

General issue	Specific issue	Issue arena
Growth		planning commission, county supervisors
Housing	affordable housing	planning commission, county supervisors
	housing discrimination	county human rights commissions, realtors
	mortgage discrimination	county human rights commissions, lenders
	segregation	housing market, realtors
	home ownership	housing market, Fannie Mae
Education	funding, taxes	county supervisors, school board
	gifted & talented	school board
	school names	school board
	ESOL	school board
	desegregation	school board, federal courts
Quality of life	overcrowding	county planning boards, neighborhood associations
	street parking	county planning boards, neighborhood associations
	lawn parking	county planning boards, neighborhood associations
	zoning	county planning boards, neighborhood associations
	day laborer sites	county supervisors
	small business	county supervisors
Crime	police brutality	police
	crime	police
	hate crime	police
Social services	bilingual translation	courts, county/city agencies
Political incorporation		
	redistricting	county and school boards
	minority representation	county and school boards

Each of these issue areas has been subtly, or less subtly, transformed by the increasing ethnic diversity of suburban Washington, D.C.

Growth

The slow-growth–progrowth debate has driven much of metropolitan D.C. politics from the 1980s onward (see Siskind in this volume). Much of this debate has centered on disagreements over the costs and benefits of growth. Slow-growth advocates bemoan the accelerating loss of green space in the metro area. They point out that development implies significant public outlays, in terms of investments in municipal sewers, roads, and schools, all of which imply higher levels of taxation for individual homeowners. Finally, they argue that development has translated into a reduction in the quality of life for residents in the area. Progrowth partisans, for their part, see public investments in infrastructure as simply insuring the continued economic prosperity on which suburban counties depend. Without these investments there would be a gradual slowing in the creation of new jobs, and the D.C. area would lose its attractiveness as an area for investment for new business, particularly the high-tech businesses attracted to Fairfax and Loudoun counties at the height of the Internet boom.

As the battle has grown more heated, organizations like the Federation for American Immigration Reform (FAIR)[25] began ad campaigns linking growth in D.C.'s Virginia suburbs to the arrival of increasing numbers of immigrants.[26] Stop immigration, they argued, and suburban sprawl and its attendant problems would cease. The advertisements were denounced by both pro- and anti-growth proponents, but the damage was done: the ads introduced immigration and ethnicity into the growth debate. Once introduced, the link between the two never entirely disappeared. Underlying much of the discussion around growth is the uncomfortable recognition that many of the new residents in the outer D.C. suburbs are nonwhite, and many of these are immigrants. This has complicated strategies, particularly for slow-growth proponents, who have been vulnerable to charges of class elitism and racism.

After decades of feverish growth, for example, by 2000 the slow-growth faction had succeeded in capturing majorities in both Fairfax and Loudoun counties, a coup of significant proportions. For years, developers and business leaders in Northern Virginia had been able to block any attempts to restrict the pace of growth.[27] By 2001, however, the new slow-growth majorities, particularly in Loudoun County, passed significant restrictions on future development. Under Loudoun County's new development plan, two-thirds of the county were to be preserved in their rural state. In northwestern Loudoun, one home would be allowed on every 20 acres or one per 10 acres if they were clustered to preserve open space. In the southwestern portion of the county, one house could be built for every 50 acres or one per 20 acres if clustered. Previously developers had been allowed to build one house per three acres.[28]

Progrowth advocates in Loudoun continued to press for development, seeking to build a coalition around the issues of housing affordability and property rights.[29] The latter resonated with the strain of libertarian conservatism that runs deep in Northern Virginia, but it was the issue of housing affordability that posed particularly prickly questions for slow-growth forces. Because the new development restrictions increased the ratios of land to housing, the most attractive alternative left to developers was often to build very expensive housing on very large lots—thus pricing out many middle- and working-class homebuyers seeking homes close to their jobs in the suburban economy.[30] In short, the county's development restrictions had the potential to act in class- and race-biased ways—not surprisingly, given the history and effects of other kinds of zoning restrictions. This did not go unnoticed by progrowth partisans, who in 2002 filed a lawsuit against the county arguing, among other things, that the new restrictions had racially disparate impacts, and so should be struck down.[31]

The restrictions against growth in Loudoun County were struck down in the courts on a technicality, but these disagreements were more decisively resolved by the election of a progrowth slate to the county council in 2003, which immediately scuttled any plans even hinting of slower growth for the county. According to the 2000 Census, however, Loudoun County had been the fastest growing county in the nation over the last decade, with its infrastructure—schools, roads, libraries, services—struggling to keep pace with the influx of new residents. Given these growing pains, the debate is likely still far from settled.

Education

Education, like growth, has often been at the center of suburban politics. From their inception, schools in suburban areas have been one of the principal selling points to new suburban residents. This has been the case particularly in the D.C. metro area, where three of its suburban counties rank among the ten highest income per capita counties in the United States (Fairfax, Loudoun, and Montgomery counties). The influx of a more multiracial (and sometimes non-English-speaking) population has posed some complications for the area's school systems. I focus here on its implications for the gifted and talented programs in its public schools.

The success of D.C.'s suburban school systems has rested in their ability to attract and keep the allegiance of the upper-middle class. To capture this constituency, area school systems constructed extensive "tracking" programs. Some of these "gifted and talented programs" are virtual schools within schools; students in these programs can take advanced placement courses with like students and have little contact with the broader curriculum or student body. Others are "magnet schools" designed to attract students from across the county school system (for instance, Jefferson High School in Fairfax County, with its emphasis on science and technology). Entrance into these accelerated programs is exam-based; students test as early as first grade for placement in "gifted and talented" classrooms and courses. The entering class of Jefferson High School, for instance, was, until 2002, simply selected by taking the top test scorers for the county.

These advanced placement and magnet school programs had a substantial constituency among the county's well-educated upper-middle class, who see these programs as the edge their children require for entrance into elite universities. But as suburban counties have become more ethnically and racially diverse, it has been questioned whether these programs mirror the diversity of the student body. Although blacks and Latinos, for instance, make up 25 percent of students in Fairfax County, from 1999 to 2001 they made up only 8 percent of those in gifted programs.[32] The problem, critics said, was that testing worked to the disadvantage of minority kids. "The odds are really stacked against kids who don't come from the most mainstream backgrounds and kids who aren't white," said James H. Borland, a professor and the coordinator of programs in gifted education at Teachers College, Columbia University. "If tests are the gatekeepers . . . they will systematically screen out poorer kids and children of color from their pool," he noted. "If schools are serious enough about identifying gifted kids beyond what's found in white middle-class and upper-middle-class [neighborhoods], then they have to find other ways to identify those children."[33]

Criticism that Fairfax County's classes for the "gifted and talented" were filled with mostly white and wealthy students resulted in pressure for reform. In 2001, Fairfax County's school superintendent announced that the county would be changing its criteria for entry into the program. Beginning that year, students were given a test that focused on problem-solving, patterns, and relationships in hopes of identifying gifted children who do not speak English and poorer students who don't traditionally score as high on an IQ test. In addition, the IQ test that is normally given in first grade to all gifted-program applicants was moved to second grade, to allow students another year of school before being tested. Administrators allowed students to be considered if they were referred by their parents, even if their test scores didn't immediately qualify them. And private-school students, who have usually waited until summer to be tested, were tested in the spring with every other child. The result was an increase of nearly a thousand children in the semifinalist pool, from 2,616 last year to 3,588 this year. Officials said 563 of the additional students in the pool were accepted because of testing changes and 409 because of parent and private-school referrals. Finalists were selected based on a packet of information on each student, including test scores, progress reports, other information from teachers and parents, and samples of the student's work. The changes seem to have had real effects: in 2002 there were 168 percent more Hispanics, 41 percent more African Americans, and 53 percent more Asians in the elite program. Overall, minority students in 2002 made up 36 percent of students in gifted and talented programs, up from 32 percent.[34]

At Jefferson High School, low African American and Latino enrollment for the 2001/2002 school year (two black students and seven Latinos) also prompted changes in admissions practices. Again, the Fairfax school superintendent proposed changes. The first phase of applying for the school would remain the same: students would take an entrance exam and the 800 or so with the highest scores would become semifinalists. The change would be that these semifinalists would be sorted by school, and the number of slots for each school would be determined proportionally by its eighth-grade enrollment. The greater the number of students in the school, the greater the number of slots the school would be allotted at Jefferson High. The selection committees reviewing the applications would give first preference in each school to students eligible for free or reduced lunch. Then additional students would be given the remaining seats.[35] By allocating entry slots by school and then within school to economically disadvantaged students, the proposal would most likely result in significantly higher minority enrollment at Jefferson High School.[36] Predictably, opposition, particularly from schools whose candidates for the magnet high school would likely be cut, was ferocious and succeeded in derailing the plan but not in scuttling the push for greater diversity in its entirety.[37]

Quality of Life

Historically, the maintenance of middle-class suburban lifestyles has relied on the imposition of standards, whether through deed covenants, zoning ordinances, neighborhood association by-laws, or local legislation. However, the changing demography of suburbs in the D.C. area indicates that these barriers to entry are now perhaps less effective than before, as less well-off minorities move into what had been largely white, middle-class neighborhoods. In this situation, local officials must decide how, and if, to enforce "quality of life" ordinances.

Zoning codes and regulations, for instance, set limits on how much square footage must be available per person, how many unrelated people can share space, and what rooms can be used as sleeping quarters. In Montgomery County, Maryland, zoning rules prohibit more than five unrelated adults in the same house. The county also has per-person square footage requirements and fire safety regulations relating to sleeping quarters. Homeowners can rent rooms to as many as two boarders, but only if they all share a kitchen. Separate apartments built into single-family homes are allowed only by special permit.[38] Each of these regulations is meant to guarantee health and safety standards and, not coincidentally, to preserve neighborhoods as communities of single-family homes.

In suburban Washington, D.C., affordable housing is a scarce commodity. Immigrants and other newcomers have few alternatives to more expensive housing, whether as renters or as owners. Either owning or renting a home originally intended for a single family may require newcomers to take on additional boarders—whether related by blood or not related at all—to help share costs. The need to reduce costs leads to the conversion of single-family housing into de facto subdivided apartments. The most likely target for this conversion is the lower-middle-class tract housing built in the postwar suburban boom of the 1950s and 1960s. The transformation of single-family housing into group or extended family residences pits longtime residents concerned with their property values and the maintenance of what they see as their quality of life, against newcomers who move to suburbs in order to have access to well-paying jobs, good schools, and safe neighborhoods.[39]

As longtime residents see the character of "their" neighborhood change, the handiest weapon at their disposal is zoning regulations. Neighbors call in to complain to inspection officials about overcrowding. From 1997 to 2001, the number of complaints about crowding in Montgomery County tripled, prompting 159 investigations by housing inspectors in 2001. In Fairfax County, housing inspectors conducted 285 investigations in 2001 alone. Conflicts that flared over differences in notions of decorum, noise, parking, and the like played out in these zoning complaints. Zoning enforcement became a battlefield, reflecting the tensions between newcomers and older residents.

Housing inspectors are often reluctant to enter into such disputes and careful to avoid charges of racism. Lawmakers in the metro area municipalities, however, were under increasing pressure to intervene. In 2000, a bill introduced by a representative from Fairfax County passed the Virginia Senate; the bill would have banned sleeping in any room except bedrooms. In practice the effect of the law, had it passed, would have been to set limits on the use of single-family housing by extended families or unrelated adults. The bill was subsequently withdrawn, however, after protests that it was anti-immigrant.[40] Although the measure failed, a number of municipalities passed ordinances seeking similar ends. In 2002, the Fairfax City Council passed legislation restricting the extent to which homeowners could pave their front lawns, again in the name of preserving neighborhood property values and quality of life.[41] The root of the issue lay in the fact that as suburban single-family housing is converted into multi-family use, adults in these households must get to work. In the suburbs, this often means owning a car. The driveways in older, smaller houses in D.C.'s suburban neighborhoods were not designed to handle two or more cars. The easiest solution is simply to pave over the front yard, turning it into parking. Restricting "lawn parking" was an indirect way of restricting the numbers of individuals living in homes designed as single-family residences. By 2002 Arlington, Alexandria, and the District of Columbia had already passed similar legislation.[42]

Political Representation

As the Washington metropolitan region became more ethnically and racially diverse, questions began to be raised about the adequacy of political representation. Prince George's County in Maryland, whose population is majority African American, is the only jurisdiction in the metro area to have significant minority political representation. The county executive, superintendent of schools, and a majority of the county school board are all African American. Apart from Prince George's, however, minority representation has been spotty at best. In 2002, only one member of Montgomery's County Council was nonwhite, as were two of its school board members.[43] None of the D.C. area's other suburban counties had any nonwhites elected to their boards of supervisors or school boards. That same year Alexandria had two African Americans elected to its school board, but there were no Asians or Latinos elected to any major city or county position in the metro area.

Montgomery County, historically the most liberal of the metropolitan area's suburban counties, was the only one to openly address the issue of minority representation. The county charter commission appointed by the County Council suggested that the process for electing the council needed to be overhauled. Addressing diversity, the commission announced, is "of central importance to the legitimacy of policy decisions, the assimilation of new groups . . . and the maintenance of high levels of citizen participation in the civic life of Montgomery County." The charter commission made its recommendations in May 2002, and its recommendations went on the ballot in the 2002 fall election cycle, with changes to be implemented in time for the 2006 election cycle.[44]

Among the possibilities the charter commission placed on the table for consideration for increasing representation in the county boards was changing the election system of some of the seats from at-large to single-member districts, or simply expanding the number of seats. In 2002, four seats on Montgomery County's nine-member county board were elected at large and five by district. All the seats could be made to represent districts or the number of district-based representation increased. Interestingly, these alternatives were favored by the county's Latino and Asian American groups, but opposed by the African American groups like the county's chapter of the NAACP. The NAACP argued that more districts would not necessarily elect more minority representatives in an area where minorities are geographically dispersed. One alternative would have been multiple-member districts: keeping the current five districts, but electing three representatives from each. These multiple-member districts might be more likely to elect a minority representative, but not necessarily a representative of a *particular* minority group.

The Montgomery County charter commission debate is interesting not least of all because it illustrated the manner in which the political strategies of different ethnic/racial minority communities may diverge. Latino and Asian American organizations, for instance, tended to favor the creation of districts concentrating ethnic populations, even if these districts may not have immediately resulted in the election of minority representatives. What they sought were minority "influence" districts for their particular ethnic communities. African Americans, for their part, were already more engaged in the electoral process, so any electoral system that was designed to elect a nonspecific minority representative was more likely to be to their advantage. These differences were apparent too in black-majority Prince George's County, where Latinos are the fastest growing minority

population. It is unclear in this context how African American officehold-
ers will respond to demands for increased representation from another
minority community.

———

Some of the issues raised in the preceding discussion, such as the deliberations around the desirability of growth in suburban D.C., predate the
appearance of minorities in suburbs but are given an additional twist upon
their arrival. In the case of Loudoun County, for example, antigrowth advocates have linked immigration to sprawl, while progrowth forces have
argued that the preservation of green space through low-density zoning
is a form of discriminatory housing policy, aimed at keeping out lower
income immigrants and minorities.[45] "Quality of life" issues like zoning
and parking have often been at the center of suburban politics but acquire
new prominence as larger households of immigrants increase residential density in developments originally planned for single-family homes,
prompting new regulations on sleeping arrangements in the home[46] or the
extent of parking on residents' front lawns.[47] Other issues become politi-
cized only with the emergence of sizable ethnic minority communities.
For example, gifted and talented programs in the area, originally designed
as a way of keeping upper-middle-class families in the wealthy D.C. suburbs committed to public schools, are increasingly arenas of contestation
as newer minority residents seek entrance into programs whose entrance
exams place them at a disadvantage.[48] Of course, as ethnic and racial minorities become more numerous in suburbia, local governments are often confronted with decisions about providing specialized social services,
often in other languages, and about adequate political representation.[49]
What is evident in all cases is that whether the issues are new or old, they
acquire additional emphasis as the result of the increasingly racial and
ethnic diversification of the Washington metro area and that they are
reorienting the debates and priorities of suburban politics.

We know very little, however, about the mobilization of immigrants
and other racial/ethnic groups in suburbia, and here media coverage fails
us. The *Washington Post*'s coverage can give us a sense of the way in which
suburban politics is changing, but not of how and why the issues play
out as they do. At times issues seem to get onto the agenda as the result
of "reactive" politics, the impulse many middle-class homeowners have
to resist change, any change, in suburbia, but particularly change which
might irremediably alter the value of their own property. This is true in the
case of both the growth debate and of quality of life issues. In some cases,

however, it seems that the issues are introduced proactively. The issue of gifted and talented programs in schools and the extension of political representation both seem to be a response, not to reactive politics, but to something else. This "something else" might be the mobilization of activists from among immigrant and minority communities, or it might be the result of bureaucracies anticipating change. In either case, how issues get on the table is important and would tell us much about the nature of the new suburban politics and the role immigrants and other minorities play in them. It is clear that at the moment we do not know enough.

Research Paths

The racial and ethnic politics in the Washington metro area unfolds in what many have thought of as a characterless landscape, with no "there there." The seeming absence of landmarks and the apparent irrelevance of political boundaries call for a different approach to research. Classic urban ethnographies—and their many imitators—describe ethnic organizational life and politics as an extension of a particular place or neighborhood. Neighborhood delimits "community"—the relevant social and political space for a given population. But the suburban idea of "neighborhood" is less than meaningful without the dense residential and organizational clustering of traditional urban neighborhoods. In many of the new ethnically diverse suburbs appearing in metro areas across the United States there is minimal residential clustering by new minorities, and so there are no specific "ethnic" neighborhoods.

In the D.C. metropolitan area, for instance, immigrants are widely dispersed throughout the region. In 1998 the ten zip codes with the most immigrants in the metro area (accounting for a significant swath of Montgomery, Prince George's, Arlington, and Fairfax counties) together accounted for only a fifth of all immigrants in the region.[50] There is some residential concentration of immigrants in particular zip codes,[51] but in none of these does any single national origin group make up the majority of immigrants, much less a majority of residents. In fact, in the 1990s there were no zip codes in the D.C. area where immigrants made up a majority of residents.[52] Note that this is not true for native-born blacks, who were significantly more residentially concentrated across the region.

Because suburbs are spatially organized in different ways from older urban areas and because many minorities (particularly immigrants) tend to be residentially dispersed in these suburbs, neighborhood-based analysis is

TABLE 9.3 **Concentration of immigrant national origin groups in the top ten zip codes in the Washington area, 1990–98**

County	Zip Code	All Countries	El Salvador	Percent Salvadoran
South Arlington	22204	7823	1143	14.6
Adams Morgan/Mt. Pleasant	20009	6534	1443	22.1
Langley Park/Hyattsville	20783	5763	1336	23.3
Silver Spring/Wheaton	20906	5365	595	11.1
Silver Spring/Colesville	20904	4812	171	3.6
Gaithersburg	20878	4811	237	4.9
Annandale	22003	4731	276	5.8
Landmark	22304	4605	370	8.0
Bailey's Crossroads	22041	4526	637	14.1
Petworth/Brightwood Park	20011	4378	755	17.2
		53321	6963	13.1

Source: Audrey Singer et al., *The World in a Zip Code* (Washington, DC: Brookings Institution, 2001), 5, table 3.
Note: There is no zip code in the Washington, DC, metropolitan area where any one immigrant group is the majority. The 10 largest groups in this area are (in descending order) El Salvadoran, Vietnamese, Indian, Chinese, Philippino, Korean, Ethiopian, Iranian, Pakistani, and Peruvian. Salvadorans are the largest group, constituting 13% of the total population of these 10 groups.

unlikely to be the optimal research strategy. The study of politics in suburbia must take into account a very different form of spatial organization. Just as the earlier bifurcation of work from place of residence had profound political implications,[53] so also does the spatial fragmentation/disassociation of residential and social life. Far-flung social networks overlapping only intermittently in physical space likely mean that local political mobilization is no longer "place-based"—organized around one's immediate residential surroundings—or at the very least that the meaning of "place-based" mobilization shifts considerably. In short, the physical layout of suburbia shapes all political mobilization in suburbs.

The distinct spatial organization of suburbs calls for alternative approaches to research. One possibility is giving research an organizational, not place-centered, locus. For instance research might consist of an in-depth study of the social networks generated by a key institution such as a church, mosque, or temple, networks that might extend across the metropolitan region. This approach could be quite fruitful in generating a thick narrative of the immigrant experience in suburbs. The weakness of this approach, however, is likely to be its limitation in scope—the very intensity of its focus precludes study of more than one or two organizations, and thus restricts drawing more generalized conclusions. A second possibility, the randomized survey, addresses this problem, giving a sense of the range of attitudes and behavior across populations but at the cost of some of the explanatory richness of the first approach. Finally, a third possibility—the approach followed in this chapter—is an examination of immigrant and ethnic politics in suburbia through the lens of a set of issues, using these issues to organize the scope of research. The manner in which issues are approached and dealt with presumably varies across political jurisdictions and ethnic groups, allowing for analysis of this variation, as well as illuminating interactions across individuals and organizations, and providing room for in-depth description.

Conclusion

As immigrants and ethnic minorities themselves become more diverse, it is no longer possible to look solely to central cities as the main locus for their study. However, as new immigrants and ethnic minorities have moved to suburbs, it is clear we know remarkably little about how they are changing, or are changed by, the experience of suburbia. In this chapter I have taken some initial steps toward remedying this, focusing on the changing nature of suburban political systems as the result of interactions between immigrants and other racial and ethnic groups on the one hand and suburban structures on the other. In particular I have focused on changes in issues discussed in the suburban political arena of Washington, D.C, an important immigration gateway and an increasingly racially and ethnically diverse metropolitan area. I have also posed questions as to the changing nature of ethnic mobilization in suburbia, particularly the way in which the distinct spatial organization of suburbs might influence this mobilization; however, this theme awaits further investigation before any conclusions can be drawn. If one thing is clear as the result of the research thus far it is that the increasing diversity of suburbia is changing the politics of the suburbs, and this in turn will likely have profound effects on American politics as a whole. As the center of gravity of American politics continues to shift to metropolitan suburbs, understanding the political incorporation of these newest suburban residents is essential for a broader understanding of the challenges facing democracy in the United States today.

TEN

The Legal Technology of Exclusion in Metropolitan America

GERALD FRUG

An essential feature of the transformation of metropolitan America since World War II has been the erosion of public space through legal measures that foster exclusion and privatization. By public space I mean areas that are open to anyone who decides to enter them. These are the places that provide people with the experience of encountering unfamiliar strangers. As a result, they give those who enter them the experience of being members of what I call a fortuitous association: a group within which people simply find themselves—a group that they have to learn to get along with whether they like it or not.

Over the last half century—and at an accelerating rate in recent decades—American pubic policy and law have eroded the existence of this kind of public space. Suburbanization is a major factor in this erosion. But central cities are playing an important part in this process as well. Many, although not all, of the legal devices that have fueled the privatization of urban space have been adopted as public policy throughout the metropolitan area. Privatization is a pervasive aspect of current metropolitan political and legal culture—not just in the organization of land use, schools, and transportation (the first topic below) but in the very conception of what cities are and what they can do (the second topic below).

Here are ten ways that prevailing legal rules are now undermining the availability of public space in America.

(1) *Suburbanization.* State law currently empowers American suburbs to engage in exclusionary zoning. The widespread expansion of local zoning power dates to the early twentieth century, and zoning power has proved to be a very effective technique for creating and maintaining class and racial homogeneity in suburbs. By specifying minimum standards for housing development (allowing only single-family housing, prescribing minimum lot sizes), prosperous suburbs have excluded not only the poor but anyone who cannot afford a house priced at a specific level. As Margaret O'Mara has shown, exclusionary zoning was a decisive factor in the creation of "cities of knowledge" in places like Silicon Valley. And, as Peter Siskind argues, both legislative and judicial efforts to override local zoning and land-use laws for the sake of equitable housing have been met with fierce resistance. (See O'Mara and Siskind in this volume.)

State law has also authorized suburbs to spend the money they raise from property taxes solely on local residents. This rule of taxation enables local residents to make sure that their tax money is not spent on anyone poorer than they are because, as we have just seen, they have already excluded such people from town. The benefits of local taxation have been particularly pronounced in wealthy suburbs, but as Robert Self has shown, middle-class suburban communities like Fremont and San Leandro, just outside of Oakland in California's East Bay, have been able to provide excellent public services and well-funded schools, while keeping property taxes low, by relying on tax revenue generated by local businesses and industries. Oakland residents, by contrast, have faced growing tax burdens as businesses suburbanized and as whites followed them. (See Self.)

The legal rules that permit exclusionary zoning and local taxation enable those with enough money to move across city lines and thereby dramatically improve their quality of life by leaving other people behind. Some people move to wealthy communities, if they can afford it, simply to save the money that they would have spent on the poor had they remained in a class-integrated jurisdiction. These two legal rules, in short, create a sprawl machine—a legally generated incentive to move out of central cities. As the wealthy move to their suburbs with cost-consciousness in mind, taking their resources with them, the cities they abandon begin to decline. As a result, people in the middle class who have remained in these jurisdictions move to their own suburbs and exclude those poorer than they are, and the cities they leave behind decline even further. When this sprawl machine becomes fully operational, neither the central cities nor the individual suburbs have a truly diverse population. Class—and racial—segregation become the norm.

(2) *Segregating Land Uses*. It is not just the places where people live that have grown increasingly segregated. By the middle of the twentieth century, land-use rules in most suburbs required that residential life, shopping, and work take place in three different, separated spaces. As a result, residential neighborhoods became closed to outsiders simply because there was no reason to go there. Outsiders are attracted to shopping and entertainment, not to houses occupied by strangers. Moreover, the office parks and shopping centers that have proliferated in American metropolitan areas beginning in the mid-twentieth century are private property. Office parks have taken a distinctive architectural form, one organized to exclude anyone not invited. Suburban high-tech campuses often have a single entrance road, security booths or desks, and few, if any, means of access by foot or public transportation. Malls have used other legal means to exclude "undesirables." Under the 1972 Supreme Court ruling in *Lloyd v. Tanner*, shopping centers can exclude people the property owners think detract from the shopping experience, such as protestors. It is not surprising, therefore, that most office parks and shopping centers provide little opportunity to encounter unfamiliar kinds of strangers. In fact, most shopping malls are designed to attract only a limited range of people. Shopping centers with a Nieman Marcus do not have a Kmart.[1]

(3) *Homeowners' Associations*. The kind of segregation of housing and land use that I have just described has not provided a space that is sufficiently isolated or exclusionary for some people in America. By the mid-twentieth century, neighborhood associations became important nongovernmental organizations in many cities. These voluntary organizations banded together to enforce restrictive covenants and to preserve neighborhood homogeneity. Their strategies often worked in the short run, but neighborhood associations lacked control over land use and, because they relied on voluntary contributions, seldom had the power or resources to stem long-term racial or economic change in their neighborhoods.[2] More recently, the most common form of housing being built in the suburbs, as well as in some central cities, have taken the form of private, often gated, communities governed by homeowners' associations. Homeowners' associations have been far more effective exclusionary devices than neighborhood associations because they have control over property use and can employ enforceable contracts to reinforce exclusion. Homeowners' associations invoke private law rules rather than local government law to isolate themselves from outsiders. Like the suburbs, they exclude outsiders, but they do so by relying on

property owners' right to exclude rather than on zoning. They too spend the money they raise from taxes—which they call assessments—solely on themselves, but they do so by relying on contract law rather than tax law. To protect themselves from outsiders, these communities rely on interpretations of property and contract law that are highly controversial, given the effect that this "secession of the successful" has on those who live outside the walls.[3] Nevertheless, their interpretation is widely accepted. As a result, many people move to residential subdivisions populated by people like themselves and, once there, accept with pleasure detailed restrictions on their lives—age restrictions on who can live in their house, limits on what they can plant in their yard, and prohibitions against parking vehicles in their driveways—in exchange for the security that sameness generates. Guests are screened by security guards.[4]

(4) *Combining 1–3 Above.* Throughout the country, suburbanization, segregation of land uses, and homeowners' associations have been combined into a single package. Consider the situation in the fastest growing metropolitan area in America in the 1990s: Las Vegas. As Evan McKenzie has analyzed in detail,[5] Las Vegas requires new developments to have certain features (open space, landscaping plans) and then requires the formation of a homeowners' association to maintain them. It is not hard to figure out why Las Vegas has such requirements. If the homeowners' association provides services (recreational space and sanitation, for example), the city does not have to. The scheme saves the city money. As a result of this policy, it is not accurate to think of Las Vegas homeowners' associations in terms of voluntary contracts entered into by property owners. Home buyers cannot buy a house in a new development without a homeowners' association because they are mandated by law. The Las Vegas requirement is not unique (some Dallas suburbs do the same thing, and Chicago has a similar rule for certain townhouse developments). Even in the parts of the country without such a rule, it is often hard to find a new home not governed by a homeowners' association.

(5) *The Organization of Public Schools.* Many American suburbs have good public schools—that is one of the main reasons people move to them. But these public schools are not public in the sense that they are open to anyone who decides to enroll in them. Quite the contrary. The suburbs in which these schools are located rely on zoning law, rather than an admissions office, to screen out the kind of students thought not to fit in. Moreover, because school districts in most states are funded through local property taxes, school funding and classroom resources are closely correlated to local property values. Federal court decisions have reinforced this structure of place-based segregation and local financing. In *San Antonio*

Independent School District v. Rodriguez (1973), the Supreme Court ruled that states did not have to equalize funding between school districts. And in the landmark *Milliken v. Bradley* decision (1974), the Supreme Court struck down interdistrict busing between Detroit and its suburbs. To be sure, some state supreme courts have adopted a different path, holding unconstitutional their state's school financing system because of the inequality it has generated. Even so, the legal system as a whole has helped produce and reinforce the segregation of American schools by race and class. School segregation is as intense now as it was in the 1950s. In 1994–95 (twenty years after the *Milliken* decision), 82 percent of African American students in metropolitan Detroit attended school in just three of eighty-three school districts.[6] When John Dewey described the social function of the public schools, he said that in a public school "each individual gets an opportunity to escape from the limitation of the social group in which he was born, and to come into contact with a broader environment."[7] This no longer describes a vast number of the public schools that exist in America today.

(6) *Tracking within the Public Schools*. Even when public schools admit a diverse group of students, it does not follow that the schools are organized so that the students can learn to engage each other. On the contrary, academic tracking—the division of the student body into fast, average, and slow classes—is standard educational policy in America's public schools, and not just for English and math. Academic tracking is one of the ways Americans first learn that a heterogeneous group should be divided into different spaces—spaces not just for smart and dumb but for whites and blacks, college-bound and vocationally tracked, cool and nerd. This process has helped Americans learn an important, and destructive, lesson from an early age: being in the same space with different kinds of people not only feels uncomfortable but impedes personal advancement. The same attitude helps generate, later in life, support for exclusive suburbs and gated communities.[8]

(7) *Crime Policy*. Schooling is not the only city service that has contributed to the privatization of formerly public spaces. The other principal reason that people move to exclusive suburbs and gated communities—along with the desire for good schools—is the fear of crime. In America, the predominant strategy that individuals employ in dealing with crime is to move away from it. True, escape is usually not enough: once located in the right kind of neighborhood, people isolate themselves further by relying on security guards, alarm systems, locks, window bars, surveillance cameras, doormen, dogs, speed bumps, mace, and guns—far more than they rely on city police.[9] The very presence of a young black male

triggers security concerns in many neighborhoods; so does the presence of any one else who seems different. This reliance on isolation, rather than crime prevention, as America's principal crime control strategy, divides metropolitan areas into separate areas for different kinds of people and, perhaps more than any other single policy, erodes the vitality of public space in America.

(8) *Funding Highways Rather Than Mass Transit.* One final city service seems worth mentioning here. Since the mid-twentieth century, the rules adopted by federal, state, and local governments have privileged highways at the expense of mass transit. Mass transit and walkable streets are two of the major sources of public space in America: they enable the daily experience of crossing paths with different kinds of people. Driving, on the other hand, is a privatized affair: it fosters focusing on oneself (day-dreaming, putting on makeup), interaction with people one knows (car phones), or, at its most expansive, listening to the radio. The governmental decisions that favor cars over mass transit have thus helped ensure that the commute between the gated community and the office park—and between the two of them and the shopping mall—requires no more contact with unfamiliar strangers than these places themselves. The concept of a "public street" does not mean much if one is moving at 60 miles per hour. The public feel of streets is produced by pedestrians.[10]

(9) *Designing Central Cities.* As I have already suggested, it is a mistake to think of the privatization of public space as simply a suburban phenomenon. Although some of the devices listed above—exclusionary zoning and tax policy, for example—are not used by large central cities, many similar legal tools divide and separate the central city population. Like suburban jurisdictions, central cities segregate land uses into residential, commercial, and industrial areas (the creation of "downtowns" as well as residential neighborhoods); they establish attendance zones within a single school district that differentiate the nature of the public schools; they track students in schools wherever located; they fail to support adequate public transportation and fail to maintain public parks at a level at which their citizens would feel like using them. And that's not all. Urban renewal in the 1950s and 1960s was predominantly a central city phenomenon, and, as Arnold Hirsch shows in his chapter, the exclusionary politics that undergirded it were those that also reinforced suburbanization. Central cities' use of eminent domain in those years resulted in the massive displacement of the urban poor to other parts of the city and to the suburbs ("Negro removal," it was often called).[11] Although the urban renewal style of massive land-clearing for highways and upscale development has largely disappeared, central city efforts to distinguish parts of the city from

others continue apace. These include programs that foster gentrification in selected neighborhoods, that enable tourists to visit city centers without ever having access to public streets or city populations, and that locate undesirable land uses in the poorer parts of town. Rationales for policies such as these are easy to come by. Central cities, after all, need to compete with the suburbs, attract business and tourist revenue, and locate garbage dumps where land is cheapest. The end result is visible enough. No one walking down Newbury Street in Boston's Back Bay could tell that Boston is now a majority minority city.[12]

(10) *BIDs.* Of course, we still have large, open cities in America. And many of them have mass transit, public schools, streets lined with stores, vital public parks, and housing close to work. Yet even in these cities efforts are being made to privatize public space. One form this effort has taken has been the creation of business improvement districts—organizations that are designed to police and clean up the public streets in areas like Midtown Manhattan and Center City Philadelphia. These organizations are run by property owners, not by residents. And they adopt the perspective of these property owners when questions about the nature of public streets arise—matters such as the presence of the homeless, street peddlers, and others considered undesirable. In addition, BIDs create a two-tiered system of public service provision, further reinforcing inequality between downtowns (where property owners can afford to pay for BIDs) and poor, working-class, and even middle-class neighborhoods. Those who pay extra in the form of assessments get special services unavailable in other sections of cities. These include street sweepers and, as is the case in Philadelphia, uniformed "ambassadors" who greet tourists and discourage homeless people. The constitutionality of this kind of property owner government was upheld recently by the United States Court of Appeals in New York. The court rejected the argument that local policy governing the nature of public streets should be based on democratic—one-person, one-vote—decision making.[13]

These ten legal devices—and many others like them—provide the background legal structure for democracy in America today. They foster a privatized sense of self that structures the consciousness of people when they act as citizens. As a result, they help generate support for withdrawal rather than engagement, sameness rather than diversity, separation rather than openness, avoidance of conflict rather than building the capacity to deal with it. These laws are not simply the result of politicians' decisions to enact the kind of rules that Americans want. No doubt, many people want to move to the suburbs or to gated communities and to send their kids to good schools outside the central city. Given the structure of metropolitan

America that legal rules have helped put into place, these decisions make sense. People choose from the menu of choices that are available to them. But the background legal rules and institutions shape the world in which people are making their choices. Background legal rules frame choices; different rules frame different choices. Law is not just the product of society. Society is also the product of law. With a different legal structure, the way people would think about what they want would change. When you hear someone say "I'm moving to the suburbs for the schools," you should ask: why are good schools located in some places and not others?

There is another reason that the ten examples of legal doctrine listed above cannot be explained simply by referring to the popular desire to exclude undesirable strangers. Some of them are primarily motivated by other considerations. Las Vegas homeowners' association rules were generated by the city's desire to save money; many of the central city policies were enacted in order to compete with the suburbs; many people support highway construction for reasons that have little to do with exclusion. Nevertheless, all ten rules directly affect the organization of public space in American metropolitan areas. And these rules do not exist in isolation. Other legal rules promote a "what's-in-it-for-me" mentality toward local government, an attitude that buttresses support for the policies that promote the privatization of land use. I list below ten more examples of the kind of legal rules that I have in mind. The first three embrace a privatized version of local government finance. They favor a fee-for-service mentality toward paying for city services that mimics the consumer-oriented perspective of the market rather than a more public-oriented recognition that the ability to live in a diverse society depends on ensuring (and financing) the welfare of one's neighbors. The next three rules embrace a privatized version of the city and its services. They adopt the same kind of self-interested perspective toward municipal services as the first three rules embraced for methods of raising revenue. The final four rules deal with cities' regulatory authority. They limit the city's ability to regulate the private sector and, therefore, their power to impose public values on the privatized spaces that are spreading across the metropolitan area. These ten rules have not usually been adopted to further the desire to exclude. Yet their impact on public space is important. The rules that erode a public orientation toward city finance, services, and regulatory authority and the rules that erode the vitality of public space reinforce each other: in a circular fashion, privatization begets privatization.

(1) *Revenue Other Than Taxes*. Cities and towns generate their own revenue through the imposition of taxes, fees, or special assessments. Taxes are imposed on the jurisdiction's population as a whole; they generate

money from the collectivity and are allocated by political decision makers to support the city budget. Fees and special assessments are different. They are paid only by people who use a relevant service (fees) or by landowners who are specially benefited by a local improvement (special assessments). Fees and special assessments thus emphasize a close relationship between those who pay the cost and those who are benefited by government action. By contrast, taxes are expected to be paid even if the government program benefits others. A reliance on fees and special assessments thus strengthens a "what's-in-it-for-me" attitude toward government over a more community-minded alternative. There has been a dramatic shift in local government finance in recent decades from taxes to fees and special assessments.[14] This shift is not simply a matter of local government choice. Cities are limited by state law in their ability to raise taxes, while they are often given more latitude when it comes to setting fees and special assessments. They get the money where they can.

(2) *Taxes as Fee for Service.* Taxes themselves can be conceptualized to be like fees. Residents of America's metropolitan areas often pay taxes with the same expectations they have when they pay dues to be a member of a club: taxes are seen as the collective property of a community's residents, just as a club's dues are the collective property of club members. They therefore think it obvious that they should only pay taxes for services that directly benefit themselves. A growing number of older people, for example, have moved to senior citizen communities to avoid paying the taxes that support local schools. At the same time, many communities seek to attract seniors, rather than families with children, because, unlike children, they do not generate a demand for new schools. On the contrary, seniors often oppose the building of new schools once their kids have left home. This kind of fee-for-service mentality affects the entire range of local government services. Why should I pay to support any city service that I do not use? If I never go to the city park (because of my backyard), never use city sanitation (because my garbage is picked up by my homeowners' association), never use mass transit (because my car is more convenient), why should I pay for them?

In many parts of the country—particularly in racially divided metropolitan areas—the opting out of public services also reinforces racial polarization. In the 1950s, when Atlanta desegregated its public pools, white Atlantans engaged in a record spate of private pool construction and formed private swim clubs. And, when buses were integrated, white ridership plummeted. Whites increasingly viewed public facilities and public transportation as "someone else's problem" and began to resist paying taxes for them.[15] Others simply fled central cities to opt out of responsibility for urban public services altogether. It would be better to move to a place where I do not have to pay than to stay behind and have to spend "my" money on "those people." In recent years, although policymakers have recognized the economic advantages of regional policymaking and finance, the perception of taxation as a fee for service has hindered the prospects of city-suburban cooperation. Contrast the vision of taxes famously expressed by Oliver Wendell Holmes: "Taxes are what we pay for civilized society."[16]

(3) *Earmarking Taxes.* Major redevelopment projects are often financed these days by issuing tax-exempt municipal bonds to pay for condemning land and making site improvements. The bonds are paid for by what is commonly called tax increment financing: the additional property-tax revenues gained from the project are pledged to pay off the bonds. Tax increment financing takes money away from the general funds that support local services. It thus drains the city of revenue that might have been spent to support social services more generally. This method of financing is very attractive to cities because the bonds they issue are exempt from federal taxes and therefore carry a lower-than-market interest rate. To be sure, this scheme is expensive. It has cost the federal government a lot of lost tax revenue: twice as much in the mid-1980s as the $520 million it annually spent during the twenty-five-year history of urban renewal. And it costs central cities a lot of money, too. Not only do they use city property tax revenue to pay off their bonds, but they regularly sell the condemned land to developers below cost and, when necessary, offer tax abatements. Given the limits on city revenue (and other lack of funding), however, city officials often find that tax increment financing is the only choice available.

(4) *Public Authorities/Special Districts.* Public services are often delivered not by the city government itself but by public authorities or special districts. These specialized government-created institutions—airport authorities, transportation authorities, water districts, and the like—typically focus on a single problem, and they are organized to resemble private corporations rather than city governments. Their board of directors is not elected but appointed (usually by the governor); they are organized to be run by experts rather than to be politically accountable; they often (although by no means always) have their own source of funds. By taking important city services out of the realm of collective democratic decision making, public authorities and special districts buttress a businesslike and consumer-oriented, rather than a democratic and public-oriented, notion of government. By segregating city functions into different institutions, they undermine city responsibility for, and trade-offs between, all public

services. And they allow elected city officials to disclaim responsibility for vital public functions. "I can't do anything about the subways," they can properly say, "I don't run them."

(5) *Privatization of Services.* Another consumer-oriented option for delivering public services is to privatize them. Virtually every local government service—from transportation to jails, from sanitation to fire departments—can either be contracted out to private companies or sold to them outright. Privatization is an easy step to take if one thinks of city services as consumer goods. After all, don't private companies offer most consumer goods already? Privatization implicitly rejects the alternative conception of city services—one that emphasizes the importance of bringing a diverse population together into public schools, transportation, and parks. Its focus instead is on the bottom line, and city supervision of the contracts with the private sector concentrates on ensuring that the privatization achieves the cost-saving goal that brought it about. Only when privatization of something like the police department is proposed does the "public" nature of city services spring to mind. Privatization has not yet led to the widespread contracting out of police services. But it has had an impact on them. There are more private security guards than police officers in America, and the reliance on private security is increasing. For those who can afford them, these security guards perform the protective duties that police have traditionally offered. They thereby reorient what the police themselves do.[17]

(6) *The City as Consumer Product.* The city itself can be understood as a consumer product. The familiar notion that the city is a vehicle for providing services to its residents (the notion referred to in the previous two paragraphs) is now being supplemented, if not replaced, by the idea that the city should focus on attracting tourists, visitors, pleasure-seekers, and sports fans to town. These marketing efforts emphasize the connection between cities and outsiders and between cities and pleasure rather than between cities and insiders and between cities and the provision of necessary services. The entertainment destinations that are the result of this focus—places like Quincy Market in Boston, the Inner Harbor in Baltimore, South Street Seaport in New York City, Water Tower Place in Chicago, Ghirardelli Square in San Francisco—have often been compared to Disneyland.[18] To their critics, these efforts paper over the realities faced by city residents living in other parts of town.

(7) *Regulating Private and Civil Affairs.* An important aspect of local government law deals with the power of municipalities to regulate those who live and work within their borders. A variety of legal rules limit their ability to do so. For example, in many states even home rule cities cannot

regulate so-called "private or civil affairs" unless they are independently given such a power by the state legislature. This restriction has placed some kinds of local legislation designed to deal with issues of exclusion—such as rent control, efforts to combat racial discrimination, and inclusionary zoning—beyond city authority. A number of court cases have held that cities cannot adopt these kinds of measures to make housing more afford-able to more people.[19] Not all city policies that affect the private sector, however, have been subject to this kind of restraint. There is a relative lack of legal control on city spending to lure businesses to town. While the courts have been careful to control city regulation of the private sector, they have been very amenable to city subsidies—even condemnation of land—for potential corporate employers.

(8) *Market Participant Doctrine.* A more arcane, yet still important, legal rule is the "market participant doctrine." Local governments are limited in their ability to regulate the private sector not just by state law (the source of the private and civil affairs rule) but also by the Commerce Clause of the U.S. Constitution. It is unconstitutional, the courts have held, for a local ordinance to favor a local business over outsiders because doing so would interfere with the nationwide economy that the Commerce Clause has been interpreted to promote. There is, however, a judicially crafted exception to this rule. If the city is acting not as a regulator but as a market participant—that is, if the city (like a private corporation) is buying or selling items in the market—this rule does not apply. In other words, if the city is acting in its private ("market participant") rather than its public ("regulatory") capacity, it has more power to act in its own interest without worrying about the Commerce Clause. This is one of many legal doctrines that give greater protection to cities when they act in their private capacity than they have when they exercise their public powers.

(9) *Annexation/Incorporation.* City regulation usually affects only peo-ple within the city's boundaries.[20] One important limit on a city's power of regulation therefore takes the form of restrictions on its ability to ex-pand its boundaries—that is, its ability to annex neighboring territory. The more its borders expand, the greater its power. David Rusk's well-known argument for "elastic" over "inelastic" cities—for "cities without suburbs," to quote his book title—provides a well-known statement of this thesis.[21] All major American cities have grown through annexation, and annex-ation is still very much in use in the South and the West. But, in much of the country, state law favors inelastic cities over elastic ones. It also favors easy incorporation of new cities, thus promoting the fragmenta-tion that annexation would overcome. These two rules limit city power

no matter how annexation decisions are made. Many states, however, allow property owners, not voters, to control annexation and incorporation decisions. For example, in some states, annexation and incorporation can be initiated only if a fixed percentage of property owners asks for it. This allocation of legal authority to property owners, rather than voters at large, may seem surprising to some readers. Didn't the United States move from a property-owner government to a more general franchise in the nineteenth century? The answer is, yes it did—but, as this case demonstrates, not for every issue.[22]

(10) *Initiatives/Referenda.* It may seem odd to list initiatives and referenda as examples of privatization. Aren't initiatives and referenda the primary example of "public" decision making—of direct democracy in action? How can they be examples of privatization? The answer has been most forcefully provided by Derrick Bell.[23] Direct democracy has often been used on the local level to generate forms of racial exclusion that go beyond those enacted by state legislatures or city councils. A requirement that a new housing project be approved by a popular vote, rather than by the city council, has enabled private prejudice to have more of a scope than a reliance on the give-and-take of publicly accountable government bodies. The private nature of the vote in a referendum or initiative—the absence of public discussion and accountability—are thought to contribute to this difference in results. The city council often finds it hard to articulate a constitutionally adequate justification to exclude the housing project; voters in a secret ballot need not justify their decisions. The widespread use of referenda on matters such as these is not necessarily the result of a city policy. Decisions about whether a referendum is necessary are often made by the state. A state requirement that a local decision be made referendum (say, for additional tax authority) may be a way for the state to make its defeat more likely.

The ten rules just listed are very different from each other. They do not foster privatization in the same way or even in the same sense of the term. Nevertheless, they all contribute, like the privatization of public space, to the erosion of the concept of the "public." Even action by government— the raising of revenue, the delivery of services, regulatory policy—can be seen as fostering privatization. I think that the kinds of rules I have described in this chapter should be replaced by rules that reinvigorate the notion of the "public." Legal rules, in my view, should help people adjust to the idea that the world is filled with people different from themselves, that help them cope with the fact that this difference sometimes makes them feel uncomfortable, and that enable them to stretch their own sense of self by being introduced to unfamiliar lives. In this brief chapter, I cannot outline the kind of legal rules that might turn America's existing urban policy upside down in this way. A few broad sketches will have to suffice.

- We should, first of all, organize American metropolitan areas in a way that opens up the boundaries that now divide and separate the different cities and suburbs that make up America's metropolitan regions. We should recognize the effect that exclusionary zoning is now having on outsiders—above all, the fact that one of its consequences is the disinvestment in, and decline of, those sections of the metropolitan region where the excluded have been allowed to go.
- We should recognize that the tax revenue generated from commercial and industrial property does not belong to the residents of the jurisdiction in which it is located. Why should the taxes on a shopping mall owned by nonresidents—a place where people throughout the region shop—be spent only on people who live nearby?
- We should alter current zoning rules to reintegrate housing and commercial life, not simply to cut down on the necessity of using the car for every errand but to open up the streets to more kinds of people.
- We should recognize the impact that the proliferation of gated communities is having on America metropolitan areas as a whole. Too many residents of these communities have been led to think that they have no obligation to support public services outside their walls.
- We should open the public schools to outsiders though a metropoliswide public school choice program. Such a metropolitan program would not undermine neighborhood schools—after all, most Americans prefer sending their children to neighborhood schools—unless, of course, these schools continue to be as radically unequal as they are now.
- We should organize the suburbs, and not just those who live in high-crime neighborhoods, to support, and pay for, crime-control efforts wherever crime occurs. Crime prevention benefits more than those now most plagued by crime; it also opens up the areas of cities now closed to outsiders.
- We should allocate money to mass transit and public streets not simply for environmental reasons but to encourage the creation of the kinds of public space that they both facilitate.
- We should insist on democratic organization of business improvement districts—indeed, we should insist on a form of democratic control that would allow visitors who fear being harassed, as well as those who live nearby, to be represented.
- We should organize our tax system, our city services, and our regulatory authority to promote an inclusive form of democratic self-government rather than privatization.

Is this kind of change in legal rules politically impossible? It will not be easy. Yet concerns about the lack of affordable housing, the decline of the public schools, crime, traffic congestion, and suburban sprawl are widespread in American metropolitan areas. To be sure, the role of the privatization of public space and of current tax, service-delivery, and regulatory rules in creating these problems is largely unrecognized. That is why I think that it is important to demonstrate how the legal system generates sprawl, produces intercity and interneighborhood inequality, and limits cities' ability to address the problems facing metropolitan America. The current legal structure reinforces the common belief that the way to deal with urban problems is to run away from them—to cross city lines and protect oneself from the bad things going on elsewhere. This attitude is not going to be turned around overnight. It will be turned around only when people begin to recognize the problems that the current structure is causing them, whoever they are and wherever they live. There is no way for law to be neutral on whether we promote the values of openness or isolation. Legal rules shape the nature of our cities and metropolitan areas whether we like it or not. Our only choice is determining what kind of rules—and therefore what kind of urban life—we want to promote.

Notes

INTRODUCTION

1. William Schneider, "The Suburban Century Begins," *Atlantic Monthly*, July 1992, 33.
2. Juliet F. Gainsborough, *Fenced Off: The Suburbanization of American Politics* (Washington, DC: Georgetown University Press, 2001); Lisa McGirr, *Suburban Warriors: The Origins of the New American Right* (Princeton, NJ: Princeton University Press, 2001); J. Eric Oliver, *Democracy in Suburbia* (Princeton, NJ: Princeton University Press, 2001); Matthew D. Lassiter, "Suburban Strategies: The Volatile Center in Postwar American Politics," in Meg Jacobs, William J. Novak, and Julian E. Zelizer, eds., *The Democratic Experiment: New Directions in American Political History* (Princeton, NJ: Princeton University Press, 2003), 325–349; Kevin M. Kruse, *White Flight: Atlanta and the Making of Modern Conservatism* (Princeton, NJ: Princeton University Press, 2005).
3. Arnold R. Hirsch, *Making the Second Ghetto: Race and Housing in Chicago, 1940–1960* (Chicago: University of Chicago Press, 1983); Thomas J. Sugrue, *The Origins of the Urban Crisis: Race and Inequality in Postwar Detroit* (Princeton, NJ: Princeton University Press, 1996).
4. Robert B. Reich, "Secession of the Successful," *New York Times Magazine*, 20 January 1991, 16–17, 42–45; Evan McKenzie, *Privatopia: Homeowner Associations and the Rise of Residential Private Government* (New Haven, CT: Yale University Press, 1994); Edward J. Blakely and Mary Gail Snyder, *Fortress America: Gated Communities in the United States* (Washington, DC: Brookings Institution, 1999); Thomas J. Sugrue, "All Politics Is Local: The Persistence of Localism in Twentieth-Century

America," in Jacobs, Novak, and Zelizer, eds., *The Democratic Experiment*, 301–326; Kruse, *White Flight*, chap. 9.

5. Elaine Tyler May, *Homeward Bound: American Families in the Cold War Era* (New York: Basic Books, 1988); Joanne Meyerowitz, ed., *Not June Cleaver: Women and Gender in Postwar America, 1945–1960* (Philadelphia: Temple University Press, 1994); Leland T. Saito, *Race and Politics: Asian Americans, Latinos, and Whites in a Los Angeles Suburb* (Bloomington: University of Illinois Press, 1998); Rosalyn Baxandall and Elizabeth Ewen, *Picture Windows: How the Suburbs Happened* (New York: Basic Books, 2000); Sylvie Murray, *The Progressive Housewife: Community Activism in Suburban Queens, 1945–1965* (Philadelphia: University of Pennsylvania Press, 2003); Becky Nicolaides, *My Blue Heaven: Life and Politics in the Working-Class Suburbs of Los Angeles* (Chicago: University of Chicago Press, 2002); Robert O. Self, *American Babylon: Race and the Struggle for Postwar Oakland* (Princeton, NJ: Princeton University Press, 2003); Stephen J. Pitti, *The Devil in Silicon Valley: Northern California, Race, and Mexican Americans* (Princeton, NJ: Princeton University Press, 2003); Andrew Wiese, *Places of Their Own: African American Suburbanization in the Twentieth Century* (Chicago: University of Chicago Press, 2004).

6. Bruce J. Schulman, *From Cotton Belt to Sunbelt: Federal Policy, Economic Development, and the Transformation of the South, 1938–1980* (New York: Oxford University Press, 1991); Robert M. Collins, *More: The Politics of Economic Growth in Postwar America* (New York: Oxford University Press, 2000); Lizabeth Cohen, *A Consumers' Republic: The Politics of Mass Consumption in Postwar America* (New York: Vintage, 2003); Stephanie Dyer, "Markets in the Meadows: Department Stores and Shopping Centers in the Decentralization of Philadelphia, 1920–1980," Ph.D. diss., University of Pennsylvania, 2000; Alison Isenberg, *Downtown America: A History of the Place and the People Who Made It* (Chicago: University of Chicago Press, 2004); Margaret Pugh O'Mara, *Cities of Knowledge: Cold War Science and the Search for the Next Silicon Valley* (Princeton, NJ: Princeton University Press, 2005).

7. Adam Rome, *The Bulldozer in the Countryside: Suburban Sprawl and the Rise of American Environmentalism* (New York: Cambridge University Press, 2001); Peter Siskind, "Growth and Its Discontents: Localism, Protest, and the Politics of Development on the Postwar Northeast Corridor," Ph.D. diss. University of Pennsylvania, 2002; McGirr, *Suburban Warriors;* Kruse, *White Flight.*

8. For recent assessments of the dominance of the suburban majority in American life, see Schneider, "The Suburban Century Begins"; Stanley B. Greenberg, *Middle-Class Dreams: The Politics and Power of the New American Majority,* rev. ed. (New Haven: Yale University Press, 1996); Nicholas Lemann, "The New American Consensus: Government of, by, and for the Comfortable," *New York Times Magazine,* 1 November 1998, 37–42; G. Scott Thomas, *The United States of Suburbia: How the Suburbs Took Control of America and What They Plan to Do with It* (New York: Prometheus Books, 1998); Thomas,

"Suburbs Rule: How the Suburban Majority is Changing America," *New York Times Magazine,* 9 April 2000.

9.   Kenneth T. Jackson, *Crabgrass Frontier: The Suburbanization of the United States* (New York: Oxford University Press, 1985), 283–296; Thomas Hanchett, "U.S. Tax Policy and the Shopping Center Boom of the 1950s and 1960s," *American Historical Review* 101 (1996): 1082–1110. For useful syntheses and overviews of this literature, see William Sharpe and Leonard Wallock, "Bold New City or Built-Up 'Burb'?: Redefining Contemporary Suburbia," *American Quarterly* 46 (March 1994): 4–6; Timothy J. Gilfoyle, "White Cities, Linguistic Turns, and Disneylands: The New Paradigms of Urban History," *Reviews in American History* 26 (1998): 175–204; Richard Harris and Robert Lewis, "The Geography of North American Cities and Suburbs, 1900–1950: A New Synthesis," *Journal of Urban History* 27 (March 2001): 262–292; Mary Corbin Sies, "North American Suburbs, 1880–1950," *Journal of Urban History* 27 (March 2001): 313–346.

10.   Lewis Mumford, *The City in History: Its Origins, Its Transformations, and Its Prospects* (New York: Harcourt, Brace & World, 1961), 486.

11.   Jackson, *Crabgrass Frontier,* 6.

12.   Robert Fishman, *Bourgeois Utopias: The Rise and Fall of Suburbia* (New York: Basic Books, 1987), 4.

13.   Robert Lewis, ed., *Manufacturing Suburbs: Building Work and Home on the Metropolitan Fringe* (Philadelphia: Temple University Press, 2004). For other studies with relevance to the rise of working-class suburbia, see Herbert J. Gans, *The Levittowners* (New York: Columbia University Press, 1982); David Halle, *America's Working Man: Work, Home and Politics among Blue-Collar Property Owners* (Chicago: University of Chicago Press, 1984); Bennett Berger, *Working-Class Suburb: A Study of Auto Workers in Suburbia* (Berkeley: University of California Press, 1968); Richard Harris, "Working-Class Home Ownership in the American Metropolis," *Journal of Urban History* 17 (November 1990): 46–69; Harris, "Self-Building in the Urban Housing Market," *Economic Geography* 67 (January 1991): 1–21; Richard Harris and Matt Sendbuehler, "The Making of a Working-Class Suburb in Hamilton's East End, 1900–1945," *Journal of Urban History* 20 (May 1994); Margaret Crawford, *Building the Workingman's Paradise: The Design of American Company Towns* (New York: Verso, 1995); James Borchert, "Residential City Suburbs: The Emergence of a New Suburban Type, 1880–1930," *Journal of Urban History* 22 (March 1996): 283–307; Richard Harris, *Unplanned Suburbs: Toronto's American Tragedy* (Baltimore: Johns Hopkins University Press, 1996); Becky M. Nicolaides, "'Where the Working Man Is Welcomed': Working-Class Suburbs in Los Angeles, 1900–1940," *Pacific Historical Review* 68 (November 1999): 517–599; Minna Ziskind, "Labor Conflict in the Suburbs: Organizing Retail in Metropolitan New York, 1954–1958," *International Labor and Working-Class History* 64 (October 2003): 55–73.

14.   For additional explorations of African American suburbanization, see Ronald Johnson, "From Romantic Suburb to Racial Enclave: LeDroit Park,

Washington, D.C., 1880–1920," *Phylon* 45 (1984): 264–270; Bruce B. Williams, *Black Workers in an Industrial Suburb* (New Brunswick, NJ: Rutgers University Press, 1987); W. Edward Orser, "Secondhand Suburbs: Black Pioneers in Baltimore's Edmondson Village, 1955–1980," *Journal of Urban History* 10 (September 1990): 227–262; William H. Wilson, *Hamilton Park: A Planned Black Community in Dallas* (Baltimore: Johns Hopkins University Press, 1998); Andrew Wiese, "The Other Suburbanites: African American Suburbanization in the North before 1950," *Journal of American History* 85 (March 1999): 1495–1524; Thomas J. Sugrue, "Black Suburbanization," in Kwame Anthony Appiah and Henry Louis Gates, Jr., eds., *Encarta Africana 2000* (Redmond, WA: Microsoft, 1999); Shirley Ann Wilson Moore, *To Place Our Deeds: The African American Community in Richmond, California, 1910–1963* (Berkeley: University of California Press, 2000); Bruce D. Haynes, *Red Lines, Black Spaces: The Politics of Race and Space in a Middle-Class Suburb* (New Haven: Yale University Press, 2001); for an ahistorical and optimistic view of black suburbanization, see Stephan Thernstrom and Abigail Thernstrom, *America in Black and White: One Nation, Indivisible* (New York: Simon & Schuster, 1997), 211–213. Quote from Wiese, *Places of Their Own,* 5.

For an appreciation of the meaning of suburbanization for other racial minorities, see for example Matt García, *A World of Its Own: Race, Labor and Citrus in the Making of Greater Los Angeles* (Chapel Hill: University of North Carolina Press, 2001); Pitti, *Devil in Silicon Valley.*

15. Charles Tilly, "What Good Is Urban History?" *Journal of Urban History* 22 (September 1996): 710.

16. Historians of nineteenth-century suburbanization were more likely to situate their histories in a broad urban context than their post–New Deal counterparts, who have largely cordoned off the history of suburbs and their cities. Jackson, *Crabgrass Frontier;* Sam Bass Warner, Jr., *Streetcar Suburbs: The Process of Growth in Boston, 1870–1900* (Cambridge, MA: Harvard University Press, 1962); Gwendolyn Wright, *Building the Dream: A Social History of Housing in America* (New York: Pantheon, 1981), chap. 13; Henry Binford, *The First Suburbs: Residential Communities on the Boston Periphery, 1815–1860* (Chicago: University of Chicago Press, 1984); Mary Corbin Sies, "The City Transformed: Nature, Technology, and the Suburban Ideal, 1877–1917," *Journal of Urban History* 14 (November 1987): 81–111; John R. Stilgoe, *Borderland: Origins of the American Suburb, 1820–1939* (New Haven, CT: Yale University Press, 1988); Michael H. Ebner, *Creating Chicago's North Shore: A Suburban History* (Chicago: University of Chicago Press, 1988); Margaret Marsh, *Suburban Lives* (New Brunswick, NJ: Rutgers University Press, 1990); David R. Contosta, *Suburb in the City: Chestnut Hill, Philadelphia, 1850–1990* (Columbus: Ohio State University Press, 1992); Barbara M. Kelly, *Expanding the American Dream: Building and Rebuilding Levittown* (Albany: State University of New York Press, 1993); Michael Birkner, *A Country Place*

No More: The Transformation of Bergenfield, New Jersey, 1894–1994 (Rutherford, NJ: Farleigh Dickinson University Press, 1994).

An early exception to this trend was the work of Jon C. Teaford. See, for instance, *City and Suburb: The Political Fragmentation of Metropolitan America, 1850–1970* (Baltimore: Johns Hopkins University Press, 1979). More recently, see Paul H. Mattingly, *Suburban Landscapes: Culture and Politics in a New York Metropolitan Community* (Baltimore: Johns Hopkins University Press, 2001), 7, which argues for close attention to the "suburban-urban interactive process."

17. For examples of the "urbanization of the suburbs" trope, see Jack Rosenthal, "The Outer City: U.S. in Suburban Turmoil," *New York Times*, 30 May 1971; Gurney Breckenfeld, "'owntown' Has Fled to the Suburbs," *Fortune*, October 1972, 80–87, 156, 158, 162; Louis H. Masotti, "Prologue: Suburbia Reconsidered—Myth and Counter-Myth," in Louis H. Masotti and Jeffrey K. Hadden, *The Urbanization of the Suburbs*, Urban Affairs Annual Reviews (Beverly Hills, CA: Sage Publications, 1973), 15, 21; Jack Rosenthal, "Suburban Land Development: Towards Suburban Independence," in *Suburbia in Transition*, ed. Louis H. Masotti and Jeffrey K. Hadden (New York: New Viewpoints, 1974), 298; Peter O. Muller, *The Outer City: Geographical Consequences of the Urbanization of the Suburbs* (Washington, DC: Association of American Geographers, 1976); Peter O. Muller, *Contemporary Suburban America* (Englewood Cliffs, NJ: Prentice Hall, 1976); Christopher B. Leinberger and Charles Lockwood, "How Business Is Reshaping America," *Atlantic*, October 1986, 43–52; Paul Goldberger, "When Suburban Sprawl Meets Upward Mobility," *New York Times*, 26 July 1987. For an excellent overview of the changing terminology of such scholars, see Sharpe and Wallock, "Bold New City or Built-Up 'Burb'?"

18. Fishman, *Bourgeois Utopias*, 183.

19. Joel Garreau, *Edge City: Life on the New Frontier* (New York: Random House, 1991), 398–399.

20. Fishman, *Bourgeois Utopias*, 186.

21. For a compelling argument for the metropolitan approach, see Raymond A. Mohl, "City and Region: The Missing Dimension in U.S. Urban History," *Journal of Urban History* 25 (November 1998): 3–21. For studies that skillfully incorporate surrounding regions into the study of the city, see Richard C. Wade, *The Urban Frontier: The Rise of Western Cities* (Cambridge, MA: Harvard University Press, 1959); David R. Goldfield, *Cotton Fields and Skyscrapers: Southern City and Region, 1607–1980* (Baton Rouge: Louisiana State University Press, 1982); William Cronon, *Nature's Metropolis: Chicago and the Great West* (New York: W. W. Norton, 1991). One recent suburban historian who has usefully examined intergovernmental relations and city-suburban competition is Jon Teaford, *Post-Suburbia: Government and Politics in the Edge Cities* (Baltimore: Johns Hopkins University Press, 1997).

22. John R. Logan, "Growth, Politics, and the Stratification of Places," *American Journal of Sociology* 84 (1978): 404–415; Sugrue, "'All Politics Is Local'";

Richard Briffault, "Our Localism, Part II: Localism and Legal Theory," *Columbia Law Review* 90 (1990); Nancy Burns, *The Formation of American Local Governments: Private Values in Public Institutions* (New York: Oxford University Press, 1994); Teaford, *Post-Suburbia;* Gerald Frug, *City Making* (Princeton, NJ: Princeton University Press, 1999); Richard Thompson Ford, "The Boundaries of Race: Political Geography in Legal Analysis," in Kimberle Crenshaw, et al., eds., *Critical Race Theory: The Key Writings That Formed the Movement* (New York: New Press, 1995), 449–464; Kathryn M. Doherty and Clarence N. Stone, "Local Practice in Transition," in Martha Derthick, ed., *Dilemmas of Scale in America's Federal Democracy* (Washington, DC: Woodrow Wilson Center Press and Cambridge: Cambridge University Press, 1999), 157–160; Robert Wood, *1400 Governments: The Political Economy of the New York Metropolitan Region* (Cambridge, MA: Harvard University Press, 1961); Charles Tilly, *Durable Inequality* (Berkeley: University of California Press, 1999), chap. 5.

23. Nicolaides, *My Blue Heaven;* Wiese, *Places of Their Own.*

24. See, for instance, Kenneth T. Jackson, "Race, Ethnicity, and Real Estate Appraisal: The Home Owners' Loan Corporation and the Federal Housing Administration," *Journal of Urban History* 6 (August 1980): 419–452; "The Spatial Dimensions of Social Control: Race, Ethnicity, and Government Housing Policy in the United States," in Bruce M. Stave, ed., *Modern Industrial Cities: History, Policy, and Survival* (Beverly Hills: Sage Publishers, 1981), 79–128; and, for his fullest discussion of these issues, *Crabgrass Frontier.*

25. See, among others, Hirsch, *Making the Second Ghetto;* Michael B. Katz, ed., *The "Underclass" Debate: Views from History* (Princeton, NJ: Princeton University Press, 1993); Douglas S. Massey and Nancy A. Denton, *American Apartheid: Segregation and the Making of the Underclass* (Cambridge, MA: Harvard University Press, 1993); Sugrue, *The Origins of the Urban Crisis.*

CHAPTER ONE

For their invaluable comments on drafts of this chapter, special thanks to Michael Berk, Karen Caplan, Arnold Hirsch, Robert Self, and the readers for the University of Chicago Press.

1. Among the best introductions are Mark Gelfand, *A Nation of Cities: The Federal Government and Urban America, 1933–1965* (New York: Oxford University Press, 1975); Arnold R. Hirsch, *Making the Second Ghetto: Race and Housing in Chicago, 1940–1960* (New York: Cambridge University Press, 1983); Kenneth Jackson, *Crabgrass Frontier: The Suburbanization of the United States* (New York: Oxford University Press, 1985); Gregory R. Weiher, *The Fractured Metropolis: Political Fragmentation and Metropolitan Segregation* (Albany: State University of New York Press, 1991); Douglas S. Massey and Nancy A. Denton, *American Apartheid: Segregation and the Making of the Underclass* (Cambridge, MA: Harvard University Press, 1993); Jill

Quadagno, *The Color of Welfare: How Racism Undermined the War on Poverty* (New York: Oxford University Press, 1994); Melvin L. Oliver and Thomas M. Shapiro, *Black Wealth/White Wealth: A New Perspective on Racial Inequality* (New York: Routledge, 1995); Thomas J. Sugrue, *The Origins of the Urban Crisis: Race and Inequality in Post-war Detroit* (Princeton, NJ: Princeton University Press, 1996); Michael K. Brown, *Race, Money, and the American Welfare State* (Ithaca: Cornell University Press, 1999); Robin D. G. Kelley, "Into the Fire: 1970 to the Present," in *To Make Our World Anew: A History of African Americans,* Robin D. G. Kelley and Earl Lewis, eds. (New York: Oxford University Press, 2000); and Lizabeth Cohen, *A Consumers' Republic: The Politics of Mass Consumption in Post-war America* (New York: Knopf, 2003).

2. See, for example, Hirsch, *Making the Second Ghetto;* Sugrue, *Origins of the Urban Crisis;* George Lipsitz, *The Possessive Investment in Whiteness: How White People Profit from Identity Politics* (Philadelphia: Temple University Press, 1998); Becky Nicolaides, *My Blue Heaven: Life and Politics in the Working Class Suburbs of Los Angeles, 1920–1965* (Chicago: University of Chicago Press, 2002); Robert O. Self, *American Babylon: Race and the Struggle for Postwar Oakland* (Princeton, NJ: Princeton University Press, 2003); and Cohen, *Consumers' Republic.*

3. Ira Katznelson and Bruce Pietrykowki, "Rebuilding the American State: Evidence from the 1940's," *Studies in American Political Development* 5 (Fall, 1991), quoted from 302, 306–307; Alan Brinkley, *The End of Reform: New Deal Liberalism in Recession and War* (New York: Knopf, 1995).

4. Other recent treatments of the Keynesian revolution include David M. Kennedy, *Freedom from Fear: The American People in Depression and War, 1929–1945* (New York: Oxford University Press, 1999), 350–361, and Robert M. Collins, *More: The Politics of Economic Growth in Postwar America* (New York: Oxford University Press, 2000), 6–16. For an introduction to the vast scholarship on New Deal reform, see Anthony J. Badger, *The New Deal: The Depression Years, 1933–1940* (Chicago: Ivan R. Dee, 2002), and the important critiques of the state-building literature by Michael Brown, "State Capacity and Political Choice," *Studies in American Political Development* 9 (Spring 1995), and Julian E. Zelizer, *Taxing America: Wilbur D. Mills, Congress, and the State, 1945–1975* (Princeton, NJ: Princeton University Press, 2003).

5. Before the New Deal, the nation's money supply was relatively "inelastic," because the Treasury's specie reserves limited the amount of new money that banks could inject into the economy (either through lending or draft withdrawals). Following abandonment of the gold standard and the creation of a multifaceted federal regulatory, reserve, and insurance system, the money supply became "elastic," enabling private lenders to provide a potentially unlimited amount of liquid capital to both businesses and consumers.

6. Among the most important interventions were the Banking Acts of 1933 and 1935, the Gold Reserve Act of 1934, and the selective credit programs

discussed below. For an introduction, see Robert Guttman, *How Credit Money Shapes the Economy: The United States in a Global System* (Armonk, NY: M. E. Sharpe, 1994); Ronnie J. Phillips, "An End to Private Banking: Early New Deal Proposals to Alter the Role of the Federal Government in Credit Allocation," *Journal of Money, Credit, and Banking,* 26, 3, Pt. 2: *Federal Credit Allocation: Theory, Evidence, and History* (Aug., 1994), 552–568; Raymond W. Goldsmith, *The Flow of Capital Funds in the Post-war Economy* (New York: National Bureau of Economic Research, 1965); Ann Meyerson, "The Changing Structure of Housing Finance in the United States," in *Housing Issues of the 1990s,* Sarah Rosenberry and Chester Hartman, eds. (New York: Praeger, 1989); and Sherman J. Maisel, *Financing Real Estate: Principles and Practices* (New York: McGraw-Hill, 1965). Giovanni Arrighi situates these reforms in the context of international political and economic transformations in *The Long Twentieth Century: Money, Power, and the Origins of Our Times* (London: Verso, 1994), esp. chap. 4. The few general treatments of postwar growth in the United States that address the credit revolution are those studies whose focus is money and credit, such as James Grant, *Money of the Mind: Borrowing and Lending in America from the Civil War to Michael Milkin* (New York: Farrar Straus & Giroux, 1992), and Lendol Calder, *Financing the American Dream: A Cultural History of Consumer Credit* (Princeton, NJ: Princeton University Press, 1999).

7.   Quotes from Brinkley, *End of Reform,* 13, and Cohen, *Consumers' Republic,* 30. See also Kennedy, *Freedom from Fear,* 363–370. Notably, selective credit programs are seldom discussed in studies of New Deal reform and modern state-building.

8.   Technically, the VA program "guaranteed" its loans.

9.   Cohen, *Consumers' Republic,* 122–123; U.S. Federal Housing Administration, *Underwriting Manual: Underwriting and Valuation Procedure under Title II of the National Housing Act* (Washington, DC: Government Printing Office, 1936), Pt. 2, Secs. 229 and 233. See also Sec. 266 (on keeping "incompatible racial element[s]" out of the schools) and Sec. 284(3)(g–h). If a floor plan for new construction met FHA approval, an agency stamp indicated that structures "shall be located on the plot so as to comply with all restrictions" and all "F.H.A. property standards." Examples in National Archives II, Record Group (RG) 31, Case Files for Homes, 1934–1938, box 8. On restrictive covenants, see samples and memos in RG 31, Commissioner's Correspondence and Subject File, 1938–1958 (CCSF), box 6.

10.   U.S. Department of Commerce, Bureau of the Census data (1965, 1975); Department of Commerce, *Statistical Abstract* (1965); U.S. Housing and Home Finance Agency, *Housing Statistics,* Historical Supplement (1958) and *Twelfth Annual Report;* Leo Grebler, *The Role of Federal Credit Aids in Residential Construction* (New York: National Bureau of Economic Research, 1953), 16, 18, 29–30, 42; Maisel, *Financing Real Estate,* 99–100; Jackson, *Crabgrass Frontier,* 190–218; Cohen, *Consumers' Republic,* 121–123, 200–227; Andrew

Wiese, *Places of Their Own: African American Suburbanization in the Twentieth Century* (Chicago: University of Chicago Press, 2004), chaps. 4–7.

11. Carl E. Parry, "Selective Instruments of National Credit Policy," in Karl R. Bopp, et al., *Federal Reserve Policy* (Post-war Economic Studies, no. 8) (Washington, DC: Board of Governors of the Federal Reserve System, 1947), 73–74; Grebler, *Role of Federal Credit Aids,* 29–30, 36, 42; Thomas B. Marvell, *Federal Home Loan Bank Board* (New York: Praeger, 1969), 19, 27–29, 31; Milton P. Semer et al., "Evolution of Federal Legislative Policy in Housing: Housing Credits," in J. Paul Mitchell, ed., *Federal Housing Policy and Programs: Past and Present* (New Brunswick, NJ: Rutgers University Center for Urban Policy Research, 1985), 69–106; Frederick E. Balderston, *Thrifts in Crisis: Structural Transformation of the Savings and Loan Industry* (Cambridge, MA: Ballinger Publishing Co., 1985); Jackson, *Crabgrass Frontier,* 216.

12. Cohen quoted in *Consumers' Republic,* 404 (see also 122, 196–197). Compare Jackson, *Crabgrass Frontier,* 215–217. Depending on the account, selective credit policies are alternatively described as "subsidizing" businesses and consumers, as "stabilizing" existing markets, or even as "proceed[ing]" on the same philosophy of supply and demand that governs private firms," essentially "liberating" existing capital. Many general texts in U.S. economic history ignore the programs completely. In addition to works cited above, compare discussions in Robert C. Wood, *1400 Governments: The Political Economy of the New York Metropolitan Region* (Cambridge, MA: Harvard University Press, 1961); Edward C. Banfield and James Q. Wilson, *City Politics* (Cambridge, MA: Harvard University Press, 1963); Jeremy Atack and Peter Passel, *A New Economic View of American History: From Colonial Times to 1940* (New York: Norton, 1994); and Tom Martinson, *American Dreamscape: The Pursuit of Happiness in Post-war Suburbia* (New York: Carroll & Graf, 2000).

13. Miles Colean, *The Impact of Government on Real Estate Finance in the United States* (New York: National Bureau of Economic Research, 1950), 106, and chap. 7; Balderston, *Thrifts in Crisis,* 21; Raymond J. Saulnier, *Constructive Years: The U.S. Economy under Eisenhower* (Lanham, MD: University Press of America, 1991), 42; George F. Break, *The Economic Impact of Federal Loan Insurance* (Washington, DC: National Planning Association, 1961), 45; William E. Dunkman, *Money, Credit and Banking* (New York: Random House, 1970), 394; James Gillies, "Federal Credit Programs in the Housing Sector of the Economy: An Aggregate Analysis," in Stewart Johnson et al., eds., *Federal Credit Programs* (Englewood Cliffs, NJ: Prentice-Hall, 1963), 427, 434, 457–460; Goldsmith, *Flow of Capital Funds,* 277–279, 303, 446; William L. Silber, "Selective Credit Policies: A Survey" and Jack M. Guttentag, "Selective Credit Controls," in Ira Kaminow and James M. O'Brien, *Studies in Selective Credit Policies* (Philadelphia: Federal Reserve Bank of Philadelphia, 1975), 95–121, 35–40.

14. The FHA's collaboration with the private sector is documented in reports, correspondence, agency memoranda, and speeches before business leaders. For an introduction, see "Suggested Agenda for Industry Meeting," "Combined Home Builders and FHA Conference, Fort Pitt Hotel, Sept. 22, 1948," and "Summary of the Housing Act of 1948 for September Meetings with Industry," all in (folder) "Meetings—Industry, 1948," RG 31, CCSF, box 4; "Mortgage Conferences—Suggestions for Conducting," in RG 31, Program Correspondence for the Assistant Commissioner for Operations, 1936–1956, box 9; and assorted correspondence regarding postwar operations, in RG 31, Interoffice Policy Memos, boxes 41 and 43. Foley quoted in letter to Walter Greene, Aug. 14, 1945, in "Committee-Planning, 1945–1946," RG 31, CCSF, box 1. Metropolitan data collected in: RG 31, Records Relating to Housing Market Analysis, 1935–1942; RG 31, State and City Data Re. Economic Conditions, c. 1934–1942; RG 31, Housing Market Data, 1938–1952; and RG 31, Reports of Housing Market Analysts, 1937–1963. For a detailed treatment, see David M. P. Freund, *Colored Property: State Policy and White Racial Politics in the Modern American Suburb* (Chicago: University of Chicago Press, forthcoming), chaps. 3–5.

    For discussions of public-private collaboration in other agencies, see C. Lowell Harriss, *History and Policies of the Home Owners' Loan Corporation* (New York: National Bureau of Economic Research, 1951) and Marvell, *Federal Home Loan Bank Board.* The HOLC, a short-lived but very influential experiment in direct federal mortgage lending created in 1933, set critical precedents for FHA appraisal and lending practices; see Jackson, *Crabgrass Frontier,* chap. 11, and Freund, *Colored Property,* chap. 3.

15. "Address delivered by Mr. James A. Moffett . . . at a luncheon of the Advertising Club of New York," Dec. 13, 1934, in "Early Moffett Speeches," RG 31, Speeches (SP), box 29.

16. Cohen, *Consumers' Republic,* 124–129 (quoted on 127). In addition to the postwar studies cited above, see the excellent monographs by Charles Abrams, Joseph T. Howell, David Halle, Jonathan Rieder, Elaine Tyler May, Mike Davis, Ronald P. Formisano, Stephanie Coontz, and Elizabeth Fones-Wolf.

17. Freund, *Colored Property,* Pt. 1.

18. Arnold R. Hirsch, "'Containment' on the Home Front: Race and Federal Housing Policy from the New Deal to the Cold War," *Journal of Urban History* 26, no. 2 (Jan., 2000): 158–180; Hirsch, "Searching for a 'Sound Negro Policy': A Racial Agenda for the Housing Acts of 1949 and 1954," *Housing Policy Debate* 11, no. 2 (2000); Hirsch, "Choosing Segregation: Federal Housing Policy between *Shelly* and *Brown,*" in John F. Bauman, Roger Biles, and Kristin Szylvian, eds., *From Tenements to Taylor Homes: In Search of an Urban Housing Policy in Twentieth-Century America* (University Park: Pennsylvania State University Press, 2000); David M. P. Freund, "Democracy's Unfinished

Business: Federal Policy and the Search for Fair Housing, 1961–1968" (see *Poverty and Race* 13, no. 3, 2004).

19. The agency would later compare their promotional efforts to "a Government war bond drive"; Federal Housing Administration, *The FHA Story in Summary* (Washington, DC: Government Printing Office, 1959), 9. For Moffett's characterizations and the reach of early PR efforts, see radio addresses and talks collected in "Early Moffett Speeches," RG 31, Speeches, 1935–1954, box 29, including talks before the Bankers Forum of American Institute of Banking, New York City (Dec. 12, 1934), the Advertising Club of New York (Dec. 13, 1934), and the Oklahoma City Chamber of Commerce (March 1, 1935). Also see Mathew F. Bokovoy's excellent reconstruction of an elaborate FHA "Better Housing" installation in "The FHA and the 'Culture of Abundance' at the 1935 San Diego World's Fair," *Journal of the American Planning Association* 68, no. 4 (Autumn 2002): 371–386.

20. Ibid; and Moffett's "New U.S. Housing Plan," NBC national broadcast (August 15, 1934), in "Early Moffett Speeches," RG 31, SP, box 29.

21. Ibid.

22. Ibid.; and Moffett's speech over the Columbia Broadcasting System hookup (under auspices of the U.S. Building and Loan League), Sept. 28, 1934, in "Early Moffett Speeches," RG 31, SP, box 29; *FHA Story,* 9.

23. Moffett over the CBS hookup, Sept. 28, 1934; Moffett, "New U.S. Housing Plan"; and Moffett over CBS and NBC hookup, Sept. 19, 1934; all in "Early Moffett Speeches," RG 31, SP, box 29; Ferguson address on WCFL, Chicago, March 16, 1938, in "Speeches, 1935–1939," RG 31, SP, box 29.

24. Speeches and memoranda from 1935 to 1954 in RG 31, SP, boxes 29–34.

25. Moffett to the National Retail Lumber Dealer's Association, Washington, D.C., April 17, 1935, and to the Advertising Club of New York, Dec. 13, 1934, in "Early Moffett Speeches," RG 31, SP, box 29; Ferguson to American Title Association Convention, Memphis, Oct. 14, 1935, in "Speeches, 1935–1939," RG 31, SP, box 29.

26. On resumption of the PR campaign, see Walter Greene's correspondence in "Committee-Planning, 1945–1946," RG 31, CCSF, box 1. For an introduction to postwar programs, see Richards's speech before builders and lenders, Greensboro, N.C., March 14, 1949, in RG 31, SP, box 31; Richards before NAHB, Chicago, Jan. 24, 1951; Richards before the Mortgage Bankers Association, Chicago, Jan. 25, 1951, in RG 31, SP, box 32; and "Credit Controls—Correspondence, 1950" and "1952," in RG 31, CCSF, box 2. For one of Richards's laments that lenders were not doing their part, see his speech to the Texas Mortgage Bankers Association, Fort Worth, April 12, 1951, in RG 31, SP, box 32.

27. Speeches by Foley and Richards, 1948–1952, collected in RG 31, SP, boxes 31 and 32. See, for example, Richards to "committee of financial and building interests," New York City, Sept. 12, 1945; Richards to American Bankers

Association, Western Savings and Mortgage Conference, San Francisco, April 4, 1949; and Richards to "Washington Conference for Men Under 35, Sponsored by Mortgage Bankers Association of America," Washington, D.C., Jan. 15, 1952.

28. "Statement of Franklin D. Richards, Commissioner, FHA, before the Subcommittee of the House Banking and Currency Committee," Feb. 5, 1952, in RG 31, SP, box 32; FHA, *FHA Story,* 22. On the legislative debates and press coverage, see Freund, *Colored Property,* chaps. 3–4.

29. George H. Patterson to Ferguson, Oct. 20, 1939; J. A. Markel to Ferguson, March 8, 1940; and assorted correspondence; all in "Speeches— Correspondence (Ferguson, 1939–1941)," RG 31, SP, box 29; Moffett at Century of Progress Fair, Chicago, Oct. 24, 1934, in "Early Moffett Speeches," RG 31, SP, box 29. For an example of appraisers' post-*Shelley* treatments of race and property values, see American Institute of Real Estate Appraisers, *The Appraisal of Real Estate* (Chicago: Institute, 1960), 97, 100–101.

30. For an examination of local mobilizations in metropolitan Detroit, see Freund, *Colored Property,* Pt. 2.

31. The critique of discrimination in federal housing programs is as old as the programs themselves. For an introduction, see articles and monographs by Charles Johnson, Robert Weaver, Herman Long, Charles Abrams, Kenneth Clark, Mark Gelfand, Chester Hartman, and Kenneth Jackson, as well as Hirsch's discussion of the federal Race Relations Service in "'Containment' on the Home Front."

32. Emphasis in the original. Notably, "the barometers of" was handwritten over the original typescript, which read "responsible for." Ferguson, "Talk before Negro Business Conference, April 18, 1941, Department of Commerce," in "Speeches—Correspondence (Ferguson, 1939–1941)," RG 31, SP, box 29. In internal correspondence, Ferguson had encouraged his speechwriter to emphasize that it was "occupants who make slums far more than the structures in which they live"—advice that the author ignored.

33. Hirsch, "'Containment' on the Home Front," esp. 161–162, 170–178 (quoting Cole); Hirsch, "Choosing Segregation"; Freund, "'Democracy's Unfinished Business'"; 1948 memo re: court challenges, in "Racial Restrictive Covenants, 1938–1948," RG 31, CCSF, box 6; Flora Y. Hatcher, "Overall Summary Report of Housing Hearing of Commission on Civil Rights, Feb. 2–3, 1959, NYC," in National Archives II, RG 207, "Racial Relations, Intergroup Relations," box 25; "Material prepared for Harold Tyler, Justice Dept., re: effect of an executive order on housing activities . . ." (Oct. 4, 1960), in "Intergroup (Snowden policy memos), 1960," RG 207, box 40; National Committee against Discrimination in Housing, "Needed: 'A Stroke of the Pen,"' in "Intergroup, Exec. Order, 1961," RG 207, box 64. Hirsch also discusses the Tyler memo in "'Containment' on the Home Front," 182.

34. Indeed, even the selective credit agencies designed to support conventional market operations (such as the FHLB system) claimed exemption from federal fair housing laws, arguing that they were not authorized to influence the lending decisions of private institutions.

CHAPTER TWO

I would like to acknowledge the research assistance of Samuel Collins and Lynette Rawlings as well as the financial support of Chester Hartman and the Poverty and Race Research Action Council. Similar thanks are due Thomas Henderson of the Lawyers National Committee for Civil Rights under the Law. Helpful critical commentary was provided by Connie Atkinson, David Freund, Raymond A. Mohl, Florence Roisman, editors Thomas Sugrue and Kevin Kruse and the participants they gathered at the conference on the new suburbia at Princeton University last year. Final thanks go to the College of Liberal Arts at the University of New Orleans and the Midlo family of New Orleans for their support in facing the future.

1. National Committee against Discrimination in Housing (NCDH), press release, January 10,1955, was found attached to Frances Levenson to Maxwell Rabb, January 23, 1956, in folder GF 50-A(3), box 399, Central Files, General Files, Dwight David Eisenhower Papers (DDE Papers), Eisenhower Library (EL), Abilene, Kansas.

2. The RRS and the "equity" policy are discussed more fully in Arnold R. Hirsch, "Searching for a 'Sound Negro Policy': A Racial Agenda for the Housing Acts of 1949 and 1954," *Housing Policy Debate* 11 (Summer 2000): 393–441.

3. Frank S. Horne, "First Go 'Round Note following HST-day," November 9, 1948, in folder 4, box 1, in the Frank S. Horne Papers, Amistad Research Center, Tulane University.

4. PHA, "The Negro in Public Housing, 1933–1953: Problems and Accomplishments" (typescript, May 1954), 109–110, in folder 4, box 1, Record Group (RG) 196, National Archives (NA) II; "Racially Integrated Public Housing Programs," Draft no. 3, February 1952, Adker 067282 (LC), plaintiff's ex. 293. The author wishes to thank Tom Henderson of the National Lawyer's Committee for Civil Rights under Law for providing documents from *Adker v. HUD*. See also, Arnold R. Hirsch, "'Containment' on the Home Front: Race and Federal Housing Policy from the New Deal to the Cold War," *Journal of Urban History* 26 (January 2000): 158–189.

5. See Arnold R. Hirsch, *Making the Second Ghetto: Race and Housing in Chicago, 1940–1960* (New York: Cambridge University Press, 1983; 2d ed. University of Chicago Press, 1998); for the two-tiered housing policy, see Gail Radford, *Modern Housing for America: Policy Struggles in the New Deal Era* (Chicago: University of Chicago Press, 1996).

6. Hyde Park–Kenwood Association to Irene McCoy Gaines, July 6, 1944, box 2, Irene McCoy Gaines Papers, Chicago Historical Society (CHS).

7. Chicago Housing Authority, *Relocation of Site Residents to Private Housing* (Chicago: CHA, 1955).

8. Leverett S. Lyon to Holman D. Pettibone, September 27, 1945, box 2, Holman D. Pettibone Papers, CHS. The plan's author, an otherwise unidentified John R. Thomas, offered his outline in good faith to "advance and protect the just rights and reasonable aspirations of both elements." See John R. Thomas, "Race Relations in Chicago" (typed, n.d.), attached to Lyon to Pettibone, September 27, 1945, cited above. The exchange of "decent living conditions" for an acceptance of residential segregation as a formula for racial peace in Chicago went back at least as far as Gov. Frank Lowden's riot commission report following the city's 1919 debacle. See Arnold R. Hirsch, *Making the Second Ghetto: Race and Housing in Chicago, 1940–1960*, 1st ed., 13–14.

9. Holman D. Pettibone, Notes of telephone conversation with Mr. Ecker, October 8, 1947, box 3, Pettibone Papers (CHS).

10. *Chicago Bee,* November 28, 1943, 1.

11. Lyon to Pettibone, September 27, 1945.

12. "Address by Senator Paul H. Douglas," April 19, 1949; Sen. Paul H. Douglas to Raymond M. Foley, April 20, 1949 and Foley to Douglas, April 21, 1949, all in Chicago Commission on Human Relations, "Monthly Report of the Executive Director," October–December, 1949, folder 624, Chicago Urban League Papers, Special Collections, University of Illinois at Chicago (UIC).

13. W. Edward Orser, *Blockbusting in Baltimore: The Edmondson Village Story* (Lexington: University Press of Kentucky, 1994); Kenneth D. Durr, *Behind the Backlash: White Working-Class Politics in Baltimore, 1940–1980* (Chapel Hill: University of North Carolina Press, 2003). For a recent treatment of blockbusting in Chicago, see Amanda Irene Seligman, "Apologies to Dracula, Werewolf, and Frankenstein: White Homeowners and Blockbusters in Chicago," *Journal of the Illinois State Historical Society* 94 (Spring 2001): 70–95.

14. Metropolitan Housing Council, Minutes of the Regular Meeting of the Board of Governors, November 2, 1943, in Supplement II, Board of Governors, Metropolitan Housing and Planning Council Papers, Special Collections, UIC.

15. The documents that follow in this note are drawn from the Plaintiff's First Request for Admissions in *Carmen Thompson, et al., v. United States Department of Housing and Urban Development, et al.,* Civil Action MJG 95-309. Thanks are due to Barbara Samuels and the American Civil Liberties Union–Maryland Foundation for making them available. [NHA], "Problems of Site Selection during the War Housing Program" (Preliminary Draft, Oct.–Nov., 1944), #62 *Thompson v. HUD*; [n.a.], "Special Note on Site Selection," May 20, 1944, #61 *Thompson v. HUD*; HABC, "Effects of the Post-War Program on Negro Housing," September 25, 1945, #7 in *Thompson v. HUD*. See also Peter H. Henderson, "Local Deals and the New Deal State: Implementing Federal Public Housing in Baltimore, 1933–1968" (Ph.D. diss., Johns Hopkins University, 1993); Durr, *Behind the Backlash.*

16. Frank S. Horne to Neal J. Hardy, February 2, 1951, folder: Racial Relations, box 53, HHFA General Subject Files, 1947–1960, RG 207.

17. Frank S. Horne to Carl Feiss, September 1, in folder 1: Racial Relations, box 263, Urban Renewal Administration (URA) General Subject File, 1949–1960, RG 263; Clarence Mitchell to Nathaniel S. Keith, December 17, 1951, and Raymond M. Foley to Enrique, n.d., both in Clarence Mitchell, Untitled Speech before the Richmond Civic Council, December 6, 1951, typescript in folder 22, box 269, General Subject files, 1949–1960, RG 207.

18. HABC, "Effects of the Post-War Program on Negro Housing," September 25, 1945, #7 in *Thompson v. HUD*. An FHA marketing survey from the mid-1950s indicated that agency's perspective on black housing in Baltimore. Assessing housing demand over a two-year period ending in 1955, the FHA called for the construction of 20,000 new units, with 2,600 allocated for nonwhites (13% of the total though blacks represented nearly one quarter of the city's population). Some 2,000 of the 2,600 units (77%) were expected to be centrally located rental housing; 16,000 of the 17,400 units designated for white occupancy (88.5%) were to be single-family homes. The agency admitted the desire to promote the "general objective" of "close-in development" for blacks while describing white housing needs in terms of "the recent strong trend to suburban building." See Ralph S. Weese, "Report on the Housing Market: Baltimore, Maryland, Standard Metropolitan Area as of September 1, 1953" (typewritten, n.d.), folder 11, box 748, Racial Relations Program Files, HHFA, RG 207.

19. Frank Horne to the Administrator, July 27, 1951, in folder: Racial Relations, box 53, HHFA General Subject Files, 1947–1960, RG 207.

20. Richard O. Davies, *Housing Reform in the Truman Administration* (Columbia: University of Missouri Press, 1966), and *Defender of the Old Guard: John Bricker and American Politics* (Columbus: Ohio State University Press, 1993). See also the *New York Times*, April 15, 1949, 15:1 and April 22, 1949, 1:1.

21. PHA, "The Negro in Public Housing, 1933–1953: Problems and Accomplishments" (typescript, May 1954), 109–110 in folder 4, box 1, RG 196, NA II.

22. Office of the Administrator, Racial Relations Service, "Policy Questions—Staff Discussion of Staff Papers," April 6, 1953, Adker 116127 (LC); plaintiff's ex. 121. The author wishes to thank Tom Henderson of the National Lawyer's Committee for Civil Rights under Law for providing documents from *Adker v. HUD*.

23. George B. Nesbitt to J. W. Follin, October 19, 1954, Adker 116135 (LC); plaintiff's ex. [illegible].

24. PHA, "The Negro in Public Housing," 109.

25. "Racially Integrated Public Housing Programs," Draft no. 3, February 1952, Adker 067282 (LC), plaintiff's ex. 293.

26. Ibid.

27. Aksel Nielsen to Governor Sherman Adams, December 22, 1952, in folder: Endorsements, box 398, GF 50-A, DDE Records.

28. Ibid.
29. Gail Radford, *Modern Housing for America: Policy Struggles in the New Deal Era* (Chicago: University of Chicago Press, 1996).
30. Charles F. Willis, Jr., to Governor Adams, January 28 and 29, 1953, both in folder: Endorsements, box 398, GF 50-A, DDE Records.
31. The President's Advisory Committee on Government Housing Policies and Programs, *A Report to the President of the United States* (Washington, DC: Government Printing Office, 1953), Appendix 2: Subcommittee on Urban Redevelopment, 108–127.
32. Frank S. Horne to Albert M. Cole, Memorandum re Proposals for the President's Advisory Committee on Housing, n.d., in folder 12, box 745, Program Files, Racial Relations Files, 1946–1958, RG 207, NA II.
33. President's Advisory Committee, *Report,* n.d., attached to Albert M. Cole to Mr. President, December 14, 1953, in folder: Public Housing-1953, box 7, James Lambie Records, EL.
34. Clipping from *Business Week,* December 12, 1953 found in folder: Housing (1), box 47, Howard Pyle Records, EL.
35. Minutes of Cabinet Meeting, December 9, 1953 in folder: Cabinet Meeting, December 9, 1953, box 2, Ann Whitman File, Cabinet Series, DDE Papers.
36. The full text of the "Housing Message" may be found in the *New York Times,* January 26, 1954; a clipping is in folder: Housing (2), box 47, Pyle Records.
37. The rather distinctive handwriting commenting on the text appears to be Hauge's. The memo to which the draft is attached is also addressed to him. See the "First Draft of Housing Message," attached to Albert M. Cole to Gabriel Hauge, January 18, 1954, in folder OF-120, 1954 (3), box 613, Central Files, Official Files, DDE Papers, EL.
38. Hirsch, "Searching for a 'Sound Negro Policy,' ' 410–419; Arnold R. Hirsch, "Massive Resistance in the Urban North: Trumbull Park, Chicago, 1953–1966," *Journal of American History* 82 (September 1995): 522–550.
39. Adam Clayton Powell, Jr., to Mr. President, June 10, 1953, and Max Rabb to Governor Adams, June 15, 1953, both in file: OF 142-A-4, Segregation-Integration (1), box 731, DDE Papers.
40. Handwritten notes of January 28, 1955, Cabinet meeting, in folder C-21 (3), 1/28/55, box 3, Office of the Staff Secretary Records, 1952–1961, White House Office, DDE Records.
41. Walter White to Herbert R. Brownell, December 22, 1954, frame 615, reel 6, Part 5: Campaign against Residential Segregation, NAACP Papers; George W. Snowden to Henry M. Day, March 14, 1955, in folder: Minority Group Housing, 1955–1956, box 6, Program Correspondence of the Assistant Commissioner for Operations, 1936–1956, RG 31, NA II.
42. Robert Fredrick Burk, *The Eisenhower Administration and Black Civil Rights,* (Knoxville: University of Tennessee Press, 1984), 109–127.
43. B. T. Fitzpatrick to Mr. Cole, June 10, 1954, in folder 5, box 20, Subject Correspondence File, Albert Cole, Administrator; Joseph Guandolo to

J. W. Follin, August 24, 1954, and J. W. Follin to Albert M. Cole, May 28, 1954, in folder: Racial Relations, box 284, HHFA General Subject Files, 1949–1960, all in RG 207. See also Allan F. Thornton to Walter S. Newlin, June 28, 1954, and W. S. Newlin to Regional Directors, July 2, 1954, in folder: Minority Group Housing, General, 1954, box 3, Program Correspondence of the Assistant Commissioner for Operations, 1936–1956, RG 31; and *New York Times* clipping, November 14, 1958, in folder 5, box 10, RG 196, NA II.

44. Burk, *Eisenhower Administration and Black Civil Rights*, 109–127.
45. George B. Nesbitt, "Approaches and Objectives Useful to Intergroup Relations Officials in Connection with Local Slum Clearance and Redevelopment Programs," 1951, paper presented at the Conference of Intergroup Relations Officials, folder 715, Chicago Urban League Papers, Special Collections, UIC.
46. Metropolitan Housing Council to Planning Committee, [Chicago] City Council, October 1, 1951, folder: Redevelopment #3, Supplement III, MHPC Papers.
47. Albert M. Cole, "The Slum, the City, and the Citizen" (typewritten, February 24, 1954), speech presented to the St. Louis Chamber of Commerce, frame 0537, reel 6, Part 5: The Campaign against Residential Segregation, NAACP Papers (University Microfilms).
48. Maxwell Rabb to Robert W. Dowling, October 18, 1954, folder: Racial Relations, box 96, General Subject Files, 1947–1960, RG 207; Albert M. Cole, "Address to the Mid-Atlantic Conference," National Association of Housing and Redevelopment Officials, New York, April 1, 1954, frame 0563, reel 6, Part 5: The Campaign against Residential Segregation, NAACP Papers (University Microfilms).
49. Cole, "Address to the Mid-Atlantic Conference," and "The Slum, the City, and the Citizen."
50. Albert M. Cole to Fred M. Stuart, May 27, 1954, in folder: Racial Relations, box 96, General Subject Files, 1947–1960, RG 207.
51. Franklin D. Richards to Thurgood Marshall, November 1, 1948, folder: Restrictive Covenants, 1938–1948, box 6, Commissioner's Correspondence and Subject File, 1937–1958, RG 31. This letter is making direct reference to the Housing Act of 1937 and the Supreme Court's action in *Shelley v. Kraemer* (1948). Richards adhered to the argument, however, that the "restricted use of property rests entirely with the property owner" and that the FHA could not "withdraw its normal protection and benefits" from anyone because of their private decision even after *Brown*.
52. Frank S. Horne to the Administrator, May 27, 1952, in folder: Racial Relations, box 59, General Subject Files, 1947–1960, RG 207.
53. Minutes of the Cabinet Meeting, January 28, 1955, folder: Cabinet Meeting, 1/28/55, box 4, Cabinet Series, Ann Whitman File, DDE Papers, EL, Abilene, Kansas.
54. Cole to Stuart, May 27, 1954.

CHAPTER THREE

1. Joel Garreau, *Edge City: Life on the New Frontier* (New York: Doubleday, 1991); Robert Lang, *Edgeless Cites: Exploring the Elusive Metropolis* (Washington, DC: Brookings Institution, 2003).
2. Fishman, *Bourgeois Utopias: The Rise and Fall of Suburbia* (New York: Basic Books, 1987), 184.
3. John Seely Brown, Foreword, *Understanding Silicon Valley: The Anatomy of an Entrepreneurial Region,* ed. Martin Kenney (Stanford, CA: Stanford University Press, 2000), xii. Also see John Seely Brown and Paul Duguid, "Mysteries of the Region: Knowledge Dynamics in Silicon Valley," in *The Silicon Valley Edge: A Habitat for Innovation and Entrepreneurship,* ed. Chong-Moon Lee, et al. (Stanford, CA: Stanford University Press, 2000), 16–45; David P. Angel, "High-Technology Agglomeration and the Labor Market: The Case of Silicon Valley," and Stephen S. Cohen and Gary Fields, "Social Capital and Capital Gains: An Examination of Social Capital in Silicon Valley," both in Kenney, *Understanding Silicon Valley;* AnnaLee Saxenian, *Regional Advantage: Culture and Competition in Silicon Valley and Route 128* (Cambridge, MA: Harvard University Press, 1994); Peter Hall and Ann Markusen, *Silicon Landscapes* (Boston: Allen & Unwin, 1985).
4. Examples of entrepreneur-centered narratives include Michael Lewis, *The New New Thing* (New York: W. W. Norton, 2000); David A. Kaplan, *The Silicon Boys and Their Valley of Dreams* (New York: William Morrow, 1999); Michael Malone, *The Big Score: The Billion-Dollar Story of Silicon Valley* (Garden City, NY: Doubleday, 1985). Perhaps the most influential scholarly study of Silicon Valley to date is Saxenian, *Regional Advantage*. The literature on the Cold War research university also has made important contributions to the history of high-tech regions; see Rebecca Lowen, *Creating the Cold War University: The Transformation of Stanford* (Berkeley: University of California Press, 1997); Roger L. Geiger, *Research and Relevant Knowledge: American Research Universities Since World War II* (New York: Oxford University Press, 1993); Stuart W. Leslie, *The Cold War and American Science: The Military-Industrial-Academic Complex at MIT and Stanford* (New York: Columbia University Press, 1993); Richard M. Freeland, *Academia's Golden Age: Universities in Massachusetts, 1945–1970* (New York: Oxford University Press, 1992). Also significant are works on American scientists and science policy, including Jessica Wang, *American Science in an Age of Anxiety: Scientists, Anticommunism, and the Cold War* (Chapel Hill: University of North Carolina Press, 1999); Daniel J. Kevles, *The Physicists: The History of a Scientific Community in Modern America* (Cambridge, MA: Harvard University Press, 1995); Brian Balogh, *Chain Reaction: Expert Debate and Public Participation in American Commercial Nuclear Power, 1945–1975* (New York: Cambridge University Press, 1991). For a useful review of the debate see Balogh, *Chain Reaction,* 1–20.

5.   Important monographs exploring this regional favoritism include Bruce J. Schulman, *From Cotton Belt to Sunbelt: Federal Policy, Economic Development, and the Transformation of the South, 1938–1980* (New York: Oxford University Press, 1991); Ann Markusen et al., *The Rise of the Gunbelt: The Military Remapping of Industrial America* (New York: Oxford University Press, 1991); Roger Lotchin, *Fortress California, 1910–1961: From Warfare to Welfare* (Urbana and Chicago: University of Illinois Press, 1992).

6.   See Thomas Hanchett, "U.S. Tax Policy and the Shopping-Center Boom of the 1950s and 1960s," *American Historical Review* 101, no. 4 (October 1996): 1082–1110; Thomas J. Sugrue, *Origins of the Urban Crisis: Race and Inequality in Postwar Detroit* (Princeton, NJ: Princeton University Press, 1993); Douglas S. Massey and Nancy A. Denton, *American Apartheid: Segregation and the Making of the Underclass* (Cambridge, MA: Harvard University Press, 1993); *Urban Policy in Twentieth-Century America,* ed. Arnold R. Hirsch and Raymond A. Mohl (New Brunswick, N.J.: Rutgers University Press, 1993); Jon C. Teaford, *The Rough Road to Renaissance: Urban Revitalization in America, 1940–1985* (Baltimore: Johns Hopkins University Press, 1990); Carl Abbott, *The New Urban America: Growth and Politics in Sunbelt Cities,* rev. ed. (Chapel Hill: University of North Carolina Press, 1987); Kenneth T. Jackson, *Crabgrass Frontier: The Suburbanization of the United States* (New York: Oxford University Press, 1985).

7.   For further discussion of the spatial and political characteristics of Sunbelt cities, see Carl Abbott, *The Metropolitan Frontier: Cities in the Modern American West* (Tucson: University of Arizona Press, 1993), Raymond Mohl, ed., *Searching for the Sunbelt: Historical Perspectives on a Region* (Knoxville: University of Tennessee Press, 1990).

8.   Marketing, publicity, and economic development campaigns spearheaded by the Atlanta Chamber of Commerce and promoted by the city's mayors underscored this metropolitan approach. In the 1950s and early 1960s, downtown-based leaders actively recruited new firms and residents to Atlanta by emphasizing its suburban commercial and residential amenities and celebrated the region's growth in 1959 with "M Day," the moment at which the Census estimated the metropolitan area had gained its one millionth resident. See William A. Emerson, Jr., "Where the Paper Clips Jump . . . And 'M' Stands for Men, Money, Millions," *Newsweek,* 19 October 1959, 94–96.

9.   For a detailed case study of Atlanta's economic development efforts and the currents of race and class that shaped them, see Margaret Pugh O'Mara, *Cities of Knowledge: Cold War Science and the Search for the Next Silicon Valley* (Princeton, NJ: Princeton University Press, 2004).

10. San Francisco Bay Area Council, Industrial Development Meeting, Minutes, 13 August 1947, file folder (FF) "S.F. Bay Area Council," San Francisco History Center (SFHC), San Francisco Public Library; San Francisco Bay Area Council, *Program and Objectives* (December 1945), SFHC. The six firms pledging financial support to the Bay Area Council in its first year were the pillars of the

downtown business community: Bank of America, American Trust, Standard Oil of California, Pacific Gas and Electric, U.S. Steel and Bechtel Corporation.

11. For historical patterns, see Richard A. Walker, "Industry Builds the City: The Suburbanization of Manufacturing in the San Francisco Bay Area, 1850–1940," *Journal of Historical Geography* 27, no. 1 (January 2001): 36–57. For effect of the progrowth political economy on the development and allocation of water resources in suburban Santa Clara County (the home of Silicon Valley), see Richard A. Walker and Matthew J. Williams, "Water from Power: Water Supply and Regional Growth in the Santa Clara Valley," *Journal of Economic Geography* 58, no. 2 (April 1982): 95–119. For further discussion, see O'Mara, *Cities of Knowledge,* 103–110.

12. San Francisco Bay Area Council, *Program and Objectives.* Also see Industrial Survey Associates, *San Francisco Bay Area: Its People, Prospects, and Problems, A Report Prepared for the San Francisco Bay Area Council,* Advance Review Edition (March 1948), SFHC; Jacques F. Levy, *San Francisco Bay Region Industrial Study, Final Confidential Report to the Executive Committee and the Technical Advisory Committee,* San Francisco Bay Area Council, 28 January 1946, 18, SFHC.

13. Jackson's *Crabgrass Frontier* is the seminal work on the subject of postwar housing policy structures and mass suburbanization. For discussion of tax policy in particular, see Christopher Howard, *The Hidden Welfare State: Tax Expenditures and Social Policy in the United States* (Princeton, NJ: Princeton University Press, 1997), and Hanchett, "U.S. Tax Policy and the Shopping-Center Boom of the 1950s and 1960s."

14. National Security Resources Board, *Is Your Plant a Target?* (Washington, DC: Government Printing Office, 1951).

15. Harry S. Truman, Memorandum and Statement of Policy on the Need for Industrial Dispersion, 10 August 1951, *Public Papers of the Presidents of the United States, January 1 to December 31, 1951* (Washington, DC: Government Printing Office, 1965), no. 189.

16. See, for example, Department of Defense Directive 5220.3 on Industrial Dispersion Policy, 11 September 1951, reprinted in Armed Services Committee, U.S. Senate, *Hearings before a Subcommittee of the Armed Services Committee on S. 500, S. 1383, and S. 1875,* 86th Congress, 1st Session, 13–31 July 1959 (Washington, DC: Government Printing Office, 1959), 219; Joint Economic Committee, *The Need for Industrial Dispersal* (Washington, DC: Government Printing Office, 1951), 3; Executive Order 10172, *Federal Register* 15 (17 October 1950), 6929.

17. U.S. Department of Commerce, Office of Area Development, "The National Industrial Dispersion Program" (March 1957), 2.

18. Ibid.

19. U.S. Department of Commerce, Office of Area Development, "Industrial Dispersion Program: Progress in Urban Areas of the United States," 15 March 1957.

20. Electronics Division, Business and Defense Services Administration, U.S. Department of Commerce, Memorandum on "The Electronics Industry— Factors in Selecting Plant Locations—Methods for Approaching Industry," 23 August 1956, box 3, Accession 66A2584, RG 378, National Archives and Records Administration, College Park, MD (NARA). It is also revealing that, by the mid-1950s, publications, surveys, and programmatic activities related to dispersion all emanated from the Office of Area Development; by housing the program in the Department of Commerce rather than the Department of Defense, the Eisenhower administration signaled the degree to which dispersion had become an economic initiative rather than a strategic one.

21. By 1963, "specialists . . . in science and technology" accounted for 3.6 percent of the civilian workforce, up from 1.5 percent in 1940; *Profiles of Manpower in Science and Technology* (Washington, DC: Government Printing Office, 1963), 3.

22. Robert C. Wood, "Scientists and Politics: The Rise of an Apolitical Elite," in *Scientists and National Policy-Making,* ed. Robert Gilpin and Christopher Wright (New York: Columbia University Press, 1964), 58, 60.

23. *Science Education in the Schools of the United States,* Report of the National Science Foundation to the Subcommittee on Science, Research, and Development of the Committee on Science and Astronautics, U.S. House of Representatives, 89th Congress, 1st Session, Serial D (Washington, DC: Government Printing Office, 1965), 20.

24. J. Martin Klotsche, *The Urban University and the Future of Our Cities* (New York: Harper & Row, 1966), 85, paraphrasing John Fischer, "Money Bait," *Harper's Magazine,* September 1961, 12.

25. Robert C. Cowen, "President Talks on Research," *Christian Science Monitor,* May 15, 1959. Basic research is defined as that performed for the sake of scientific knowledge or technological advancement. Applied research was that which supported the development of a particular military or consumer product.

26. *Scientific Progress, the Universities, and the Federal Government,* Statement by the President's Scientific Advisory Committee, 15 November 1960 (Washington, DC: Government Printing Office, 1960), 11.

27. Clark Kerr, *The Uses of the University* (Cambridge, MA: Harvard University Press, 1963; New York: Harper & Row, 1966), 89.

28. Arthur D. Little, Inc., *Georgia Tech: Impetus to Economic Growth,* Report to Georgia Tech National Alumni Association, November 1963.

29. Quoted in Paul V. Turner, *Campus: An American Planning Tradition* (Cambridge, MA: MIT Press, 1984), 101.

30. Thomas Bender calls this "a major deviation from the central theme of the history of universities"; see "Introduction," *The University and the City: From Medieval Origins to the Present,* ed. Bender (New York: Oxford University Press, 1988), 3.

31. Robert E. Boley, "Industrial Districts Restudied: An Analysis of Characteristics" *Urban Land Institute Technical Bulletin,* no. 41 (Washington, DC: Urban Land Institute, 1961), 18.

32. Industrial parks were near large cities, but not in them; about 75 percent of the parks built during the first decade after World War II were "located in cities of between 25,000 and 500,000 population"; see William Bredo, *Industrial Estates: Tool for Industrialization* (Menlo Park, CA: Stanford Research Institute, 1960), 12.

33. Theodore K. Pasma quoted in "Attraction of Districts Is Increasing, Particularly for Small Plants, Firms," *Industrial Development* 3, no. 3 (May–June 1956): 48–49.

34. The major developers of early research parks in Silicon Valley and Route 128 consistently used terms like "clean" and "smokeless" in arguing that these parks were compatible with surrounding residential areas. See O'Mara, *Cities of Knowledge,* 107, 119–121.

35. Henry Bund, "Economic Problems," Remarks to New York State Symposium on Research and the Community, 1 May 1961, Sterling Forest, NY, FF "State Science and Technology Conference," box 1, Accession 76-4, RG 40, NARA.

36. The National Science Foundation published annual reports ranking top university grantees; see, for example, National Science Foundation, *Federal Support of Research and Development at Universities and Colleges and Selected Nonprofit Institutions, Fiscal Year 1968,* NSF 69-33, 15–17.

37. U.S. Department of Commerce, Economic Development Administration, "A Research Park . . . Is It for Your Community?" (Washington, DC: Government Printing Office, 1966), 8.

38. Mel Wax, "Stanford Park—Weird Success," *San Francisco Chronicle,* 16 November 1958.

39. Board of Trustees statement, 1954, quoted in Stanford University, "Land Development Fact Sheet," 2 April 1960, FF 11, box A29, SC 216, Stanford University Archives.

40. "Chamber Unit Has a Research Probe," Lawrence (KS) *Journal-World,* 12 December 1961; "Four Studies for Future Growth Urged on Chamber of Commerce," Corvallis (OR) *Gazette-Times,* 6 March 1962; "Research Parks Meet Need," Editorial, Lubbock (TX) *Avalanche-Journal,* 9 April 1963; "Bringing Research Center to City is Object of Plan Launched Here," Meridian (MS) *Star,* 20 February 1964; Quayne Kenyon, "City Encourages Start of Light Industry Center," *Idaho State Journal* (Pocatello, ID), 21 August 1964; Stanford Lands Scrapbooks VI and VII, 1961–1962 and 1962–1965, Subject Files 1300/9, Stanford University Archives.

41. University of Pennsylvania official Jean Paul Mather, described in "Dr. Mather's Summing Up," Editorial, *Philadelphia Evening Bulletin,* 26 June 1969.

42. Another important example is that of the University of Chicago, whose effort to combat neighborhood racial change and shore up its campus

through urban renewal was masterfully documented by Arnold R. Hirsch in *Making the Second Ghetto: Race and Housing in Chicago, 1940–1960* (New York: Cambridge University Press, 1983). Hirsch's narrative focuses on the way in which federal policymakers, local economic development officials, and university administrators worked to *prevent* racial and economic change in its neighborhood; the cases here add to this story by showing how these actors simultaneously worked to *create* a new kind of settlement, built around scientific industry and its managerial and technical workers.

43. Hugh Scott, "University City: Brainsville on the March," *Philadelphia Inquirer Magazine*, 19 July 1964, 4.

44. Michael I. Luger and Harvey A. Goldstein, *Technology in the Garden: Research Parks and Regional Economic Development* (Chapel Hill: University of North Carolina Press, 1991); Raymond W. Smilor, George Kozmetsky, and David V. Gibson, "The Austin/San Antonio Corridor: The Dynamics of a Developing Technopolis," in Smilor, Kozmetsky, and Gibson, eds., *Creating the Technopolis: Linking Technology, Commercialization, and Economic Development* (Cambridge, MA: Ballinger Publishing Co., 1988), 145–184.

45. See Greg Hise, *Magnetic Los Angeles: Planning the Twentieth-Century Metropolis* (Baltimore: Johns Hopkins University Press, 1997); Robert O. Self, *American Babylon: Race and the Struggle for Postwar Oakland* (Princeton, NJ: Princeton University Press, 2003). For discussion of the West's influence on postwar urban landscapes, see John M. Findlay, *Magic Lands: Western Cityscapes and American Culture after 1940* (Berkeley: University of California Press, 1992).

46. Two compelling recent monographs address these inequities: Glenna Matthews, *Silicon Valley, Women, and the California Dream: Gender, Class, and Opportunity in the Twentieth Century* (Stanford, CA: Stanford University Press, 2003) and Steven J. Pitti, *The Devil in Silicon Valley: Northern California, Race, and Mexican Americans* (Princeton, NJ: Princeton University Press, 2002), esp. 173–201.

47. Silicon Valley's stunningly high number of Superfund sites—places deemed highly toxic and of high priority for cleanup by the U.S. Environmental Protection Agency—attests to the polluting effects of high-tech activity. By 2004, Santa Clara County alone contained 23 of them. See U.S. Environmental Protection Agency, National Priorities List, <http://www.epa.gov/superfund/sites/npl/ca.htm> (accessed 3 September 2004).

CHAPTER FOUR

The author would like to thank Matt Lassiter, Tom Sugrue, Kevin Kruse, Stephen Macedo, and Denise Spooner for their insights, suggestions, and support.

1. For an overview of these critics, see Bennett M. Berger, "The Myth of Suburbia," *Journal of Social Issues* 12, no. 1 (1961): 38–49; Scott Donaldson, *The Suburban Myth* (New York: Columbia University Press, 1969); on the cultural

critics, see Catherine Jurca, *White Diaspora: The Suburb and the Twentieth-Century American Novel* (Princeton, NJ: Princeton University Press, 2001); Robert Beuka, *SuburbiaNation: Reading Suburban Landscape in Twentieth-Century American Fiction and Film* (New York: Palgrave Macmillan, 2004).

2. William Whyte's *Organization Man* particularly influenced cultural producers of the period, who used this work as a jumping off point for their own.

     For an excellent treatment of the national discourse over postwar cities, see Robert Beauregard, *Voices of Decline: The Postwar Fate of U.S. Cities,* 2d ed. (New York: Routledge, 2003). Beauregard focuses mostly on the urban rather than suburban part of the story. Although he does document popular reactions to the "decentralizing" trend, the focus is more on its impact on cities rather than life in suburbia itself.

3. A good argument for a more fluid definition of community is in Thomas Bender, *Community and Social Change in America* (Baltimore: Johns Hopkins University Press, 1978). Jane Jacobs was perhaps the most notable exception in this regard, describing how city people enjoyed a "fluidity of use and choice" in their lives, allowing them to partake of many options for jobs, goods, entertainment, and sociability in different areas of the city. She asserted that city neighborhoods should not be "self-contained units," either economically or socially. Jane Jacobs, *The Death and Life of Great American Cities* (New York: Vintage, 1961), 115–117.

4. Beauregard, *Voices of Decline*, 89.

5. Mumford, Jacobs, and Whyte had varying opinions about the state of cities by the 1950s and 1960s. For example, Mumford believed cities were being taken over by what he termed the megamachine, while Jacobs decried the trend of intrusive large-scale planning. Yet they also shared a fundamental faith in the superiority of city life, if only these forces could be counteracted. I think they saw suburbanization as yet another threat to their own, pure vision of what a city should be, as well as a manifestation of the very trends they believed were threatening cities—like massive planning (Jacobs) and the megamachine (Mumford). The suburbs, too, were products of these forces.

6. Beauregard, *Voices of Decline,* 8–10. The work of Lewis Mumford is something of an exception here; it does not fit an easy framework that links modernization with urbanization. He dates the rise of big cities much earlier than the modern period. See Mumford, *The City in History: Its Origins, Its Transformations, and Its Prospects* (New York: Harcourt, Brace, 1961), and see note 21.

7. Andrew Lees, *Cities Perceived: Urban Society in European and American Thought, 1820–1940* (Manchester: Manchester University Press, 1985), 299–304, Wirth quoted at p. 302.

8. R. D. McKenzie, "The Ecological Approach to the Study of the Human Community," in Robert E. Park, Ernest W. Burgess, and Roderick D. McKenzie, *The City*, with an Introduction by Morris Janowitz (Chicago: University of Chicago Press, 1967), 63.

9. Robert E. Park, "The City: Suggestions for the Investigation of Human Behavior in the Urban Environment," in Park, Burgess, and McKenzie, *The City,* especially 22–38; quote at 22. A good overview of this social theory is in Bender, *Community and Social Change in America,* chap. 2.

10. Louis Wirth, "Urbanism as a Way of Life," *On Cities and Social Life,* ed. Albert J. Reiss, Jr. (Chicago: University of Chicago Press, 1981), 71, 80.

11. Sociologist Herbert Gans would later criticize Wirth for this theoretical imprecision, that is, for Wirth's vagueness in pinpointing exactly what was causing an "urban way of life"—the nature of cities, the pecuniary culture, etc. See Gans, "Urbanism and Suburbanism as Ways of Life: A Re-evaluation of Definitions," in Arnold M. Rose, ed., *Human Behavior and Social Processes* (Boston: Houghton Mifflin, 1962), 626–627.

12. Wirth, "Urbanism," 76.

13. Ibid., 81.

14. Lees, *Cities Perceived,* 302–303; Michael P. Smith, *The City and Social Theory* (New York: St. Martin's Press, 1979), 172–173.

15. His main subjects were the history and criticism of architecture, cities, literature, art, and technology. As his biographer Donald Miller put it, Mumford was a generalist but also "made his mark as a specialist in at least half a dozen fields. Although he helped found two scholarly disciplines, American studies and history of technology, he is best known as a writer on cities and architecture." Donald L. Miller, "Lewis Mumford: Urban Historian, Urban Visionary," *Journal of Urban History* 18 (May 1992): 281.

16. Lewis Mumford, "What Is a City?" *Architectural Record* 82 (November 1937): 58–62.

17. I hesitate to use the word "theory" (instead of philosophy), since Mumford himself seemed to loathe the academic penchant for theories divorced from values and conviction.

18. Leo Marx, "Lewis Mumford: Prophet of Organicism," in Thomas Hughes and Agatha Hughes, eds., *Lewis Mumford: Public Intellectual* (New York: Oxford, 1990), 167–168. Marx offers a good discussion of the intellectual roots of this philosophy, derived from the counter-Enlightment, otherwise known as "the romantic reaction," in Alfred North Whitehead's words. See p. 168 for details.

    Mumford has also been placed within a "long line of urban theorists that includes Percival Goodman, Christopher Alexander, and Peter Calthorpe." See Richard LeGates and Frederic Stout, eds., *The City Reader* (New York: Routledge, 1996).

19. Mumford used the same terminology—organic and mechanical—as Emile Durkheim; however, Mumford conceived the terms more broadly. Durkheim proposed the idea of mechanical and organic solidarity as the basis for different kinds of community experiences—along the lines of Tönnies. In *The Division of Labor in Society* he defined mechanical solidarity this way: "We all know that a social cohesion exists whose cause can be traced to a certain

conformity of each individual consciousness to a common type, which is none other than the psychological type of society. Indeed under these conditions all members of the group are not only individually attracted to another because they resemble one another, but they are also linked to what is the condition for the existence of this collective type, that is, to the society that they form by coming together." In contrast, the heart of organic solidarity is the recognition and valuing of the difference between individuals. As such, rather than the existence of one common conscience based upon the similarity of all the people, there exist as many consciousnesses as there are types of people. Emile Durkheim, *The Division of Labor in Society,* trans. by W. D. Halls, 2d ed. (London: Macmillan Publishers, 1984), 60–61, 85; Emile Durkheim, *On Morality and Society: Selected Writings,* ed. Robert N. Bellah (Chicago: University of Chicago Press), xxvi; Whitney Pope and Barclay D. Johnson, "Inside Organic Solidarity," *American Sociological Review* 48 (1982): 683–685. Many thanks to Denise Spooner for clarifying this for me.

20. From Mumford's *The Myth of the Machine,* vol. 1: *Technics and Human Development,* vol. 2: *The Pentagon of Power* (New York: Harcourt, Brace & World, 1967, 1970), quoted in Kenneth Stunkel, "Lewis Mumford's Idea of Community in an Urban World," *Urban History* 26 (1999): 251.

21. It is important to note that Mumford did not reject technology; in fact, he believed it to be essential to human existence but only if it served life rather than commanded it. This point is noted in Stunkel, "Lewis Mumford's Idea," 250.

22. Here, he referred to labor machines. In hinging the crux of his social critique on the "megamachine" and dating its emergence in ancient times, Mumford diverges from "classical social" and modernization theories, which see the critical social transformations of modernity happening much later. Mumford was still a critic of modernization; however, he historicized and conceptualized these processes in a very different way. See Eugene Rochberg-Halton, "The Transformation of Social Theory," in Hughes and Hughes, eds., *Lewis Mumford: Public Intellectual,* 134–135.

23. See Mumford, *The City in History.* Other "urban" manifestations of this mechanistic tendency were modern architecture, mass-produced suburbs, and the bigness and overcentralization of city life, wherein simpler human needs were trammeled by technology gone amok. The triumph of mechanism was ultimately embodied in the nuclear-armed nation state. Mumford wrote, "In our own time, the mechanical world picture at last reached the state of complete embodiment in a multitude of machines, laboratories, factories, office buildings, rocket-platforms, underground shelters, control centers. But now that the idea has been completely embodied, we can recognize that it had left no place for man. He is reduced to a standardized servo-mechanism: a left-over part from a more organic world"; Mumford, *The Myth of the Machine,* vol. 2:*The Pentagon of Power,* 430, as quoted in Marx, "Lewis Mumford," 172.

24. Miller, "Lewis Mumford," 287; "The City as Both Heaven and Hell: A Conversation between Graeme Shankland and Lewis Mumford," *Listener,* September 28, 1961, 471.

25. Ibid., 464.

26. Ibid.

27. Quote is from Mumford's review of Jane Jacobs in *New Yorker,* December 1962, quoted in Miller, "Lewis Mumford," 296; also see p. 282, for a good description of Mumford's vision.

28. Lewis Mumford, "What Is a City?" *Architectural Record* 82 (November 1937).

29. Mumford, *The City in History,* 518.

30. He claimed the earliest suburbs appeared alongside the earliest cities, begun in ancient Egypt. A wonderful quote that expresses Mumford's notion of the organicism of this earlier ideal suburb: "Thus in its earliest form, the suburb acknowledged the varieties of human temperament and aspiration, the need for change, contrast, and adventure, and above all, for an environment visibly responsive to one's personal efforts, as even the smallest flower garden is responsive. Here nothing was too absurd to be attempted in architecture or gardening: hardly anything too private or too neurotic to be openly expressed. Domestic whimsy offset productive rigor and utilitarian monotony." This is a classic statement of the organic versus mechanical impulse; *The City in History,* 483, 491.

31. Lewis Mumford, "The Wilderness of Suburbia," *New Republic,* September 7, 1921, 44–45.

32. Mumford, *The City in History,* 486.

33. Ibid., 494, 495.

34. Ibid., 512–513.

35. David R. Hill, "Jane Jacob's Ideas on Big, Diverse Cities," *Journal of the American Planning Association* 54 (Summer 1988): 302.

36. Gans quote is from "The Dream of Human Cities," *New Republic,* June 1969, 28. Also see Herbert Gans, "City Planning and Urban Realities," *Commentary* 33 (February 1962): 170–175.

37. Hill, "Jane Jacobs' Ideas," 302.

38. See Jacobs, *Death and Life,* 428–435; and the fine summary in Hill, "Jane Jacobs' Ideas," 303–304.

39. Jacobs, *Death and Life,* 339. Harvey Choldin notes that Jacobs virtually ignored the relevant sociology scholarship, despite her use of sociology methods and the fact that her work is "sociologically compelling." He wrote, "By the 1950s, the main corpus of the Chicago School was complete, and there were numerous works available on neighborhoods . . . But Jacobs' lengthy book, which reflects several years of work, takes no cognizance of sociology. It is as though Wirth, McKenzie, Firey, and the others had said nothing useful." See Harvey M. Choldin, "Retrospective Review Essay: Neighborhood Life and Urban Environment," *American Journal of Sociology* 84 (September 1978): 458.

40. Jacobs believed that this form of dense, mixed-use cities also promoted economic vitality in cities, spawning new jobs and keeping urban economies healthy. She expanded upon these themes in *The Economy of Cities* (New York: Vintage Books, 1969).

41. Jacobs, *Death and Life,* passim, quote at p. 339; and Choldin's useful review, "Retrospective Review Essay," 457–463.

    Jacobs criticized Los Angeles for many things: its high crime rate, its ridiculous and monotonous architecture, its cultural vacuity, its lack of public life, its segregation, and its car-dependency which degraded air quality, among other things. She claimed Los Angeles was "almost all suburban"; *Death and Life,* 32.

42. Choldin, "Retrospective Review Essay," 459. It is worth noting that Jacobs acknowledged that low-density urban areas, suburbs, villages, and exurbs could serve certain noncity functions for a "city region." For example, suburbs might serve as a site for "old work." However, these functions were always of the old, stagnant kind, lacking the "youthful creativity of city diversity." This point is made in Hill, "Jane Jacobs' Ideas," 304, 308.

43. She wrote that the Garden City approach influenced city planners to "aim for at least an illusion of isolation and suburban privacy. . . . And every significant detail must be controlled by the planners from the start and then stuck to"; *Death and Life,* 20.

44. Jacobs, *Death and Life,* 220.

45. Ibid., 53.

46. Like Mumford, Jacobs also believed that suburbia was destructive for draining off urban resources. She developed this idea in *Cities and the Wealth of Nations* (New York: Random House, 1984). In her latest book, Jacobs continues her attack on suburbia and especially the automobile industry that made it possible; *Dark Age Ahead* (New York: Random House, 2004).

    In a 2000 interview, Jacobs seemed to have softened her view of surburbia somewhat, seeing it as one of many choices. See Mitchell Duneier, "Joys in the Hood," *New York Times Magazine,* April 9, 2000, 33.

47. Jacobs made an oblique reference to Whyte's work in one passage: "'Togetherness,' apparently a spiritual resource of the new suburbs, works destructively in cities"; *Death and Life,* 62. Here, she elaborated on her thesis that cities struck the optimal balance between public and private life, allowing urbanites the healthiest mix of the two.

48. There were a number of social critics writing in the 1950s, concerned about the disturbing underpinnings of postwar affluent consensus, including David Riesman, C. Wright Mills, Vance Packard, John Kenneth Galbraith, the Frankfurt school theorists, and later Herbert Marcuse, among others. One important work that paralleled Whyte's was David Riesman, "The Suburban Sadness," in William Dobriner, ed., *The Suburban Community* (New York: G. P. Putnam's Sons, 1957). For a brief discussion of this, see Jackson Lears, "A Matter of Taste: Corporate Cultural Hegemony in a

Mass-Consumption Society," in Lary May, ed., *Recasting America: Culture and Politics in the Age of Cold War* (Chicago: University of Chicago Press, 1989).

49. William H. Whyte, Jr., *The Organization Man* (New York: Simon & Schuster, 1956), 365.

50. Ibid., quotes at 7, 13, 157, 382.

51. Ibid., 267.

52. Ibid., 280, 284–287.

53. Ibid., 276.

54. One example of this nuance was Whyte's characterization of the role of consumption in the Park Forest community. He found not an impulse to buy recklessly to show off, but rather a tendency to "keep down with the Joneses." This was all part of the social compact. Sensitive to the fact that they were all in a critical, vulnerable stage in their careers, neighbors refrained from buying extravagantly so it wouldn't make the others look bad: "If you find you're going ahead, it's rubbing it in unfairly to make it obvious to the others who aren't. You have broken the truce" (p. 313). The concern with Social Ethic thus guided even purchasing choices. Whyte had much more to say about this issue, including describing a process whereby the group itself collectively decides—through a kind of critical mass—when a luxury becomes a necessity. The result was that the "good life standard" was being revised upward quite rapidly. He concluded by describing the tendency of suburban families to buy on credit and live constantly in debt, in a rather ignorant and irresponsible way. "For a future capitalist, the Organization Man displays a remarkable inability to manipulate capital" (p. 326). See chap. 24 on this topic.

55. Ibid., 335, 344–345, 348. Later in the book, Whyte's discussion took a turn that complicated (and contradicted somewhat) his views about the power of the built environment to shape social behavior. In his conclusion, he argued passionately that humans cannot allow themselves to acquiesce before the material trappings of a prosperous industrial society, nor to blame science and technology for causing the social problems facing modern man. This was a pessimistic view that ceded too much power to "the machine." People needed to stand up to these pressures and assert themselves against these dehumanizing influences. In this context, he wrote that it wasn't mass-produced housing that produced the desire to conform—that outcome was not inevitable. He asserted this as part of his call to stand up and fight the power.

56. Ibid., 361, 365.

57. Ibid., 399.

58. William Whyte, "Are Cities Un-American?" *Fortune* (September 1957), 123–125, 213–214, 218; Adam Rome, "William Whyte, Open Space, and Environmental Activism," *Geographical Review* 88 (April 1998): 259–274; Nathan Glazer, "The Man Who Loved Cities," *Wilson Quarterly* 23 (Spring 1999); Michael Kaufman, "William H. Whyte, 'Organization Man' Author

and Urbanologist, Is Dead at 81," *New York Times,* January 13, 1999, B7; William Whyte, *The Last Landscape* (New York: Doubleday, 1968); William Whyte, *The Social Life of Small Urban Spaces* (Washington, DC: Conservation Foundation, 1980).

Whyte continued to evince a real interest in the ways that the built environment impacted social life, a theme he especially explored in *The Social Life of Small Urban Spaces*. And see John Cook, "The Observation Man," *New York Times Magazine,* January 2, 2000, 23.

59. Robert Putnam makes a useful distinction between bridging (inclusive) and bonding (exclusive) types of social capital; the same concept is applicable to community. I think the writers here made implicit judgments about these different kinds of community as well; indeed, a pervasive critique of suburbia has been its "bonding" tendencies, its tendency to exclude others on the basis of race, ethnicity, class, etc. But these distinctions were not always carefully drawn in these writing, and the result is some conceptual confusion. See Robert Putnam, *Bowling Alone: The Collapse and Revival of American Community* (New York: Simon & Schuster, 2000).

60. And it was also unlikely that any particular "way of life" could really characterize urban or suburban living, a point made well by Herbert Gans in his influential 1962 essay, "Urbanism and Suburbanism."

To his credit, Whyte did not blame the suburban environment per se for the "other directedness" of Organization Man; yet he did ascribe great power to the built environment in shaping the character of social life, evident in his detailed description of neighborhood layout and its impact on social interaction. Also see note 55.

61. Gans, "City Planning and Urban Realities," 172. Gans wrote several seminal works that challenged this "physical fallacy," including *The Levittowners* (New York: Columbia University Press, 1967) and "Urbanism and Suburbanism as a 'Way of Life.'"

62. It should be emphasized that Wirth, Mumford, Jacobs, and even Whyte all critiqued the suburban trend for draining resources away from the city. In this regard, they aligned with the urban commentators, described earlier by Robert Beauregard, who saw suburbanization as a kind of "zero sum" equation: suburban growth meant urban depletion.

Jane Jacobs, in fact, was very interested in the economy of cities, themes she explored in *The Economy of Cities* and *Cities and the Wealth of Nations*. She held what one reviewer called a "curiously bimodal" strain of political thought, at the moderate edge of both right and left. For example, she supported unfettered entrepreneurship, a hands-off government policy to allow new work to flourish, and skepticism that the government could solve material inequity. At the same time, she distrusted a hierarchical order, supported the decentralization of power to local neighborhoods, and detested the inequities of urban renewal. Her biggest economic critique of suburbs: they drained precious resources from the city. See Hill, "Jane Jacobs' Ideas," 308.

63. This is a common critique waged of Jacobs's work. For example, see Gans, "City Planning and Urban Realities," 170–175; Choldin, "Retrospective Review Essay," 461–462.

64. Even Robert Putnam, who is deeply concerned about the need for community rejuvenation in America, found that ethnic and racial diversity lowered levels of community trust. Yet he emphasized the possibility that those differences can be overcome through diligent effort. Robert Putnam, *Better Together: Restoring the American Community* (New York: Simon & Schuster, 2003).

65. See Jackson Lears, "A Matter of Taste." Work over the past decade is finally offering a real correction to this portrayal; for a brief overview of that revisionism, see Thomas J. Sugrue, "Reassessing the History of Postwar America," *Prospects* 20 (1995): 493–509.

66. In the 1960s, sociologists like Herbert Gans, Bennett Berger, and William Dobriner all produced works that showed a much healthier, less insidious life in the suburbs. They swung the pendulum of environmental determinism far in the other direction, suggesting that it wasn't the environment that shaped behavior, it was factors like class and ethnicity. Gans, *The Levittowners* and "Urbanism and Suburbanism"; Bennett Berger, *Blue Collar Suburb: A Study of Auto Workers in Suburbia* (Berkeley: University of California Press, 1960); William M. Dobriner, *Class in Suburbia* (Englewood Cliffs, NJ: Prentice Hall, 1963); Scott Donaldson, *The Suburban Myth* (New York: Columbia University Press, 1969). Donaldson's book reviews the literature and surveys the formation of a "suburban myth" that emphasized conformity, conservatism, and consumption.

67. Examples of the "new suburban history" include Richard Harris, *Unplanned Suburbs: Toronto's American Tragedy, 1900–1950* (Baltimore: Johns Hopkins University Press, 1996); Richard Harris and Robert Lewis, "The Geography of North American Cities and Suburbs, 1900–1950" *Journal of Urban History* 27 (March 2001): 262–292; Andrew Wiese, *Places of Their Own: African American Suburbanization in the Twentieth Century* (Chicago: University of Chicago Press, 2004); Becky Nicolaides, *My Blue Heaven: Life and Politics in the Working-Class Suburbs of Los Angeles, 1920–1965* (Chicago: University of Chicago Press, 2002); Steven Pitti, *The Devil in Silicon Valley: Northern California, Race, and Mexican Americans* (Princeton, NJ: Princeton University Press, 2003).

    Women's history has likewise shown a new appreciation for women's postwar associational life, seeing it as integral to politics and a meaningful civic life. For example, see Susan Ware, "American Women in the 1950s: Nonpartisan Politics and Women's Politicization," in Louise Tilly and Patricia Gurin, eds., *Women, Politics and Change* (New York: Russell Sage Foundation, 1990), 281–299; Joanne Meyerowitz, ed., *Not June Cleaver: Women and Gender in Postwar America, 1945–1960* (Philadelphia: Temple University Press, 1994).

68. Robert Putnam, *Bowling Alone*.

69. Mary Corbin Sies has made a very persuasive case for studies that carefully analyze the white suburban middle class. Just as scholars are uncovering insurgent histories that challenge blanket concepts like "ghetto," "urban crisis," and "slums," showing instead the variations in human experience and assertiveness from the "inside out" (i.e., see work by Robin Kelley, Steven Gregory, and Earl Lewis on African Americans), scholars working on white suburban communities need to adapt a parallel research strategy that deals with empirical realities, rather than mass-mediated misrepresentations of middle-class lifestyles. Sies is attempting to do this for the early period (1877–1917); I think the same thing needs to be done for the postwar period.

70. Bender, *Community and Social Change in America*, passim.

71. As Catherine Jurca notes, popular novelists borrowed heavily from the sociologists and social critics, even adopting "quasi-sociological techniques in fiction dealing with the suburbs"; Jurca, *White Diaspora*, 135–136. This point is also emphasized in Beuka, *SuburbiaNation*, 68.

CHAPTER FIVE

1. The names are pseudonyms. See Dorothy Sutherland Jayne, "First Families: A Study of Twenty Pioneer Negro Families Who Moved into White Neighborhoods in Metropolitan Philadelphia" (masters thesis, Bryn Mawr College, 1960), Appendix B, 66–70.

2. Ibid., 66–67.

3. Following the U.S. Census, I refer here to "suburbanites" as people living within Census-defined metropolitan districts but outside the central city. By this definition, southern suburbs gained 330,000 people (despite aggressive annexation of outlying areas by central cities). Suburbs outside the South added almost 700,000. In the Northeast and Midwest, black suburban population ballooned from 468,000 to 905,000. The number of western suburbanites grew from just 32,000 to 274,000, which accounted for more than a quarter of black population growth in the region. U.S. Census of Population: 1960, vol. III, *Selected Area Reports*, pt. 1D (Washington, DC: Government Printing Office, 1963), 2–5.

4. Reynolds Farley, "The Changing Distribution of Negroes within Metropolitan Areas: The Emergence of Black Suburbs," *American Journal of Sociology* 75 (January 1970): 345–346; Clarence Dean, "Negroes Facing Test in Suburbs: Major Shift from the City Poses Housing Question," *New York Times*, May 21, 1961.

5. On African American's symbolic uses of domestic space to challenge white supremacy in the nineteenth and early twentieth century, see Barbara Burlinson Mooney, "The Comfortable Tasty Framed Cottage: An African American Architectural Iconography," *Journal of the Society of Architectural Historians* 61 (March 2002): 49–67.

6. Housing and Home Finance Agency, *The Housing of Negro Veterans: Their Housing Plans and Living Arrangements in 32 Areas* (Washington, DC: Government Printing Office, 1948), 9–10.

7. Frederick Gutheim, "Failure to Build for Negroes Will Create New Blight Areas," *New York Herald Tribune,* July 4, 1948, VI-1.

8. Robert Kleiner, Seymour Parker, and Haywood Taylor, Social Status and Aspirations in Philadelphia's Negro Population, prepared for and edited by the Commission on Human Relations (Philadelphia: Commission on Human Relations, 1962), 9.

9. Philadelphia Commission on Human Relations, Some Factors Affecting Housing Desegregation: A Summary and Analysis of Five Papers Concerning Non-White Attitudes and Behavior (Philadelphia: Commission on Human Relations, 1962), 1.

10. See Andrew Wiese, *Places of Their Own: African American Suburbanization in Twentieth-Century America* (Chicago: University of Chicago Press, 2004), chap. 5, n. 23.

11. Clydie Smith, interview by author, July 1986.

12. City of Pasadena, Department of Planning and Permitting, Letter to Owner of 523 Pepper Street, April 4, 1952, Building Permit Files (Hall Building, Pasadena, California); also letters to owners of 525 and 545 Hammond Avenue, ibid.

13. David Doles, interview by Elizabeth Langley, October 25, 1979, "Black History in Mount Vernon, New York" (Local History Room, Mount Vernon Public Library). On gardening in other suburbs, see Harold Rose, "The All Black Town: Suburban Prototype or Rural Slum," *Urban Affairs Annual Reviews* 6 (1972): 414; David J. Dent, *In Search of Black America: Discovering the African American Dream* (New York: Simon & Schuster, 2000), 69; Felix James, *The American Addition: History of a Black Community* (Washington, DC: University Press of America, 1979), 58–60. Even newly wealthy entertainers like Pearl Bailey, Eartha Kitt, and Josephine Baker indulged working-class roots by keeping chickens on estate properties. Pearl Bailey, *The Raw Pearl* (New York: Harcourt Brace & World, 1968), 141–144; Eartha Kitt, *Alone with Me: A New Autobiography* (Chicago: H. Regnery Co., 1976), 234; "Josephine Baker, Modern Cinderella," *Baltimore Afro American Magazine,* October 25, 1947, 1.

14. Lorraine Hansberry, *A Raisin in the Sun; Sign in Sidney Brustein's Window* (New York: New American Library, 1966), 41, 78.

15. U.S. Census of Housing: 1940, *Block Statistics, Evanston, Illinois* (Washington, DC: Government Printing Office, 1942), 5, 8–9; U.S. Census of Housing: 1950, vol. V, *Block Statistics,* pt. 61, *Evanston, Illinois* (Washington, DC: Government Printing Office, 1952), 3–11; ibid., pt. 17, *Berkeley, California,* 3–17; ibid., pt. 56, *East Orange, New Jersey,* 3–8; ibid., pt. 124, *New Rochelle, New York,* 3–10; ibid., pt. 138, *Pasadena, California,* 3–17.

16. "Get Tough Policy on Housing Urged at Interracial Meeting," *Evanston Review,* September 17, 1959.

17. See "Lots for Sale," Chicago *Defender,* May 11, 1946, 11; "Special Sale, Choice Homesites, Morgan Park," ibid., October 13, 1945, 11; "$10 a Month Pays for a Large Lot," ibid., May 25, 1946, 8; "It's Cheaper to Own than to Pay Rent," ibid., October 13, 1945, 2. In New York, "Gordon Heights, L.I," *Amsterdam News,* December 31, 1949; "Help Me, I Want to Own My Own Home," ibid.; "Bungalow, Farm or Homesite," ibid., July 12, 1947. In Detroit, "Little Farms, 90′ × 126′," *Michigan Chronicle,* October 13, 1945, 4.

18. "Farm Homesites," *Amsterdam News,* July 12, 1947.

19. "You Too Can Beat the High Cost of Living," Chicago *Defender,* January 31, 1948, 4.

20. Smith, interview by author; William Hagler, interview by author, August 11, 1986; Clara Adams, interview by author, July 29, 1986.

21. E. P. Stephenson, testimony, U.S. Commission on Civil Rights, *Hearings Held before the United States Commission on Civil Rights, Hearings Held in Los Angeles, Calif., Jan. 25–26, 1960; San Francisco, Calif., Jan. 27–28, 1960* (Washington, DC: Government Printing Office, 1960), 622; Harold Lindsay, "From Fields to Ford's: The Development of Inkster, Michigan" (Ph.D. diss., University of Michigan, 1992); James, *The American Addition,* 58–60.

22. "Port-o-Cottage," Chicago *Defender,* August 14, 1948, 9; "Phoenix, Ill. Properties. . . . Owner Completed or Finished Homes on Your Paid Up Lot," ibid., April 1, 1950, 19; "Quonset Makes an Attractive Home," Cleveland *Call and Post,* December 21, 1946, 13B; Floris Barnett Cash, "Long Island by Design, Segregation's Brand of Housing," New York *Newsday,* December 29, 1997, A25.

23. Eunice Grier and George Grier, *In Search of Housing: A Study of Experiences of Negro Professional and Technical Personnel in New York State* (New York: State Committee against Discrimination, 1958), 18.

24. Dorothy Sutherland Jayne, "First Families: A Study of Twenty Pioneer Negro Families Who Moved into White Neighborhoods in Metropolitan Philadelphia," Summary Report (Philadelphia: Commission on Human Relations, 1960), 1–4; Jayne, "First Families" (masters thesis), 22.

25. "St. Alban's: New York Community Is Home to More Celebrities than Any Other U.S. Residential Area," *Ebony* 6 (September 1951): 34.

26. "Period Styles for Elegance: Detroit's Dr. Saulsbury Chooses Eighteenth Century Motif to Furnish Home in Restful Tone," *Ebony* 6 (December 1950): 64; "Louis Jordan Birthday Party," ibid., 6 (November 1950): 91–92; "Rochester: Radio Star Finds Long Greens Buy Lots of Comfort and Ease," ibid., 1 (November 1945): 13–20; "Push Button Home," ibid., 9 (November 1954): 42–46; "The White House," ibid., 1 (April 1946): 3–7.

27. "St. Alban's," 34–39.

28. Ibid.

29. On equality through consumption, see Lizabeth Cohen, "Citizens and Consumers in the Century of Mass Consumption," in *Perspectives on Modern America: Making Sense of the Twentieth Century,* ed. Harvard Sitkoff (New York:

Oxford University Press, 2001), 152–158. On middle-class suburban dreams, see Kenneth T. Jackson, *Crabgrass Frontier: The Suburbanization of the United States* (New York: Oxford University Press, 1985), 243–245; Barbara Kelly, *Expanding the American Dream: Building and Rebuilding Levittown* (Albany: State University of New York Press, 1993), 59–88; Elaine Tyler May, *Homeward Bound: American Families in the Cold War Era* (New York: Basic Books, 1988), 3–6, 16–20.

30. "Hempstead Park Detached," *Amsterdam News,* July 12, 1947.

31. "Pacoima's Quality Circle," Pasadena *Crown City Press,* February 7, 1957, 5.

32. Clara Adams, interview.

33. Jayne, "First Families (Summary), 1, 4.

34. "Interracial Unit Ready," *New York Times,* August 22, 1950; advertisement, *New York Daily News,* October 14, 1951; Eardlie John, "Bring Up Your Children in This Suburban Paradise," *Amsterdam News,* December 31, 1949, 25.

35. "It's Cheaper to Own Than to Pay Rent," Chicago *Defender,* October 13, 1945, 2.

36. Grier and Grier, *In Search of Housing,* 17.

37. Chelsea Carter, "Unlikely Musical Mecca: Jazz Fans Take Journey through Neighborhoods Where the Greats Lived," Cedar Rapids *Gazette,* January 10, 1999, 2G.

38. On black middle-class values related to children, see St. Clair Drake and Horace Cayton, *Black Metropolis: A Study of Negro Life in a Northern City* (New York: Harcout, Brace & Co., 1945), 663–668.

39. U.S. Commission on Civil Rights, *Hearings before the United States Commission on Civil Rights, Hearings Held in New York, February, 2–3, 1959* (Washington, DC: Government Printing Office, 1959), 272.

40. "Poitier Says Bias Exists on Coast," *New York Times,* August 19, 1960, 14.

41. Winston Richie, "Pro-Integrative Policy and Incentives," transcript, National Federation for Neighborhood Diversity Conference, Cleveland, Ohio, June 15, 1990.

42. Mary Patillo-McCoy, *Black Picket Fences: Privilege and Peril among the Black Middle Class* (Chicago: University of Chicago Press, 1999), 19.

43. U.S. Commission on Civil Rights, *Hearings before the United States Commission on Civil Rights, Hearings Held in Los Angeles, Calif., Jan. 25–26, 1960,* 260–261. See also John Kain, "Housing Market Discrimination, Homeownership, and Savings Behavior," *American Economic Review* 62 (June 1972): 263–277.

44. Eunice Grier and George Grier, *Negroes in Five NY Cities: A Study of Problems, Achievements, and Trends* (New York: State Commission against Discrimination, 1958), 78; U.S. Commission on Civil Rights, *Hearings before the United States Commission on Civil Rights, Hearings Held in Detroit, Michigan, December 14–15, 1960* (Washington, DC: Government Printing Office, 1961), 259; Jayne, "First Families" (Summary), 3; Thomas Trevor, *San Francisco's Housing Market—Open or Closed? Civil Rights Inventory of San Francisco, Part II, Housing: A Report* (San Francisco: Council for Civic Unity of San Francisco, 1960), 9.

45. Grier and Grier, *In Search of Housing,* 41–42; Trevor, *San Francisco's Housing Market,* 9. Gwendolyn Brooks also pointed to the internalization of harm caused by housing discrimination in the poem, "Beverly Hills, Chicago."

46. Jayne, "First Families" (masters thesis), 68–69.

47. Ibid.

48. Ibid., 37, 40–41, 57.

49. Ibid., 32, 70. Also Marvin Bressler, "The Myers' Case: An Instance of Successful Racial Invasion," *Social Problems* 8 (Fall, 1960): 126–142.

50. Jayne, "First Families" (master thesis), 45, 70.

51. Ibid., 48, 73.

52. Drake and Cayton, *Black Metropolis,* 531.

53. Jayne, "First Families" (master thesis), 52; Harold Goldblatt, "Open Occupancy Housing in Westchester County," Urban League of Westchester County, New York (November, 1954), 36, box 96, Housing and Home Finance Agency Files, National Archives, Washington, DC.

54. Philadelphia Commission on Human Relations, "Some Factors Affecting Housing Desegregation," 1–6.

55. Ossie Davis and Ruby Dee, *With Ossie and Ruby: In This Life Together* (New York: William Morrow, 1998), 302–303.

56. Philadelphia Commission on Human Relations, "Some Factors Affecting Housing Desegregation," 5.

57. See, for example, Molly McCarthy, "North Amityville: Where Freed Slaves Could Make a Home," *Newsday,* February 22, 1998, H:7–8; U.S. Commission on Civil Rights, *Hearings Held in Los Angeles,* 244, 279–280.

58. Philadelphia Commission on Human Relations, "Some Factors Affecting Housing Desegregation," 5.

59. May, *Homeward Bound,* 3. See also Margaret Marsh, *Suburban Lives* (New Brunswick, NJ: Rutgers University Press, 1990); Mary Corbin Sies, *The American Suburban Ideal: A Cultural Strategy for Modern American Living, 1877–1917* (Philadelphia: Temple University Press, forthcoming).

60. Bart Landry, *The New Black Middle Class* (Berkeley: University of California Press, 1987), 59.

61. "St. Alban's," 34–39; "Period Styles for Elegance," 64; "Louis Jordan Birthday Party," 91–92; "Designer for Living: America's Ace Architect Paul Williams Attains Fame and Fortune Blueprinting Stately Mansions," *Ebony* 1 (February, 1946): 24–28.

62. "St. Alban's," 34–39.

63. Willard B. Gatewood, *Aristocrats of Color: The Black Elite, 1880–1920* (Bloomington: Indiana University Press, 1990), x, 182–190.

64. Ibid.

65. Drake and Cayton, *Black Metropolis,* in Patillo-McCoy, *Black Picket Fences,* 26; Gatewood, *Aristocrats of Color,* 194–195. See also Steven Gregory, *Black Corona: Race and the Politics of Place in an Urban Community* (Princeton, NJ: Princeton University Press, 1998), 17–18; Arthur S. Evans, Jr., "The

New American Black Middle Classes: Their Social Structure and Status Ambivalence," *International Journal of Politics, Culture, and Society* 7 (Winter 1993): 209–228.

66. Patillo-McCoy, *Black Picket Fences,* 23, 27.

67. Grier and Grier, *In Search of Housing,* 17.

68. U.S. Commission on Civil Rights, *Hearings Held in San Francisco, 1960,* 575.

69. Goldblatt, "Open Occupancy Housing in Westchester County," 23.

70. Grier and Grier, *In Search of Housing,* 17; Clarence Q. Pair, *The American Black Ghetto* (New York: Carlton Press, 1969), 13; Joseph Moore, *Pride against Prejudice: The Biography of Larry Doby* (New York: Greenwood Press, 1988), 88.

71. Leslie Gourse, *Unforgettable: The Life and Mystique of Nat King Cole* (New York: St. Martin's Press, 1991), 104.

72. Jayne, "First Families," 35, 50.

73. Ibid., 46.

74. Preston H. Smith, II, "The Quest for Racial Democracy: Black Civic Ideology and Housing Interests in Postwar Chicago," *Journal of Urban History* 26, no. 2 (January 2000): 133; Testimony of Carl Fuqua, U.S. Commission on Civil Rights, *Hearings before the United States Commission on Civil Rights, Hearings Held in Chicago, May 5–6, 1959* (Washington, DC: Government Printing Office, 1959), 828.

75. See, for example, Fred E. Case and James H. Kirk, *Housing Status of Minority Families, Los Angeles, 1956* (Los Angeles: Los Angeles Urban League, 1958), 78.

76. Grier and Grier, *The Search for Housing,* 17.

77. Council for Civic Unity, U.S. Commission on Civil Rights, *Hearings Held in San Francisco, Jan. 27–28, 1960,* 575.

CHAPTER SIX

1. Richard Nixon, "Acceptance Speech," *Campaign Speeches of American Presidential Candidates, 1948–1984,* ed. Gregory Bush (New York: Frederick Ungar, 1985), 153–163; Nixon, "The Philosophy of Government" (Oct. 21, 1972), *Weekly Compilation of Presidential Documents* (Washington, DC: Government Printing Office, 1972), 1546–1548; *Report of the National Advisory Commission on Civil Disorders* (New York: New York Times Co., 1968), 2; *Charlotte Observer (CO),* Sept. 12–13, 1968.

2. *Swann v. Charlotte-Mecklenburg,* 402 U.S. 1 (1971); Matthew D. Lassiter, *The Silent Majority: Suburban Politics in the Sunbelt South* (Princeton, NJ: Princeton University Press, 2006), chaps. 5–8. On differences between fragmented and "elastic" metropolitan regions, see David Rusk, *Cities without Suburbs,* 3d ed. (Washington, DC: Woodrow Wilson Center, 2003).

3. Mrs. T. L. Paige to Julius Chambers, Nov. 19, 1969, folder 16, box 3, Julius L. Chambers Papers, University of North Carolina at Charlotte Library (UNCC); *CO,* Aug. 3, 1970.

4. "Man and Woman of the Year: The Middle Americans," *Time,* Jan. 5, 1970, 10–17; "The Troubled American: A Special Report on the White Majority," *Newsweek,* Oct. 6, 1969, 28–59. On reactionary populism, see Ronald P. Formisano, *Boston against Busing: Race, Class, and Ethnicity in the 1960s and 1970s* (Chapel Hill: University of North Carolina Press, 1991); Michael Kazin, *The Populist Persuasion: An American History* (New York: Basic Books, 1995); Thomas Byrne Edsall with Mary D. Edsall, *Chain Reaction: The Impact of Race, Rights, and Taxes on American Politics* (New York: W. W. Norton, 1991).

5. Paul Leonard, "A Working Paper: Charlotte, An Equalization of Power through Unified Action," April 22, 1970, folder 19, box 3, Chambers Papers, UNCC.

6. Leonard, "Research Report," March 1970, folder 5, box 9, Chambers Papers, UNCC; "Transcript of Hearing," March 10, 1969, 29a–64a, March 13, 1969, 173a–219a, U.S. Supreme Court Records and Briefs, *Swann v. Charlotte-Mecklenburg,* 402 U.S. 1, no. 281; *CO,* June 26, 1968, July 7, 1970, June 10, July 6, 1971; Thomas W. Hanchett, *Sorting Out the New South City: Race, Class, and Urban Development in Charlotte, 1875–1975* (Chapel Hill: University of North Carolina Press, 1998). Because of Charlotte's aggressive annexation policy, many of the neighborhoods labeled as suburbs in this essay were technically located inside the expansive city limits, including the prewar garden suburbs of the Myers Park area. The city incorporated most of the outer-ring suburbs of southeast Mecklenburg County that formed the base of the antibusing movement in the midst of the desegregation crisis of the 1970s.

7. Pat Watters, *Charlotte* (Atlanta: Southern Regional Council, 1964); *CO,* May 27, Aug. 22, 1969, March 8, 1970, Jan. 22, May 2, 1971.

8. Leonard, "Research Report." On housing protests, see *CO,* March 3–5, 8, April 25–29, May 8–11, 1969. On the hospital dispute, *CO,* Jan. 16, Feb. 16, April 5, 10, 1971. On district elections, *CO,* June 24, 1970 (quotation), and general coverage from Dec. 1970 through March 1971. The interracial resolution of the busing crisis led to a successful grassroots campaign to replace at-large voting with district elections in 1977.

9. Mrs. William A. Cox to Charles Jonas, July 28, 1969, folder 827, Mrs. A. J. Woodle to Jonas, April 22, 1971, folder 906, series 2, Charles Raper Jonas Papers, Southern History Collection, University of North Carolina at Chapel Hill (SHC); *CO,* Aug. 24, 1969. Election results in *CO,* Nov. 6, 1968, May 7–8, 1972.

10. *Swann v. Charlotte-Mecklenburg,* 300 F. Supp. 1358 (W.D.N.C. 1969); *CO,* May 3–6, 14, 1969; *Charlotte News,* May 3, 10, 1969; William Overhultz interview, Aug. 20, 1997, Charlotte, North Carolina; Sharon McGinn interview, Aug. 20, 1997, Charlotte, North Carolina.

11. Watters, "Charlotte, North Carolina: 'A Little Child Shall Lead Them,'" *The South and Her Children: School Desegregation, 1970–1971* (Atlanta: Southern Regional Council, 1971), 29–33.

12. *CO*, May 6, 1969; Edwin Byrd to Richard Nixon, Feb. 2, 1970; James E. McDavid, Jr., to Jonas, Feb. 5, 1970; Thomas Conder to Nixon, Feb. 5, 1970, folder 494, series 1.1, Jonas Papers, SHC.

13. Nixon, "Desegregation of America's Elementary and Secondary Schools," March 24, 1970, *Weekly Compilation of Presidential Documents*, 424–440; *New York Times*, March 25–26, 1970.

14. CPA, "A Struggle for Freedom Is Coming," 1970; CPA, "Beverly Woods Bulletin," Feb. 26, 1970, folder 20, box 14, Fred Alexander Papers, UNCC; *CO*, Jan. 29, Feb. 2–9, Sept. 22, 1970.

15. *CO*, May 3, June 1, 1970.

16. *CO*, Aug. 24, 1969; Aug. 9, 12, 26, 28, 31, Sept. 2–3, 8–16, 1970, April 30, 1971; *New York Times*, Sept. 10, 1970.

17. *Swann v. Charlotte-Mecklenburg*, 402 U.S. 1 (1971); "Plaintiffs' Preliminary Response," June 17, 1971, folder 22, box 2, Chambers Papers, UNCC; *CO*, April 30, May 19, June 3, 19, 1971.

18. "Pupil Assignment Plan, 1971–1972," June 25, 1971, folders 23–24, box 5, William Waggoner Papers, UNCC; *Swann v. Charlotte-Mecklenburg*, 328 F. Supp. 1346 (W.D.N.C. 1971), 1349; *CO*, July 15, Aug. 3, 1971, Jan. 6, 1974.

19. CUFF Petition, Aug. 1971, folder 8, box 9, Chambers Papers, UNCC; *Swann v. Charlotte-Mecklenburg*, 334 F. Supp. 623 (W.D.N.C. 1971); *CO*, July 28, Aug. 3–4, 6, 22, 26–27, Sept. 4, 1971.

20. Cloyd Goodrum, Jr., to Rolland Jones, March 29, 1974, folder 3, box 4, Hidden Valley PTA Committee, Homeowner Survey, 1973, folder 7, box 3, Chambers Papers, UNCC.

21. "Community Relations Committee Hearing," Transcript Nos. 1–4, Nov. 21, 28, Dec. 5, 10, folders 5–6, box 39, Fred Alexander Papers, UNCC.

22. "Report of the Charlotte-Mecklenburg Community Relations Committee," March 14, 1972, folder 7, box 39, Fred Alexander Papers, UNCC; "Pupil Assignment Plan Study," March 6, 1973 (revised Sept. 27, 1973), folder 14, box 29, Kelly Miller Alexander, Sr., Papers, UNCC; *CO*, May 8, June 4, 1972, March 7, 1973.

23. "Northeast Concerned Parents" flier, May 21, 1973, personal papers of Julian Mason, copy in author's possession; Mason to Julius Chambers, June 15, 1973, Mason to James B. McMillan, May 21, 1973, Mason, Statement to Board of Education, May 30, 1973, folder 2, box 4, Chambers Papers, UNCC; Frye Gaillard, "Charlotte's Road to Busing," *Christianity and Crisis*, Oct. 29, 1973, 216–219; *CO*, May 15, 19, 23, 31, June 2, 4, 1973; Julian and Elsie Mason interview, Charlotte, North Carolina, April 29, 1998.

24. *CO*, June 11, 13, 15–16, 20, 1973.

25. *Swann v. Charlotte-Mecklenburg*, 362 F. Supp. 1223 (W.D.N.C. 1973), 1233, 1237; *CO*, June 23–24, July 3, 1973.

26. CAG, "Report to Court," April 22, 1974, folder 11, box 3, Chambers Papers, UNCC; "Charlotte-Mecklenburg Schools: A Joint Proposal for School

Assignment of Students," July 9, 1974, folder 6, "Order," April 3, 1974, folder 7, box 1, Margaret Whitton Ray Papers, UNCC; *CO*, April 4–5, 1974.

27. William Poe, "Five Years of Busing in Charlotte," Sept. 25, 1974, folder 12, box 2, series II, Frye Gaillard Papers, SHC; *CO*, May 8, June 5, July 10–11, Aug. 27, Sept. 12, 1974. Community studies of busing in Charlotte include Frye Gaillard, *The Dream Long Deferred* (Chapel Hill: University of North Carolina Press, 1988); Davison M. Douglas, *Reading, Writing, and Race: The Desegregation of the Charlotte Schools* (Chapel Hill: University of North Carolina Press, 1995); Stephen Samuel Smith, *Boom for Whom? Education, Desegregation, and Development in Charlotte* (Albany: State University of New York Press, 2004).

28. Peter Schrag, "The Forgotten American," *Harper's Magazine*, Aug. 1969, 134–141; Barbara Ehrenreich, *Fear of Falling: The Inner Life of the Middle Class* (New York: HarperPerennial, 1990), 97–143; Formisano, *Boston against Busing,* 237–238.

29. *Milliken v. Bradley,* 418 U.S. 717 (1974); Gary Orfield, *Must We Bus? Segregated Schools and National Policy* (Washington, DC: Brookings Institution, 1978); Jennifer L. Hochschild, *The New American Dilemma: Liberal Democracy and School Desegregation* (New Haven: Yale University Press, 1984).

30. Gary Orfield and Franklin Monfort, *Racial Change and Desegregation in Large School Districts: Trends through the 1986–87 School Year* (Alexandria: National School Board Association, 1988); Lassiter, *Silent Majority,* chaps. 4, 11–12; *Raleigh News and Observer,* Oct. 6, 1972.

31. *CO*, May 31, 1974; CBS, *Busing: Complying with Swann in 1976* (Films for the Humanities and Sciences, 2002), broadcast May 28, 1976; Lee A. Daniels, "In Defense of Busing," *New York Times Magazine,* April 17, 1983, 34–37, 92–93, 97–98; *Capacchione v. Charlotte-Mecklenburg,* 57 F. Supp 2d 228 (1999); Lassiter, *Silent Majority,* chap. 8, epilogue.

CHAPTER SEVEN

1. Much of the argument presented here is distilled from chapters 3, 7, and 8 of my book, *American Babylon: Race and the Struggle for Postwar Oakland* (Princeton, NJ: Princeton University Press, 2003). For treatments of postwar California politics, see Mike Davis, *City of Quartz: Excavating the Future in Los Angeles* (London: Verso, 1990); Peter Schrag, *Paradise Lost: California's Experience, America's Future* (Berkeley: University of California Press, 1999); Allen J. Scott and Edward Soja, *The City: Los Angeles and Urban Theory at the End of the Twentieth Century* (Berkeley: University of California Press, 1996); Lisa McGirr, *Suburban Warriors: The Origins of the New American Right* (Princeton, NJ: Princeton University Press 2001); Matthew Dallek, *The Right Moment: Ronald Reagan's First Victory and the Decisive Turning Point in American Politics* (New York: Free Press, 2000); Eric Avila, *Popular Culture in the Age of White Flight: Fear and Fantasy in Suburban Los Angeles* (Berkeley: University of California Press, 2004); Mark Brilliant, *Color Lines: Civil*

Rights Struggles on America's "Racial Frontier," 1945–1975 (New York: Oxford University Press, forthcoming).

2. Schrag, *Paradise Lost;* Davis, *City of Quartz;* David O. Sears and Jack Citrin, *Tax Revolt: Something for Nothing in California* (Cambridge, MA: Harvard University Press, 1982).

3. See the sources from note 2 as well as George G. Kaufman and Kenneth T. Rosen, eds., *The Property Tax Revolt: The Case of Proposition 13* (Cambridge, MA: Ballinger, 1981); Jaffrey Chapman, *Proposition 13 and Land Use: A Case Study of Fiscal Limits in California* (Lexington, MA: Lexington Books, 1981); Terry Schwadron and Paul Richter, *California and the American Tax Revolt: Proposition 13 Five Years Later* (Berkeley: University of California Press, 1984); Steven M. Sheffrin and Terri Sexton, *Proposition 13 in Recession and Recovery* (San Francisco: Public Policy Institute of California, 1998). For work on the conjuncture of race and taxes in New Right politics and in local battles in the postwar period, see Thomas Byrne Edsall and Mary D. Edsall, *Chain Reaction: The Impact of Race, Rights, and Taxes on American Politics* (New York: W. W. Norton, 1992); Raymond Wolters, *Right Turn: William Bradford Reynolds, the Reagan Administration, and Black Civil Rights* (New Brunswick, NJ: Transaction, 1996); Lizabeth Cohen, *A Consumers' Republic: The Politics of Mass Consumption in Postwar America* (New York: Knopf, 2003); Robert O. Self, *American Babylon: Race and the Struggle for Postwar Oakland* (Princeton, NJ: Princeton University Press, 2003).

4. On the urban politics of growth liberalism and the "growth machine," see Harvey Molotch, "The City as a Growth Machine: Toward a Political Economy of Place," *American Journal of Sociology* 82 (1976): 309–330; John H. Mollenkopf, *The Contested City* (Princeton, NJ: Princeton University Press, 1983); Andrew E. G. Jonas and David Wilson, *The Urban Growth Machine: Critical Perspectives Two Decades Later* (Albany: State University Press of New York, 1999).

5. John Logan and Harvey Molotch, *Urban Fortunes: The Political Economy of Place* (Berkeley: University of California Press, reprint, 1988).

6. Kenneth Jackson, *Crabgrass Frontier: The Suburbanization of the United States* (New York: Oxford University Press, 1985); Mollenkopf, *The Contested City;* Logan and Molotch, *Urban Fortunes.*

7. U.S. Department of Commerce, *Census of Population: 1950, Characteristics of the Population, California* (Washington, DC: Government Printing Office, 1951); *1970 Census of the Population, Characteristics of the Population, California* (Washington, DC: Government Printing Office, 1973).

8. Barry Bluestone and Bennett Harrison, *The Deindustrialization of America: Plant Closings, Community Abandonment, and the Dismantling of Basic Industry* (New York: Basic Books, 1982); Thomas J. Sugrue, *Origins of the Urban Crisis: Race and Inequality in Postwar Detroit* (Princeton, NJ: Princeton University Press, 1996); Judith Stein, *Running Steel, Running America* (Chapel Hill: University of North Carolina Press, 1998); Jefferson Cowie and Joseph

Heathcott, *Beyond the Ruins: The Meanings of Deindustrialization* (Ithaca: Cornell University Press, 2003).

9. *Fremont News Register (FNR)*, 14 June 1956, 31 October 1957, 27 March 1958, 21 December 1960, 18 and 19 March 1964; General Motors file, Fremont Public Library.

10. The term "white racial nationalism" is used here as a variation of "whiteness." I simply mean a self-conscious investment in racialized hierarchies governing resource distribution (including the advantages of racialized property markets) in which "white" or, in the legal language of the period, "Caucasian," acts as a marker of intrinsic citizenship, national belonging, and privilege. I find the concept less problematic and more specific than "whiteness."

11. For other examples of this kind of suburban city-building, see Greg Hise, *Magnetic Los Angeles: Planning the Twentieth-Century Metropolis* (Baltimore: Johns Hopkins University Press, 1997); Becky Nicolaides, *My Blue Heaven: Life and Politics in the Working-Class Suburbs of Los Angeles* (Chicago: University of Chicago Press, 2002). For another dimension of the public policy of suburbanization, see Cohen, *A Consumers' Republic.*

12. *Wall Street Journal (WSJ)*, 4 March 1966; *San Leandro News Observer (SLNO)*, 27 August 1948; "San Leandro California: Land of Sunshine and Flowers" pamphlet in "Historical Scrapbook of San Leandro," vol. 1, Local History Room, San Leandro Public Library; "Your Success Story—Annual Report 1951," San Leandro Chamber of Commerce, San Leandro Public Library; Alameda County Taxpayers Association, "News and Facts," 1955–1970, Institute of Governmental Studies, University of California, Berkeley (IGS). See also *SLNO*, 27 June, 4 and 18 July, 28 November 1947; Jack Maltester, interviewed by the author, San Leandro, California, 1 March 1999; Wes McClure, interviewed by the author, 16 February 1999.

13. Barbara Burbank quoted in *SLR*, 13 February 1948 (italics in original). See also, *SLNO*, 27 June, 4 and 18 July, 28 November 1947; Jack Maltester, interviewed by the author, San Leandro, California, 1 March 1999; Wes McClure, interviewed by the author.

14. *SLNO*, 17 December 1948; for pamphlets and other materials related to the program to sell industry to San Leandro residents, see "Historical Scrapbook of San Leandro," vols. 1–7, Local History Room, San Leandro Public Library. See also Elizabeth Fones-Wolf, *Selling Free Enterprise: The Business Assault on Labor and Liberalism, 1945–1960* (Urbana: University of Illinois Press, 1995).

15. *SLNO*, 12 September 1947, 9 January 1948; *San Francisco Chronicle*, 4 January 1948. For the use of racial covenants to restrict and contain Oakland's Chinese community, see Willard T. Chow, *The Reemergence of an Inner City: The Pivot of Chinese Settlement in the East Bay Region of the San Francisco Bay Area* (San Francisco: R & E Research Associates, 1977); for San Francisco, see, among others, Judy Yung, *Unbound Feet: A Social History of Chinese Women in San Francisco* (Berkeley: University of California Press, 1995).

16. *WSJ*, 4 March 1966.

17. *FNR*, 18 February 1966, 3 April 1967, 22 and 23 February 1971; Ronald Bartels, "The Incorporation of the City of Fremont: An Experiment in Municipal Government" (masters' thesis, University of California, Berkeley, 1959), 12–14, 20, 31–38; Stanley Weir, "Separate Efforts, Similar Goals and Results: A Study of the New Public City of Fremont, California, for Comparison with Private New Communities" (Berkeley, 1965), 10–15; Patricia O'Rourke, "Trend Surface Analysis of Urban Development: A Study of the Growth of the City of Fremont, California, 1956–1970" (masters' thesis, California State University, Hayward, 1973); Oral History Associates, *City of Fremont: The First Thirty Years, A History of Growth* (Sausalito: Oral History Associates, 1989), 33; Jack Parry, interviewed by the author, Fremont, California, 5 May 1999.

18. *FNR*, 2 June, 10 November 1955, 3 May 1956; Weir, *Separate Efforts, Similar Goals and Results,* 10–12; Oral History Associates, *City of Fremont,* 34–37; Jack Parry, interviewed by the author.

19. *FNR*, 14 June 1956, 31 October 1957, 27 March 1958, 21 December 1960, 19 March 1964; General Motors file, Fremont Public Library; *Preliminary General Plan, Fremont, California.*

20. Catherine Bauer Wurster, *Housing and the Future of the San Francisco Bay Area* (Berkeley: Institute for Governmental Studies, 1963), 32; Weir, *Separate Efforts, Similar Goals and Results,* 45–48; *FNR*, 3 April 1967; Bureau of the Census, *1970 Census of Population and Housing, San Francisco–Oakland, California* (Washington, DC: Government Printing Office, 1973).

21. Bureau of the Census, *U.S. Census of Housing and Population: 1960, San Francisco–Oakland, California* (Washington, DC: Government Printing Office, 1961); Bureau of the Census, *1970 Census of Population and Housing, San Francisco–Oakland, California;* "News/Facts: Property Tax Rates," published by the Alameda County Taxpayers Association, IGS; Alameda County Tax Rates, Fiscal Year, Auditor of Alameda County, Bancroft Library, University of California, Berkeley; Tax Rates, County of Alameda, Fiscal Year, Auditor-Controller of Alameda County, Bancroft Library, University of California, Berkeley.

22. *SLNO*, 7 September 1962; "Draft Report to the Governor's Advisory Committee on Housing Problems," 4.

23. Legislative Analyst, "An Analysis of Proposition 13: The Jarvis-Gann Property Tax Initiative" (Sacramento, 1978).

24. Sears and Citrin, *Tax Revolt: Something for Nothing in California;* Kaufman and Rosen, *The Property Tax Revolt;* Chapman, *Proposition 13 and Land Use.*

25. *SLR*, 1 and 2 June 1978; *Fremont Argus (FA)*, 28 May 1978.

26. Arthur Slaustein, "Proposition 13: The Morning After," *New Spirit,* February 1979, 6–9; Eric Smith and Jack Citrin, "The Building of a Majority for Tax Limitation in California, 1968–1978" (unpublished ms. IGS); "Jarvis-Gann vs. SB 1 (Proposition 8), A Summary Report," *San Francisco Business,*

June 1978, 20–23; Richard P. Simpson, "Spotlight on Proposition 13," *Western City,* April 1978, 9–12.

27. *FA,* 24 and 25 May 1978.

28. *FA,* 28 May 1978; *Hayward Daily Review,* 2 June 1978; Slaustein, "Proposition 13: The Morning After," 7.

CHAPTER EIGHT

1. William K. Reilly, ed., *The Use of Land: A Citizens' Policy Guide to Urban Growth* (New York: Thomas Y. Crowell Co., Rockefeller Brothers Fund, 1973), 33.

2. Randall W. Scott, ed., *Management and Control of Growth,* vols. 1–3: *Issues— Techniques—Problems—Trends* (Washington, DC: Urban Land Institute, 1975); quote from 1:xvi.

3. For recent evaluations and overviews of the political localism and suburban literatures respectively, see Thomas J. Sugrue, "All Politics Is Local: The Persistence of Localism in Twentieth-Century America," and Matthew D. Lassiter, "Suburban Strategies: The Volatile Center in Postwar American Politics," in Meg Jacobs, William J. Novak, and Julian E. Zelizer, eds., *The Democratic Experiment: New Directions in American Political History* (Princeton, NJ: Princeton University Press, 2003), 301–349.

4. Montgomery County Planning Board, *Framework for Action: First Annual Growth Policy Report for Montgomery County* (1974), 6.

5. Barbara Wurtzel, "The Politics of Suburban Growth Management" (Ph.D. diss., American University, 1976), chaps. 3–5; Neal Potter oral history (1997), in box 4, RG 16 (Oral Histories), Montgomery County Archives (MCA); League of Women Voters of Montgomery County, *The Planning Process in Montgomery County* (February 1976), FS-1, 2, in box 67, folder "Planning—Planning Process Study 1975–6," RG 2 (Potter Papers), MCA; Lynn Darling, "Good Guys Bow Out," *Washington Post,* February 7, 1978; Norman L. Christeller, "Local Government: Why It's in Trouble," *Washington Post,* February 13, 1978.

6. Rivkin/Carson, Inc., *The Sewer Moratorium as a Technique of Growth Control and Environmental Protection* (Washington, DC: U.S. Department of Housing and Urban Development, 1973), 22–30; Fact Research, Inc., *Beyond the Mid-Million Mark: Life, Change, and Government in Montgomery County, Maryland* (Washington, DC: Fact Research, 1974), 54–56; Montgomery County Council to Citizens of Montgomery County, "The Sewer Crisis and Council Action since 1970" (July 12, 1973), in box 117, folder "Water and Sewerage—Crisis 1973," RG 2 (Potter Papers), MCA; Wurtzel, "The Politics of Suburban Growth Management," 304ff., 372ff.

7. Montgomery County Office of Planning Policies, *A Generation of Change in Montgomery County: 1960–1990* (1991), 18; Idamae Garrott, "Planning Our Way," Council Comments column, July 16, 1973, in box 3, folder "Council Comments 1973," RG 2 (County Council Printed Materials), MCA;

"Chronology: Studies and Actions Pertaining to Solid Waste Disposal," January 17, 1971, and James Gleason to Montgomery County Council re: "Solid Waste Disposal: Recommended System and Sanitary Landfill Site," November 27, 1973, both in box 95, folder "Solid Waste—General 1971–73," RG 2 (Potter Papers), MCA.

8. Sidney Kramer, "The Solution to the Reassessment Dilemma," Council Comments column, December 31, 1973, in box 3, folder "Council Comments 1973," RG 2 (County Council Printed Materials), MCA; Montgomery County Council, *Budget Choices . . . Your Views Count: Fiscal Year 1977* (1976), 1; this overview of tax and fiscal issues is drawn from a general reading of much archival material, but see especially Neal Potter, "Assessments and Tax Reform" (1977), in box 1, folder "Budget 1972–78," RG 2 (Potter Papers), MCA and numerous Council Comments columns in box 3, RG 2.

9. "Biography—Neal Potter" (c. 1997) and "Neal Potter for County Council" (c. 1974), both in box 1, folder "Biography," RG 2 (Potter Papers), MCA; Neal Potter oral history (1998), box 4, RG 16 (Oral Histories), MCA.

10. Wurtzel, "The Politics of Suburban Growth Management"; Sears, "Growth Control in Montgomery County, Maryland" (thesis, Catholic University of America, 1980); Norman L. Christeler, "Wrestling with Growth in Montgomery County, Maryland," in Douglas R. Porter, ed., *Growth Management: Keeping on Target?* (Washington, DC: Urban Land Institute, with the Lincoln Institute of Land Policy, 1986), 81–91; on planning and zoning issues related to the Washington Metro, see Zachary M. Schrag, "The Washington Metro as Vision and Vehicle, 1955–2001" (Ph.D. diss., Columbia University, 2002), chap. 9.

11. Kenneth Bredemeier, "The Slowing of Suburbia," *Washington Post,* December 30, 1973—January 4, 1974, as reprinted in Scott, ed., *Management and Control of Growth,* 3:188–210; Marion Clawson, *Suburban Land Conversion in the United States: An Economic and Governmental Process* (Baltimore: Johns Hopkins University Press, 1971), 238–239.

12. Book-length overviews of Fairfax County land-use politics include Grace Dawson, *No Little Plans: Fairfax County's PLUS Program for Managing Growth* (Washington, DC: Urban Institute, 1977), and Terry Spielman Peters, *The Politics and Administration of Land Use Control: The Case of Fairfax County, Virginia* (Lexington, MA: Lexington Books, 1974); see also Moran E. Griggs, "Fairfax County: An Update," in Frank Schnidman and Jane Silverman, eds., *Management and Control of Growth,* vol. 5: *Updating the Law* (Washington, DC: Urban Land Institute, 1980), 204–207; Shelley Smith Mastran, "The Evolution of Suburban Nucleations: Land Investment Activity in Fairfax County, Virginia, 1958–1977" (Ph.D. diss., University of Maryland, 1988), 43.

13. Dawson, *No Little Plans;* John T. Hazel, "Growth Management through Litigation: A Case Study of Fairfax County, Virginia," in Schnidman and Silverman, eds., *Management and Control of Growth,* 5:193–203.

14. Griggs, "Fairfax County: An Update," 204; Hazel, "Growth Management through Litigation," 203.

15. Dawson, *No Little Plans,* 110–111.

16. Ibid., 149–50.

17. Robert H. Freilich, "Comment," in Scott, ed., *Management and Control of Growth,* 2:36; Manuel S. Emanuel, "Ramapo's Managed Growth Program: After Five Years Experience," in Scott, ed., *Management and Control of Growth,* 3:302; Rockland County Planning Board, *Rockland County Data Book, 1981;* Alan S. Oser, "Innovator in Suburbs under Fire," *New York Times,* March 28, 1971.

18. Gary K. Duberstein, "The Politics of Controlled Growth in Suburbia: A Case Study of Ramapo, N.Y." (senior thesis, Princeton University, 1976), esp. 79–109.

19. Ibid., 96, 109; Freilich, "Comment," and Emanuel, "Ramapo's Managed Growth Program," both review the town's planning history and process from an insiders' perspective; the actual 1969 zoning amendments are reprinted in Scott, ed., *Management and Control of Growth,* 2:7–13.

20. The Court of Appeals of New York case is *Golden v. Planning Board of Ramapo,* 285 N.E.2d 291 (1972) and both majority and minority opinions are reprinted in Scott, ed., *Management and Control of Growth,* 2:14–31; for comments by Ramapo's lead attorney, see Freilich, "Comment," in Scott, ed., *Management and Control of Growth,* 2:37.

21. Oser, "Innovator in Suburbs under Fire"; Herbert M. Franklin, *Controlling Urban Growth—But for Whom? The Social Implications of Development Timing Controls* (Washington, DC: Potomac Institute, 1973), 13, 26.

22. Oser, "Innovator in Suburbs under Fire"; Court of Appeals of New York opinion as quoted by Israel Stollman, "Ramapo: An Editorial," in Scott, ed., *Management and Control of Growth,* 2:6; Duberstein, "The Politics of Controlled Growth in Suburbia," 148ff.

23. David W. Silverman, "A Return to the Walled Cities: Ramapo as an Imperium in Imperio," 53–55, and Fred P. Bosselman, "Town of Ramapo: Binding the World?" 107, both in Scott, ed., *Management and Control of Growth,* vol. 2; Franklin, *Controlling Urban Growth—But for Whom?* 14–15, 27; John F. McAlevey, "A Method for Suburb to Aid Poor," *New York Times,* May 14, 1972.

24. Michael Danielson, *The Politics of Exclusion* (New York: Columbia University Press, 1976), 290–300; Louise Campbell, "Paul Ylvisaker: The Art of the Impossible," *City* 3 (April 1969): 17–24.

25. David L. Kirp, John P. Dwyer, and Larry A. Rosenthal, *Our Town: Race, Housing, and the Soul of Suburbia* (New Brunswick, NJ: Rutgers University Press, 1995); Charles M. Haar, *Suburbs under Siege: Race, Space, and Audacious Judges* (Princeton, NJ: Princeton University Press, 1996).

26. Kirp, Dwyer, and Rosenthal, *Our Town;* Haar, *Suburbs under Siege,* quote from p. 30, statistic from p. 131; Robert Hanley, "After 7 Years, Town Remains under Fire for Its Zoning Code," *New York Times,* January 21, 1983.

27. Karen Jean Schneider, "Innovation in State Legislation: The Massachusetts Suburban Zoning Act" (thesis, Radcliffe College, 1970), chaps. 3–5.

28. Lawrence Susskind, ed., *The Land Use Controversy in Massachusetts: Case Studies and Policy Options* (Cambridge, MA: MIT, Special Commission on the Effects of Growth Patterns on the Quality of Life in the Commonwealth of Massachusetts, 1975), 111–123; "A Proposal for a moderate income apartment complex in Concord submitted by Concord Home Owning Corporation" (n.d.), "Background Material on CHOC Case" (January, 1975), and various other documents in Swamp Brook Preservation Association Records, 1970–77, Concord Free Public Library; Charles M. Haar and Demetrius S. Iatridis, *Housing the Poor in Suburbia: Public Policy at the Grass Roots* (Cambridge, MA: Ballinger Publishing Co., 1974), chaps. 4–5.

29. Haar and Iatridis, *Housing the Poor in Suburbia,* 253; Melvin R. Levin, Jerome G. Rose, and Joseph S. Slavet, *New Approaches to State Land-Use Policies* (Lexington, MA: D. C. Heath & Co., 1974), 104; Danielson, *The Politics of Exclusion,* 103; *Boston Globe,* January 1, 1989.

30. The most useful overview of the UDC's powers and activities is Eleanor L. Brilliant, *The Urban Development Corporation: Private Interests and Public Authority* (Lexington, MA: Lexington Books, 1975); Logue quote from UDC Annual Report, 1970.

31. Rockefeller to Michaelian, June 19, 1972, in folder 3j, box 271, Logue Papers (LP), Sterling Memorial Library, Yale University; Edwin Michaelian speech, June 20, 1972, in folder 535, box 297, LP; Brilliant, *The Urban Development Corporation,* 90–98; UDC Annual Reports, 1969–1972. For details about the public opinion survey, see Logue to Rockefeller, January 5, 1973, Reel 51, 4th Nelson A. Rockefeller (NAR) Administration (1971–1973), Rockefeller Archive Center (RAC), Sleepy Hollow, NY.

32. Brilliant, *Urban Development Corporation,* 132–146; for additional details about United Towns for Home Rule, see Daniel Miller to Files, August 23, 1972, in folder 537, box 297, LP.

33. Logue to Rockefeller, January 14, 1972, in folder 3j, box 271, LP; Logue to Rockefeller, February 5, 1973, in folder 3l, box 271, LP; memos and correspondence referred to appear in various folders in box 271, LP; Reel 51, 4th NAR Administration, RAC.

34. "Statement by Westchester's Republican State Legislators" with J. Edward Meyer to Rockefeller, October 12, 1972, on Reel 51, 4th NAR Administration, RAC; Brilliant, *Urban Development Corporation,* 142.

35. Brilliant, *Urban Development Corporation,* 132–146; Rockefeller to nine Westchester town supervisors, September 27, 1972, and Nicholas C. Russo to Logue, January 15, 1973, both on Reel 51, 4th NAR Administration, RAC.

36. Brilliant, *Urban Development Corporation,* 132–146; UDC Annual Report, 1973; Logue to Rockefeller, February 5, 1973, in folder 3l, box 271, LP.

CHAPTER NINE

1. Meaning "non-Hispanic" white; "black" in this chapter refers to "non-Hispanic black," and "Asian" to "non-Hispanic" Asian.
2. Reynolds Farley, "The Changing Distribution of Negroes within Metropolitan Areas: The Emergence of Black Suburbs," *American Journal of Sociology* 75 (January 1970): 512–529; Harold Rose, *Black Suburbanization* (Cambridge, MA: Ballinger, 1976).
3. Mark Schneider and Thomas Phelan, "Black Suburbanization in the 1980s," *Demography* 30 (May 1993): 2; John M. Stahura, "Changing Patterns of Suburban Racial Composition, 1970–1980," *Urban Affairs Quarterly* 23 (March 1988): 3; John Logan and Mark Schneider, "Racial Segregation and Racial Change in American Suburbs, 1970–1980," *American Journal of Sociology* 89, no. 4 (1984): 874–888.
4. William Frey and Douglas Geverdt, "Changing Suburban Demographics: Beyond the 'Black-White, City-Suburb' Typology" (paper presented at the Suburban Racial Change Conference, Harvard University, 28 March 1998); Nancy Denton and Richard Alba, "Suburban Racial and Ethnic Change at the Neighborhood Level: The Declining Number of All-White Neighborhoods" (paper presented at the Suburban Racial Change Conference, Harvard University, 28 March 1998).
5. Doug Massey and Nancy Denton, "Suburbanization and Segregation in U.S. Metropolitan Areas," *American Journal of Sociology* 94, no. 3 (1988): 592–626.
6. Some important recent scholarship on racial and ethnic issues draws on fieldwork in suburbia, but makes little of the fact. See, for example, Leland Saito, *Race and Politics: Asian Americans, Latinos, and Whites in a Los Angeles Suburb* (Urbana: University of Illinois Press 1998); Timothy Fong, *The First Suburban Chinatown: The Remaking of Monterey Park* (Philadelphia: Temple University Press 1994); John Horton, *The Politics of Diversity: Immigration, Resistance, and Change in Monterey Park, California* (Philadelphia: Temple University Press 1995); Sarah Mahler, *American Dreaming: Immigrant Life on the Margins* (Princeton, NJ: Princeton University Press 1995). While all these books describe immigration and ethnic relations in suburbia, there is little analysis of what might make ethnic politics in suburbia different from the experience described in the traditional urban case study.
7. A. Dianne Schmidley and Campbell Gibson, *Profile of the Foreign Born Population in the United States,* Current Population Reports, U.S. Census Bureau (Washington, DC: Government Printing Office, 1999).
8. Jesse McKinnon and Karen Humes, *Black Population in the United States, March 1999,* Current Population Reports, U.S. Census Bureau (Washington, DC: Government Printing Office, 2000); Karen Humes and Jesse McKinnon, *Asian and Pacific Islander Population in the United States, March 1999,* Current Population Reports, U.S. Census

Bureau (Washington, DC: Government Printing Office, 2000);
www.census.gov/populationsocdemo/hispanic/cps99/tab16-1.txt.

9. In 2000 the comparable figures for all groups edged up slightly: 54 percent of whites lived in suburbs, as well as 45 percent of Latinos, 51 percent of Asian Americans and 33 percent of blacks (Census 2000 Summary File 1, 100 Percent Data.)

10. J. Eric Oliver, *Democracy in Suburbia* (Princeton, NJ: Princeton University Press 2001). Oliver notes, however, that suburban homogeneity also results in declines in more issue-oriented forms of political participation.

11. Juliet Gainsborough, *Fenced Off: The Suburbanization of American Politics* (Washington, DC: Georgetown University Press 2001).

12. Ibid.

13. Oliver, *Democracy in Suburbia*.

14. Ibid.

15. Michael Danielson, *The Politics of Exclusion* (New York: Columbia University Press, 1976).

16. Richard Alba and John Logan, "Variations on Two Themes: Racial and Ethnic Patterns in the Attainment of Suburban Residence," *Demography* 28, no. 3 (1991): 431–453.

17. Gainsborough, *Fenced Off*, appendix, table 6, p. 145.

18. Mark Schneider and John Logan "Suburban Racial Segregation and Black Access to Local Resources," *Social Science Quarterly* 63 (1982): 762–770; Schneider and Phelan, "Black Suburbanization."

19. M. P. Baumgartner, *The Moral Order of Suburbia* (New York: Oxford University Press, 1988), and Evan McKenzie, *Privatopia: Homeowner's Associations and the Rise of Residential Private Government* (New Haven: Yale University Press, 1994).

20. Oliver, *Democracy in Suburbia*, 123.

21. Massey and Denton "Suburbanization and Segregation in U.S. Metropolitan Areas"; George C. Galster, "Black Suburbanization: Has It Changed the Relative Location of Races?" *Urban Affairs Quarterly* 26 (1991): 621–628.

22. "Dillon's rule" refers to court decisions indicating that states retain complete authority over localities and that local governments have only those powers explicitly delegated to them by their state. States vary greatly in the powers they delegate to their localities: those delegating substantial control over taxation and administration to their localities allow "home rule"; those delegating little authority are "Dillon's rule" states.

23. In particular, any comparison would bring out the difference between the greater leeway granted by the Maryland state constitution to its municipalities in contrast with the strict oversight on the delegation of powers to municipalities in Virginia (a "Dillon's rule" state).

24. Though by no means a complete list of likely issues, the *Washington Post* coverage of the area suburbs is quite good for a major metropolitan

newspaper—considerably better than comparable coverage by the *Los Angeles Times* or *New York Times*—reflecting the interests and composition of its readership, the majority of whom reside in the surrounding counties rather than the city itself. The paper's coverage is better at recognizing issues than it is at following them and better at noting trends after the fact than at spotting them as they emerge. These deficiencies are common to journalism as a whole and suggest that the generation of this table of issues should in fact be supplemented, preferably by fieldwork. In this case, the author conducted fieldwork in the Washington, D.C., area in 2003–2004, with the support of the Russell Sage Foundation and the Woodrow Wilson International Center for Scholars.

25. And related organizations like Negative Population Growth, Americans for Better Immigration, and the Coalition for the Future American Worker.

26. "Virginia Ads Linking Immigration, Sprawl," *Washington Post,* September 21, 2000, p. B01.

27. In the 1980s, when the Fairfax Board of Supervisors had sought to reduce the allowable density of construction on 15,000 acres in the county, developers and others persuaded the Virginia State Assembly to overturn the local restrictions. Then Governor Douglas Wilder, who had received significant amounts of campaign contributions from Northern Virginia developers, signed into law the bill overriding local restrictions; Glenn Frankel and Stephen Fehr, "As the Economy Grows, the Trees Fall," *Washington Post,* March 23, 1997, p. A01.

28. Michael Laris and Peter Whoriskey, "Loudoun's Ambitious Search for Perfection: County Aims to Keep Vast Acreage Rural," *Washington Post,* July 22, 2001, p. A01.

29. Ibid.

30. Particularly because land-to-housing ratios are increased without any corresponding increase in permits for multifamily housing. See Peter Whoriskey, "Prosperity Feeds Housing Pinch," *Washington Post,* March 17, 2002, p. A01.

31. Michael Laris, "Suit Takes on Loudoun Slow-Growth Plan: Filing Says Policies Keep Minorities Out," *Washington Post,* July 24, 2002, p. B03.

32. Liz Seymour, "Too Few Make Cut As Fairfax's Gifted," *Washington Post,* April 28, 2002, p. C01.

33. Ibid.

34. Liz Seymour, "Minorities Swell Pool of Gifted in Fairfax," *Washington Post,* July 3, 2002, p. B01.

35. Liz Seymour, "Parents Decry Minority Plan: Proposal Would Alter Admissions at Jefferson," *Washington Post,* October 11, 2001, p. B01.

36. The proposal's strategy is similar in some ways to the alternatives to affirmative action adopted in Texas and Florida, which guarantee entry to the state's publicly financed universities to the top 10 percent of each high school's student body. Because the racial makeup of schools' student bodies reflect their neighborhoods, and because neighborhoods themselves tend to be racially

segregated, then guaranteeing entry to the best students of every school in essence acts much like the affirmative action programs they replaced.

37. See Michael Jones-Correa, "Racial and Ethnic Diversity and the Politics of Education in Suburbia," paper presented at the American Political Science Association Meeting, Chicago, September 2–5, 2004.

38. Jo Becker, "Suburban Crowding Arouses Tensions: Immigrants Jam Affordable Housing," *Washington Post,* May 3, 2002, p. A01.

39. Mary Beth Sheridan, "Deaths Draw Attention to Illegal Housing," *Washington Post,* January 11, 2002, p. B8.

40. Jonathan Kaufman, "Immigrant Homebuyers See Bias against Many Relatives Sharing the Same Roof," *Wall Street Journal,* January 10, 2002.

41. The new Fairfax law forbids drivers to park on anything but the pavement on their property. In the case of a lot of one-third to three-quarters of an acre, no more than 25 percent of the front yard can be paved over. See Lisa Rein and David Cho, "In Defense of the Front Lawn," *Washington Post,* June 4, 2002, p. A01.

42. David Plotz, "A Suburb All Grown up and Paved Over," *New York Times,* June 19, 2002.

43. Jo Becker, "Activists, Politicians Court Minorities," *Washington Post,* April 26, 2001, p. GZ16.

44. Jo Becker, "Diversity Warrants Changes, Panel Says," *Washington Post,* December 20, 2001, p. GZ03.

45. "Virginia Hits Ads Linking Immigration, Sprawl," *Washington Post,* September 21, 2000, p. B01; Kate Snow, "Ads Linking 'Urban Sprawl' with Immigration Stir Controversy in Virginia" *CNN,* October 3, 2000; Laris, "Suit Takes on Loudoun Slow-Growth Plan."

46. Jonathan Kaufman, "Immigrant Homebuyers See Bias against Many Relatives Sharing the Same Roof."

47. Rein and Cho, "In Defense of the Front Lawn"; Plotz, "A Suburb All Grown Up and Paved Over."

48. Seymour, "Too Few Make Cut as Fairfax's Gifted"; Liz Seymour, "Minorities Swell Pool of Gifted in Fairfax."

49. On service provision see, for example, Chris Jenkins, "Picking Up a Spanish Influence," *Washington Post,* December 11, 2000, p. B01; Ruben Castañeda, "Language Differences a Challenge for Courts," *Washington Post,* June 21, 2001, p. G15. On representation see, for example, Eugene Meyer, "Majority Black District Proposed for Prince George's," *Washington Post,* October 10, 2001; Becker "Diversity Warrants Change, Panel Says."

50. None of the top ten zip codes accounted for more than 3.3 percent of the metro area's immigrant population.

51. There are 14 zip codes in the District of Columbia area, for example, in which there are more than 500 Salvadorans residing, but no other immigrant group has more than two zip codes with this number of co-nationals.

52. Audrey Singer et al., *The World in a Zip Code* (Washington, DC: Brookings Institution, 2001), 5, fig. 3.
53. Ira Katznelson, *City Trenches: Urban Politics and the Patterning of Class in the United States* (Chicago: University of Chicago Press, 1981).

CHAPTER TEN

1. *Lloyd v. Tanner,* 407 U.S. 551 (1972); Lizabeth Cohen, *A Consumers' Republic: The Politics of Mass Consumption in Postwar America* (New York: Knopf, 2003), chap. 6; Bryant Simon, *Boardwalk of Dreams: Atlantic City and the Fate of Urban America* (New York: Oxford University Press, 2004); David Nasaw, *Going Out: The Rise and Fall of Public Amusements* (New York: Basic Books, 1993); Joel Garreau, *Edge City: Life on the New Frontier* (New York: Random House, 1991); Neil Wrigley and Michelle Lowe, *Reading Retails: A Geographic Perspective on Retailing and Consumption Spaces* (Oxford, UK: Oxford University Press, 2002); Stephanie Dyer, "Markets in the Meadows: Department Stores, Shopping Centers, and the Decentralization of Retailing in Philadelphia, 1920–1980" (Ph.D. diss., University of Pennsylvania, 2000).
2. See Charles Abrams, *Forbidden Neighbors: A Study of Prejudice in Housing* (New York: Harper, 1955); Steven Grant Meyer, *As Long as They Don't Move Next Door: Segregation and Racial Conflict in American Neighborhoods* (Lanham, MD: Rowman & Littlefield, 2000); Thomas J. Sugrue, *The Origins of the Urban Crisis: Race and Inequality in Postwar Detroit* (Princeton, NJ: Princeton University Press, 1996), chaps. 3, 8, 9.
3. See generally, Robert Reich, "The Secession of the Successful," *New York Times,* January 20, 1991, sec. 6, p. 16; Kevin M. Kruse, *White Flight: Atlanta and the Making of Modern Conservatism* (Princeton, NJ: Princeton University Press, 2005), chap. 9.
4. Evan McKenzie, *Privatopia: Homeowner Associations and the Rise of Residential Private Government* (New Haven: Yale University Press, 1994); Edward J. Blakely and Mary Gail Snyder, *Fortress America: Gated Communities in the United States* (Washington, DC: Brookings Institution, 1999); Setha Low, *Behind the Gates: Life, Security, and the Pursuit of Happiness in Fortress America* (New York: Routledge, 2003); Robert Dilger, *Neighborhood Politics* (New York: New York University Press, 1994).
5. Evan McKenzie, "Constructing the *Pomerium* in Las Vegas," *Housing Studies* (forthcoming 2005).
6. *San Antonio Independent School District v. Rodriguez,* 411 U.S. 1 (1973);*Milliken v. Bradley,* 418 U.S. 717 (1974); for a New Jersey case study, see Cohen, *Consumers' Republic,* 240–251; Thomas J. Sugrue, "The Compelling Need for Diversity in Higher Education: Expert Report of Thomas J. Sugrue," *Michigan Journal of Race and Law* 5 (1999): 289–290. On school segregation more generally, see Jennifer Hochschild and Nathan Skovronick, *The American Dream and the Public Schools* (New York: Oxford University Press, 2003); and

Gary Orfield and Susan Eaton, *Dismantling Desegregation: The Quiet Reversal of Brown v. Board of Education* (New York: New Press, 1996).

7. John Dewey, *Democracy and Education* (New York: Macmillan, 1916), 20–21.

8. Hochschild and Scovronick, *American Dream,* esp. 159–167; Jeannie Oakes, *Keeping Track: How Schools Structure Inequality* (New Haven: Yale University Press, 1986); Jonathan Kozol, *Savage Inequalities: Children in America's Schools* (New York: Crown Books, 1991).

9. Mike Davis, *City of Quartz: Excavating the Future in Los Angeles* (New York: Verso, 1990), esp. 250–260; James F. Pastor, *The Privatization of Police in America: An Analysis and Case Study* (Jefferson, NC: McFarland, 2003); Camilo José Vergara, *The New American Ghetto* (New Brunswick: Rutgers University Press, 1995), 101–119.

10. Kenneth Jackson, *Crabgrass Frontier: The Suburbanization of the United States* (New York: Oxford University Press, 1985), esp. 283–296; Tom Lewis, *Divided Highways: Building Interstate Highways, Transforming American Life* (New York: Penguin, 1999); Stephen B. Goddard, *Getting There: The Epic Struggle between Road and Rail in the American Century* (Chicago: University of Chicago Press, 1996); Owen Gutfreund, *Twentieth-Century Sprawl: Highways and the Reshaping of the American Landscape* (New York: Oxford University Press, 2004); Loren Demerath and David Levinger, "The Social Qualities of Being on Foot: A Theoretical Analysis of Pedestrian Activity, Community, and Culture," *City and Community* 2 (September 2003): 217.

11. Jon Teaford, *The Rough Road to Renaissance: Urban Revitalization in America, 1945–1980* (Baltimore: Johns Hopkins University Press, 1990); Arnold R. Hirsch, *Making the Second Ghetto: Race and Housing in Chicago, 1940–1960* (Cambridge: Cambridge University Press, 1983).

12. Alison Isenberg, *Downtown America: A History of the Place and the People Who Made It* (Chicago: University of Chicago Press, 2004).

13. *Kessler v. Grand Central District Management Association, Inc.,* 158 F.3d 92 (2d Cir. 1998). Cf. Richard Briffault, "A Government for Our Time? Business Improvement Districts and Urban Governance," *Columbia Law Review* 99 (1999): 365.

14. Laurie Reynolds, "Taxes, Fees, Assessments, Dues, and the 'Get What You Pay For' Model of Local Government," *Florida Law Review* 56 (2004): 373.

15. Kevin M. Kruse, "The Politics of Race and Public Space: Desegregation, Privatization and the Tax Revolt in Atlanta," *Journal of Urban History* 31, no. 5 (July 2005): 610–633; see Robert Self in this volume.

16. *Compania General de Tabacos de Filipanas v. Collector of Internal Revenue,* 275 U.S. 87, 100 (1927)

17. David Sklansky, "The Private Police," *U.C.L.A. L. Rev.* 46 (1999): 1165.

18. Michael Sorkin, "See You in Disneyland" (pp. 205–232), Margaret Crawford, "The World in a Shopping Mall" (pp. 3–30), and M. Christine Boyer, "Cities for Sale: Merchandising History at South Street Seaport" (pp. 181–204) in Michael Sorkin, ed., *Variations on a Theme Park: The New American City and*

the End of Public Space (New York: Hill & Wang, 1992); Simon, *Boardwalk of Dreams,* chap. 8.

19. David Barron, "Reclaiming Home Rule," *Harv. L. Rev.* 116 (2003): 2255, 2347–2361.

20. I say "usually" because some cities exercise extraterritorial regulatory powers. See, e.g., *Holt Civic Club v. City of Tuscaloosa,* 439 U.S. 60 (1978).

21. David Rusk, *Cities without Suburbs* (Washington, DC: Woodrow Wilson Center Press, 1993).

22. Jackson, *Crabgrass Frontier,* 138–156, 276–278; see Lassiter in this volume.

23. Derrick Bell, "The Referendum: Democracy's Barrier to Racial Equality," *Wash. L. Rev.* 54 (1978): 1.

Contributors

DAVID M. P. FREUND is currently a visiting assistant professor of history at Rutgers University at Newark. He is the author of *Colored Property: State Policy and White Racial Politics in the Modern American Suburb* (University of Chicago Press, forthcoming). Freund earned his doctorate from the University of Michigan at Ann Arbor.

GERALD FRUG is the Louis D. Brandeis Professor of Law at Harvard Law School. He is the author of *City Making: Building Communities without Building Walls* (Princeton University Press, 1999) and co-author of *Local Government Law* (West Publishing, 3d ed., 2001) and *Dispelling the Myth of Home Rule: Local Power in Greater Boston* (Rappaport Institute for Greater Boston, 2004), among others. Frug has also written several articles on topics such as home rule, property rights, metropolitan divisions, and regional government.

MICHAEL JONES-CORREA is an associate professor of government at Cornell University. He is the author of *Between Two Nations: The Political Predicament of Latinos in New York City* (Cornell University Press, 1998), and the editor of *Governing American Cities: Inter-Ethnic Coalitions, Competition and Conflict* (Russell Sage Foundation, 2001). Jones-Correa is currently completing a book looking at the renegotiation of ethnic relations after civil disturbances in New York, Los Angeles, Miami, and Washington, D.C., and engaged in two additional projects: one on the increasing ethnic diversity of suburbs and its implication for local and national politics and the other the design of a new national and state-by-state survey of Latinos in the United States.

ARNOLD R. HIRSCH is the Ethel and Herman L. Midlo Professor for New Orleans Studies and University Research Professor at the University of New Orleans. He is the author of *Making the Second*

Ghetto: Race and Housing in Chicago, 1940–1960 (University of Chicago Press, 1983, 2d ed. 1998). Hirsch is also the co-editor and a contributor to *Creole New Orleans: Race and Americanization* (Louisiana State University Press, 1992) and *Urban Policy in Twentieth-Century America* (Rutgers University Press, 1993). He has also written articles on the role of government in fostering segregation, the rise of black mayors, urban renewal, and public housing.

KEVIN M. KRUSE is an assistant professor of history and the David L. Rike University Preceptor of History at Princeton University. He is the author of *White Flight: Atlanta and the Making of Modern Conservatism* (Princeton University Press, 2005). Kruse has written several articles and book chapters on civil rights and the courts, residential desegregation, the connections between the desegregation of urban spaces and the politics of suburban conservatism, and the ideology and strategy of segregationist resistance. He is currently working on a book locating the origins of the modern religious right in suburbia.

MATTHEW D. LASSITER is an associate professor of history at the University of Michigan at Ann Arbor. He is the author of *The Silent Majority: Suburban Politics in the Sunbelt South* (Princeton University Press, 2006) and the co-editor of *The Moderates' Dilemma: Massive Resistance to School Desegregation in Virginia* (University Press of Virginia, 1999). Lassiter has written articles on suburban political developments and is currently working on a wide-ranging study of postwar American suburbs entitled "The Suburban Crisis: The Pursuit and Defense of the American Dream."

BECKY NICOLAIDES is an associate professor of history at the University of California at San Diego. She is the author of *My Blue Heaven: Life and Politics in the Working-Class Suburbs of Los Angeles, 1920–1965* (University of Chicago Press, 2002), as well as articles on the history of working-class suburbia and pedagogical approaches to urban history. She is currently researching several projects, including a transnational study of suburbanization, a study of California's postwar suburbs, and an intellectual and cultural history of the city and suburbs.

MARGARET PUGH O'MARA is the deputy director of the Center for the Study of the North American West and an acting assistant professor of history at Stanford University. O'Mara is the author of *Cities of Knowledge: Cold War Science and the Search for the Next Silicon Valley* (Princeton University Press, 2004). Her next book project is about public policy and high-tech entrepreneurship in the West and Pacific Rim. O'Mara previously served in the White House and the U.S. Department of Health and Human Services as a political aide and policy analyst, working on health care, welfare, and urban economic development programs.

ROBERT O. SELF is an assistant professor of history at Brown University. He is the author of *American Babylon: Race and the Struggle for Postwar Oakland* (Princeton University Press, 2003), which won the James A. Rawley Prize from the Organization of American Historians, the Ralph J. Bunche Award from the American Political Science Association, and best book prizes from both the Urban History Association and the Urban Affairs Association. He is currently at work on a project entitled "This Is a Man's World: Los Angeles and the Politics of Gender in Mid-Century America."

PETER SISKIND is an assistant professor of history at Arcadia University. He is currently revising his dissertation, a study of suburban growth and its discontents along the Northeast Corridor during the postwar era. Siskind earned his doctorate in history from the University of Pennsylvania.

THOMAS J. SUGRUE is the Edmund J. and Louise W. Kahn Professor of History and Sociology at the University of Pennsylvania. He is the author of *The Origins of the Urban Crisis: Race and Inequality in Postwar Detroit* (Princeton University Press, 1996), which won the Bancroft Prize in American History, the Philip Taft Prize in Labor History, the President's Book Award of the Social Science History Association, and the Urban History Association Award for Best Book in North American Urban History, among other prizes. He is currently finishing "Sweet Land of Liberty: The Unfinished Struggle for Racial Equality in the North" (under contract with Random House) and is also co-writing a history of twentieth-century America and co-editing a collection of essays on race, class, and the transformation of American law in the twentieth century.

ANDREW WIESE is an associate professor of history at San Diego State University. Wiese is the author of *Places of Their Own: African American Suburbanization in the Twentieth Century* (University of Chicago Press, 2004). He has also published several articles on suburban history, such as "The Other Suburbanites: African American Suburbanization in the North before 1950," *Journal of American History* (March 1999), which won prizes for best scholarly article of 1999 from the Urban History Association and the Oral History Association. He is currently working on a co-edited collection on North American suburbs and a co-authored book on the relationships between white and black suburbs in the early twentieth century United States.

Index